To Stand with
Nations of the World

To Stand with the Nations of the World

Japan's Meiji Restoration in World History

MARK RAVINA

OXFORD
UNIVERSITY PRESS

OXFORD
UNIVERSITY PRESS

Oxford University Press is a department of the University of Oxford. It furthers
the University's objective of excellence in research, scholarship, and education
by publishing worldwide. Oxford is a registered trade mark of Oxford University
Press in the UK and certain other countries.

Published in the United States of America by Oxford University Press
198 Madison Avenue, New York, NY 10016, United States of America.

Library of Congress Cataloging-in-Publication Data

Names: Ravina, Mark, 1961- author.
Title: To stand with the nations of the world : Japan's Meiji Restoration in
world history / Mark Ravina.
Description: New York, NY : Oxford University Press, 2017. | Includes
bibliographical references and index.
Identifiers: LCCN 2017016155 (print) | LCCN 2017037952 (ebook) |
ISBN 9780190656096 (Updf) | ISBN 9780190656102 (Epub) |
ISBN 9780195327717 (hardcover : alk. paper) | ISBN 9780190088378 (paperback : alk. paper)
Subjects: LCSH: Japan—History—Meiji period, 1868-1912. |
Japan—Foreign relations—1868-1912.
Classification: LCC DS882 (ebook) | LCC DS882 .R38 2017 (print) |
DDC 952.03/1—dc23
LC record available at https://lccn.loc.gov/2017016155

In memory of Hamano Kiyoshi

Contents

Acknowledgments

IN THE LONG course of writing this book I have benefited from the help of so many colleagues that a full accounting would itself amount to a short book. What follows is, therefore, a limited and selective list of those to whom I owe a particularly large intellectual debt.

In the early stages of this work, Mitani Hiroshi spent an afternoon guiding me through the Tokyo University Komaba bookstore, pointing out every "must read" work in Tokugawa and Meiji Japanese history. While I am still working through that list, it proved invaluable in navigating the enormous Japanese-language bibliography on the Meiji Restoration. In subsequent conversations, I benefited from Professor Mitani's insightful and creative approaches to historiography and methodology.

I first began exploring the Meiji Restoration as world history at a 2001 workshop on globalization sponsored by Emory's Halle Institute and hosted by Boğaziçi University (Istanbul). In 2002, I presented two research papers, first at a conference on the teleologies of the nation-state at Princeton's Institute for Advanced Study (IAS), and then at a conference on state-making at the University of Leiden. Those early thoughts on globalization appeared in conference volumes edited by Joshua Fogel and by Richard Boyd and Ngo Tak-Wing. I am thankful to the conference participants and the editors for their comments and insights. I owe special thanks to Josh Fogel for his support and advice over many years.

A Fulbright Senior Research Award allowed me an extended residence in Japan at the International Research Center for Japanese Studies (Nichibunken) in 2005 and 2006, where I learned much from Kasaya Kazuhiko in his seminar on early modern Japan. Kasaya's graduate student Yokoyama Mitsuteru spent many hours helping me with handwritten manuscripts. My family joined me in Kyoto for the first half of that sabbatical and dutifully pulled me away from my desk for various adventures, including trips to Osaka, Kōyasan, and Amanohashidate. Initially overwhelmed by family obligations, I briefly despaired that my progress reports to Fulbright might focus primarily on Kyoto's little league baseball off-season training schedule and teen volleyball practices. My fears were unfounded and instead those experiences were not just delightful but revitalizing, helping me to appreciate Japan anew, and I returned to the classroom a better and more enthusiastic teacher. I offer my thanks to my wife Nora Levesque and our blended family for their love, support, good humor, and constant reminders of life beyond the printed page and computer screen.

From August through December 2011, the Institute for Research in the Humanities (Jinbunken) in Kyoto hosted me as a visiting professor, with additional support from a Japan Foundation Research Grant. I offer my deepest appreciation to the faculty and staff of the Institute for creating a glorious environment in which to explore and refine ideas. My sponsor, Iwaki Takauji, spent many hours guiding me through difficult manuscripts and fielding my many questions on Tokugawa social and political history. I benefited enormously from his erudition, graciousness, and generosity. I was invited to present my work-in-progress at the Institute's seminar series, where I received valuable comments from Takagi Hiroshi, Nara Katsuji, Haga Yōji, John Breen, and Hatakayama Kazuhiro. At other presentations in Kyoto and Tokyo I benefited from the comments of Neil Waters, James Baxter, Bruce Batten, Leonard Blussé, and Silvio Vita. My special thanks to Professor Vita for hosting a dinner with Iwakura Tomotada, history professor and great-great-grandson of Iwakura Tomomi. That evening of fine food, wine, and conversation was both delightful and enlightening. Matthew Stavros and Francesco Campagnola were wonderful lunch and dinner companions, who would listen to the messiest, protean ideas.

I benefited greatly from a series of conferences in 2014 and 2015, organized in anticipation of the Meiji Restoration sesquicentennial. My thanks to Rob Hellyer for arranging the meeting at Wake Forest and to Harald Feuss for two meetings at Heidelberg University. I learned much from the fellow participants at those sessions, especially Jong Chol An, Sven Saaler, Toru Takenaka, Hans Martin Kraemer, Fabian Drixler, and Kären Wigen. Thanks also to Ethan Segal, Luke Roberts, Aaron Skabelund, Yabuta Yutaka, and Fujita Teiichirō for advice and support over the years.

My colleagues at Emory University have offered an invaluable mix of supportive comments and incisive criticism. I learned much from the fellow participants in an East Asian Studies faculty writing group (Julia Bullock, Sun-chul Kim, Maria Sibau, and Jenny Chio), who read drafts of many chapters. Their patient and exacting readings helped me to clarify my thinking at several key stages. Team-teaching an undergraduate East Asian history survey with Tonio Andrade has been an intellectual windfall. The multi-year, iterative process whereby Tonio and I gradually knitted our national history lectures into a transnational history of East Asia was both demanding and exhilarating. If our students learned as much in class as I did, they received a superb education. Team-teaching a graduate seminar in comparative empires with Clifton Crais helped me to situate the Meiji Restoration in a broader perspective. I hope this volume reflects how much I learned from both Clifton and the students in that class. Graduate students Stephanie Bryan and Tim Romans were extremely helpful— Stephanie for refining and improving my maps, and Tim for enduring many drafts. When a family crisis threatened to derail my sabbatical at Jinbunken, Michael Elliot, then dean of faculty, responded with flexibility and magnanimity. At the Emory libraries, Lawrence Hamblin got obscure books on the shelf faster than I could have hoped or imagined, and the interlibrary loan staff supported my many unusual requests. Archivists and staff at the Tojō Rekishikan and Library of Congress helped track down and get copies of rare prints and photographs.

Susan Ferber at Oxford University Press guided this project with patience and wisdom. In an era when most everything seems to be outsourced, it was a rare and great gift to get her thoughtful and judicious line edits. In pencil, no less! I am indebted to her steady editorial hand. Two readers for the Press offered valuable suggestions and saved me from errors of fact and interpretation.

For their support and guidance over many years, I owe special thanks to Dani Botsman, Kevin Doak, and Sheldon Garon. Julia Thomas was a careful reader who offered both insightful criticism and effusive praise. My mother, Ruth Ravina, and mother-in-law, Ann Levesque, listened with interest to the details of my research and writing struggles.

I am particularly grateful to several scholars who are also dear friends. Matthew Payne endured the most inchoate early versions of my ideas in conversations over lunch, coffee, or beer. He was also a careful reader of many draft chapters and grant applications. Ari Levine has spent many hours helping me through classical Chinese texts. He has also been a marvelous source of advice not only on historiography and the philosophy of history but also on sources of artisanal free-range lamb, local micro-distilleries, and which National Book Award and Booker Prize finalists to skim rather than read. I have relied on him as a sympathetic ear when wrestling both with major intellectual challenges and the minor indignities of midlife.

During the latter part of my year at Nichibunken, I dined regularly with Robert Eskildsen and his late wife Mariko, enjoying home cooking in exchange for bringing Spanish red wine and washing dishes. I undoubtedly got the better end of that arrangement. More recently, Rob and I met via Skype to read each other's work. This book scrupulously cites Rob's many publications, but that does not convey how much I learned from his questions and criticism. His exacting knowledge of 1870s politics saved me from many point-of-fact errors and glib conclusions. I am grateful to Rob for his years of generosity as a scholar and a friend.

It is with a heavy heart that I offer thanks to the late Hamano Kiyoshi. A great scholar and gentle soul, Kiyoshi was an unstinting source of support, advice, and friendship. I am thankful for the many hours we spent on questions of history and historiography, but also for many extra-academic moments. During his sabbatical at Emory, Kiyoshi and his family taught my family what has become our favorite card game. During stays in Kyoto, he introduced us to the city's marvelous hidden restaurants. And I remember fondly our tacit but strict "home field" rule: our conversations were in English in the United States, but in Japanese in Japan. His premature passing is a great loss, and this book is dedicated to his memory.

Note to Reader

Romanization

Japanese is romanized in the Hepburn system, Chinese in Pinyin, and Korean in McCune-Reischauer. The following abbreviations are used to indicate the target language: J. for Japanese, Ch. for Chinese, and K. for Korean.

Personal Names

Japanese, Chinese, Korean, and Ryukyuan names are presented in the traditional fashion, family name followed by given name. Individuals are commonly identified by family name, but where that might point to many individuals (e.g., Tokugawa and Matsudaira), the given name is used for clarity. Given names are also used to follow convention. Thus Ogyū Sorai, whose followers are known as the Sorai School, is identified as Sorai, but Hirata Atsutane is identified as Hirata. Because most Japanese characters have multiple readings, some Japanese given names have multiple readings. Tokugawa Yoshinobu, for example, is also known as Tokugawa Keiki. Prominent secondary readings, as well as common pseudonyms, are noted in the text and index.

Place Names

Several places in this book are known by different names in different languages—for example, the Liancourt Rocks are called Takeshima in Japanese but Tokto in Korean. In such cases I have used the most common English toponym followed by the alternatives in parentheses.

Early modern domains (daimyo territories) were commonly known by the name of their castle town, the local government seat, but there are numerous exceptions. Larger domains, for example, often went by the name of their province. The Shimazu family's holdings in Satsuma province, for example, are known as Satsuma domain rather than Kagoshima domain, the name of the castle town. Some names are irregular. The Mōri house's holdings in Nagato province, for example, are commonly known as Chōshū, a variant term for Nagato. Rather than artificially systematize domain names, I have followed convention and relied on the standard reference work Kodama and Kitajima, eds., *Hanshi sōran*.

Dates

Dates with named months (e.g., January, February) are in the Gregorian calendar. Dates in year/month/day format are in the Japanese lunar-solar calendar. Prior to 1873, the Japanese calendar had twelve months each of twenty-nine or thirty days for a total year of about 354 days. Intercalary or "leap" months were used to keep this lunar calendar synchronized with the solar year. Following historiographic convention I have converted Japanese years, but not months or days, to the Gregorian calendar. Thus, the fifth day of the eleventh lunar month of the sixth year of the Hōreki era is rendered as 1756/11/5, corresponding to November 26, 1756. Intercalary months are represented by the letter "i." Thus, 1756/11i/5 represents the fifth day of the eleventh intercalary (or twelfth) month of 1756, corresponding to December 26, 1756. On the Gregorian calendar, the Japanese year began "late," falling between January 21 and February 19. Therefore, some key events in the Meiji Restoration fall before New Year's Day on the Japanese calendar, but after on the Gregorian. The imperial declaration of the "revival of ancient kingly rule," for example, occurred on the ninth day of twelfth month of the third year of Keiō (1867/12/7), corresponding to January 3, 1868, on the Gregorian calendar.

Weights and Measures

Daimyo holdings were assessed by their annual rice harvest, measured in *koku*, equal to 47.66 gallons or 180.39 liters.

*To Stand with the
Nations of the World*

Introduction

ON APRIL 28, 1871, Itō Hirobumi, a future prime minister of Japan, spoke before a group of prominent Americans at Welcker's Restaurant in Washington, DC. Itō was then merely an official in the finance ministry, returning to Japan after on-site study of the US financial system, but the dinner resembled an official state banquet. The attendees included President Ulysses S. Grant, Vice President Schuyler Colfax, Speaker of the House James Gillespie Blaine, and Secretary of State Hamilton Fish, as well as Japan's ambassador to the United States, Mori Arinori. Itō took the opportunity both to promote Japan's recent political accomplishments and to celebrate US-Japanese friendship. Addressing the group in English, Itō proceeded to explain the Meiji Restoration, the revolution that had overthrown the last Tokugawa shogun in the name of the emperor just three years before. Itō insisted that Japan was eager to learn from the West. While officials of the Tokugawa regime had stifled Japanese material and cultural progress, the Meiji government was determined to catch up to the rest of the world.

Much of Itō's account was nonsense, but it was savvy and diplomatic nonsense, designed to flatter his American hosts. As a result, more than a century later, accounts like Itō's still appear in standard English-language descriptions of the Meiji Restoration. Rebutting Itō's speech, even 150 years later, is thus an ideal way to begin rethinking the Meiji Restoration: cleaning out seductive and pervasive but erroneous ideas. Itō, for example, drew a stark contrast between the new Meiji government and the Japanese past. According to Itō, Japan had been isolated for most of its history: "the recorded existence of the nation extends over something more than two-thousand five hundred years, during which time its intercourse with foreign nations has been exceedingly limited." Then in 1853, the United States "opened" Japan to the world, "kindly" advising it to open its ports to foreign intercourse. From that moment, Itō explained, the Japanese people began to appreciate their own backwardness: they were centuries behind the West. Eager to reach "the highest stage of civilization" they began reforms based on European and American models. Having found in America "a people who would encourage and assist us in every way possible," Itō was confident that Japan was now on a trajectory to "the front rank of advanced and civilized nations." Japan would soon "stand among the first nations in its civilization and progress."[1]

Most of this is wrong. The United States had not "kindly" advised the Tokugawa to open their ports. Rather, it had sent a squadron of state-of-the-art warships to the shogun's capital and forced the regime to sign unpopular treaties. That humiliation was the beginning of the end of Tokugawa rule, which collapsed fifteen years later. The 1800s were the heyday of imperialism, and compared to British and French actions in China, US policy toward Japan was peaceful and restrained. But there was no mistaking the threat of force behind US actions. Commodore Matthew Perry, the commander of the 1853 mission, was fully prepared to seize outlying Japanese territories in order to compel the shogunate to accept US demands. Itō, like many young men of his day, had railed against the shogunate for defiling the "land of the gods" by signing unequal treaties with Western powers. Those compacts allowed for foreign settlements in Japan, so-called treaty ports, and placed foreigners under the jurisdiction of their own consular courts. In 1861, Itō himself was so outraged by these humiliations that he helped set fire to the British legation in Edo. The following year, however, he was persuaded to study in England, where he became convinced that Japan had much to learn from the West. When he returned to his homeland in 1864, he sought to convince his friends that xenophobic violence was not in Japan's best interests. By the time he spoke in DC in 1872, Itō's respect for American institutions was genuine, but he wisely chose not to describe his path from xenophobia to xenophilia. It was best not to tell a group of Americans that a decade earlier he had vilified their civilization as barbarous, and Itō eliminated the story of how American gunboat diplomacy had once driven him to arson. Instead, he praised the nation for awakening a slumbering Japan to the glories of Western civilization.

Itō's revision of earlier Japanese history was still more skewed and selective. Japan had not been closed to the outside world before 1853. Rather, the long arc of Japanese history is characterized by waves of intense international engagement. The Meiji Restoration was not Japan's first encounter with the outside world, just the most recent. For millennia, the Japanese people had not only interacted with the rest of the world, but they had also transformed their state and society in order to adapt to that world. Flattering his American audience, Itō chose to describe Japan's modern encounter with the West as unique and unprecedented. In fact, Meiji-era cultural borrowing had ample precedent. In the 600s and 700s, for example, Japan was deeply connected to the rest of East Asia and borrowed heavily from Chinese and continental culture. Japanese officials, scholars, and monks traveled to China and Korea to learn advanced political, social, and material technologies. The nascent imperial court also employed numerous foreign advisors, many of whom were immigrants or refugees or from the Korean peninsula. In that way, the 700s resembled the late 1800s: Japanese leaders embraced foreign ideas and advisors to show that they had caught up to the great powers of the day. Like the Meiji state, the ancient Japanese imperial state was eager to display its accomplishment. In the eighth century, the court built a massive temple, Tōdaiji in Nara, and invited representatives from as far away as India to participate in the consecration of a 250-ton bronze Buddha statue. This was

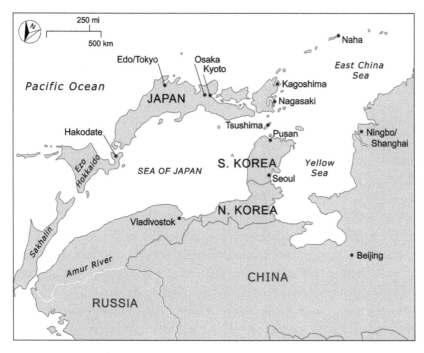

Conventional maps of the Japanese archipelago emphasize its isolation. This alternative orientation, inspired by the work of Amino Yoshihiko, highlights connectedness instead.

FIGURE INTRO.I Japanese Archipelago and East Asia.

the eighth-century equivalent of hosting the Olympics Games: a costly but peaceful way of displaying power and technological prowess. This earlier example of international engagement served as a powerful precedent for Meiji-era cultural borrowing.

From a Japanese perspective, the United States and Europe in the nineteenth century were like the Chinese Tang dynasty in the seventh and eighth centuries: powerful foreign empires worthy of both fear and emulation. In both cases, there was no avoiding these expansive foreign regimes. The Japanese state would need to master and redeploy their social, political, and material technologies in order to establish its own legitimacy and defend its territory. But Itō wisely chose not to explain ancient Japan's cultural debt to Tang China. Better to simply indulge his American hosts by extolling the virtues of Western civilization.

Itō also glossed over a second wave of global engagement, from the 1400s to the early 1600s, when Japanese pirates and traders roamed across East Asia. There were Japanese expatriate communities as far away as Siam, and official Japanese envoys reached the Vatican. Far from being isolated, Japan was part of an emerging global economy: silver from Japanese mines entered an integrated market, with prices moving in sync around the world. In that context, Japan's most powerful warlord, Toyotomi Hideyoshi, sought to establish a great empire: in 1592 he led an invasion of Korea as part of a plan to topple the Chinese Ming dynasty. Hideyoshi's invasion ended in defeat, and the Tokugawa chose not to repeat his mistake of starting a major war on the continent. They did, however, push back against other empires. In 1628, for example, when the Dutch attempted to limit Japanese trade with Taiwan, an angry Japanese ship captain took the Dutch colonial governor hostage and brought him back to Nagasaki. Such stories inspired men like Itō as they struggled with Western imperialism 250 years later. But Itō wisely omitted this aspect of Japanese history as well. It was best not to suggest to an American audience that Western imperialism had revived Japanese territorial ambitions.

Itō's account of the Meiji Restoration, so shrewd and flattering in the 1870s, continues to shape writing about Japan to this day. The idea that the United States "opened" Japan is a compelling fiction, but bad history. It creates a false contrast between "traditional Japan" and the "modern Western world."[2] Making sense of the Meiji Restoration requires moving beyond that contrast, paying attention instead to the continuities between the long arc of Japanese history and the modern state. The Restoration was not only about emulating Western practices but also about restoring and reviving older Japanese institutions. It was not a clash between "modern" and "traditional" or between "Western" and "Japanese" but a struggle to transcend those dichotomies and to create new institutions and practices that could simultaneously evoke both Japanese uniqueness and Western progress. The Meiji Restoration was a revolution, but its bold innovations were grounded in precedents from the ancient imperial state. The leaders of the Restoration deliberately ransacked the Japanese past in their search for the Japanese future.

In many places this combination of the ancient and modern was overt and explicit. Consider, for example, the creation of the modern Japanese military, a cornerstone of the Meiji state. In its radical reform of the military, the Meiji government smashed one tradition while restoring another. The creation of the Meiji army and navy was an explicit rejection of Tokugawa social and political traditions. Since the late 1500s, Japanese rulers had separated warriors from commoners; commoners were effectively disarmed, while samurai were distinguished by their right to carry two swords. In 1872, however, the Meiji state attacked samurai tradition, even though most government leaders were themselves samurai. Hereditary warriors were no longer needed. Instead, Japan's new military would comprise Japanese subjects from all classes. Commoners would be trained to fight for their country, and samurai would need to adapt to this new reality. In the edict that announced conscription, the government loudly declared its defiance of tradition: "the samurai are not the samurai of former days and the commoners are not the commoners of former days." They were now all equal in their "rights" and "duties" to the state. Inspired by the military success of Western conscript armies, the Japanese government dissolved its own warrior elite. The Meiji government openly declared that it would copy the best practices of Western militaries. Since Western countries had been studying military organization for centuries, Japan could learn from their efforts. Conscription was thus a modernizing Western-style reform.

At the same time, however, Meiji leaders described the conscription system as a return to ancient ways. In the ancient past, they declared, all strong young men had offered military service to the state in times of crisis and then returned to their fields when the enemy was defeated. In the government's account, the Japanese emperor had served as the direct commander of this ancient national army. The rise of a hereditary warrior elite, the samurai, came only centuries later, with the decline of imperial power. The traditions of the samurai class were thus relatively recent innovations that had replaced the older tradition of a Japanese national army. Thus, in attacking the "traditions" of the samurai, the Meiji government claimed that it was actually returning to ancient ways. It was abolishing one tradition in the name of another. The Westernizing, modern innovation of a conscript army was also a return to the ancient Japanese past.

The Meiji government's depiction of ancient conscription was impossibly rosy, as factually challenged as Itō's speech in Washington, DC. The ancient state did, in fact, draw conscripts from across the land, but ancient commoners viewed the draft as forced labor rather than as loyal service. They were unruly and unreliable troops, prone to desertion. But those facts did not trouble Meiji leaders. Instead they insisted that modern Western reforms were a necessary means to reviving ancient imperial practices. After a millennium of neglect, the glories of the ancient state would be restored with the help of Western models.

Such combinations of the ancient and modern were a defining feature of the Meiji Restoration, but they did not arise in a vacuum. They were part of the Meiji state's strategy for integration into nineteenth-century world politics. The Meiji Restoration occurred amid a global political transformation: the rise of nationalism and nation-states. The world's great multi-ethnic empires—Ottoman, Qing, Romanov, and Hapsburg—were on the decline, besieged from within and without.[3] They were challenged by a new type of polity, the nation-state. Unlike the declining empires, nation-states asserted an essential cultural identity between ruler and ruled. However much, for example, Frenchmen might differ from one another, they were, in theory if not in practice, bound together by common ties of culture, language, religion, and tradition. French rulers, be they emperors, presidents, or prime ministers, ruled over the French but they were also Frenchmen themselves, sharing a common history and heritage. Such rhetoric proved toxic to multi-ethnic empires: how could a German-speaking Hapsburg monarch claim authority over Italy? How could an ethnically Manchu Qing emperor be the sovereign of China?

Nation-states established a distinctive form of empire. Older empires were commonly stitched together by dynastic alliances, often the intermarriage of elite households. But nineteenth-century empires were increasingly based on a hierarchical vision of civilization. Some superior national cultures, primarily in Europe, were deemed capable of forming nation-states. Much of the rest of the world, however, was seen as temporarily or permanently incapable of self-governance.[4] India and China, for example, were commonly described as the atrophied or somnolent remnants of great ancient civilizations. Perhaps these cultures could be "awakened," but in the interim, neither was civilized or advanced enough to form a nation-state and thus could be legitimately subjugated. Like minor children, flawed civilizations required guidance from Europe.[5] Even the venerable humanitarian Albert Schweitzer described Africans as eternal children needing adult supervision.[6] Seen from Japan, this new international order was both terrifying and exhilarating. Clearly, if Japan failed to establish itself as a "civilized" sovereign power it might fall under foreign control. A Japanese nation-state was thus essential as a defense against foreign predation. But the volatility of the nineteenth-century world order was also enthralling. The speed with which new empires were devouring the old suggested new avenues for Japanese political ambition. A Japanese nation-state could soon become the metropole of a new Japanese empire.

For nineteenth-century Japanese observers, the power of the nation-state was most obvious in military affairs. The British, French, and Americans could give their commoners state-of-the-art weapons and send them around the world to fight for the homeland. The Tokugawa state, by contrast, had kept weapons away from commoners lest they use them to attack the state. In the late Tokugawa and Meiji periods, Japanese leaders struggled to understand how Japanese commoners could be mobilized to support the state. How could Japanese culture be invoked to instill respect for the state and the obedience of its people? In short, how could Japanese commoners be transformed into Japanese nationals, loyal and willing servants of their sovereign? How could the Japanese polity be turned into a Japanese nation-state? In this way, narrowly conceived questions of national defense came to encompass broad questions of culture, politics, and society.[7]

When Meiji leaders sought to build a nation-state they emulated what they understood as Western best practice. They created Japanese analogues to the rituals and institutions that were associated with powerful Western nation-states. Creating these analogues required a double move: the institutions of the Japanese nation-state needed to resemble Western models, but they also needed to be distinctly Japanese. Meiji leaders could not just copy, for example, the national institutions of Great Britain. Rather, they needed to make new institutions that were Japanese parallels. Consider, for example, the creation of the Japanese national anthem, "Kimigayo," in 1870. In the 1800s, Western nation-states began using national anthems to cultivate a sense of national unity. Having soldiers (or students, or subjects) declare in unison their loyalty to state and sovereign, praising the glories of the homeland, was a powerful evocation of common purpose. The very act of singing together instilled the sense of unity the national anthem was designed to celebrate. Thus, such rituals both created and extolled national unity.

Tokugawa Japan had no such rituals, but Meiji leaders quickly understood that a Japanese nation-state needed a national anthem. The first attempt at a Japanese national anthem was largely a copy of European models: it was written for a Western-style military band and played on Western musical instruments. But in order for "Kimigayo" to function as a Japanese national anthem, it needed to be distinctly Japanese, not just an adaption of a Western form.[8] The lyrics to the new anthem therefore used distinctive imagery drawn from Japanese verse, primarily the *Kokinshū*, a tenth-century imperial poetry anthology. "Kimigayo" expresses the hope that the emperor will reign long enough for small stones to grow into boulders covered in moss.[9] As later nationalists were proud to observe, this image of rocks growing larger with time, rather than shrinking from erosion, is the opposite of a Western sensibility. In this way, "Kimigayo" is not an imitation of the West but a defiant statement of a Japanese vision of nature. This combination of Western-inspired music with ancient Japanese poetic imagery signified the double move of Meiji radical reform: "Kimigayo" was both a modern copy of "God Save the King" and a declaration of an ancient and distinctive Japanese sensibility.[10] It was modern and Western, but also ancient and Japanese.

When described with adjectives such as "Western" and "Japanese," these combinations can seem like ungainly hybrids. The very words "Western" and "Japanese" suggest a choice between distinct and irreconcilable options. But late Tokugawa and Meiji leaders were strikingly untroubled by such concerns. Instead they employed a language in which radical hybridity was both laudable and unremarkable. Western practices worthy of emulation were described as "enlightened" (*kaika*), "civilized" (*bunmei*), "universal" (*udai*), or "international" (*bankoku*) rather than uniquely Western. By contrast, local practices needing reform were described as "conventional and routine" (*injun*) or corrupt (*rōshū*), rather than distinctly Japanese. Radical reformers of the late Tokugawa and early Meiji era routinely wrote that Japan should "rank with the nations of the world" (*bankoku ni heiritsu*). The term "heiritsu," literally "to stand side by side," implied both equality and distinctiveness; the goal was to make Japan equal to, but still different from, the great powers.

Many histories of Japan describe these processes in terms of "modernization" or "modernity." But those terms inherently efface continuities with the ancient past.[11] A major aspect of the Restoration was intense technological borrowing, but that was common to previous epochs as well. The concept of global isomorphism helps to situate the Restoration in that longer historical context: polities become more like each other during periods of intense interaction, whether through trade, war, or a combination. That process is driven partly through the borrowing of best practices: polities copy what seems to work best. Further, polities that fail, either in trade or war, can be absorbed by their rivals. But some commonalities are based in less tangible, utilitarian advantages. Often the cultural practices of dominant polities are appealing simply because they are associated with military or economic dominance. Thus, in the seventh century, the Japanese political elite adopted the garb of the Tang dynasty court, but in the nineteenth century, British-style frock coats. Those uniforms conveyed no practical advantage but worked instead as symbols, marking the Japanese as civilized. In that sense, globalism is not especially modern. Rather, the Japanese adoption of Tang-style court caps was "ancient global isomorphism," while frock coats were "modern global isomorphism."[12]

A related but distinct question is how did the Japanese explain the Restoration to themselves? How did they combine the seemingly contradictory goals of glorifying the Japanese past while embracing radical, Western-oriented change? Full of optimism and revolutionary ardor, Meiji reformers saw themselves as revitalizing their Japanese heritage and culture rather diluting it through Westernization. What could possibly be wrong with strengthening Japan by adapting "international" and "universal" best practices? How could the benefits of "civilization" possibly make Japan less Japanese? Because terms such as "civilization" were culturally and temporally non-specific, late Tokugawa and Meiji-era reformers could combine their admiration for the ancient Japanese past with an eagerness for radical change and foreign models. The revival of ancient Japanese custom was part of a rush toward a cosmopolitan future.

In order to describe the logic of Tokugawa and Meiji thought, this book focuses on two critical tensions: radical nostalgia and cosmopolitan chauvinism. Radical nostalgia refers to the invocation of the distant past to promote radical change in the present—for example, citing the ancient conscript army to advance military reform eleven centuries later. Meiji reformers used ancient precedents to justify revolutionary change within a discourse of deference to authority: the elimination of the daimyo ruling class, for example, was explained not as the overthrow of a pampered and feckless elite but as a return to ancient origins.[13] Radical nostalgia explains how men like Itō could shift from xenophobia to xenophilia without a sense of having recanted or abandoned their earlier views. Itō's desire to purge Japan of foreigners was based on a vision of ancient Japan that was pure and unsullied by foreign influence. But, as cooler heads observed, the ancient imperial state had graciously received foreign emissaries. Such hospitality was a measure of its power, not its weakness. As early as the 1850s, Itō's own mentor, Yoshida Shōin, abruptly abandoned his calls to "expel the barbarian" from Japan and instead sought to travel to the United States and learn from Americans. In this way, Itō and many other Meiji activists could embrace foreign ideas without any sense of betrayal or transgression: they had merely refined their understanding of the glories of ancient Japan.[14]

Radical nostalgia was not new to the Meiji era. On the contrary, Tokugawa-era radical nostalgia paved the way for Meiji-era reforms. Tokugawa-era reformers had advocated change under the guise of reverence for the past, but they were constrained in their choice of historical precedent. Reformers who wanted to repair rather than replace the Tokugawa regime could go back only as far as the early 1600s, the origins of the Tokugawa shogunate, or to the late 1500s, the rise of the Tokugawa warrior house. If they looked at pre-Tokugawa precedents, they would have implicitly suggested that the Tokugawa regime itself could be replaced. As a result, they were less bold than their Meiji counterparts, who could look back more than ten centuries. But even within this narrower time frame, Tokugawa-era reformers used the past to challenge the present. They advocated the reform of hereditary privilege by looking back to the late 1500s and early 1600s, when class distinctions were more fluid. In foreign affairs, they criticized isolationist policies by noting that the early Tokugawa shoguns had allowed Japanese traders to travel across East Asia. Such arguments appeared in a diverse range of Tokugawa-era writings, including the works of Ogyū Sorai, Hayashi Shihei, and Hirata Atsutane. These men agreed on little except that the Tokugawa regime should be reinvigorated and legitimized by returning to its earlier principles. Tokugawa-era radical nostalgia could not save the regime, but it paved the way for Meiji-era discourse.

Cosmopolitan chauvinism refers to the strategy of integrating Japanese cultural distinctiveness with cross-cultural norms.[15] Much as radical nostalgia made the past compatible with the future, cosmopolitan chauvinism made foreign ideas compatible with local practice. Cosmopolitan chauvinism posited that certain great universal truths had been discovered outside Japan. Although discovered abroad, these ideas were universally applicable and would therefore enhance rather than degrade Japanese culture. This approach transcended the potential opposition of "Japanese" and "foreign." Instead, within the discourse of cosmopolitan chauvinism, Japan's full military, economic, political, and even cultural potential could be realized only by looking outside Japan. Cosmopolitan chauvinism thus made cross-cultural borrowing compatible with local pride.

Cosmopolitan chauvinism figured prominently in the Japanese study of modern European political institutions. As early as 1862, Katō Hiroyuki argued that Japan should adopt the Western principle of separation of powers. Examining the various polities of the world, Katō had concluded that "weaker" governments could actually produce stronger nations because autocracies enervated their own people. For Katō, this was "an inevitable trend of the times." Around the world, nascent constitutional monarchies and republics were replacing old empires. Prussia, for example, was growing at the expense of the Habsburg Empire. The choice, for Katō, was thus between good government and bad government, not between East and West. China, Russia, Austria, and Turkey were all failing because they would not adopt constitutions. Japan should instead emulate Prussia, adopting a modern constitutional monarchy.[16]

As with radical nostalgia, Meiji-era discourse built on Tokugawa precedents. Early modern thinkers had long invoked the strategy of treating Western ideas as universal rather than foreign. Satō Nobuhiro, for example, insisted that Western astronomy was more compatible with Japanese culture than with that of Europe. In 1825, he published a detailed summary of European astronomical thought, complete with seven planets in elliptical orbits around the sun. He then showed how this model was fully compatible with ancient Japanese mythology: the centrality of the sun goddess Amaterasu in Japanese culture, for example, corresponded to the centrality of the sun in heliocentric theory. In Europe, however, modern astronomy collided with religious notions of geocentrism. Because discussions of the Bible were illegal in Tokugawa Japan, Satō wrote with great caution, but his intent is clear. Modern Western astronomy actually disproves the Bible but confirms the truth of the *Kojiki*, Japan's ancient chronicle.[17]

Japanese thinkers had also applied cosmopolitan chauvinism to Chinese and Indian thought, treating Confucianism and Buddhism as universal truths rather than foreign ideas. In Buddhism, religious theorists matched Shinto deities to incarnations of the Buddha, arguing that the Japanese gods were local manifestations of various forms of Buddhist truth. Instead of positing a conflict between a "foreign" religion and local tradition, Japanese religious practitioners created a symbiosis. A famous Buddhist-Shinto pairing was that of Vairocana, the most abstract and universal manifestation of the Buddha, with Amaterasu. That association meant that the largest temple and Buddha image in Japan, Tōdaiji and its huge bronze statue of Vairocana, were also venerations of Amaterasu.[18] In the Tokugawa era, nativist philosophers began to push back against this syncretism, insisting that Buddhism was corrupting a pure Japanese tradition. But that hostility toward Buddhism did not diminish the broader impact of cosmopolitan chauvinism: foreign ideas could be localized and made essential to Japanese culture.

Japanese thinkers also claimed Confucian thought as their own cultural heritage. In the 1600s, for example, the philosopher Yamazaki Ansai insisted that Japan could claim Confucian thought as its own. In an oft-cited exchange, Yamazaki was asked what he would do if Chinese forces attacked Japan, led in person by Confucius and Mencius. Yamazaki responded that he would capture Confucius and Mencius alive and have them serve Japan: "That is what Confucius and Mencius would teach us to do."[19] Yamazaki thus treated these men as universal sages, great philosophers who were incidentally born in China, rather than Chinese philosophers. Because of their universality, they could be made to serve Japan. Thus, for Yamazaki, Japanese cultural pride was fully compatible with a reverence for Confucius and Mencius. Meiji thinkers took a parallel approach to Western thought, separating powerful ideas from their geographic origins: intriguing European ideas were just universal truths that happened to be discovered first in Europe.[20]

Because cosmopolitan chauvinism encompassed both Chinese and European ideas, it helped produce the vibrant eclecticism of early Meiji thought. Rather than contrast "Eastern" and "Western" thought, many nineteenth-century thinkers freely combined both traditions, bringing together complementary universal truths. Kurimoto Joun, for example, embraced both Confucian idealism and Western legal thought. While serving as the Tokugawa shogun's ambassador to France, Kurimoto became convinced of the value of Western jurisprudence, but he reconciled this with his earlier education in the Confucian classics. It was true, he wrote, that in a society governed by Confucian sages, detailed written law would be unnecessary. The problem was that such sages were in short supply. Thus, in reality, judges were often ordinary men, full of bias and moral weakness. The solution to this quandary was to introduce an explicit and exacting legal code, such as the Napoleonic Code. The encyclopedic detail of the Napoleonic Code was therefore a brilliant supplement to Confucian thought, since it addressed how ordinary men, rather than sages, might adjudicate legal disputes.[21] Astute and intellectually omnivorous, Kurimoto served the shogunate but also thrived after its demise. In the Meiji period, he became editor of a major newspaper (*Yūbin Hōchi Shinbun*), and his cosmopolitan chauvinism shaped public discourse on politics, society, and culture.

These forces of cosmopolitan chauvinism and radical nostalgia explain a central tension of the Meiji Restoration. In their cosmopolitan chauvinism, reformers embraced Western ideas in defense of local distinctiveness. In their radical nostalgia, they pushed Japan into the future while extolling the glories of the past. Since Meiji radical nostalgia looked backed to ancient Japan, explaining the Restoration requires examining the ancient past. Chapter 1 surveys Japanese history from the 700s to the 1700s, focusing on the precedents for state-building invoked in the 1800s. Faced with the challenge of European imperialism, late Tokugawa and Meiji reformers looked back to earlier eras of Japanese globalization. How had Japan defended and legitimized itself in the ancient and medieval periods? How had the state mobilized people and resources for war? Many Tokugawa-era reformers looked to the early 1600s for precedents. That was the apex of Tokugawa power and overseas engagement, and reformers urged later shoguns to restore the policies of the early years of the dynasty. Meiji reformers, by contrast, looked beyond the Tokugawa era, going further back to the Nara and Heian periods, the zenith of imperial state power.

Chapter 2 describes reform efforts from the 1700s until the crisis of imperialism in the 1840s. For Meiji reformers, the Tokugawa regime was a failure because it could not defend Japan against imperialism. By other metrics, however, the Tokugawa shogunate was a remarkable success: it kept Japan at peace, both foreign and domestic, for more than two centuries. Beginning in the 1600s, the Tokugawa regime carefully avoided any overseas engagements that might lead to diplomatic or military disgrace. With no external threats, the government saw little need to maintain a robust military or to extend the powers of the central state. This chapter explores how perceived Tokugawa weakness in the 1800s was largely a consequence of Tokugawa successes in the 1700s; in the absence of interstate conflict, the regime had no need to prepare for war.

Chapter 3 discusses the rise of radical imperial loyalism and the overthrow of the shogunate in 1868. The rebels who fought against the Tokugawa in 1868 insisted that they were attacking a traitorous regime, an enemy of the Japanese imperial house. Yet, both Tokugawa reformers and imperial loyalists were motivated by similar concerns. As a result, shogunal reforms in many ways presaged Meiji reforms. Activists on both sides embraced cosmopolitan chauvinism, adopting Western practices and technologies in order to strengthen Japan. Employing radical nostalgia, they wrapped their bold visions of the future in reverence for the past. Because of these commonalities, imperial loyalists quickly pardoned and employed many Tokugawa officials.

Chapter 4 explores the early years of the Meiji Restoration, from 1868 to 1871, and the dissolution of daimyo domains. Although imperial loyalists had toppled the shogunate, they moved cautiously against the daimyo, Japan's regional lords. Indeed, rather than eliminate the daimyo, the new government attempted to rule through them, even creating new daimyo territories and convening daimyo councils. The Meiji state's deference to daimyo domains had the unexpected consequence of speeding their collapse. Many astute daimyo recognized that the goal of an internationally recognized Japanese nation-state could not be achieved through hundreds of regional reform movements. Rather than defend their traditional privileges, many daimyo invoked radical nostalgia and advocated a return to the central power of the ancient imperial state. Rewarded for their cooperation with lavish pensions, the elite stratum of the samurai estate quietly disappeared from political life.

Chapter 5 examines a period of radical reform and intense discord, 1871 to 1873. The government was united by cosmopolitan chauvinism and radical nostalgia but divided by the question of which nations to emulate. Members of the new government shared a common goal: to create a powerful Japanese nation-state based on both the ancient Japanese monarchy and modern Western models. But within that ambit of agreement, the government confronted divisive practical questions. How had the great Western powers become so strong? Was it superior technology? Better education? Greater freedom? Greater loyalty? And which Western models should Japan adopt? Should they look to French, Prussian, British, or American models? And what made Western nation-states so powerful? Was it the power of the state? Or did national power originate with the people and their devotion to their state? In 1873, these fierce disagreements tore the government apart. Several major leaders of the

Restoration quit in protest, setting the stage for violent rebellions in subsequent years.

Chapter 6 focuses on the new government's consolidation of political power and the emergence of a new political opposition between 1874 and 1881. Both the modern Japanese bureaucracy and modern popular opposition movements can be traced to the crisis of 1873. After a period of revolutionary fervor, the government shifted to more cautious and systematic reform. The goal was still "to stand with the nations of the world," but this was now understood as a generation-long process. In the place of revolutionary ardor, charisma, and courage, the government increasingly valued administrative competence, such as the ability to keep a ministry on budget. Increasingly structured and focused, this post-crisis administration established the basic functions and organizational form of the modern Japanese bureaucracy. Meanwhile, the opposition articulated alternative visions of the Japanese future. They extolled Japanese martial valor and criticized the government for its cowardice. They also accused the government of autocracy. The regime was failing, they argued, either to inspire the "people" or to follow the popular will. But the opposition did not agree on a single definition of the "people." Conceived narrowly, the "people" only included disgruntled samurai, but considered broadly, it encompassed millions of farmers and merchants. Both capacious and chaotic, this opposition movement transcended such standard distinctions as "progressive" and "conservative." Working within the discourse of cosmopolitan chauvinism, the opposition invoked samurai valor as an emblem of national pride but also cited Western theories of natural rights. In pursuing their goals, members of the opposition embraced both violent insurrection and peaceful petitions. The early Meiji opposition demonstrated the appeal of both a belligerent foreign policy and demands for a more inclusive political system. It is thus the antecedent of both popular support for Japan's militarism and modern mass movements for democracy.

By the 1880s, Japan was a stable nation-state, not a revolutionary regime. Its leaders no longer imagined that they could transform Japan overnight into a world power. When Itō spoke in Washington, DC, in 1872, for example, he still hoped that charm and good intentions might convince the United States to renegotiate the unequal treaties. By the 1880s, he understood that such negotiations would take decades of legal and constitutional reform. Katō Hiroyuki, who introduced Western political thought to Japan in the 1860s, looked back on his early writings with dismay. Who, he wondered, was that dangerous young radical? After Katō became president of

Tokyo Imperial University, he banned reprinting of his early work. Katō and Itō were representative of a new patience and caution. Instead of passion and courage, the Japanese leadership instead esteemed planning and consistency. That conservative turn can be understood as the maturation of the modern Japanese state. For this book, however, it marked the end of an era of revolutionary potential and change.[22]

The central theme of the book is thus that the Meiji Restoration needs to be considered, simultaneously, in three different contexts. First, and most obvious, is the local diachronic context. Japan in the 1860s and 1870s was shaped by policies and practices of preceding decades. Many of the boldest reforms of the Meiji state, for example, can be understood as radical variants of Tokugawa-era reform initiatives. At the same time, the Restoration was shaped globally and synchronically. As Japan grew more embedded in world politics, the impact of decisions made in London, Paris, Washington, and St. Petersburg increased accordingly. Japanese leaders were active in this process, seeking to legitimize the Japanese state in a new international order. The Meiji Restoration was thus part the "long nineteenth century," with the decline of old empires and the rise of powerful new states. Finally, the Restoration needs to be understood asynchronically: shaped by the distant past. Many passionate imperial loyalists hoped for the return of a mythical age in which emperors and their subjects were united by an effortless spiritual immediacy, sanctified by religious rites. They dreamed of a pure Japanese civilization, unspoiled by Chinese and Western influence. They were crushingly disappointed. Meiji leaders looked to a different aspect of the ancient past. Ancient imperial rule was relevant for how it responded to Sui and Tang China, coopting and adapting foreign ideas to build a powerful new Japanese state. Ancient imperial policies, such as the creation of national taxation and a national army, gave Meiji leaders ancient precedents for modernizing reforms. In the context of modern globalization, the process of ancient globalization felt immediate and vital.[23]

I

An Almost Perpetual Peace

THE REVOLUTIONARIES WHO toppled the Tokugawa shogunate disparaged it as feeble and backward. They faulted it for abetting social and economic stagnation and impeding advances in critical military technologies. The shogunate had failed to defend Japan against a foreign threat and thereby undermined Japan's rightful status as a world power. Those Meiji-era accusations reflect the challenges of the nineteenth century, primarily the threat of Western imperialism. By that criterion, the Tokugawa was indeed a failure: it was never able to mobilize Japan's people or resources in a unified and effective response to foreign aggression.

By other criteria, however, the Tokugawa regime looks quite different. The Tokugawa state system kept Japan at peace, both foreign and domestic, for over two centuries. That long peace witnessed a flourishing of Japanese culture. A surge in literacy and a thriving publishing industry fed growing demand for everything from pulp fiction to classical poetry. The Tokugawa capital of Edo, today known as Tokyo, emerged as one of the largest and most vibrant cities in the world, with a full range of intellectual, aesthetic, and carnal diversions. A new consumer culture, complete with ephemeral trends in clothing and hairstyle, started in cities and slowly spread to the countryside, where new technologies, such as better farm tools and new crops, raised living standards. Many domestic critics viewed these changes as decadent, but, prior to the crisis of imperialism, few saw the Tokugawa regime as fragile.

The Tokugawa regime fell not because it was "weak" but because it could not adapt to an increasingly violent international environment. For centuries, the Tokugawa shoguns had assiduously avoided foreign entanglements, maintaining limited but peaceful relations with China and Korea and strictly limiting contact with other polities. That long Pax

Tokugawa had obviated the need for a powerful national military: there was no one to fight. Without a national army, the shoguns lacked a key incentive to establish national institutions, such as national taxation. Why would the Tokugawa risk sparking domestic discontent by collecting taxes for a national army it did not need? In other parts of Eurasia, fierce inter-state rivalries drove rulers to seek ever-expanding control over their people. From Western Europe to Southeast Asia, monarchs demanded more power in order to defeat rival kingdoms. Warfare was expensive, and as kings sought more income from their subjects they became increasingly concerned with quotidian aspects of their subjects' lives: where did commoners live, what did they do, how much did they produce, and how much tax could they pay? In preparation for war, rulers counted, taxed, drafted, trained, and indoctrinated their people with increasing intensity. War-making was thus central to state-building, or, in the words of sociologist Charles Tilly, "war made the state and the state made war."[1]

Beginning in the 1600s, the Tokugawa took a different approach. Having made peace with China and Korea, they chose stability over conflict, claiming only enough power to maintain the status quo. Domestically, they were content with indirect rule. Rather than crush regional warlords, they sought instead to guarantee their submission and compliance. In foreign policy, the Tokugawa sought to avoid open conflict. This strategy was ideally suited to its contemporaneous international environment: neither China nor Korea were eager to refight the disastrous wars of the 1590s. Instead, Japan and the major powers of Northeast Asia engaged in a highly attenuated but peaceful web of relations. When that international environment changed, however, the Tokugawa regime began to seem fragile and malformed. The spread of Western imperialism to Northeast Asia meant that war-making was again essential to statecraft. The Tokugawa regime's carefully considered policies began to appear feckless and outdated. The regime was not so much weak as endangered by a changed ecosystem.

Making sense of the fall of the Tokugawa thus requires examining its broader political environment. For nineteenth-century reformers, looking at an environment shaped by Western imperialism, the Tokugawa regime offered only negative precedents: it had failed to prepare for a violent and competitive interstate order. Meiji reformers, in their search for a usable past, looked beyond the Tokugawa regime, to previous eras of globalization, when Japanese leaders had faced similar challenges. How had Japan responded to the first great Chinese empires, the Sui (581–618 CE) and Tang China (618–907 CE)? How had it responded to Western imperial ambitions in the sixteenth and early seventeenth centuries? During both of those eras, local leaders built powerful, centralized Japanese states in the face of foreign threats and rivalries.

The long sweep of Japanese history can be understood in terms of three great waves of globalization and global isomorphism.[2] The first wave of Japanese globalization began in the sixth century, when Japan adapted to the rise of Sui and Tang China, and lasted through the tenth century.[3] In this first wave of globalization, direct contacts were limited to East Asia, but precious objects reached Japan from as far away as Persia. The second wave began in the fifteenth century and lasted into the seventeenth, as Japan engaged with new global markets and empires. This globalization involved the creation of world markets and direct personal contacts between the peoples of Japan, Europe, and the New World. The third wave began in the mid-1800s and continues to the present.

Japan's first era of globalization triggered the creation of the ancient Japanese imperial state. In the 600s, as in the 1800s, Japanese leaders sought to defend Japan against encroaching empires, and that required both emulating foreign best practices and legitimizing Japan in a broader international discourse. In the Meiji era, the foreign threat was Western imperialism, but in the ancient period, it was the Chinese empire. The Sui and then the Tang dynasties created massive empires, stretching from parts of modern Vietnam in the southeast to modern Turkmenistan in the west and Manchuria in the northeast. The Tang tributary system covered a still wider sphere, including the Korean peninsula and much of Central and Southeast Asia. Under that system, local "kings" were described as the servants of the Tang emperor, a singular monarch, invested by the will of heaven.

As in the 1800s, ancient Japanese leaders felt threatened by this foreign empire, and they were especially alarmed by events on the Korean peninsula. In the 660s, the Tang intervened on behalf of the Korean kingdom of Silla in a multi-sided civil war. Silla was then able to destroy its main rival Paekche. Japanese troops had supported Paekche and were humiliated in battle by the joint forces of Tang and Silla. After that debacle, it seemed the Tang and its allies might move against Japan.[4]

As in the 1800s, it was unclear what made this massive foreign empire so powerful. Was it merely military technology? Or was it also the political systems that allowed the mobilization and command of people and resources? Or perhaps a still broader philosophical and religious system? Unsure, Japanese reformers were expansive in their adoption of foreign practices. They undertook a massive centralization of the Japanese state, based largely on Tang models. The Nara-Heian state attempted the first nationwide population and land surveys in Japanese history. The imperial state claimed control over all the arable land in Japan, overriding the claims of noble lineage groups (*uji*). From the late seventh century, in theory, all farmland was redistributed every six years, with equal parcels for each type of cultivator: male or female, free or indentured. Similarly, the entire population of Japan was, in law if not in practice, redistricted into equally sized villages, which paid taxes into a central treasury. Adult males owed both military and labor service to the central state. A new central administration was created, and titles based on lineage were replaced with Tang-style imperial offices. The Japanese sovereign was now, in theory if not in practice, served by ministers with portfolios rather than by chieftains. Since, in Tang thought, legitimate monarchs disseminated Buddhist teachings, the ancient Japanese state built a nationwide system of Buddhist temples and promoted the study of Buddhist texts. To look "civilized," ancient Japanese officials adopted the Tang dress code. As in the 1800s, Japanese rulers were willing to coopt their enemies' ideas and technologies in defense of a Japanese state. In these parallel instances of global isomorphism, cooptation extended from rarified philosophical abstractions to mundane aspects of daily life.

Even as they adapted Chinese institutions and technologies, ancient Japanese rulers insisted on the unique glories of the Japanese state. The name "Japan" itself reflects this combination of mimesis and chauvinism. "Japan" comes from the Japanese "*Nihon*" (via the Chinese "*Riben*") and means "origin of the sun" or "land of the rising sun." The term was first used in the 600s and makes sense primarily as a description of Japan relative to Sui and Tang China. Japan is the "land of the rising sun" only when seen from lands to the west, namely, China. By describing Japan as the land of the "rising" sun, and China as the land of the "setting" sun, Japanese diplomats asserted their own cultural superiority, but at the same time they hinted at the centrality of Chinese civilization. Notably, earlier terms for Japan, such as "land of the eight islands" (Ōyashima), referred to local geography and made no reference to the continent. The word Nihon, by contrast, is relational, establishing Japan's position as an eastern outpost in a China-centered international order.

Japan's first wave of globalization ended in the early tenth century. The Japanese imperial court ceased embassies to China in the late 800s, and the Tang itself collapsed in 907. The collapse of the Tang tributary system did not halt non-state relations. On the contrary, cultural and economic exchange between Japan and the continent continued unabated, with deep and lasting consequences. Zen Buddhism, for example, was brought to Japan by intrepid monks, who traveled to China for study in the twelfth and thirteenth centuries. But interstate travel decreased and these exchanges occurred outside formal structures of power.[5] Within Japan, after the 1100s, the imperial court steadily lost power to its military officers. The shogun emerged as an independent source of power rather than merely an imperial officer. The first shogunal dynasty, the Minamoto, created new rituals and institutions that shaped Japanese politics into the 1870s. Centuries later, the Tokugawa shoguns not only employed Minamoto rituals, such as vows of loyalty, but also claimed genealogical descent from Minamoto no Yoritomo, the first shogun.

The first shogunate set many precedents for warrior rule, but it was vastly less powerful than the Tokugawa regime. The second shogunal dynasty, the Ashikaga, was still weaker. Indeed, from the 1300s until the late 1500s, political power shifted from the capital to the countryside: neither the imperial court nor the shogunate could exert national control. One nascent political force in these years was a new type of local ruler called *daimyō*. These warlords based their legitimacy on their ability to win battles against their rivals, to reward their followers, and to stop feuding and turmoil within their territories. The daimyo of the Warring States era (1467–1568) seized the authority necessary to rule their domains: they issued legal codes, established courts, took population surveys, and directed public works. They routinely acted without reference to higher authority, either the imperial house or the beleaguered shoguns. Commoners also developed increasingly sophisticated systems of self-government. Village councils took charge of civil affairs and public safety, regulating matters such as the lodging of travelers, the keeping of dogs, and the maintenance of temples and shrines. To defend against banditry and plunder, they constructed moats and palisades. These sub-national institutions outlasted the Tokugawa shogunate itself. In fact, it was daimyo armies that defeated the Tokugawa in 1868. At the local level, village headmen and councils remained in control while the Meiji government developed new institutions of national control.

Powerful central authority reemerged only in the late 1500s. From 1568 to 1600, three successive warlords beat their rivals into submission and reestablished institutions of national control. The new policies and practices of those hegemons became the basis of Tokugawa rule. The first

unifier, Oda Nobunaga, seized the capital city of Kyoto in 1568 and proceeded to conquer much of central Japan. Nobunaga initially styled himself
as a defender of the Ashikaga shogunate, and he claimed to be restoring the
shogun Ashikaga Yoshiaki to power. In 1573, however, Nobunaga expelled
Yoshiaki, destroying even the façade of Ashikaga control. Nobunaga's successor, Toyotomi Hideyoshi, pushed further. Between 1582 and 1590, he
forced every daimyo in Japan to acknowledge his supremacy, building the
most powerful central government since the apex of the imperial state in
the 700s.

Hideyoshi demanded vows of loyalty from all daimyo and crushed
those who contested his decrees. Daimyo sent family members as noble
hostages to live in Kyoto, Hideyoshi's capital, as a sign of their submission.
Hideyoshi ordered the daimyo to compile detailed land surveys (*Taikō
kenchi*) and used them to increase, decrease, or move their investitures
according to his strategic vision. Compliance with the land survey edict
was often more nominal than real: daimyo patched together fragmentary
land records and presented them as comprehensive surveys. But no one
thought to challenge Hideyoshi's authority to demand the surveys or to
specify new national standards for weights and measures. Hideyoshi also
proclaimed a strict distinction between farmers and samurai, constraining the social fluidity of the Warring States era, when he himself had risen
from commoner origins to rule Japan. Instead, Hideyoshi restricted mobility, ordering severe punishments for farmers who left their villages and let
land fall fallow. To secure commoner submission, Hideyoshi ordered the
collection of weapons, including swords, bows, spears, and firearms. This,
he declared, would lead to peace and happiness by ensuring that farmers worked diligently in their fields rather than contesting tax collection.
Samurai were barred from changing masters without formal permission
and from living as merchants or farmers. This later became known as
a four-estate system of warriors, farmers, artisans, and merchants. After
seizing control over Japan's major gold and silver mines, Hideyoshi issued
the first Japanese government coins since the 900s, replacing imported
Chinese coins. He attacked independent religious institutions, forcing
powerful temples to acknowledge his superior authority. By the 1590s,
Hideyoshi had created the most powerful Japanese government in eight
centuries.[6]

Hideyoshi's quest for domestic hegemony was linked to his international ambitions. Like the ancient *ritsu-ryō* state, Hideyoshi was concerned
with military control of the Korean peninsula. Unlike the ancient imperial

state, his approach was unmistakably aggressive. Hideyoshi sought to conquer Korea and to establish a massive international empire. That ambition required complete domestic hegemony in order for Hideyoshi to marshal Japanese human and material resources without fear of non-compliance or dissent. As in ancient Japan, war-making inspired state-making.

Hideyoshi's imperial ambitions were part of a second wave of Japanese globalization. That wave had begun in the 1400s, when Ming China's expanding economy and growing demand for silver promoted overseas commerce. Trade surged after the discovery of large silver deposits in western Japan in 1530s and the introduction of new smelting techniques. Unlike Japan's first wave of globalization in the Asuka-Nara-Heian period, this second wave featured an integrated world economy. The founding of Manila in 1571 connected the East Asian silver trade with New World silver, bringing Japan into an emerging world economy. By the early 1600s, international trade was so extensive that the relative prices of gold and silver converged in markets as distant as Japan, China, and France.[7] At the peak of this trade cycle (1540–1640) Japanese silver exports were as high as 200 tons per year and accounted for as much as 30 percent of the world's silver production.[8] In addition to precious metals, Japan exported swords, spears, fans, and room screens (*byōbu*) and it imported coins, silk thread and cloth, linen, spices, and medicines.[9]

These global flows of goods were enabled by a surge in human mobility: traders, smugglers, and pirates moved freely in and out of the Japanese islands, creating large expatriate communities. Within Japan there were Chinese and Korean settlements throughout the southwest and substantial European trading posts in Hirado and Nagasaki.[10] Japanese traders established settlements across Southeast Asia, including Macao, Hội An (now Vietnam), Ayutthaya (now Thailand), and Luzon (now the Philippines).[11] As in the 1800s, Japanese rulers employed foreign advisors. Perhaps the most famous is William Adams (also known as Miura Anjin, 1564–1620), the English mariner who inspired James Clavell's novel, *Shogun*. Adams arrived in Japan in 1600 as a pilot for the Dutch and was befriended by Tokugawa Ieyasu, the first Tokugawa shogun. Adams served Ieyasu as shipbuilder, interpreter, and advisor, and he was granted official support for trading missions to Tonkin and Ayutthaya. Chinese and Korean vassals are less famous but were more numerous. The Chinese captain Zhang Zhong (? –?) arrived in Hirado when his two ships drifted ashore. He was recruited by a daimyo as a doctor and military advisor. His son received a large investiture, as did his two grandsons.[12] Zhu Shunhui (1600–82), a Confucian scholar and Ming loyalist, became an important advisor to Mito domain, while another Ming refugee, Yinyuan (J., Ingen; 1592–1673), introduced Ōbaku (Ch., Huangbo), a new sect of Zen, with the support of the shogunate.[13] Many Koreans were brought to Japan as hostages during Hideyoshi's invasion. Some escaped and roughly 7,500 were eventually repatriated as part of peace negotiations, but others became hereditary retainers in Japanese vassal bands.[14] A parallel process occurred abroad, as Japanese expatriates entered the service of foreign rulers. Yamada Nagamasa (1590?–1630), leader of the Japanese community in Ayutthaya, was given an official title by King Songtham for his military service. After Songtham's death in 1628, Yamada led a large army of Siamese and Japanese soldiers to secure the throne for Songtham's son, Chetthathirat.

This global exchange contributed to the rapid dissemination of new ideas and technologies. The most striking new ideology was Christianity, introduced by Portuguese and Spanish missionaries in the 1540s. Several prominent daimyo were intrigued by this doctrine and allowed the Jesuits to establish churches, seminaries, orphanages, and hospitals. Hideyoshi himself issued orders protecting the Jesuits from interference in their proselytizing.[15] Some lords saw Christianity primarily as means of securing reliable access to gunpowder and firearms, but several daimyo were sincere converts and promoted the conversion of their retainers and commoners. In 1582, three Christian daimyo sponsored an embassy to Rome, sending representatives to the Vatican for an audience with Pope Gregory XIII. By the early 1580s, the Jesuits counted nearly 150,000 Japanese Christians and by the 1600s the total may have reached 700,000, roughly 5 percent of the population.[16] As in modern Japan, Christianity was disproportionately influential among elites: Christian daimyo (in the 1500s) and Christian prime ministers (in the 1900s) were surprisingly common.

In technology, the most transformative innovation was the firearm. The Ming had used firearms from at least the 1300s, and they were used in the Japanese archipelago and Ryukyu from the 1400s.[17] But the widespread use of guns in Japan did not begin until the introduction of matchlocks by the Portuguese in 1543. Japanese warriors were impressed by their superior range and accuracy, and daimyo began promoting domestic production. Japanese smiths were proficient enough that by the late 1500s they were making guns in large numbers and developing new techniques to improve accuracy. In battlefield reports from the early 1600s, gunshot wounds outnumbered arrow wounds by four to one.[18] The adoption of firearms promoted social mobility. A well-disciplined deployment of peasant musketeers could destroy an elite brigade of mounted archers, whose skills reflected years of training and noble privilege.[19] As in the Meiji period, globalization and military competition transformed the social order.

Despite an abundance of Western contacts, Japanese interstate politics remained focused on China. Accordingly, Hideyoshi's dream of empire was centered on the Ming. Historians still debate whether Hideyoshi truly hoped to march into Beijing and take control of the Ming throne or whether this bluster concealed more modest goals. At a minimum, he wanted the Ming court to recognize him as an equal. These goals explicitly challenged the notion that the Chinese emperor was superior to other sovereigns.[20] Ironically, even as Hideyoshi challenged the Ming, he reproduced the logic of the Chinese world order. He considered and rejected, for example, a plan to conquer Luzon.[21] In Hideyoshi's worldview, subjugating the Spanish or the Dutch in East Asia would not have made him a great monarch. Only by forcing recognition from China could he legitimize his conquests. Thus, Japan's second epoch of globalization reveals the "softer" ontological aspect of global isomorphism: the power of ideas to shape politics, independent of military or economic force. The Ming did not compel Hideyoshi to accept the notion of China as the center of civilization. Rather, Hideyoshi unwittingly reproduced Sinocentrism when he insisted on building his empire by going through, rather than around, Beijing. Thus, even as he fought the Ming, Hideyoshi confirmed the centrality of China in East Asian civilization.

Hideyoshi's dreams of empire ended in disaster. His armies invaded Korea in 1592 and, after a series of swift victories, became bogged down in a protracted struggle against Korean forces and their Ming allies. By 1598, a combination of Ming troops, a revitalized Korean navy, and Korean guerillas had driven his troops back to a defensive perimeter in the southeastern corner of the peninsula. When Hideyoshi died later that year, his generals decamped for home, many delighted to be free of his folly. Hideyoshi's hubris undermined his domestic legacy. His heir, Hideyori, was only five years old in 1598, and he needed the support and cooperation of his father's allies to succeed. In the wake of the Korean debacle, that help was not forthcoming. Hideyoshi's governing council fractured and Tokugawa Ieyasu, an erstwhile ally, emerged supreme, crushing a rival coalition in 1600. In 1615 the Tokugawa killed Hideyori, Hideyoshi's heir, and eliminated the Toyotomi line.

Hideyoshi's Korean debacle was a powerful negative precedent for the Tokugawa. The early Tokugawa shoguns extended Hideyoshi's efforts to establish domestic hegemony, but they were leery of his international aspirations. Imperial ambition, it seemed, was bad for dynastic longevity. Instead, the Tokugawa steadily disengaged from the broader world. Starting in the 1630s, they restricted the ability of Japanese to live and travel overseas and limited the movement of foreigners in Japan. In the 1700s, they began to limit Japan's international trade. The cliché that Tokugawa Japan was a "closed country" is an exaggeration, but the late 1700s were a nadir for Japan's global integration.

The Tokugawa state's cautious and restrained approach to interstate engagement produced a paradox. The Tokugawa shogunate was, nominally, a warrior government, but its great accomplishment was two centuries of peace. This Pax Tokugawa was supported, if tacitly and indirectly, by Japan's major neighbors: China and Korea. Once the Tokugawa foreswore imperial ambitions, those kingdoms were amenable to an enduring, if frosty, peace. In that international climate, the Tokugawa's neglect of a powerful national army was frugal rather than cowardly. It was only in the 1800s, in the face of Western imperialism, that Tokugawa military weakness became a threat to the dynasty's legitimacy.

Pax Tokugawa and East Asian Diplomacy

Understanding the fall of the Tokugawa regime requires examining its central paradox: the shogunate was a warrior government that for two centuries deftly avoided war. The first three Tokugawa shoguns (Ieyasu, Hidetada, and Iemitsu) built their government largely on domestic precedents laid down by Hideyoshi. They inherited a uniquely powerful system of rule and strengthened it still further. But Ieyasu and his successors had little interest in foreign conquest. Rather than expend resources on an overseas empire, they focused on consolidating their domestic hegemony and they severed foreign contacts that seemed to threaten the regime. This decrease in international contacts coincided with a slowing in state formation: after the mid-1600s, the Tokugawa ceased their drive to centralize power. Without the threat of domestic or international conflict, Tokugawa shoguns lost the drive to crush their domestic rivals. In the 1800s, when the shogunate confronted Western imperialism, it became a victim of its own success. The shogunate had so successfully adapted to peace that it could no longer mobilize for war.

Central to the Pax Tokugawa was the restriction of Japanese contacts with the outside world. By the 1700s few Japanese ever left the home islands. Like Hideyoshi, Ieyasu worried that Christianity could undermine his regime, and he turned against the faith when two prominent Christian daimyo were accused of bribery, forgery, and conspiracy. In 1614, Ieyasu ordered the expulsion of all missionaries, declaring that Christianity was leading his subjects to wickedness and subversion.[22] Unlike Hideyoshi, the Tokugawa shoguns systematically followed through on these prohibitions. Converts were given the choice of apostasy or death, and the government actively searched for hidden Christian communities. When the Spanish continued to proselytize, the shogun prohibited Japanese nationals from sailing to Manila and severed relations with Spain.[23]

The Tokugawa also chose to cut ties with Japanese traders and expatriates. It viewed those groups more as a liability than an asset. Expatriate communities were full of potential threats to Tokugawa hegemony: pirates, Christians, and *rōnin* (masterless samurai). The Japanese community in Ayutthaya, for example, absorbed many refugees from the Tokugawa suppression of Christianity.[24] To eliminate the danger posed by such elements, the shogunate drastically curtailed foreign interactions. In 1635, the shogunate issued orders to the Nagasaki magistrate barring Japanese ships from leaving for "other countries" (*ikoku*) and prohibiting, upon pain of death, the return of Japanese from abroad.[25] In practice, "other countries" did not include the Japanese trading post in Pusan, the northern frontier of Ezo, or the Ryukyu Islands, but the edict severely limited other foreign contacts. The Tokugawa also limited the size of Japanese ships, effectively banning oceangoing vessels.

A final round of suppression came after the Shimabara Uprising of 1637. That insurrection confirmed the shogunate's worst fears: Japanese Christians joined with rōnin and disaffected peasants in a massive rebellion, taking control of a castle in Shimabara, near Nagasaki. The shogunate mobilized more than 100,000 soldiers to suppress the uprising, even requesting support from the Dutch. After months of siege, shogunal forces took the castle, massacred over 30,000 defenders, and then burned the castle to the ground. Determined to crush missionary activity, the shogunate barred the Portuguese from coming to Japan in 1639. Those who violated the edict were executed.

The Tokugawa continued to tolerate non-missionary foreigners but drastically curtailed their freedom of movement. By the late 1600s, the Chinese were confined to a small Chinatown in Nagasaki and the Dutch were restricted to a gated artificial island in Nagasaki harbor. Since the English had abandoned their trading post for financial reasons, the

Dutch became the only European power with a regular presence in Japan. Remarkably, the end of Japanese overseas traders did not mean the end of Japanese exports: Japan continued to provide much of the world's silver and copper. But this cargo was carried by Dutch and Chinese ships, and direct Japanese contact with the rest of the world was sharply curtailed.[26]

The implicit but clear goal of Tokugawa policy was to sever international relations that might undermine Tokugawa hegemony. But this restriction of interstate relations was not isolationism. Ieyasu was not averse to combat, only to conflicts that might damage his aura of supremacy. In that spirit he authorized the daimyo of Satsuma to invade and conquer the kingdom of Ryukyu (today Okinawa Prefecture). That contest produced a quick and clear victory, and the Ryukyuan king, Shō Nei, became the vassal of both the Tokugawa shoguns and the Shimazu, the daimyo house of Satsuma. The Ryukyu campaign followed the logic that Japanese foreign relations should unerringly enhance Tokugawa legitimacy. In his 1609 surrender, King Shō Nei pledged that he and his people would "forever be the humble servants of Satsuma and obedient to all commands, and never will be traitors to our lord."[27] Because the daimyo of Satsuma had sworn fealty to the Tokugawa, the Shō kings were now, by extension, vassals of the Tokugawa as well. Accordingly, representatives of the Shō dynasty traveled to Edo to receive confirmation as well as to celebrate the succession of a new shogun.[28] Ryukyuan embassies were important as public spectacles celebrating shogunal power. The Ryukyuan legations were instructed to wear distinctive Ryukyuan garb to dramatize how "foreign" dignitaries were paying homage to the shogun.[29]

The Japanese conquest of Ryukyu could have precipitated a war with China. The Shō king sent tribute missions to the Ming, so Ryukyu was nominally a Chinese vassal. Thus, as in the case of Hideyoshi's invasion of Korea, Japan was attacking a Chinese ally. Unlike Hideyoshi, however, the Tokugawa and Shimazu did not want a broader war. Rather than antagonize the Ming with their conquest, the Shimazu sought to minimize the impact of their actions. The Ryukyu archipelago was most valuable to Japan as a source of trade and information. The Ming allowed trade as part of Shō diplomatic missions, and Ryukyuan officials were a valuable source of information about China, since their envoys met with high-ranking government officials in Beijing. But China allowed regular missions only because they understood the Shō to be vassal kings of the Ming emperor. Had the Shimazu bragged about their conquest, the Ming would have cut ties with Ryukyu.

The Shimazu thus described Ryukyu in two contradictory manners. Within Japan, they celebrated their victory, claiming that their conquest of Ryukyu gave them unique status among the daimyo. Internationally, however, the Shimazu concealed their conquest from China. Over the years, they developed specific protocols for masking their presence in Ryukyu. By the 1700s, for example, it was official policy that, during Chinese embassies, Japanese officials should leave Shuri, the capital of Ryukyu, and hide in a nearby village. By the mid-1700s, these ruses had developed into a formal system of disinformation, complete with protocols and handbooks. The Japanese conquest of Ryukyu was thus strikingly different from Hideyoshi's invasion of Korea. Hideyoshi aspired to challenge the Ming and lost. The Tokugawa won in Ryukyu but endeavored not to offend the Ming lest that interrupt trade.[30] Tokugawa strategies worked because Chinese officials were amenable to the deception and chose to ignore evidence of the Japanese conquest, such as Ryukyuan men with Japanese hairstyles, and a temple bell dated according to the Japanese calendar.[31] The Chinese court was willing to tolerate Japanese influence in Ryukyu so long as the dignity of the Chinese embassy was respected.

So detailed were these deceptions that they produced an imaginary country: Tokara, known in English as Tsuchara. In order to sustain the conceit that Ryukyu was not under Japanese control, Satsuma also concealed its control over the nearby Amami and Tokara Islands. They referred to the Amami archipelago as the Michinoshima Islands and pretended that it was Ryukyuan territory.[32] They described the small and unremarkable island of Tokara itself (also known as Takarashima) as a semi-autonomous polity. This fictional land of Tokara was then invoked to conceal Japanese influence over Ryukyu. If Chinese diplomats discovered Japanese-looking people or objects, the protocol was to describe them as coming from Tokara, which was said to maintain ties with both Japan and Ryukyu. People from Tokara could therefore look and sound Japanese, even though Ryukyu itself did not (according to this ruse) have direct contact with Japan. So compelling was this fantasy that it was reproduced in official Ryukyuan histories and then made its way into Western sources.[33] Based on Ryukyuan accounts, Western explorers imagined that "Tsuchara" was a substantial territory and were surprised to learn that it was a tiny island, less than three square miles in area (7.14 km^2).[34]

Tokugawa relations with the Chosŏn dynasty in Korea were equally creative, and the shoguns were willing to countenance deceit if it enhanced their legitimacy and kept the peace. The 1609 compact normalizing Japanese-Korean relations, for example, was based on forged documents.

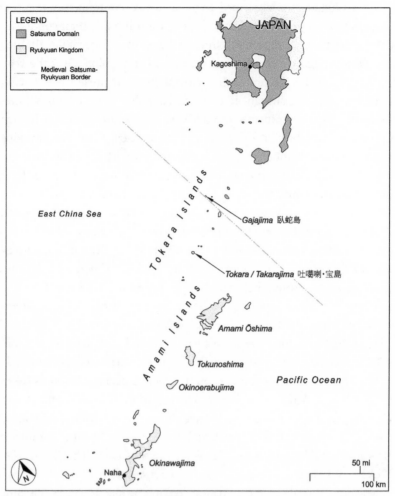

FIGURE I.I Tokara Archipelago before 1609.

The daimyo of Tsushima, Sō Yoshitoshi, was eager to mend relations between Edo and Seoul since his island domain was almost entirely dependent on trade with Korea. Faced with a deadlock over protocol, Yoshitoshi's representatives "fixed" the problem by forging a letter from Tokugawa Ieyasu to King Sŏnjo. The letter referred to Ieyasu as the "King of Japan" and was dated according to the Ming calendar. Korean officials were immediately suspicious: the combination of the Chinese calendar system and title "king" implied that the Japanese shogun saw himself as a vassal of the Ming emperor. Those were precisely the concessions Ieyasu was unwilling to make. The shogunate itself seems to have known of the forgery and chose to ignore it, instead using the opening to conclude a treaty.

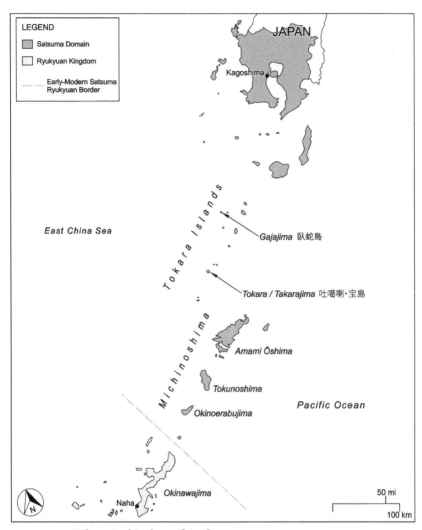

FIGURE 1.2 Tokara Archipelago after 1609.

The shogunate took action only in 1635, when the forgery was exposed due to factional infighting within Tsushima. Even then the shogun's response was surprisingly lenient. The shogun might well have seized Sō holdings and destroyed their lineage, but he ordered nothing so severe. The forgers themselves were executed, and two high-ranking officials were punished, but the Sō house itself escaped with a reprimand.[35]

More remarkably, the shogunate kept the Sō in place as intermediaries in Japanese-Korean diplomatic relations. On the vexing questions of calendars and title, the Yi and Tokugawa regimes developed a compromise. They used the zodiac system as a neutral calendar and used the

term "great prince" (*taikun*) to refer to the shogun. *Taikun* (K. *taejŏn*)
sounded regal in both Japanese and Korean but had never been used in
diplomatic correspondence.[36] It was thus unclear whether a "taikun" was
superior or inferior to a king, and how such a noble related to the Ming,
Qing, and Japanese emperors.[37] This was an effective means of resolving conflict between the Yi and the Tokugawa: either side could imagine
itself as superior.[38] As with Ryukyu, relations between the Sō, Tokugawa,
and Yi required tactical ignorance. Functionally, the Sō were vassals of
the Tokugawa, but when their emissaries repatriated shipwrecked sailors
in Pusan, they bowed four times before a wooden tablet representing the
Korean king. Yi officials therefore argued that Tsushima was, in fact, a tributary state of Korea. Rather than go to war over these contradictory views,
Korea and Japan chose studied, tactical ignorance.[39]

The Yi dynasty was initially interested in Japanese-Korea amity partly
to counterbalance other threats. In 1616, the Manchus declared war on
the Ming, the last ethnically Chinese monarchs of China. The Manchus
steadily gained control over Northeast Asia and in 1637 they forced King
Injo of Korea to become their vassal. In 1644, Manchu forces moved south
of the Great Wall, seized Beijing, and declared the foundation of the Qing
dynasty (1644–1911). Ming loyalists fought doggedly until 1662 and resistance on Taiwan lasted until 1683, but the Manchu conquest was complete.
The victory of the Qing over the Ming transformed the cultural dynamics
of Northeast Asia: the ruling dynasty of China was no longer Chinese.

In Korea, the fall of the Ming was understood as the disintegration
of civilization.[40] Early modern Korea was a deeply Confucian society. So
thoroughly did the Yi court conform to Chinese diplomatic protocol that
Ming texts cited Korea as a model tributary state.[41] Under the Qing, the
Korean intelligentsia began to describe itself as the last bastion of civilization. The Ming might have fallen, but Korea would sustain the virtues of Confucian culture. Ming loyalism became an important part of
Korean cultural identity. The Yi dynasty maintained a shrine to the Ming,
reflecting their continued loyalty to the old regime. Korean literati made
"Revere the Ming, resist the Qing" a favored couplet. This fear and loath-
ing of the Qing had a paradoxical impact on Yi-Tokugawa relations. Seen
from Seoul, the Japanese were vicious invaders who had despoiled Korea.
But compared to the Manchus, the Japanese were at least marginally less
offensive. At a minimum, the Tokugawa, unlike the Qing, had disavowed
a desire to subjugate Korea.[42] The Yi dynasty thus tolerated renewed relations with Japan, including diplomatic innovations such as the title taikun.

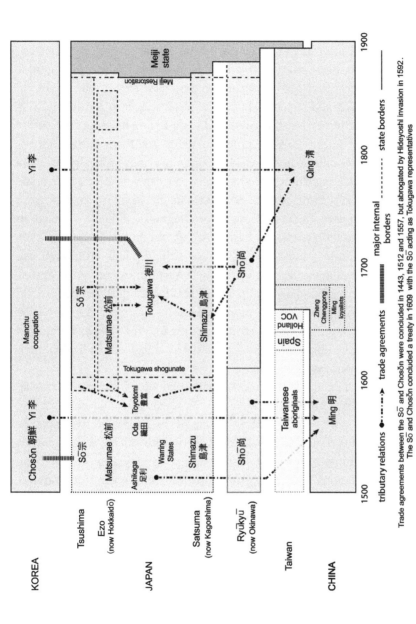

FIGURE 1.3 East Asian Interstate Relations, 1500–1900.

KOREA

Tsushima

Ezo
(now Hokkaidō)

JAPAN

Satsuma
(now Kagoshima)

Ryūkyū
(now Okinawa)

Taiwan

CHINA

Chosŏn 朝鮮 Yi 李

Sō 宗

Matsumae 松前

Ashikaga 足利   Oda 織田   Toyotomi 豊臣

Warring States

Shimazu 島津

Shō 尚

Taiwanese aboriginals

Ming 明

Tokugawa shogunate

Matsumae 松前

Manchu occupation

Sō 宗

Tokugawa 德川

Shimazu 島津

Spain

Holland VOC

Zheng Chenggong Ming loyalists

Meiji Restoration

Meiji state

Yi 李

Sō 宗

Shō 尚

Qing 清

1500   1600   1700   1800   1900

tributary relations ●∙∙∙∙∙▶   trade agreements ●−∙−▶   major internal borders ▪▪▪▪   state borders ——

Trade agreements between the Sō and Chosŏn were concluded in 1443, 1512 and 1557, but abrogated by Hideyoshi invasion in 1592.
The Sō and Chosŏn concluded a treaty in 1609 with the Sō acting as Tokugawa representatives

Tokugawa relations with the Qing also relied on diplomatic ingenuity. The historian Iwai Shigeki coined the term "silent diplomacy" to describe how the Tokugawa and Qing interacted without formal diplomatic relations.[43] Until 1684, trade between China and Japan was technically a violation of Ming maritime prohibitions. Chinese junks continued to visit Nagasaki, but according to Ming law, this trade was smuggling. When the Qing abolished Ming restrictions after the conquest of Taiwan (1683), trade surged and more than 190 junks reached Nagasaki in 1688. Alarmed by the outflow of silver and copper, Japanese officials sought to restrict and regulate Chinese junks, but this raised difficult diplomatic questions. What was Japanese authority over Chinese traders? What was Qing authority over expatriate Chinese in Nagasaki? In order to avoid conflict between the Tokugawa and Qing China, the shogunate concealed its efforts to regulate Japanese-Chinese trade. Instead of direct state intervention, the Tokugawa regulated Chinese traders through the Nagasaki Chinese Translation Bureau (Nagasaki tōtsūji). Beginning in 1715, the bureau began to issue trading certificates (shinpai) to Chinese ship captains. Although the bureau was under Tokugawa control, these certificates omitted any reference to either the Tokugawa or the Qing. This tactic effectively dodged the question of Tokugawa-Qing relations. When Chinese merchants appealed to the Qing court, the Kangxi emperor ruled that the shinpai were not a question of sovereign power, but a private matter between individual merchants and interpreters in Nagasaki.[44]

The shinpai system was also used to maintain ties with Southeast Asia, including Siam, Cambodia, and Patani. These states would hire Chinese captains for semi-official trading missions to Nagasaki: the captain's authorization to trade was private, but government officials were accorded special recognition. This created something of a gray area of diplomatic and trade relations. Describing relations with Cambodia, for example, the shogunal advisor Arai Hakuseki wrote that diplomatic relations had ended in 1627, but that Khmer officials continued to "pay their respects" at Nagasaki.[45] Relations with the Khmer kingdom thus involved more than trade but less than full diplomatic relations. Because the risk of war with the Khmer kingdom was vanishingly small, the Tokugawa were amenable to low-level, informal relations.

A final component of the Tokugawa international order was Ezo, the Tokugawa state's northern periphery. Ezo (now Hokkaido) was Japan's point of contact with a vast Amur River trading network and there is evidence of a robust trade in pelts and other animal products from at least the fifteenth century.[46] In the 1400s, the Matsumae house gained a foothold in the southeast corner of Ezo and then, under Hideyoshi and Ieyasu, secured exclusive trading rights with the indigenous Ainu.[47] The Matsumae steadily expanded their territory, pushing north the border of the Japanese zone (*wajinchi*), but their land holdings remained small. In this way, Matsumae territory was similar to Tsushima: a gateway to a foreign territory, heavily dependent on trade because of its small agricultural base.[48]

As with Tsushima and Ryukyu, the shogunate chose to rule Ezo indirectly. It gave the Matsumae considerable autonomy in their handling of foreign affairs. In Ezo, as in Tsushima, the Tokugawa tolerated daimyo malfeasance, even when they might have seized control. In 1669, for example, Matsumae provoked an Ainu rebellion through exploitative trading practices and the expansion of mining, which disrupted salmon runs. The Matsumae needed shogunal support to suppress the rebellion and such incompetence was ample reason for the Tokugawa to seize Ezo. Instead, the Tokugawa left the Matsumae in control.[49]

In one key respect, Tokugawa policy in Ezo was different from that on its other borders: unlike the Koreans and Ryukyuans, the Ainu were considered an uncivilized people. In period documents the Ainu were described as "barbarians" (*teki*) rather than "people." The tribute items offered by Ainu elders to Japanese officials reproduced the image of the Ainu as crude, frontier people: animal pelts, hawks, and eagle feathers. These rituals continued even after Ainu became paid workers in the Japanese commercial economy. By the 1800s, many Ainu worked as laborers on Japanese fishing fleets, catching and processing fish like herring for use as fertilizer. Nonetheless, in diplomatic ceremonies, the Matsumae continued to depict the Ainu as primitive trappers.[50]

Despite these differences, Tokugawa policy toward Ezo reflected the regime's broader strategy of ambiguous borders. There was a formal boundary to the Japanese zone (*wajinchi*) in Ezo, but this was a porous border and there were many Japanese trading posts in Ainu territory. Japanese merchants traveled well beyond the *wajinchi* in pursuit of resources such as lumber, and their labor contracts with the Ainu transformed the regional economy. Matsumae officials directly intervened outside the *wajinchi* to ensure Ainu dependence on Japanese grain by, for example, destroying Ainu rice fields.[51] There was thus no single border between Japanese and

Ainu territory but rather a series of overlapping and contested spheres of interactions and influence. Only in the late 1700s, with the arrival of Russian representatives in Ezo, did the Tokugawa become concerned with establishing a single clear border.[52] Thus, at both its northeastern and southwestern peripheries, Tokugawa power was distinct from territoriality: overt and extensive control over land. This strategy of vague borders was part of a broader Tokugawa strategy of carefully negotiated ambiguities. For generations, Qing, Chosŏn, and Tokugawa rulers chose not to fight over exact borders or sovereign honor. Instead, they sustained a distant but perduring peace.

In this way, from the 1600s until the mid-1800s, Northeast Asian international politics was strikingly un-"modern." Rather than emphasize exclusive territorial control, the major powers tolerated ambiguity and contradiction. The contrast with twenty-first century politics is striking. Today, Russia, China, Japan, and South Korea are all embroiled in complex and protracted disputes over uninhabited or sparsely inhabited islands, some small enough to be described as rocks. These disputes would have been inconceivable in the early modern East Asian international order. Tokugawa Japan and Chosŏn Korea not only ignored minor islands; they found it mutually advantageous to disagree quietly over major territories like Tsushima. Similarly, officials knew not to press for a definitive opinion on the sovereignty of Ryukyu but to allow for different views in Edo, Kagoshima, Shuri, and Beijing. These ingenious diplomatic inventions avoided the very questions of state sovereignty and territoriality that define the modern nation-state and modern international politics.

Because exclusive sovereign claims to territory are part of modern international law, it is tempting to see the Tokugawa system as "premodern" and therefore as an antecedent to modern politics. The Meiji state "modernized" Japanese diplomacy by insisting on clear borders and consistent diplomat protocols. But on such a scale, Hideyoshi's invasion of Korea in the 1590s was more "modern" and "Western" than the Pax Tokugawa of later centuries. Hideyoshi aspired to overt and complete domination over East Asia and he had no patience for clever diplomacy. For Hideyoshi, there was no merit in avoiding an overt conflict with China: he wanted the Ming to recognize his authority as an equal, if not superior, sovereign. In that way, Hideyoshi's approach resembled the emerging sense of state power in Europe: an international system in which states were supposed to fight ruthlessly for territory, not to obscure their borders in the interests of peace. Diplomats were supposed to defend their sovereign's rights and powers, not to discreetly finesse irreconcilable views.

Tokugawa diplomacy rejected such overt displays of state power in favor of flexibility and ambiguity. That different view of sovereignty supported two centuries of international peace, but it also created a Japanese state that was radically different not only from the nascent nation-states of Europe but also from Hideyoshi's Japanese state. The Tokugawa were not interested in expanding singular hegemony over clearly demarked territory. They were warlords who appreciated the advantages of avoiding war.

Rituals of Domestic Control

The Tokugawa regime was vastly more powerful and centralized than any Japanese government after the ninth century. But this trend toward increasing centralization slowed markedly after the Tokugawa limited their exposure to interstate conflict. Since there were no longer foreign conflicts requiring the nationwide mobilization of people or resources, the Tokugawa house stopped expanding its domestic authority. On the contrary, Tokugawa control was based on the continued authority of daimyo in their own domains. Daimyo retained much of their autonomy from the Warring States era. They set and levied their own taxes, commanded their own armies, issued their own legal codes, ran their own courts, issued their own currencies, and set their own local economic policies. Rather than subvert daimyo authority, the Tokugawa built on it, ruling Japan by making the shogun the supreme commander of the daimyo. The Tokugawa state was thus a "compound state," built on the combined authority of the shogun, the daimyo, and the imperial house.[53]

According to law and practice, the shogun could seize a daimyo's territory for any infraction of Tokugawa policy, including unauthorized castle repairs, dissent within the domain, improper funeral arrangements, and lack of an approved plan of succession. In the early 1600s, shoguns vigorously exercised this authority. In 1619, for example, the second shogun, Tokugawa Hidetada, cut the holdings of Fukushima Masanori by more than 90 percent (498,220 *koku* to 48,000 koku) for repairing his castle after a typhoon. Masanori had dutifully informed the shogunate of his intent to repair the castle but had not waited for official authorization.

When Masanori died in 1624, the shogunate cut his heir's investiture by another 93 percent, to 3,000 koku, because Masanori had been cremated without official verification of his death. Those cumulative reductions of more than 99 percent eliminated the Fukushima as a noble house: with a holding of under 10,000 koku, the Fukushima were no longer ranked as daimyo. In 1664, the shogunate seized half the holdings of the Uesugi house when Uesugi Tsunekatsu died suddenly of appendicitis. The Uesugi had opposed the Tokugawa in 1600 and the domain survived only because its allies convinced the shogunate to allow the posthumous designation of an heir.

Such measures cowed the most recalcitrant daimyo, and by the 1700s the regime saw little need to continue such aggressive actions. Shogunal attainder became rare, and between 1808 and 1835 the shogunate did not punish a single lord.[54] Even when the shogunate seized daimyo territory, it commonly transferred the lands to other daimyo. Once their control was secure, the Tokugawa regime was more inclined to reward its allies than to directly arrogate power. The goal of Tokugawa governance was not to eliminate the daimyo but to ensure that they did not challenge Tokugawa hegemony.

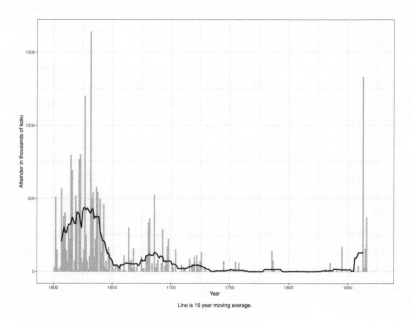

Line is 15 year moving average.

FIGURE 1.4 Decline in Rates of Attainder.
Line is fifteen-year moving average. Data from Fujino, *Shintei bakuhan taiseishi*, appendix 39-45. The graph includes attainders after 1860 (such as Chōshū) that the Tokugawa ordered but could not enforce.

These policies produced a distinct pattern of political geography. *Tozama*, literally "outsider" lords, were daimyo who swore allegiance to Ieyasu late in his rise to power or opposed the Tokugawa at the Battle of Sekigahara in 1600. The Tokugawa weakened, rather than destroyed, many tozama by seizing parts of their holdings. They tolerated some larger, contiguous tozama holdings but primarily at the periphery of Japan, far from the main Tokugawa cities of Edo, Nagoya, and Osaka. By contrast, *fudai* were lords distinguished by their long-standing loyalty to the Tokugawa and they were allowed to serve as shogunal officers. The Tokugawa surrounded their key castle towns with strategically placed fudai and rewarded them with additional parcels. This meant that prominent fudai lords often had fragmented holdings near the center rather than the periphery. Indeed, much of the land around Edo was a patchwork of direct shogunal lands, fudai lands, and the holdings of liege vassals (*hatamoto*), shogunal vassals with less than 10,000 koku.

This landholding pattern was established in the early 1600s and held to the end of the Tokugawa era. In the 1860s, most fudai domains were less than 150 miles from Edo Castle, while most tozama were more than 250 miles. Virtually all the domains within fifty miles of Edo Castle were fudai with holdings under 100,000 koku. By contrast, most of the large domains at the periphery were tozama. Scattered across Japan were *kamon* daimyo, primarily the descendants of Tokugawa Ieyasu's younger sons. Kamon lords could provide a shogunal heir in case of a succession crisis, but they were commonly excluded from key shogunal offices.

Because the shogunate, or *bakufu*, relied on the daimyo to govern their own domains, historians often refer to the early-modern political system as the *bakuhan* system: *baku* for *bakufu* and *han*, a somewhat anachronistic term for domain. But the shogunate's willingness to tolerate alternative sources of authority extended beyond the daimyo. The early shoguns cowed but did not eliminate the imperial house. In a series of edicts from the early 1600s, the shogunate banned the imperial court from interfering in military affairs and restricted its authority to make religious and ceremonial appointments. Instead of politics, the emperor's "primary efforts should be directed to the arts."[55] In 1634, the third shogun Iemitsu visited the imperial court with some 300,000 troops, a show of force thinly disguised as a gesture of respect. After curtailing the court's political authority, the shogunate was willing to show support by paying, for example, for repairs to the imperial palace. In general, the Tokugawa created new institutions of indirect control rather than assert national authority. In the Kantō region, for example, the Tokugawa elected not to claim direct control over the *eta*, a caste charged with animal slaughter and leatherwork. Instead they created a hereditary leader of the *eta*, the Danzaemon house, and entrusted it with managing *eta* affairs and representing the *eta* in legal disputes with non-*eta*. This suggests something distinct from the archetypal European model of state-building: rather than fight to destroy rival sources of authority, the Tokugawa regime created new ones.

The centerpiece of Tokugawa control over daimyo was a mandatory residence system known as *sankin kōtai*, wherein daimyo spent alternate years in the shogunal capital of Edo. Sankin kōtai had its roots in earlier warrior practices. The Ashikaga shoguns, for example, compelled daimyo to live in Kyoto in order to reduce the risk of rebellion. Hideyoshi continued this practice. As a sign of subservience, daimyo were to remain in Kyoto unless dispatched on official business, and their wives and children were to reside there permanently. Daimyo resisted this practice at great risk. Hideyoshi told the Hōjō of Odawara, for example, that he would recognize their holdings if they paid homage to him at Nijō Castle. When they refused, Hideyoshi destroyed them.[56]

Forced residence in Kyoto bound the daimyo to Hideyoshi but degraded their military abilities. As early as 1591, Shimazu Yoshihiro, second son of the daimyo of Satsuma, lamented the impact of regular life in Kyoto. "[In Kyoto] the Shimazu cannot be of any use to Hideyoshi (*kanpaku*)," he declared. If Hideyoshi asked them to suppress a rebellion, they would not have enough troops ready to make a difference. And fighting alongside Hideyoshi with just a few men was a painful indignity for a great warrior house like the Shimazu. Yoshihiro further lamented that his men were becoming unreliable as soldiers: they seemed interested primarily in borrowing money to pay for the temptations of urban life. He feared that they were losing their fighting spirit and wondered if the Shimazu would long survive as a major daimyo house.[57] Such fear and despair were exactly what Hideyoshi desired. The Shimazu had been defiant, and Hideyoshi was determined to impress upon them the cost of their insubordination. But Hideyoshi was too ambitious to squander the services of a capable commander. In 1592–94, convinced of Yoshihiro's loyalty, Hideyoshi dispatched him to Korea. Yoshihiro fought furiously for his new lord and secured one of the last victories of the campaign, a triumph at the Battle of Sach'ŏn.[58]

The Tokugawa continued Hideyoshi's policies of forced residence, and after 1600 daimyo began attending Ieyasu in Edo. But unlike Hideyoshi, the Tokugawa were concerned with domestic stability rather than an international empire. Tokugawa foreign policy was designed to minimize the need for military mobilization. Thus, the regime could degrade the military abilities of the daimyo without undermining national security. The military weakness that Yoshihiro lamented became a cornerstone of the Tokugawa policy.

The system of alternate attendance was formalized in the 1630s and 1640s, just as the Tokugawa were drastically restricting foreign contacts. Daimyo were ordered to spend alternate years in Edo according to a strict schedule determined by their relationship with the Tokugawa house. In 1635, tozama lords were ordered to travel to Edo in the fourth month and return to their domains twelve months later. The schedule was staggered so that roughly half the tozama were either entering or departing Edo each year. In 1642, sankin kōtai was extended to fudai, who traveled to Edo in either the sixth or the eighth month.[59] Both groups of daimyo were required to leave their families in Edo year-round. A few daimyo were allowed exemptions from sankin kōtai based on familial ties. Three collateral lines of the Tokugawa house, descendants of Ieyasu's younger sons, were exempted or allowed reduced attendance. The Tokugawa also allowed exemptions for military or diplomatic duties. The Sō of Tsushima, for example, came to Edo only once in three years and the Matsumae came only once in six. The Kuroda and the Nabeshima, who patrolled Nagasaki harbor, stayed in Edo for three months rather than twelve. These dispensations reflected the goal of sankin kōtai: because attendance in Edo degraded the military abilities of daimyo, those lords with security duties received special exemptions. But the limited scope of these exceptions also reflects the shogunate's limited security concerns. Unlike Hideyoshi, the Tokugawa did not need capable warriors ready for overseas engagements.

The Domestic Transformation

The end of warfare and the concentration of samurai in Edo were part of a broader transformation of Japanese society. Between 1600 and 1720, the Japanese population soared from 12 million to 31 million.[60] This growth was supported by the development and dissemination of new technologies. New types of irrigation, using treadmills, allowed for the expansion of arable land, which roughly doubled over the Tokugawa era. Farmers increased land productivity through the use of a variety of fertilizers: fishmeal; the residue from sake and soy sauce production; and human manure

FIGURE 1.5 "Bustle outside the Nakamuraza Kabuki Theatre." An 1854 urban scene by the famous print artist Andō Hiroshige (1797–1858). LACMA (M.2000.105.35a–c). Reprinted with permission.

(or "night soil"). The rise in demand for "night soil," which was free for the taking in the 1600s, caused it to rise in price by 200 percent between 1740 and 1789.[61] New technologies also increased labor productivity. A series of inventions made rice processing easier and quicker while reducing waste. The development of a tool called the "Bitchū hoe" made it easier to open new land.[62] Improvement in food production allowed farmers to focus on non-food crops and market-oriented farming production. By the 1700s, farmers in many regions were heavily invested in cash crops such as cotton, rapeseed, tobacco, tea, indigo, flax and hemp, mulberry, and lacquer.[63]

This shift to commercial agriculture was stimulated by the growth of Edo as a consumption center. In the late 1500s, the village of Edo had fewer

than 200 people. By 1600 the population had grown to 30,000, and with the introduction of sankin kōtai it reached 500,000 by the 1650s. By the 1730s, the residents numbered more than 1 million, roughly half of whom were samurai.[64] The city was known for both the range and magnitude of its conspicuous consumption. By the eighteenth century, Edo consumed annually nearly 800,000 casks of sake, over 100,000 casks of soy sauce, and over 18 million bundles of firewood. By the early 1800s, Edo boasted dozens of theaters, more than 600 book lenders, and over 6,000 restaurants. Trends in arts and letters, fashion, and popular culture started in Edo and spread to the rest of Japan.[65]

Samurai transformed the city of Edo, but Edo transformed them as well. Indeed, by the 1700s, rivalries between daimyo houses had moved fully from the battlefield to the salon, where lords competed in connoisseurship and consumption rather than warrior prowess. A daimyo could elevate his standing through a more refined performance of tea ceremony or a more elegant or exotic banquet than achieved by his contemporaries. Unlike his battle-hardened ancestors, Shimazu Shigehide, the eighth daimyo of Satsuma, won fame for his connoisseurship and lavish entertaining: he hosted an exotic Chinese feast which featured more than fifty separate dishes, including nine-year-old preserved winter melon.[66] Elaborate gifts became essential to political advancement. A newly appointed shogunal officer was required by custom to provide a banquet for his new colleagues, with the food and wine from appropriately exclusive vendors. The costs of such an event were often several times the annual income of an ordinary samurai.[67] The changes lamented by Shimazu Yoshihiro in the 1590s thus became a defining feature of Tokugawa society: samurai became familiar with urban pleasures but unfamiliar with war.

The costs of life in Edo strained the budgets of most daimyo. Some sought to control spending through austerity campaigns, and exhortations to avoid luxury were a common part of eighteenth-century political discourse. But even a frugal lord could not avoid the basic demands of sankin kōtai. Every daimyo needed an Edo residence, and the daimyo and his family, as well as domain officers, advisors, attendants, and guards, needed to be housed, fed, and clothed. Daimyo with large holdings often had multiple compounds in Edo with thousands of retainers. Contemporary observers, such as the economist Kaiho Seiryō, estimated that daimyo incurred most of their expenses in Edo. A careful examination of domain ledgers suggests that Kaiho was exaggerating, but not by much: many domains spent between 30% to 50% of their income on sankin kōtai and related expenses.[68]

In order to pay for sankin kōtai, daimyo turned to merchant intermediaries. Daimyo needed to sell part of their land's harvest to pay for their expenses in the capital, and merchant brokers (kuramoto) soon became an essential part of samurai government. As the temptations of life in Edo drove up expenses, kuramoto became creditors, treating the next year's tax revenue as collateral. Lending to daimyo could be immensely lucrative. The Kōnoike merchant house of Osaka, for example, started as sake brewers, but the owners made their fortune by lending to daimyo, eventually becoming the banking house of more than thirty daimyo families. Between 1670 and 1706, their assets grew seventy-fivefold to over 24,000 silver kanme (900,000 kg.), mostly from money lending. The head of the Kōnoike house was also paid a salary for his brokerage and trading services, and by the mid-eighteenth century that revenue exceeded the income of many daimyo.[69]

The consumption demands of the capital and the expansion of commercial networks transformed the rural economy. Farmers increasingly grew crops for market instead of local consumption, often encouraged by domain governments. In order to meet the expenses of life in the capital, daimyo began to promote cash crops and to intervene in commodity markets. A striking example is the case of indigo cultivation in Tokushima domain, across the Inland Sea from the market center of Osaka. Indigo had long been grown in the lower reaches of the Yoshino River, but by the mid-eighteenth century it had spread across the domain: in 1740, 237 of the 331 villages in northern Tokushima, over 70 percent, were growing indigo. Many of these villages were highly specialized. In 1764, nearly 90 percent of the arable land in Takenose village was planted with indigo, roughly 7 percent with potatoes, and only 0.2 percent with rice. When the Meiji government conducted a systematic survey in the 1870s, they found that less than one-third of the agricultural output of Tokushima was rice.[70]

This changing economy transformed samurai rule. In Confucian discourse, the samurai ruling elite was distinguished by its remove from petty commercial concerns. In practice, however, samurai could not ignore how commerce affected their daimyo's coffers. In Tokushima, as farmers became dependent on indigo sales, the domain became concerned with indigo prices. Because indigo sales were concentrated in Osaka, prices were susceptible to manipulation by Osaka merchant cartels. Beginning in the 1760s, Osaka merchants used their coordinated buying power to force down prices. To break this cartel, Tokushima insisted that buyers come to Tokushima and make purchases at a domain-supervised market. The government also began offering loans to indigo farmers to break their financial dependence on credit from Osaka buyers. The Osaka cartel sued, insisting that the new market would cause them economic distress. In 1766, the Osaka city magistrate, a Tokugawa officer, ruled in favor of the merchants, ordering the Tokushima to allow sales in Osaka. Tokushima tried to evade this ruling, but in 1790 the merchants sued again and Tokushima complied. In 1802, Tokushima chose a new strategy: rather than oppose the Osaka cartel with an official domain agency, they organized a rival cartel. The Osaka cartel sued again, but this time the settlement favored Tokushima. Indigo sellers were allowed to restrict sales of Tokushima indigo to their own cartel of buyers.[71]

This long legal struggle over indigo prices was emblematic of the transformation of the samurai estate. The Osaka city magistrates were shogunal officers, and the struggle over the indigo market was thus a contest between the Tokugawa and the Hachisuka. The heirs of two great warlords who had fought together at Sekigahara were now battling over indigo prices. While this change was the result of unprecedented peace and prosperity, it was difficult to avoid the sense that something was awry. If questions of commerce were central to government finances, how could the warrior elite avoid ruling on mundane matters such as trade? But if samurai became enmeshed in commercial affairs, how could they maintain their status as a warrior elite and justify their monopoly on government offices? Beyond their lineage, what distinguished samurai from commoners? This was an inherent tension of the *Pax Tokugawa*: in the absence of war, there were no battles in which the samurai could show their courage and publicly distinguish themselves from mere commoners.

The Pax Tokugawa also transformed the way samurai held land. In the early 1500s, most samurai were rural fief-holders who drew their income from a specific village or parcel. Beginning in the late sixteenth century, however, many daimyo removed samurai from their rural fiefs and resettled them in designated neighborhoods of the lord's castle town. By separating samurai from their holdings, daimyo were able to increase their own financial authority by collecting taxes directly from peasant villages and paying their samurai a regular stipend. But lords could also cut their retainers' stipends, a practice euphemistically known as "borrowing." The urbanization of the samurai also pulled them into the commercial economy. Whereas rural fief-holders might demand sandals or sake from local farmers as tax payments in-kind, urban samurai needed to sell their share of the annual harvest through a broker and then buy the products they needed for cash. This process was most pronounced in the more economically developed regions of the Kantō and the Kinai, and less so in Tōhoku and Kyūshū. But overall, by the eighteenth century, samurai were a salaried urban class.[72]

Historians now view the spread of a money economy and expansion of commerce as precursors to Japan's modern economic transformation. But many contemporary observers were more concerned with how commercialization seemed to invert the social order, making the samurai ruling class dependent on their merchant inferiors. Urban samurai households commonly developed intergenerational ties with merchant families, who also extended them credit. Merchants thus developed substantial influence over the affairs of samurai houses. In 1750, for example, Tani Tannai, a retainer in Tosa domain, appealed to his merchant broker, Saitaniya Naomasu, for advice and support. Tani lamented that rising expenses had forced him to repeatedly borrow against his future income. He was determined to live within his means, but had no idea what that might entail:

> Somehow we must make do with our present yearly income. Being unfamiliar with these [financial] matters, however, I am uncertain whether or not this is possible; but I would like to try. Please write and inform me in detail as to how much my yearly income is in rice (*fuchi*) and in rice vouchers (*kippu*), and how much is being "borrowed" (*kariage*) by the lord. Also, please inform me how much the remaining income is once converted into silver and copper coins. Then, I request that you prepare a monthly budget for my consideration.

Like many samurai, Tani had little idea how his rice stipend was converted into cash and still less of an appreciation of how to live within his means. His indebtedness was due partly to the high cost of living in the castle

FIGURE 1.6 "Samurai Selling Their Weapons." Andō Hiroshige is best known for his landscapes and cityscapes, but in this 1854 print he depicted financially struggling samurai selling their armor for scrap. LACMA (M.2006.136.334). Reprinted with permission.

town of Kōchi and the temptations of urban life. But his lord had also "borrowed" 25 percent of his stipend, and he needed 14 percent of his income just to service old loans from Saitaniya.[73]

Tani's relations with his creditor were an extreme case of a broader phenomenon: formal notions of the social order were increasingly at odds with daily experience. In much public discourse, Tokugawa society consisted of four distinct estates, each with a special function: samurai were the ruling elite, farmers grew food, artisans crafted tools, and merchants transported goods. Those distinctions were always more hortatory than descriptive, but over the Tokugawa era they became utterly detached from lived experience. Samurai, the highest estate, became increasingly dependent on merchants, the lowest estate, for credit and market services. The spread of commercial agriculture, in which farmers grew cash crops for distant markets, effaced distinctions between farmers and merchants. When the Meiji government dissolved formal status distinctions, it was merely acknowledging this transformation.

The Politics of Reform

Unlike the Meiji government, the Tokugawa regime could not attack the notion of an estate-based society: its own legitimacy was tied to the idea of an elite samurai estate. But the shogunate did attempt to confront the most egregious problems of the Tokugawa order. The Tokugawa shogunate engaged in three periods of intense reform: the Kyōho reforms (1716–45), the Kansei reforms (1787–93), and the Tenpō reforms (1841–43). The boldest and most successful was the first, led by the eighth shogun Tokugawa Yoshimune. Yoshimune became shogun as an adult, having already served as the daimyo of Kii domain. Confident, pragmatic, and intellectually intrepid, he confronted the central questions of Tokugawa rule: how would the regime adapt to a peacetime, commercial economy, and would such reform change the balance of power between the shogun and the daimyo? Many of Yoshimune's policies foreshadowed the more radical reforms of the Meiji Restoration: he asserted greater national authority, intervened in the national economy, and challenged hereditary privilege in remarkable ways. Unlike the Meiji reforms, however, his policies were designed to repair the Tokugawa system rather than replace it.[74]

Yoshimune's immediate challenge was a budget crisis. Although shogunal revenues had risen with economic growth, expenses had grown even faster because the regime had taken on additional retainers. The output of shogunal mines was also dropping, and by the 1690s, the shogunate was running regular budget deficits.[75] Yoshimune tried to cut expenses through conventional austerity measures, but when that approach failed, he asserted new authority over daimyo, demanding direct payments into the shogunal treasury. In 1721, Yoshimune ordered daimyo to pay 1 percent of their income annually into shogunal warehouses in Osaka and Edo, a tax known as *agemai*. Such direct payments were unprecedented and suggested that the Tokugawa had a claim on lands outside their own holdings.

At the same time, Yoshimune sought to reduce daimyo expenses and radically curtailed sankin kōtai obligations; both tozama and fudai lords were now to spend six months in Edo, traveling in the third month and ninth month, cutting their time in Edo by half. The shogun also reduced the sankin kōtai obligations of the lords' heirs and curtailed the exchange of gifts between the daimyo and the shogun. This was a fundamental change in Tokugawa policy, but Yoshimune insisted that he was actually returning to the original principles of the regime. Alternate attendance, he argued, was not the will of Ieyasu or Hidetada but the mandate of the third shogun Iemitsu, who was concerned that Edo was a lonely place and thus ordered daimyo and their families to reside there.[76]

Yoshimune also expanded shogunal authority over daimyo in areas such as river control. Riparian projects such as levee building commonly cut across domain lines, especially in the Kantō and Kinai regions, and since 1703 the shogunate had demanded that daimyo provide laborers for such projects. These obligations were a peacetime extension of a daimyo's wartime service: in addition to sending troops to aid the shogun, daimyo were to provide corvée labor. In 1720, Yoshimune changed these obligations to payments in cash. The shogunate would calculate the total cost of the project, underwrite 10 percent, and demand the balance from the affected daimyo, up to ten gold ryō per 100 *koku* of holdings.[77] Although daimyo with extremely large or contiguous investitures were unaffected, this policy changed the relationship between shogun and daimyo. In a commercial economy, the shogunate was interested in properly allocating the cost of public works rather than marshaling direct labor service.[78]

Yoshimune made fundamental changes in the shogunate's tax system. Prior to Yoshimune, the land tax was based on annual assessments of the harvest. These inspections had the advantage of reducing the tax burden on farmers after a poor harvest. But the annual system was burdensome and intrusive, and it had the unintended consequence of discouraging capital investments in land because the government would promptly tax the increase in yield. Annual inspections also made for erratic government tax receipts. Beginning in 1718, the shogunate began shifting to fixed assessments based on average yields over five, ten, or twenty years. Initially the government refused any tax relief except for catastrophic harvest failures, but that rigidity provoked angry rural protests, and thereafter the shogunate cut taxes whenever yields fell by more than 30 percent. This revised tax system raised government revenue without sparking unrest. In the long term, these reforms likely exacerbated a trend toward increased rural inequality: large landholders were most able to capitalize on the benefits of the fixed assessment system, whereas small holders suffered the most from reduced tax relief. In the short term, however, the reforms generated a large budget surplus, which the government used for relief grain in times of acute crisis.[79]

Under the Kyōho reforms, the shogunate promoted a range of new crops and industries, including food crops such as Japanese sweet potatoes (*Satsumaimo* or *Ipomoea batatas*), ginseng and other medicinal plants, sugarcane and sugar refining, and silk production. Underlying these projects were Yoshimune's fascination with the natural world and a more practical concern with Japan's international balance of trade.[80] Trade with China had surged after the consolidation of Qing control in the 1680s and the end of Ming maritime prohibitions, and Japan began exporting large quantities of precious metals in exchange for Chinese imports. Since Japanese mine production was dropping, the outflow of specie was especially noticeable. The shogunate had attempted to restrict imports through quotas at Nagasaki and limits on trade through Tsushima and Ryukyu. Yoshimune took a different approach, promoting the production of domestic substitutes for Chinese and Korean imports.[81] To develop these new technologies, Yoshimune eased restrictions on foreign books. Under prior practice, books were banned for any mention of Christianity, and this eliminated many scientific texts. In 1720, Yoshimune permitted the importation of scientific texts with incidental references to religion and established horticultural stations to test new crops.[82]

Several of the agricultural ventures promoted by Yoshimune had long-lasting impacts. His promotion of domestic sugar led to commercial production in several domains, including Owari, Kii, and Tosa. By the mid-1700s the price of sugar had dropped enough that middling samurai considered it a staple rather than a luxury, and by the 1800s, domestic production had almost completely displaced imports.[83] In an 1837 appeal to the Nagasaki city magistrate, local merchants complained that "domestic production of sugar has expanded, leading to a decrease in the price for imported Chinese sugar, which has also reduced profits for merchants here." In similar fashion, domestic silk began to challenge Chinese and Korean imports. With new domestic production, silk prices began dropping in the 1720s and continued to fall thereafter. Korean imports declined precipitously in the 1750s, and although Chinese silk maintained its reputation for high quality, by the 1800s, silk produced domestically exceeded imports.[84] The sweet potato had little impact on international trade but became an important part of the Japanese diet. Hardy, nutritious, and suitable for upland fields, it was widely grown both as a regular food crop and insurance against the failure of grain. Yoshimune personally ate *satsumaimo* with high-ranking officials to demonstrate that it was not merely edible but tasty.[85] One of Yoshimune's abiding concerns was domestic ginseng, which was used for a range of ailments including fevers, infections, and nervous disorders. Under Yoshimune, the Edo magistrate's office secured cuttings of both Korean and Chinese ginseng root, although export was illegal in both countries. In 1733, the shogunate began public sales of domestic ginseng in five major cities through special government offices.[86]

Yoshimune also changed the shogunate's system for promoting retainers, introducing greater meritocracy while still respecting hereditary privilege. Prior to the Kyōho reforms, high-ranking posts in the shogunal administration were reserved for retainers with large hereditary stipends. For example, before 1723, only samurai with a stipend of 1,000 *koku* or larger were appointed city magistrates (*machi bugyō*). A shogun could appoint capable men with lesser stipends only by increasing their hereditary investitures. Yoshimune broke with this tradition by creating *tashidaka*, supplemental stipends linked to a retainer's term of office. Capable retainers could thus hold two stipends: their hereditary stipend and a term-limited *tashidaka*. This system allowed Yoshimune to appoint samurai of lower rank to high office without permanently increasing shogunal spending, and this greatly increased the range of men appointed to high office. As the historian Kasaya Kazuhiko observed, *tashidaka* created a salary system within the structure of samurai investitures.[87]

Yoshimune did not articulate a single ideology behind his reforms, but his policies reflect the thinking of two iconoclastic philosophers: Ogyū Sorai and Nishikawa Joken. Yoshimune favored both men with personal audiences, and his Kyōho reforms correspond to ideas in their published works. Yoshimune's decision to ease restrictions on Western and Chinese books was likely influenced by Nishikawa, an astronomer and geographer

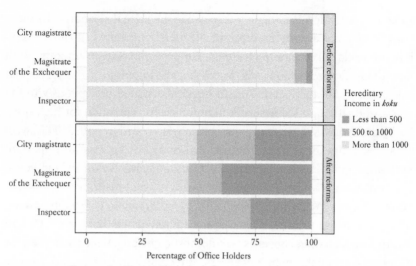

FIGURE I.7 Shogunal Office Holders before and after Yoshimune's Stipend Reform.

who wanted access to Dutch astronomical texts for calendar reform. Sorai's influence was indirect but extensive: many of Yoshimune's reforms correspond closely to Sorai's policy recommendations.[88] Sorai was broadly critical of sankin kōtai, which he famously compared to having daimyo "living in an inn," fully dependent on the innkeeper for day-to-day essentials.[89] Urban life, he argued, had made samurai reliant on merchants and inclined toward luxuries. His radical solution involved cutting sankin kōtai to as little as one month and resettling ordinary samurai in the countryside, where they could farm and support themselves directly.[90] He also advocated increased meritocracy, insisting that giving government offices to "capable men of the lower orders" would benefit the state and produce social harmony.[91] In some ways, these recommendations anticipated the Meiji government's attacks on hereditary privilege, but with a key difference. Sorai was seeking to save samurai rule from its most pronounced defects, whereas Meiji reformers saw samurai rule as beyond repair.

Nishikawa's approach to reform also presaged late Tokugawa and Meiji cosmopolitan chauvinism. In Nishikawa's vision, there was thus nothing "foreign" about imported technologies once they were adapted to Japanese needs. The oldest books on agriculture, Nishikawa observed, were from China, and cotton farming had come to Japan from Korea in the 1500s. Rather than proscribe Western learning, Nishikawa urged Japanese farmers to read translations of Western texts on hydraulics in order to improve irrigation. More remarkably, Nishikawa extended this cosmopolitan vision to morality. Japan was a virtuous and prosperous land because it was exceptionally good at realizing universal norms of good behavior. Japan had wisely adopted the best of Indian thought (the teachings of the Buddha) and the best of Chinese learning (the wisdom of the Confucian sages). Japan had not discovered these moral principles but had merely done better than China or India at manifesting them. Since morality was universal, Japan could learn from the West as well. As an example, Nishikawa noted that the Dutch showed respect for their parents even though they were unfamiliar with Confucian teachings. Clearly, all civilized peoples shared the value of filial piety; they merely described it in different ways. Thus, Western thought, like Chinese and Indian thought, might offer Japanese reformers insights into creating a more virtuous society.[92]

In this way, Nishikawa presaged the approach of Meiji reformers. His notion of universality allowed for the adoption of European ideas without abandoning ethnocentric pride. Western ideas were not "foreign" if they stood to sustain Japan's economic and moral health. Based on this cosmopolitan chauvinism Nishikawa insisted that everyone, from the shogun down to farmers, could benefit from Western texts.

Sorai's writings reconciled reverence for the past with radical reformism and thereby presaged Meiji-era radical nostalgia. Sorai was an ardent classicist, acclaimed for his mastery of ancient Chinese philosophy. He insisted, however, that the genius of the ancient sages lay in their ability to harness human talent through political ritual. Emulating the sages meant understanding how they adapted institutions to changing socioeconomic conditions. The key to good governance was therefore to match policy to social and economic conditions, not to mimic past practice. Sorai's classicism thus had a radical edge, making him a somewhat paradoxical figure. In the 1700s, he was criticized as a Sinophile, but in the Meiji era he was rediscovered as a Japanese utilitarian, advocating the greatest good for the greatest possible number. In the twentieth century, the public intellectual Maruyama Masao famously compared Sorai to Machiavelli, emphasizing how Sorai understood politics as a field of empirical inquiry, distinct from the moral conduct of the ruler himself. For present purposes, Sorai's lasting influence is how he combined a reverence for the past with a critique of convention. Much as the Meiji government invoked ancient Japanese institutions in the cause of radical reform, so Sorai's willingness to challenge convention was based on his understanding of ancient Chinese sage kings. Thus, Sorai could recommend radical changes to Tokugawa policy in the name of Tokugawa rule.[93]

Both practically and philosophically, Yoshimune's Kyōho reforms antic- ipated many policies of the Meiji Restoration but on a considerably smaller scale. Yoshimune centralized political and economic power, demanding direct payments from daimyo and asserting greater central authority over public works. The Meiji government eliminated daimyo entirely, replac- ing them with centrally appointed governors, and redirected domain tax receipts to the central treasury. Yoshimune's *tashidaka* system promoted meritocracy within the shogunal administration, giving non-heritable benefits to qualified administrators. The Meiji reforms abolished the Tokugawa status system completely, eliminating not only hereditary sti- pends but also virtually all other benefits of samurai status. Government service, including the military, became officially based solely on merit. The Kyōho reforms focused on developing domestic substitutes for key imports to reduce the outflow of specie. In the Meiji era, the government intervened to promote general industrialization, subsidizing industries from spinning to shipbuilding. The Kyōho reforms loosened restrictions on imported books. The Meiji government loosened restriction on people and actively sent students around the world to study foreign languages, laws, and technologies.

The Kyōho reforms were more modest, in part, because the crisis was more modest. Yoshimune grappled with gradual economic change, whereas the Meiji government faced the political, military, and economic challenges of imperialism. Yoshimune's central concern was the shogu- nal budget deficit; once that was resolved, he could abandon some of his less popular reforms. In 1730, for example, he canceled his sankin kōtai reforms and allowed daimyo to follow the older schedule of alternate years in Edo.[94] After increasing his power and authority as a national sover- eign, Yoshimune happily restored the status quo ante. Since he was not in rivalry with other national sovereigns, he could afford to give power back to the daimyo. Yoshimune's policies were thus predicated on the stability of the Tokugawa international order, the peaceful relationships established in the mid-seventeenth century. Yoshimune had neither the need nor the desire to fight a war, which tempered his appetite for power. Instead, he focused on the more modest goal of bequeathing to his descendants a stable and solvent regime. By that measure, he was a great success.

Beginning in the 1790s, the Japanese government faced a crisis of a dif- ferent magnitude: establishing Japanese sovereignty in a new and hostile international environment. Imperialism shattered the Tokugawa interna- tional system. Japan's intricate web of diplomatic ties made no sense to

European statesmen. Under European international law, Ryukyu could no longer be three things at once: Chinese, Japanese, and independent. If Japan wanted control over Ryukyu, it would need to assert direct sovereignty. The king of Korea could not be, simultaneously, the shogun's superior, his inferior, and his equal. The Tokugawa policy of treating Ezo as a buffer zone also became a liability. Imperial Russia did not see Japan's vague northern borders as a neutral buffer but as an invitation to expand its own empire.

The crisis of the late-Tokugawa era thus stemmed from a clash of two radically different views of international politics. Beginning in the 1600s European states began developing an increasingly exclusive sense of territorial power: ideally, a single sovereign held exclusive political and legal power over a clearly delineated territory. This doctrine is often described as "Westphalian" and linked to the 1648 Treaty of Westphalia, but it became dominant only centuries later.[95] This European sense of power stood in utter contrast to the interstate system developed by the states of Northeast Asia, where powerful sovereigns kept peace by avoiding clear borders and exclusive claims to power.[96] Under the Westphalian international order, Tokugawa policies could no longer maintain interstate peace or secure Japanese sovereignty. On the contrary, imperialism required that the Japanese state justify its territorial claims in a new language and defend those claims with a new military. Shogunal reformers struggled to meet those challenges. In the end, however, the Tokugawa regime could not rise to the challenge. It had mastered the arts of peace but forgotten those of war.

2

The Crisis of Imperialism

MODERN WESTERN IMPERIALISM destroyed the Tokugawa regime by destroying its international environment. The Tokugawa government created a peaceful international order in the early 1600s, and its domestic policies assumed the continuation of that order. For late Tokugawa and Meiji reformers, who faced belligerent and powerful Western militaries, that approach to statecraft seemed dangerously naïve. How had Japanese warlords become so ill-equiped for war? In context, however, the Tokugawa approach was entirely sensible. Until the 1800s, the West was not a military threat and as late as the 1840s, Japanese confrontations with Western powers were small and episodic, characterized by brief skirmishes, primarily with Russian and British forces. Even after Britain defeated Qing China in the Opium War (1839–42), it was still easy to dismiss the threat of imperialism. By the time the Western threat became self-evident, the task of reform seemed overwhelming. Rather than confront that challenge, many Japanese officials embraced an increasingly desperate policy of isolationism, hoped that these dangerous foreigners would simply ignore Japan and go away.

When Tokugawa officials rebuffed Western requests for trade, they explained that Japan had an ancient policy of national isolation, a "closed country" (*sakoku*) policy. Itō Hirobumi referred to such an "ancient" policy when speaking in Washington, DC, in 1871. But there was nothing ancient about Tokugawa isolationism. On the contrary, the policy emerged only in the 1790s and because Westerners could not understand Tokugawa diplomacy. Since the 1600s, Japan had avoided conflict with China and other Asian nations by avoiding direct communication between sovereigns. That approach had circumvented potentially explosive questions such as whether the Tokugawa shogun was the equal of the Qing emperor. Instead

Chinese-Japanese bilateral trade was conducted as a private affair through the Nagasaki Chinese Translation Bureau, and trade documents (*shinpai*) were scrubbed of politically fraught language. The Tokugawa were willing to include Western nations in this limited form of trade: commerce divorced from state authority. But that Tokugawa approach clashed with the European notion that trade was directly linked to sovereign power, later summarized by the aphorism "trade follows the flag." When Russia first attempted to open trade with Japan in the 1790s, negotiations fell into this conceptual chasm. The shogunate granted the Russians a *shinpai* permit to enter Nagasaki, but the Japanese insisted that documents be scrubbed of references to the Russian throne. The Russian side, by contrast, was determined to impress Japanese officials with the czar's grandeur. Practical problems of translation exacerbated this clash of worldviews, and the result was armed conflict rather than a peaceful trade. Although the two sides avoided a full-scale war, the encounter deepened suspicions on both sides. In Japan, Russian behavior was seen as evidence that Westerners were dangerous barbarians to be kept away from Japan at all costs. In Europe, the encounter confirmed the misapprehension that Japan was isolated and needed to be "opened" by the West.[1]

These early clashes sparked a lively debate within Japan on the West and world politics. What were Westerners doing on the other side of the world? How did their countries work and how did their kings rule? Examining imported books, Japanese scientists encountered the products of the Scientific Revolution, such as detailed anatomical and astronomical texts. How had "barbarians" arrived at these new insights into nature? Was this a distinctly Western science or a new form of universal knowledge? This debate dovetailed with a growing sense that the Japanese domestic order needed radical reform. The samurai estate had become a class of indolent urban rentiers rather than a rugged martial elite. What might restore their moral vigor? How could the samurai again become a powerful military force? Such questions of reform struck at the core of the Tokugawa settlement. Disarming commoners, for example, had supported domestic peace but also had weakened the Japanese nation. So had excluding ordinary Japanese from discussions of national security. Did strengthening Japan require challenging these founding principles? An equally fraught question was the shogun's relationship with the daimyo. The shogun was responsible for the defense of Japan, but it had delegated much of that responsibility to key daimyo. Could that domestic balance of power be maintained while undertaking radical military reform?

Like the more radical reforms of the Meiji era, Tokugawa-era reformers justified their calls for change in terms of both the Japanese past and
the foreign present, embracing both chauvinistic nostalgia and cosmopolitan reformism. Harkening back to Tokugawa precedents of the late
1500s, reformers called for a rural military with close ties to agriculture.
Critics also noted that Japanese warriors and traders had once roamed
across Asia: the isolation of the late Tokugawa was a recent policy decision, not a core principle of the regime. These calls for a return to origins
were coupled with calls for greater international engagement. While laud-
ing the superiority of the Japanese "spirit," reformers advocated vigorous
cultural borrowing as a means of defending local culture. That fusion of
cosmopolitanism and chauvinism anticipated Meiji reform efforts.

Russia, Britain, and the Foreign Threat

In the early 1770s, the Japanese political elite was suddenly wracked by
fear of the Russian Empire. The cause of these concerns had little to do
with Russian policy in East Asia but was the indirect result of Polish
nationalism. In 1771, Maurice Benyowsky, a minor Hungarian noble of
Polish and Hungarian ancestry, escaped from Kamchatka, where he had
been sent as a prisoner for his political activities. Stopping in western
Japan on his way south, Benyowsky exacted vengeance on his captors by
spreading wild rumors of an impending Russian invasion. The shogunate
quietly ordered an investigation of Benyowsky's rumors and found them
to be false. There were no massive Russian armies ready to attack Japan.
Nonetheless, the specter of a Russian attack led a small circle of intellectuals to investigate Japan's northern frontier and generated a series of
reform proposals.[2]

One influential report came from Kudō Heisuke, a politically well-
connected physician. Kudō concluded that there was no threat of an
impending Russian attack, but he was convinced, nonetheless, that
Russian traders were active in Ezo. That, in turn, suggested that Matsumae
domain was concealing evidence of Russian activity. Kudō advocated a
radical change in policy: allowing trade with Russia at Nagasaki, while
promoting vigorous defense and economic development.[3] Kudō's study
caught the attention of Tanuma Okitsugu, the powerful shogunal cham-
berlain and senior councilor. Tanuma dispatched a survey team, which
learned that Matsumae officials were indeed concealing evidence of direct
Japanese contact with Russian traders. In the Kuriles and Sakhalin, the

investigators found not only Russian traders but also Russian crosses, a clear violation of the Tokugawa ban on Christianity.[4]

Tanuma was concerned with these security violations, but he was equally intrigued by the possibility of increasing shogunal revenue through economic development. He began plans for land reclamation in Ezo, employing impoverished commoners, Ainu, as well as *eta* (lit. "much filth"), a pariah caste. Tanuma's plans to defend and develop Ezo by settling "undesirables" foreshadowed Meiji reforms, which sought to resettle landless commoners and displaced former samurai. Tanuma's plan was abandoned when he was forced from power in 1787, but concerns over the northern frontier remained high.[5] Not only was the Matsumae house leaving Japan's northern frontier unprotected but it was also exploiting the Ainu and provoking unrest.[6]

Unaware of these concerns, in 1792 the Russians sent a peaceful mission to Japan. The pretext of the expedition was to repatriate shipwrecked Japanese sailors, but the long-range goal was trade relations with Japan. Russian colonies in the Pacific were rich in pelts but short on grain, and St. Petersburg hoped that trade with Japan might help remedy this problem. More broadly, the mission was part of an emerging Anglo-Russian rivalry in the Pacific. Among the European powers, Britain was dominant on the high seas while Russia was superior in Eastern Europe and northern Asia. Those two empires clashed repeatedly in the Ottoman Empire, Persia, and Central Asia, a struggle that Rudyard Kipling famously dubbed "The Great Game." In Japan, Anglo-Russian tensions did not lead to open warfare, unlike in Afghanistan and Crimea. But British officials were concerned that a successful Russian mission might tip the balance of power in the Pacific. The British foreign secretary even sought to get the Japanese castaways away from Russian in order to use them as translators on Lord George Macartney's planned mission to East Asia. Unbeknownst to Tokugawa officials, Japan was becoming a prize in Great Power politics.[7]

Despite those broader tensions, the 1792 Russian mission itself was decidedly low-key—more of a tentative step toward closer relations than a formal request for a treaty. Letters and gifts to the shogunate were offered in the name of General Pihl, governor-general of Siberia, rather than Empress Catherine. The commander of the mission was not a high-ranking officer, but Lieutenant Adam Laxman, the son Eric Laxman, a well-connected scientist and key proponent of the mission. The low profile of the expedition meant that the dignity of the Russian crown was not at risk. Thus any progress toward a trade agreement could be celebrated as progress.[8]

When Laxman arrived on 1792/9/3 (October 7) at Nemuro, Japanese officials in Ezo were completely unprepared. Despite high-level discussions of a possible Russian threat, there were no clear guidelines on engaging a Russian envoy. Local officials requested orders from Edo, and while waiting for a reply, they erred on the side of courtesy and generously provisioned the expedition. After persuading the Russians to relocate to Hakodate, the capital of Ezo, Japanese officials rebuilt a local home in Western style, with individual rooms for the members of Laxman's delegation and a wooden floor. Laxman was showered with lavish gifts, including teacups, lacquer trays, and three ceremonial swords.[9]

Behind this veneer of generosity, the shogun's senior council debated how to respond. After lengthy discussion the members resolved to integrate Russia into Japan's existing trading system and to treat Russia like a Southeast Asian nation. The most commonly cited precedent in shogunal debate was the Khmer kingdom, Cambodia. Viewed from Edo, Russia and Cambodia were similar in key ways. Both were civilized people who understood norms of good behavior. Both were polite and well mannered, and both seemed interested primarily in peaceful relations. Indeed, the Russian pretense of returning Japanese castaways required that Japan respond with corresponding gestures of goodwill. But neither the Russians nor the Khmer could communicate freely in classical Chinese, the common language of Northeast Asian diplomacy. That made it impossible to establish state-to-state relations. The shogunate would therefore reject direct state-to-state ties with Russia, just as it had rejected appeals from the Khmer throne. The shogunate would, however, tolerate more limited contacts, and it granted Laxman a single *shinpai* permit for entry to Nagasaki. Following Khmer precedents, the Tokugawa were prepared to tolerate regular, if limited, trade, so long as it did not involve formal diplomatic relations. Accordingly, Laxman was instructed to go to Nagasaki but he was also informed that Japan had an "ancient policy" limiting international relations.[10] No such policy existed, but this was the shogunate's way of conveying its rejection of state-to-state relations. Viewed from the perspective of Western imperialism, the Tokugawa policy made no sense: if Japan had an "ancient" policy barring new foreign relations, why did it give Laxman a trading permit? Within a Tokugawa worldview, however, these instructions were clear: Russians could trade in Nagasaki so long as they minimized their connection to the Russian crown.

Intriguingly, Tokugawa officials did not think of Russia as a "Western" country; they emphasized the precedents of Japan's relations with Southeast Asian countries, not with the Dutch East India Company (VOC), Spain, Portugal, or England. For the shogunate, Laxman did not represent the European international order. On the contrary, although Russia was a Christian country, Japanese officials thought it could be accommodated by the *shinpai* system. Russia was threatening enough to be taken seriously but not so scary or different as to require a new international order. This logic was lost on the Russians, who were convinced that they were "opening" Japan and incorporating it into the European world order. Thus, while the Tokugawa were comparing the Russians to the Khmer, the Russians saw themselves in rivalry with other European powers. The Russians were especially concerned with the Dutch, whom they imagined to be scheming against Russian interests. This made no sense to Tokugawa officials, who made no association between the Laxman mission and the Dutch East India Company.[11]

This 1792–93 encounter suggests a path not taken. Although Edo and St. Petersburg had different long-term goals, in 1793 their interests still overlapped. St. Petersburg may have hoped for full diplomatic relations but would likely have been content with regular exports of grain. Edo primarily wanted the Russians to go away but was prepared to allow trade in the interests of peace. Critically, trade under the *shinpai* system would have incorporated Russia into the Tokugawa system. Had Laxman presented himself in Nagasaki as a private merchant, who just happened to be Russian, rather than as a Russian envoy, the Nagasaki administration would have been able to fit his mission into an existing framework for trade. Much as Japan and China had maintained peace by avoiding direct state-to-state relations, so too might Japan and Russia have initiated limited peaceful ties. Instead, Laxman misread the *shinpai* as an invitation to negotiate a treaty, and since that was beyond his rank, he returned to Russia.[12]

St. Petersburg followed up on Laxman's *shinpai* in 1804, but that mission led only to discord. Working within the discourse of European interstate relations, Russian officials assumed that Laxman's mission had been too unassuming and that a larger, more imposing expedition to Japan would yield a better response. This was the reverse of Tokugawa logic: Edo had granted Laxman a *shinpai* precisely because his approach was so modest.[13] Nonetheless, in 1804 St. Petersburg dispatched a high-ranking ambassador, Nikolai Rezanov, with a letter from Emperor

Alexander addressed directly to the shogun, or "his Tenjin-kubō Majesty, the Autocratic Potentate of the extensive Japanese Empire."[14] Such direct state-to-state contact was exactly what the Tokugawa had hoped to avoid by granting Laxman a *shinpai* permit. Rezanov's mission shattered the hope that the Russians might behave like the Khmer.

This clash of worldviews ended in violence. The shogunal council was unsure how to respond to Rezanov, but after lengthy debate, isolationist voices prevailed and the shogunate unequivocally rejected his requests. Ancestral law, the shogunate declared, forbade both trade and diplomatic relations with Russia. Trade itself was pernicious and was permitted only in cases of special and preexisting relationships. Japan had tolerated two Russian requests for trade, but henceforth Russian ships should avoid Japan. Rezanov was to leave immediately and never return. This response was markedly harsher than the 1793 response to Laxman. The Russians were now unwelcome in Japan in any form.[15]

Humiliated and vindictive, Rezanov left for Alaska, but he ordered his subordinates to attack Japanese settlements in Ezo and Sakhalin. His hope was that violence would force the shogunate to allow trade. In October 1806, Russian forces raided Sakhalin, looting food, salt, and sake before setting fire to homes and ships. The following year they extended their raids to Hakodate and the islands of Urup (J. Uruppu), Rishiri, and Iturup (J. Etorofu), before leaving for Ohotsk with some 18,000 rubles in booty.[16] In 1811, Japanese forces retaliated by capturing the Russian explorer Vasily Golovnin, who was mapping the Kurile Islands. The Russians responded by seizing a Japanese ship captain, Takadaya Kahei. Japan and Russia seemed destined for war.

Ultimately, calmer heads prevailed. The Russian commander in Ohotsk had no interest in a war with Japan; growing British naval power in the Pacific and the Napoleonic Wars in Europe were greater priorities. St. Petersburg explicitly disavowed the Rezanov raids, which had indeed been conducted without official authorization. The two sides exchanged hostages, and Russian-Japanese relations descended into a frosty peace.[17] Attitudes hardened on both sides. In Japan, isolationists argued that Westerners were uncivilized brigands but not dangerous enough to warrant radical reform. In Europe, the shogunate's rejection of Rezanov confirmed the notion that Japan was isolated. Western belligerence had created precisely the Japanese policy it was intended to challenge.[18]

Over those same years, the shogunate became alarmed by British lawlessness and violence. On 1808/8/15 (October 4), a single British ship, the

Phaeton, entered Nagasaki harbor and terrorized the city. The incident was spillover from the Napoleonic Wars: with the French conquest of Holland, Dutch ships in East Asia were seen as enemies of Britain. In an expansive reading of his orders to interdict Dutch shipping, the captain of the *Phaeton*, a headstrong eighteen-year-old, chose to attack the Dutch factory in Nagasaki. Here again, Western actions reinforced the suspicion that Westerners were lawless barbarians: he ordered the *Phaeton* to fly a Dutch rather than a British flag, kidnapped the Japanese officials who approached his ship in peaceful greeting, and then threatened to kill the hostages and destroy all ships in the harbor if he were not provided with water and supplies. The Nagasaki magistrate (*Nagasaki bugyō*) considered a counterattack but decided to comply with British demands and then commit ritual suicide to atone for the debacle.[19] As in Ezo, the conflict resolved without full-scale war. In Nagasaki, the British commander found that there were no Dutch ships to plunder, since the trading season was over. He took his supplies and departed.

These two crises prompted calls for radical reform but also equally determined defenses of the status quo. In the case of Ezo, conservatives insisted that since the Russians had sued for peace, there was no need for radical change. Others insisted that the Russian threat required a new level of national mobilization. These opposing views produced an erratic and contradictory policy toward Ezo. The shogunate began to treat Ezo as a national security threat but then reversed itself once the immediate crisis had passed. The shogunate began increasing its authority in Ezo after Laxman, and in 1799 it established the Hakodate magistrate's office (*Hakodate bugyō*), which took control of eastern Ezo. In 1807, after Rezanov's raids, the shogunate assumed direct control over the entire island.[20] In 1821, however, the shogunate reversed itself and restored the Matsumae to power in Ezo. Then in 1854, after another confrontation with Russia, the shogunate reversed itself again and reestablished direct shogunal control.

The question of how to defend Ezo was particularly fraught because it touched on deeper structural issues within the Tokugawa state system. Did the security crisis in Ezo warrant direct intervention by the shogun? The creation of a national military? Or could the problem be solved through a better mobilization of daimyo armies? If Ezo was Japanese territory, then were the Ainu, by extension, Japanese subjects? If so, shouldn't they follow Japanese customs? Could the Ainu be Japanese subjects and still follow distinct and "barbaric" practices such as long, undressed hair? If Ainu moved freely across the Japanese-Russian frontier, how could Japanese officials distinguish their own subjects from foreigners? Was Ainu cultural distinctiveness a security threat? The border crisis thus raised questions of sovereignty and national identity.

In this way, the Russian crisis precipitated new policies on Ainu ethnicity. Before the 1790s, the Ainu were treated primarily as barbarians on Japan's northern frontier. Matsumae domain had traditionally emphasized the exotic, foreign, and primitive nature of the Ainu, even when the Ainu were drawn into contract labor at Japanese-run fisheries. After 1799, however, the shogunate began looking for ways to assimilate the Ainu as Japanese subjects.[21] The shogunate became involved in Ainu daily life, encouraging the Ainu to speak Japanese, discouraging polygamy, and promoting Japanese-style haircuts. The shogunate became concerned with Ainu public health, mandating reports on infectious diseases such as tuberculosis.[22]

The conflict with Russia also prompted a new understanding of national territory. When Japanese explorers encountered evidence of Russian influence on the Kurile Islands, they responded by claiming the territory for Japan. Finding Russian crosses on Iturup in 1801, for example, explorers knocked them down and erected a signpost declaring that the island was part of "Great Japan for as long as Heaven abides and Earth endures." In the absence of Russian claims, however, the same explorers were strangely unconcerned with borders. Their signposts on Kunashiri, roughly a hundred miles southwest of Iturup, listed the date and the names of the explorers but did not mention Japanese sovereignty. The need to demarcate Japanese territory was thus contingent on competing foreign claims. Furthermore, this new sense of territoriality was improvised on the ground by the explorers themselves. There were no orders from the shogunate to establish a northern border for the Japanese empire.[23]

On the contrary, the shogunate remained commited to its long-standing policy of reliance on daimyo authority. Even after the shogunate asserted direct control over Ezo, it relied on daimyo domains for support. Most of the troops in Ezo were from northeastern domains such as Hirosaki, Akita, Morioka, Nambu, Shōnai, Sendai, and Aizu. Each domain maintained its own systems for tactics and logistics, and those multiple systems undermined effective coordination.[24] Further, although the Matsumae house had failed to protect Ezo, the shogunate did not seize or reduce its holdings. In the seventeenth century, the shogunate might well have eliminated the Matsumae house as a warning to other daimyo. In the nineteenth century, however, it granted the Matsumae an equivalent hold-ing (9,000 *koku*) some 300 miles to the southwest, to compensate for the loss of Ezo. The Matsumae were dismayed nonetheless since, unlike Ezo, Yanagawa did not provide revenue from trade. Rather than celebrate the shogunate's leniency, they lobbied to recover their older fief. In 1821, once the foreign crisis seemed past, the shogunate relented and returned Ezo to the Matsumae.[25] The shogunate's Ezo policy was thus firmly tied to tradi-tions of sub-national authority.

The shogunate's approach to Nagasaki was similarly deferential to daimyo control. The *Phaeton* Incident revealed the ineffectiveness of Nagasaki's defenses. The port's coastal fortifications were inadequate and obsolete. The *Phaeton* had forty-nine cannons, in contrast to seven at the nearest Nagasaki shoreline battery, and the British cannons were much larger. Japanese observers described the ship as a "small castle." Nagasaki's defenses were also severely understaffed, with fewer than sixty men guarding the harbor. In his last testament, the Nagasaki mag-istrate blamed the neighboring domains of Saga and Fukuoka for failing to provide troops in accordance with shogunal regulations. The domains had, indeed, been reducing their expenses by short-staffing Nagasaki, and the daimyo of Saga was placed under house arrest for this failure. But the gravest problem was organizational. The Nagasaki magistrate was responsible for the defense of the harbor but had only twenty-five direct vassals: his charge was to mobilize the samurai of other lords, the daimyo of Saga and Fukuoka. So diffuse was the chain of command that it is unclear whether Saga was supposed to provide 200 men or 5,000 and whether Fukuoka should have sent troops as well. This confusion was emblematic of the fragmented responsibility of the Tokugawa state system, which was designed for domestic stability rather than national mobilization.[26]

Remarkably, the *Phaeton* debacle did not lead to major institutional reforms. After punishing the daimyo of Saga, Edo left the organization of Nagasaki virtually unchanged. The government built additional shore batteries, arranged a new system of warning signals, and developed a more reliable means of identifying Dutch ships. But Fukuoka and Saga continued to dodge expensive obligations, such as increasing stockpiles of ammunition. At no point did Edo seriously consider taking direct con-trol of the port region and seizing daimyo assets to supports its defense.[27] Despite the inability of the existing system to defend Nagasaki, the shogu-nate was loath to challenge daimyo privilege.

The following years saw a series of minor encounters with European ships. On several occasions, British ships approached Uraga, at the entrance to Edo Bay, to request trade or supplies. In 1824, there were two isolated skirmishes with British whaling crews who came ashore to raid for supplies. None of these encounters resembled state-sponsored military action. These events confirmed the notion that the solution to the foreign crisis was isolation: peace could be maintained by scaring foreigners away from Japanese waters. Based on this reasoning, in 1825 the shogunate declared a newly restrictive policy on foreign contact, the so-called No Two Thoughts Edict.[28] When any Western ship approached the coast, Japanese forces were henceforth to drive it away without question, even if this meant accidentally firing on a Dutch ship. If Westerners managed to come ashore, they were to be imprisoned and handed over to the shogunate. The logic behind this policy was summarized in an 1824 report on military reform by Tōyama Kagemichi, a magistrate of the exchequer. "What we are seeing now are nothing more than pirates, wandering the world and slipping into coastal waters to make off with whatever they can get their hands on. They are not worthy of our fear." There was no need, Tōyama insisted, for a massive new navy. Instead, an improved coast guard, able to respond rapidly to incursions, would be enough to drive off and even capture Western ships. By combining superior knowledge of local waters with samurai spirit, Japan could defeat these simple brigands.[29] This was a reasonable response to Japan's initial confrontations with Europe, but Tōyama had no appreciation of European imperialism or state power. That misjudgment would prove fatal to the shogunate.

If Tokugawa politics is seen as a trajectory toward the powerful Meiji state, then these early confrontations with Western imperialism seem to reverse that course. In both Ezo and Nagasaki, the shogunate chose not to expand state power even though local daimyo had failed to defend Japan. In Nagasaki, the responsible daimyo had been unable to cooperate with each other or effectively serve the shogun. In Ezo, Matsumae domain had not only failed at defense but had also abused the local population, violated shogunal policy, and then concealed evidence of its own malfeasance. In both cases, the shogunate had ample grounds to extinguish the responsible domains, but instead restored the status quo ante, continuing the overlapping political authority of the Tokugawa compound state. In context, these decisions were understandable. The shogun's key advisors were themselves daimyo and such men were obviously disinclined to radically curtail the powers of daimyo. And the skirmishes with the British and

Russians did not lead to war. So long as the transnational Pax Tokugawa could be sustained, the shogunal elite was loath to mobilize for war.

Imperialism: The Opium War and the Tenpō Crisis

Between 1839 and 1842, the British military humiliated the Qing Empire in a conflict now known as the Opium War. Up and down the Chinese coast, from Canton to Tianjin, British forces destroyed forts, sank junks and warships, blockaded ports, and occupied key cities. In 1842, with Britain poised to take the southern capital of Nanjing, the Qing sued for peace. The resulting treaty (Treaty of Nanking, 1842) was a dramatic indignity for China. The Qing ceded Hong Kong to the English crown and agreed to pay 21 million silver dollars in damages, equivalent to over 500 US tons of pure silver. China opened five cities (thereafter known as treaty ports) to residence by British subjects and in 1844 conceded to extraterritoriality: Westerners in China would henceforth be tried in their own courts according to their own laws. Extraterritoriality made geopolitics palpable in everyday life well beyond the treaty ports. When European missionaries ransacked Chinese religious sites, purging them of Buddhist icons in the name of Christianity, the Qing could not take legal action. In that way, the Qing's loss of sovereign authority became tangible for ordinary imperial subjects. The legal impunity of foreigners made vivid the regime's defeat.

The origins of the Opium War made China's defeat even more painful. The Qing had seized and destroyed the opium stockpiles of British merchants in Canton. Opium was illegal in China, and Qing officials expected Britain to respect its campaign against drug smuggling. For the British government, however, the property rights of British subjects trumped the right of the Qing to enforce its laws against narcotics trafficking.

The impact of the Opium War on Japanese politics was enormous. Britain, a small island country on the other side of the world, had humbled the most powerful kingdom in East Asia. This defeat raised both practical and philosophical questions. Had the Qing merely blundered in military strategy? Had they failed because of internal weaknesses? Had they failed to instill reverence and awe among ordinary Chinese? Was the correct defense to emulate Western technology? Or would the introduction of European military tactics allow the broader infiltration of European ideas, leading to collapse from within?

In Japan, high-ranking officials and well-connected intellectuals learned of China's defeat quickly through Dutch reports. By early 1841, shogunal officials such as Mizuno Tadakuni, head of the shogunal council of elders, were already discussing how China's defeat posed a threat to Japan.[30] But the Tokugawa were loath to allow a broader discussion of foreign policy. In 1839, for example, the shogunate arrested for sedition a group of Nagasaki-based scholars who had obliquely criticized shogunal foreign policy in a privately circulated manuscript.[31] In 1849, Mineta Fūkō was imprisoned for publishing a history of the Opium War without authorization.[32] Despite these purges, it was impossible to contain news of such a momentous event. By the 1860s, the details of China's defeat were available from a variety of sources. Inexpensive woodblock prints showed the size and armaments of British warships while lofty tomes analyzed China's defeat in classical language, replete with references to ancient history.[33]

Within the shogunate, the war had an immediate impact, changing the course of an ongoing reform effort known as the Tenpō reforms (1841–43). Initially, the Tenpō reforms were unremarkable, with conventional exhortations to reduce expenses and eliminate luxuries. Following news of the Opium War, however, Mizuno Tadakuni, began to focus on responding to imperialism. He revoked the No Two Thoughts Edict and began a program to improve national defense. He reorganized Edo's defenses based on the advice of Takashima Shūhan, an expert on Western military methods. In 1843, he ordered the creation of the Ōzutsugumi, Japan's first modern artillery division, and began transferring personnel from other units. He created three new coastal defense positions, appointing magistrates (bugyō) in Shimoda, Haneda, and Niigata.[34]

In order to pay for these new initiatives, Mizuno took bold steps to increase shogunal revenue. He increased taxes on shogunal lands and demanded "loans" from Osaka merchants. He ordered construction of a massive canal from Edo Bay to Inbanuma Lake. That project would have opened new farmland and also improved Edo's defenses by creating a new supply route in case of a blockade by foreign ships. In 1843/6, in his boldest move, Mizuno asserted direct shogunal control over three regions: the port of Niigata and two broad regions around Edo and Osaka, Japan's two largest cities.[35]

Mizuno's claim was a bold break with precedent. The areas around Edo and Osaka were highly fragmented by design, divided into hundreds of territories controlled by liege vassals and minor daimyo. In case of war, these lords were to mobilize their own retainers in defense of the shogunate. The small size of each parcel made it difficult to coordinate military operations, discouraging rebellion but also undermining national defense. Mizuno sought to replace this arrangement with direct central control. Mizuno was prepared to compensate the displaced lords with new territories, farther away from Edo and Osaka, but he insisted that a new international environment demanded a new approach to national defense. In the wake of the Opium War, Mizuno had no interest in asking dozens of minor lords to mobilize conventional samurai battalions, with pikeman and lancers, against British warships. Instead, by creating two newly contiguous shogunal territories (roughly 2,000 sq. miles each), and defending them with state-of-the-art weapons, Tadakuni was confronting directly the challenge of imperialism.

This boldness was Mizuno's undoing. Daimyo and hatamoto dissented furiously, as did commoners, who feared that they would face new levies after the land transfers. Mizuno could not survive such deep and broad resistance, and within two weeks he had resigned as chair of the council of elders. The land transfer edicts were revoked and, over the next few years, his major reforms were systematically reversed.[36] The shogunate lasted another quarter century after the resignation of Mizuno Tadakuni. But the ability of daimyo and hatamoto to block the land transfer revealed how the stability of the compound state precluded the creation of a nation-state. In order to gain control over its own capital region, the shogunate needed to challenge the traditional privileges of its allies: hatamoto and fudai daimyo. But those long-standing allies were unsupportive of reforms that threatened rather than enhanced their own authority. The result was an abortive reform movement that left the regime no stronger than before. The failure of the Tenpō reforms left the shogunate averse to further radical change. Alarmed by the level of dissent provoked by Mizuno's efforts, the shogun Tokugawa Ieyoshi emphasized instead the need for "harmony" among his advisors. That mandate set the tone for the diplomatic crisis of the 1850s. Mizuno's successor, Abe Masahiro, understood the gravity of the foreign threat, but he had risen to power as an advocate of broad consensus. In practice this meant that the regime was paralyzed, since there was no consensus on the most pressing issues of the day.[37]

Domestic Crises and Domain Reform

The failure of the shogunate's Tenpō reforms was part of a broader shift in Japanese politics. From the late 1700s onward, the more innovative reform efforts came from daimyo domains rather than the shogunate. Two famous examples are the Tenpō-era reforms in Satsuma and Chōshū, the domains that toppled the Tokugawa house in 1868. In both domains, reforms addressed long-standing fiscal problems and generated funds for military modernization. In Satsuma, reformers repudiated the domain's massive debt of nearly 5 million ryō, bankrupting several Osaka merchant houses in the process. In order to avoid future borrowing, the domain intensified its program of sugarcane production in the Amami Islands, squeezing cultivators and raising prices in Osaka. Combined with other domain monopolies, this led to budget surpluses. In Chōshū, the domain took a different approach to monopolies, abolishing direct domain monopolies on indigo, wax, salt, sake, and cotton but selling those monopoly rights to merchant guilds. The domains also increased revenue through land reclamation projects and the promotion of shipping at ports such as Shimonoseki. The political impact in both domains was similar: Satsuma and Chōshū each had the funds to purchase modern weapons in the 1850s and 1860s.

Other domains were equally bold in confronting the challenges of late Tokugawa society. Yonezawa, for example, sought to address samurai poverty by promoting textile production in retainer households. Instead of treating side employments as a shameful violation of samurai norms, the government celebrated weaving for its contribution to the domain treasury. The domain compared the production of high-quality cloth to brave military service: both showed that a samurai was a loyal and stalwart vassal. Samurai households commonly sold their weaving through domain-regulated merchants. This promotion of samurai weaving presaged Meiji policies designed to make former samurai economically productive. Ironically, Tokugawa-era hardship made Yonezawa samurai uniquely prepared for the Meiji-era conversion of their stipends into bonds. Compared to most samurai, Yonezawa retainers were savvy in business and finance.[38]

Hirsosaki domain took an opposite approach. Rather than embrace commodity production, the domain attempted to return to a simpler agrarian economy. In the 1790s, the domain attempted to "resettle" thousands of samurai from Hirosaki city to the countryside, where they were supposed to become self-supporting farmers. The program was abandoned after several years: rather than grow their own food, Hirosaki samurai preferred to extort it from local farmers. The domain eventually resolved its debt problems with a less radical approach: providing tools, subsidies, and tax incentives to farmers who developed new cropland. Although samurai resettlement was largely a failure, it also foreshadowed Meiji reforms. The Meiji government attempted, with limited success, to establish samurai farmsteads in Hokkaido.[39]

Behind these diverse policies was a shared sense of crisis: Tokugawa society was out of order. In the countryside this discontent was reflected in new forms of popular protest. Until the mid-1700s, villagers commonly acted in concert to demand tax relief from the local government. Village headmen led these protests, representing their farm communities to samurai authority. Starting in the late 1700s, however, protesters began treating the local elite as the enemy rather than as their agents against samurai government. Rather than target the government, farmers attacked the property (although rarely the person) of wealthy villagers, destroying debt records, clothing, and furniture. These sorts of protests surged after the harvest failures of the 1780s and the 1830s.[40]

Underlying these new protests were changes in income and economic relations. The growth of a commercial economy had weakened the cohesion of farm villages and frayed the traditional safety net. In the rural economy of the 1600s, when most farmers grew crops primarily for their own consumption and to pay taxes, a harvest shortfall had a common impact on almost all farmers: less grain meant less to eat and less ability to pay taxes. Further, enlightened self-interest mandated that larger landholders help their poorer neighbors in times of crises. Without the help of smallholders and tenants, a wealthy farmer could not bring in his own crop: rich farmers needed the survival, and ideally the goodwill, of their poorer neighbors. By the late 1700s, these ties had substantially weakened. In a commercial economy, a bumper crop could be as damaging as a harvest failure since it could force down prices. In villages where farmers purchased each other's goods, one household's crisis was another's good fortune. For example, a drop in mulberry prices was a bane for mulberry growers but a boon to those who bought the leaves to feed to silkworms. In addition, landlords became less interested in their tenants' well-being. Short-term labor contracts and labor mobility undermined earlier connections between moral obligation and enlightened self-interest. Exacerbating those tensions was stagnation or decline in real wages. The data are fragmentary, but wage records for the Kinai show that real farm wages grew at roughly 1.6 percent per year from 1730 to 1762, but stagnated thereafter.[41] By the 1800s, real wages for both skilled and unskilled workers were falling in both the Kantō and the Kinai.[42]

Ordinary samurai also came under increasing economic stress. Most samurai were paid in stipends that used rice as a currency of account, and a gradual decline in rice prices, relative to other goods, meant a decrease in their real income. More serious was the pressure of expectations. Urban life and an increasing range of consumer goods drove many samurai to borrow against future income, often at high rates. Many had their incomes reduced when their lords "borrowed" part of their stipends. These problems were endemic to the Tokugawa system. Shimazu Yoshihiro had lamented the deleterious effect of urban life on samurai as early as 1591, but by the 1790s, cultural critics were describing a new level of decay: samurai were not just losing their warrior vitality; they were becoming indistinguishable from other classes. Rather than serving as moral exemplars for the rest of society, samurai were manifesting the worst excesses of greed, intemperance, gluttony, and sloth.[43]

In 1837, samurai disaffection and public discontent came together in spectacular fashion when Ōshio Heihachirō, a shogunal retainer, led a violent protest against his own government. Ōshio had served as a constable (*yoriki*) in the Osaka city magistrate's office, a position that combined, in modern US parlance, the duties of an assistant district attorney, a municipal court judge, and a police detective. He was relentless in his pursuit of malfeasance, breaking prostitution rings and uncovering illegal religious communities. He also developed a following as a public intellectual, and his academy, the Pure Heart Grotto (Senshindō), attracted both samurai and commoners. In 1830, Ōshio resigned his post as constable and devoted himself fully to education. He focused increasingly on Ōyōmei Learning, a heterodox school of Confucianism that emphasized the discovery of one's innate moral compass. The purpose of scholarship was less about acquiring knowledge than revealing inner truths, and then for the learner to act on that wisdom. Ōshio therefore experienced the shogunate's response to the Tenpō Famine (1834–37) as a personal moral crisis. Soaring rice prices should have prompted the shogunate to distribute grain from relief granaries, but instead the government was buying rice for upcoming shogunal celebrations. For Ōshio, it was impossible in good conscience to ignore such malfeasance and in 1837 he rallied his followers to attack the government he had recently served. According to Ōshio's manifesto, their goal was to seize the assets of the wealthy, distribute it to the needy, destroy tax records, execute greedy merchants, and bring heaven's wrath down upon corrupt local officials. By most standards, Ōshio's rebellion was a failure: he was betrayed by an informant, and his followers were poorly trained and organized. Ōshio himself fled to the countryside, where he committed suicide to avoid arrest. But his rebellion was enough to humiliate the shogunate. Police commanders fell from their horses while pursuing the rebels, and 20 percent of Osaka burned in the ensuing turmoil. Across Japan, wealthy commoners were terrified by rumors that Ōshio had actually escaped and was coming to their region to continue his struggle.[44]

Ōshio's revolt was not a harbinger of impending revolution. The Japanese countryside did not erupt in rebellion, and disgruntled samurai did not begin raising peasant armies. Overall, there is little evidence of class consciousness or a coherent mass movement in the public protests of the late Tokugawa era. On the contrary, the struggle to overthrow the shogunate was waged between relatively small factions within the samurai elite, a "revolution from above." But the indirect effect of public protest was enormous. It became impossible to ignore, in the face of widespread popular discontent, the need for fundamental social change. The most potent impact of peasant protest was thus indirect: it undermined the samurai estate's faith in its own elite status. After the fall of the shogunate, ordinary samurai were remarkably placid as the Meiji government eliminated their hereditary stipends and stripped them of prestige. Peasant protest did not topple the Tokugawa shogunate, but it precluded any serious defense of the status quo. In combination with the threat of imperialism, popular discontent thus inspired the samurai elite to dissolve itself.

Envisioning a New Japan

The reformist ideology of the Meiji Restoration was hybrid and syncretic. The critical tropes of radical nostalgia and cosmopolitan chauvinism appeared in rival schools across the ideological spectrum. Imperial loyalists often drew inspiration from multiple distinct movements, including orthodox Confucianism, the Sorai school, Dutch Studies, Nativism, and Mito Studies. The Tokugawa Confucian orthodoxy emerged in the late 1700s when the shogunate endorsed a single approach to Confucian learning, an approach based on work of Zhu Xi, the prominent twelfth-century Chinese philosopher. Many domain academies followed the shogunate's example, and Zhu Xi Confucianism received official support across Japan. Government sponsorship gave Zhu Xi learning a powerful but not exclusive claim to speak for Confucian learning. Ogyū Sorai's followers, for example, continued to pursue a distinctive approach to ancient Chinese texts, critical of Zhu Xi. The Dutch Studies (*rangaku*) movement began in the 1700s with the study of Western scientific texts, but it later engaged European works on history, politics, and economics. The term "Dutch Studies" reflects the importance of the Dutch in Nagasaki as a source of foreign knowledge, and in the 1800s, Dutch Studies scholars were surprised to learn that Holland was no longer a major European power. Dutch Studies scholars were influential in a range of fields, especially medicine and astronomy, where they could demonstrate the empirical strength of "foreign" knowledge.

By contrast, Nativist scholars insisted that foreign learning had corrupted Japan and destroyed its indigenous culture. To recover this lost tradition, Nativists focused on ancient Japanese texts such as the *Kojiki*, which they saw as a largely untainted account of the "age of the gods" (*jindai*). Compiled in 712 from oral histories and mythologies, the *Kojiki* described the origins of the universe, the birth of the primordial Japanese gods, the creation of the islands of Japan, and the descent of the gods from heaven to rule Japan and found the Japanese imperial line. The Kojiki was written in Japanese, rather than classical Chinese, but the orthography employed Chinese characters nonetheless. To their dismay, Nativists could find no purely Japanese records describing ancient Japan. But this Nativist quest for a "purely" Japanese culture led to important advances in philology. The scholar Motoori Norinaga, for example, pioneered the study of Japanese grammar so as to establish the superiority of Japanese culture. His commentary on the *Kojiki* made that text available for the first time to a broad readership. When Motoori began his exegesis, the *Kojiki* was as foreign to most Japanese as *Beowulf* was to English readers of Jane Austen or Charles Dickens. Indeed, just as J.R.R. Tolkien and other scholars of Old English searched *Beowulf* for the vestiges of a pre-Christian, Celtic, "noble but heathen past," so Motoori sought in the *Kojiki* a Japanese past unsullied by Buddhist and Confucian thought.[45] Unfortunately for Motoori, much of the moral and religious landscape of the *Kojiki* was bleak and choatic. According to Motoori, for example, the *Kojiki* offered no special reward for virtue. After death, everyone, both the wicked and the good, descended to a netherworld of pollution and decay. Compared to Buddhist thought, in which good works might lead to an auspicious reincarnation, this was a grim and nihilistic view of death. Instead of a coherent moral code, the *Kojiki* was full of strange mayhem: the gods desecrated each others' palaces with feces, performed lewd dances, quarreled, tortured, suffered, and lied. Motoori himself was forced to conclude that the acts of the gods were often incomprehensible.[46]

Despite these problems, Motoori's translation of the *Kojiki* transformed Japanese thought. Before Motoori, scholars of ancient Japan had relied primarily on the *Nihon shoki*, which was written in 720 in the style of a Chinese dynastic history. Accordingly, the *Nihon shoki* omitted much of the earthy, if lurid, detail of the *Kojiki*, such as gory accounts of fracticide and odes to menstrual blood. After Motoori, the *Kojiki* was treated with new respect, if not reverence. The impact of Motoori's work was roughly parallel to contemporaneous rediscoveries of ancient legends in Europe. In German lands, for example, modernized versions of the *Nibelungenlied* inspired works such as Wagner's opera series *Der Ring des Nibelungen*, while in England, Alfred Lord Tennyson's *Idylls of the King* was part of a Victorian revival of interest in King Arthur. In all three cases, ancient legends of heroes and dragons became newly relevant. Legends of a common and glorious ancient past were invoked as an antidote to a fractious and troubling present.[47]

Motoori's many followers pulled his legacy in different directions. Among the most influential was Hirata Atsutane, who turned Nativism into a popular movement. Hirata lacked Motoori's scholarly rigor and intellectual integrity, but he understood how a reinterpretation of the Japanese gods could be connected to the life experience of ordinary farmers and merchants. The Japanese people themselves were, according to Hirata, descendants of the gods and their seemingly mundane lives were therefore suffused with sacred meaning. But in order to bring Nativism to a broader audience, Hirata altered key aspects of Motoori's thought. Instead of Motoori's inevitable descent into hell, for example, he insisted that good souls ascended to heaven.[48] Remarkably, Hirata based this understanding of the afterlife largely on Chinese accounts of Christianity, but he attributed those ideas to Shinto texts.[49] Hirata also promoted the stories of a street performer, Kōzō Torakichi, who claimed to have flown to the moon with *tengu*, mountain goblins. Hirata carefully coached Kōzō, so that his performances supported Hirata's vision of Shinto thought.[50] This showmanship and eclecticism alarmed some of Hirata's contemporaries, but his imaginative writings and lectures were widely influential.[51] Hirata's cosmopolitan chauvinism allowed him to coopt foreign intellectual traditions while insisting on the cultural superiority of Japan. He argued, for example, that Chinese, Indian, or Dutch learning became indistinguishable from Japanese learning when used to help Japan.[52]

Mito Studies (*Mitogaku*), sponsored by Mito domain, fused Nativist ideas with a more conventional approach to Confucian learning. Mito scholars, for example, revered the Japanese emperor as a descendant of the ancient gods, but they discussed his virtue with references to Confucian texts. Starting in the 1600s, scholars in Mito began work on a massive history of Japan modeled on Chinese dynastic chronicles. Unlike Nativists, who struggled to write in "pure" Japanese, Mito scholars such as Fujita Tōko and Aizawa Seishisai commonly wrote in classical Chinese, the established language of scholarship. Mito Studies had a xenophobic aspect: Fujita Tōko helped coin and promote the motto "revere the emperor, expel the barbarian" (sonnō jōi). Nonetheless, Mito thinkers were often pragmatic on issues such as the adoption of Western technology. Mito domain was a branch domain of the Tokugawa house, and this produced one of the great ironies of nineteenth-century Japanese thought. The revival of imperial power was promoted by the Tokugawa family. The daimyo of Mito were descendants of a younger son of the first shogun. Mito scholars were convinced, however, that reverence for the emperor could only enhance Tokugawa authority. Japanese emperors had reigned but not ruled for centuries, and Mito scholars had no expectation that this would change.[53]

Late Tokugawa discourse was shaped by rivalries between these factions, but the antecedents of Meiji reformist thought appeared across these schools as rival thinkers began to endorse similar reform proposals. Three distinct thinkers, for example, proposed mobilizing commoners for national defense: Hayashi Shihei, Satō Nobuhiro, and Tōyama Kagemichi. Hayashi Shihei was an iconoclastic author, influenced by Dutch Studies and the Sorai School. In the 1780s and 1790s, he argued that the strict separation of samurai and commoners had led to Japan's military decline. Japan needed to return to older military traditions:

> The essence of the samurai is no different from that of today's farmers. This is because ancient samurai all lived in the countryside, and those who had a lot of land supported many vassal followers. When leaving for battle, they, of course, took their vassals, and they also trained farmers as troops.[54]

Hayashi also warned of an imminent Russian attack and called for a massive new navy and the settlement of Ezo. His outspokenness exceeded the shogunate's tolerance for public dissent: in 1792/5 his book was banned and Hayashi himself was put in jail, where he died of illness a year later.

In 1823, Satō Nobuhiro proposed a still bolder plan for territorial expansion. Satō was influenced by both Dutch Studies and Nativism, and his work reflects a passionate belief in the uniqueness of the Japanese emperor. In *A Secret Plan for World Unification* (*Kondō hisaku*), Satō proposed nothing less than Japanese control of the entire world, beginning with China and Korea.[55] That would require a new military, and Satō had no patience for traditional status distinctions. Not only did he advocate a conscript army drawn from all able-bodied men but he also planned to merge daimyo domains into larger administrative units. The new southwestern region of Ōhama, for example, would have 3 million people and roughly 600,000 men between twenty and fifty years of age. Selecting only the strongest, Satō projected 60,000 recruits from Ōhama. His ideas attracted the attention of Mizuno Tadakuni and likely inspired Mizuno's plan to reallocate daimyo territory.[56]

Writing in 1824, Tōyama Kagemichi dismissed such radical plans as absurd: he explicitly described Hayashi's thinking as "noxious." A steadfast shogunal servant, Tōyama rose through the ranks of the establishment, from page in Edo Castle to magistrate of Nagasaki and then to magistrate of the exchequer. He was not inclined to dismantle a political system that had served him so well. Nor was Tōyama convinced that Japan was facing an impending Western invasion. The main threat, he argued, was from whaling ships in search of fresh water and supplies. Japan simply needed a better coast guard.

Nonetheless, Tōyama, like Satō and Hayashi, advocated mobilizing commoners in defense of Japan. He proposed using fishing boats as a coast guard fleet. Samurai and fisherman would work together in joint units: the fisherman would sail the ships while the samurai would hide below deck to avoid detection. Western ships would ignore these ordinary-looking boats, and the element of surprise would allow Japanese forces to board and seize the foreign vessels. Within each coastal division, fishermen and samurai would wear matching colors to mark them as members of the same force.[57] Hayashi, Satō, and Tōyama disagreed on the very nature of Japan's foreign crisis. They agreed, however, that ordinary Japanese men, not just samurai, would be needed to defend the realm.

As precedent for the mobilization of commoners, nineteenth-century thinkers looked to Japan's past. Hirata Atsutane, for example, extolled the martial exploits of Hamada Yahyōe, a Nagasaki-based merchant who skirmished with the Dutch on Taiwan in the 1620s.[58] Hamada refused to pay Dutch levies, and when the Dutch seized his ships he retaliated by taking

Peter Nuyts, the colonial governor, hostage. The Dutch returned Hamada's ships and later extradited Nuyts to Japan, where he was held under house arrest from 1632 to 1636.[59] Hamada's exploits, Hirata declared, showed that Japanese warriors were once feared throughout the world.

Hamada was also celebrated by Koga Tōan, an instructor in the Shōheikō, the shogunate's Confucian academy. In a treatise on foreign policy, Koga explicitly cited Hamada as a model for the shogunate: Hamada had put terror in the hearts of the Dutch and extended the authority of the imperial house. The shogunate should take his actions as a guide, build new warships, and study naval tactics.[60] Hirata and Koga represented strikingly different schools of thought: Zhu Xi Confucian orthodoxy and Nativism. But they agreed that Japan needed men like Hamada, brave commoners ready to fight Europeans.

Such diverse support for arming commoners helps explain the relative ease with which conscription was introduced in the Meiji era. The idea of incorporating commoners into military units had been discussed for decades and was no longer radical. In practice, however, joint samurai-commoner battalions faced serious problems. In the Chōshū civil war (1864–65), for example, rebel samurai found it easy to recruit commoners, but those soldiers were quick to betray their officers, denouncing them as "lousy rōnin."[61] This reflected the deeper challenge of late Tokugawa politics. What would replace the traditional status system? What new ideas and practices would hold together Japanese state and society?

The seminal work in this quest for a national ideology was Aizawa Seishisai's *New Theses* (*Shinron*, 1825). Aizawa, a prominent Mito Studies scholar, grappled directly with nature of European power: why were European countries able to conquer so much of the world? For Aizawa, the answer lay in religion. Through the "evil and base" doctrine of Christianity, European countries destroyed their enemies from within. Preaching a deceitful doctrine, they induced people around the world to serve foreign masters. The solution, asserted Aizawa, was to invoke the Japanese emperor and unite the "hearts" of the Japanese people. In ancient Japan, civil and military elites and common people were united in their reverence for the emperor. Japan needed to restore this sense of unity. Aizawa emphasized the importance of rituals, such as the Daijōsai enthronement ceremony and annual harvest ceremonies. Although commoners did not witness such ceremonies directly, they participated through their offerings to the court. According to Aizawa, "in the autumn of each year when the grain ripened, His Majesty offered some of it to the gods as a symbolic act of thanksgiving and afterward, consumed it with His people. At such moments everyone in the realm was made to realize that the grain they consumed derived from Amaterasu's original rice seeds, and they stood in awesome veneration of Her will."[62] For Aizawa, belief in the emperor could create national unity and prevent subversion from abroad: "When the people are taught simply to revere Amaterasu and Her Divine Imperial Line, their allegiances are undivided and they are blind to all heresies. Thus we achieve both spiritual unity among the people and the union of Heaven and man."[63]

Aizawa's work was empirically flawed but also prescient. Aizawa thought that Christianity united the nations of Europe into a single coherent force. He thus conflated Christianity, nationalism, and imperialism. But he astutely understood the need for a new Japanese ideology, something that could unite the Japanese people. Aizawa's thinking thus encompassed a powerful tension: he was repulsed by Christianity but enthralled by its power. His vision of Japanese religion was thus both retaliation and imitation. "We must transform [the Western barbarians] by appropriating the very methods that they now seek to use to transform us."[64] The only way to resist the West was to emulate the West, using religion for mass mobilization. Cosmopolitan chauvinism led Aizawa to appreciate European statecraft.

A similar process led Satō Nobuhiro to endorse European science. In his study *The Pillar of Heaven* (*Tenchūki*, 1825), Satō synthesized European astronomy with Japanese creation myths. Like Hirata, whose writings he respected, Satō was adamant in his desire to reconcile Japanese mythology with scientific observation. Unlike Hirata, Satō was empirically scrupulous and his description of the cosmos was based on up-to-date European texts. *The Pillar of Heaven*, for example, featured a universe with seven planets revolving around the sun in elliptical orbits. Those planets each rotated on their own axes, and the Earth's axis of rotation was tilted twenty-three degrees, causing the seasons. Days and years on each planet varied according to the speed of rotation and revolution. Many planets, not only the earth, had moons.[65]

For Satō, this European knowledge was incomplete without Japanese insight. While Europeans could explain the mechanics of the planetary motion, only Japanese creation myths could explain the origins of the universe and the unseen forces behind it. What, Satō asked, brought the planets into being and why are they in motion? The answer lay in the actions of Izanagi and Izanami, the two primordial deities who created the world when they thrust a jeweled spear into a sea of brine. The gods stirred the brine and when they lifted the spear, "the brine dripping down from the tip of the spear piled up and became an island."[66] For Satō, the rotation of the planets was a logical consequence of the gods stirring the primordial brine. The shape of the orbits was also explained by ancient texts. Satō connected the elliptical orbits of planets with the words "chaotic mass like an egg" from the opening of the *Nihon shoki*: "like an egg," for Satō, meant egg-shaped or elliptical.[67]

Through such generous readings, Satō was able to make Japanese mythology uniquely compatible with modern astronomy. Unlike Greek, Roman, Persian, and Egyptian myths, Japanese texts alone could account for the inherent motion of the universe. Even the Bible, which Satō referenced elliptically, could not explain the mysteries of the cosmos.[68] Satō's cosmopolitan chauvinism allowed him to claim that there was nothing "foreign" about Western science. On the contrary, European science was more Japanese than European.[69]

Finally, cosmopolitan chauvinism and radical nostalgia appear in the work of Tadano Makuzu, one of a handful of women to write on political issues in the Tokugawa era. As a woman, Tadano worked at the margins of Tokugawa public life, although she grew up in an intellectually vibrant home. Her father, Kudō Heisuke, was a well-informed and well-connected physician, deeply involved in studies of Russia and Ezo. Tadano's work reflects what she learned in her father's home. She was uncommonly familiar with European customs, although she never formally pursued Dutch Studies. Tadano's knowledge of formal philosophy was also limited: as a woman, she learned to read Japanese but not classical Chinese. Nonetheless, her unique voice received both acclaim and approbation. The famous author Takizawa Bakin was both dazzled and repulsed by her "manly spirit." He praised her talents, then refused to help her publish, and still later lamented the end of their correspondence.[70]

Like Satō and Aizawa, Tadano was fascinated by Japanese mythology, especially the *Kojiki*. She discerned in these texts a challenge to conventional gender roles: Amaterasu, the Sun Goddess, was a woman. So was Empress Jingū, who conquered the Korean peninsula while pregnant. "Why, then," asked Tadano, "can't we be ambitious even though we are women?" For Tadano, the present status of women in Europe seemed to recall their status in ancient Japan. In Russia, she reported, bride and groom took identical public marriage vows, declaring that they are "of the same mind." Since the vows were equal, infidelity was considered a serious crime for both genders. European women also seemed to have greater intellectual opportunities, such as the chance to study medicine: "In a book that came from a Western country," wrote Tadano, "I saw a [picture of a] woman about to perform a dissection."[71]

Tadano crafted her fragmentary knowledge of Europe into a critique of Japanese society. As the daughter of a mid-ranking samurai household, Tadano lamented both reckless spending by samurai and the growing power of urban merchants. Neither problem, she insisted, existed in Russia. Russian merchants worked to enrich the realm, not to increase their own wealth through petty schemes. And Russian nobles did not squander their income, as with sankin kōtai in Japan. "Not even the most prominent officials have retinues," Tadano insisted, only the czar. "I feel envious," she proclaimed, "when I consider the customs of Russia." Much like Satō and Aizawa, Tadano insisted that the emulation of foreign customs could advance the rediscovery of Japanese virtue. Japanese creativity was exceptional, Tadano declared, but it was most evident in the stagecraft of kabuki theater. What would happen, she wondered, if this spirit of innovation were directed toward the common good? Kabuki theater was mesmerizing because actors and musicians worked together united by a common rhythm. What if this spirit of unity were invoked to benefit the country as a whole?[72] Like Aizawa, Tadano thought that European models could enhance rather than efface the unique strengths of Japanese culture.

What united the disparate writings of Satō, Aizawa, and Tadano was the shared sense that the contemporary West could help restore a lost Japanese past. For Aizawa, the political uses of Christianity in Europe suggested how the shogunate might revive the lost virtues of ancient Japan. For Satō, European science and Japanese mythology were mutually reinforcing, and the combination of the two would lead to unprecedented prosperity and power. For Tadano, the West offered examples of how ambition and ingenuity might be harnessed for the common good, restoring a lost sense of Japanese harmony. Satō, Aizawa, and Tadano were all prescient in suggesting the need for radical change, but their influence unfolded gradually and erratically. Aizawa's *Shinron*, for example, was revered by anti-foreign radicals in the 1850s and 1860s, although by 1862 Aizawa himself had concluded that treaties with the Western powers were inevitable. Tadano was largely unknown until the twentieth century, but modern Japanese feminists would echo her invocation of Amaterasu in the name of women's rights. More than any specific policies, what these thinkers pioneered were the themes of cosmopolitan chauvinism and radical nostalgia. By reconciling the celebration of ancient Japanese past with the emulation of the West, they prefigured the central motif of the Meiji Restoration.

3

Reform and Revolution

FROM 1844 TO 1868, Japanese leaders struggled to create a new government while preserving core elements of the political status quo. They failed. Responding to Western imperialism required national mobilization, but the great success of the Tokugawa dynasty had been avoiding war, and thereby the need for such mobilization. On the contrary, institutions such as sankin kōtai were designed to weaken the daimyo rather than enlist them as powerful allies in national defense. At a more abstract level, it was difficult to legitimize the Tokugawa system in the modern international order. With two sovereigns (shogun and emperor) and hundreds of daimyo, Japan did not look like a nation-state to the imperialist powers. Viewed from the West, the Tokugawa order was both militarily weak and politically backward. Tokugawa reformers thus faced two irreconcilable demands: maintaining the status quo while at the same time crafting a new political system compatible with emerging international standards.

Tokugawa efforts to confront imperialism failed, but they paved the way for the later reforms. The Meiji Restoration is sometimes described as a struggle by progressive imperial loyalists against a hidebound and backward shogunate. It was not. On the contrary, when the shogunate fell in 1868, many Westerners observers were concerned that the new Meiji government would be more xenophobic and insular than the old regime. By 1867, there were striking similarities between those struggling to save the shogunate and those seeking to overthrow it. Both factions were openly committed to a new state based on the sovereignty of the emperor. Both invoked radical nostalgia to challenge conventional status distinctions, using the distant past as a critique of the present. Both invoked cosmopolitan chauvinism to urge the adoption of Western practices in military, economic, and political reform. As a result, although the Meiji government publicly lambasted the Tokugawa regime for its failings, many former-Tokugawa vassals became prominent Meiji government reformers.

Despite the similarities, unlike the new Meiji government, Tokugawa reformers were always constrained by the Tokugawa settlement. If the privileges of low-level samurai status could be ignored, why not those of mid-level samurai as well? And what of the privileges of the daimyo themselves? How could reformers launch a contained attack on ascriptive status? In order to change but not destroy the Tokugawa order, reformers looked back to the late 1500s and early 1600s, when social classes were more fluid. That allowed them to call for greater social mobility since joint battalions, with samurai commanding commoners, could be explained as a return to the practices of the early 1600s. But Tokugawa-era reformers needed to approach hereditary privilege with caution, lest they threaten the entire political order. By contrast, the new imperial government could explicitly challenge hereditary privilege with precedents from the seventh and eighth centuries. An imperial restoration could sweep away all hereditary privileges except those of the monarchy.

Unable to directly confront hereditary warrior status, Tokugawa reformers attempted to cobble together a nation-state out of conventional political structures. But here, too, their efforts met the constraints of the Tokugawa settlement. The early shoguns had chosen to exploit daimyo rivalries rather than crush the daimyo entirely. Those tensions made it difficult for the shogunate and the daimyo to cooperate on national mobilization. The shogunate wanted daimyo to assume responsibility for national defense while the Tokugawa remained preeminent in political authority. Many daimyo responded by pleading financial hardship or otherwise seeking to avoid the burdens of national defense. But the shogunate was equally threatened by the alternative prospect: daimyo ambition. Satsuma and Chōshū, for example, actively embraced military reforms, thereby creating powerful new armies. In 1868, they used these against the shogunate.

An equally troublesome tension was the rivalry between different factions of daimyo. In the name of national unity, the shogunate moved against a long-standing distinction among the daimyo. It solicited the support of *tozama* daimyo, lords whose ancestors had opposed or only begrudgingly allied with Tokugawa Ieyasu, the first Tokugawa shogun. By tradition, tozama lords were excluded from shogunal affairs. This displeased the *fudai*, the descendants of Tokugawa Ieyasu's close vassals. Attempts to create a national council of daimyo foundered on these tensions. Compounding this problem was the character of the daimyo themselves. In the words of the historian Conrad Totman, "these lords were men raised in situations where they were accustomed to having advisors, not peers, and they seem to have found sustained political give-and-take very difficult when it involved making hard choices."[1] Ernest Satow, translator for the British legation, was more blunt. He described Japan's daimyo as "high-born dummies" whose intellect "was nearly always far below par."[2]

Despite these challenges, Tokugawa reforms anticipated many of the major changes of the Meiji era. Daimyo councils, for example, presaged the creation of a national legislature, and by the 1860s the idea of a broadly based assembly was unremarkable. In 1867, as part of the Tokugawa surrender, the last shogun agreed to resign and cede power to a bicameral assembly. The upper house would comprise court nobles, daimyo, and elite samurai while the lower house would include ordinary samurai and commoners. The last reform proposals of the Tokugawa era thus anticipated Meiji-era calls for broadly representative assemblies.

There were parallel moves to challenge other hereditary distinctions, such as the samurai monopoly on military service. The Tokugawa began experiments with close-order drill in 1862, and by 1867 it was assembling a large modern army, trained with the help of French advisors. The shogunate steadily replaced its conventional forces with infantry battalions of conscripted commoners, armed with modern rifles. Several of the shogunate's most ardent reformers went on to serve the Meiji government. Anti-shogunal domains were equally active. In Chōshū, for example, reformers created joint commoner-samurai battalions (*kiheitai*) in 1863. The commanders were samurai but the soldiers were a mix of commoners, often the younger sons of wealthy farmers. Those battalions cut across conventional status distinctions and drilled in Western style with modern firearms.[3] The *kiheitai* were a direct precedent for Meiji reforms. Yamagata Aritomo, founder of the modern Japanese army, was a *kiheitai* commander, and *kiheitai* forces fought against the Tokugawa in the key battles of the Meiji Restoration. Satsuma also introduced Western-style close order drill with imported weapons, although with less social leveling. Roughly a third of Satsuma men were samurai, in contrast to roughly 8 percent in Chōshū, so military reform in Satsuma broke down distinctions within the samurai estate rather than the distinction between samurai and commoner.[4]

These challenges to conventional hierarchies paved the way for the more radical reforms of the Meiji government. By 1868 there was a broad consensus that the political order was broken beyond repair. As a result, there were remarkably few defenders of the old regime. Tokugawa Yoshinobu (also known as Keiki, 1837–1913), the last shogun, actively contributed to the dismantling of the Tokugawa system. He resigned the post of shogun and peacefully surrendered Edo Castle. While there were calls for a punitive peace, he was allowed a quiet and comfortable retirement in a Tokyo villa. Yoshinobu died not in prison or in battle but of old age in 1913, wealthy and honored by the Meiji government. Many daimyo were equally cooperative, and most were relieved when the Meiji state granted them generous pensions while stripping them of political power. Only the abolition of samurai stipends in 1876 sparked widespread resistance, but that gave the new government nearly a decade to consolidate its power. In that way, both the successes and the failures of the late Tokugawa era paved the way for Meiji reformers. Tokugawa-era reformers broke down resistance to change by insisting on the need to adopt Western-style institutions and to challenge local traditions. But no amount of reform could turn the Tokugawa order into a Japanese nation-state. That failure legitimized the destruction of the old regime.

Abe Masahiro and the Quest for National Unity

After the fall of Mizuno Tadakuni in 1844, national politics was led by Abe Masahiro, the daimyo of Fukuyama and shogunal senior counselor. Abe's mandate was to avoid the open confrontation of the shogunate's Tenpō reforms. Instead, he consulted broadly with the daimyo and sought to coax and flatter powerful lords into new forms of cooperation. Abe's boldest move was to try to assemble a team of rivals. In particular, he sought the advice and counsel of two strikingly different lords: Tokugawa Nariaki, the former daimyo of Mito, and Shimazu Nariakira, son of the daimyo of Satsuma. These two men disagreed on much. Nariaki was a xenophobe and an iconoclast. His domain academy, the Kōdōkan, was founded on the motto "revere the emperor, expel the barbarian." He sought to purify Japan of foreign influence, including the "alien" faith of Buddhism: during his reign, dozens of temples in Mito were ransacked and destroyed. Throughout the 1850s and 1860s Nariaki insisted that Japan's key failing was its spiritual weakness: imperial loyalty and samurai valor were as important as acquiring new military technologies. Nariakira, by contrast, was a Europhile and technophile. He used Roman letters in his personal journals as a means of encrypting sensitive passages. He installed a telegraph system in Kagoshima Castle, running from the castle keep to a nearby tea arbor. Beyond such novelties, Nariakira was an early exponent of state-promoted industrialization. In 1851, he ordered the construction of a factory complex at Iso. Beginning with smelting, the complex eventually manufactured products as diverse as glass, farm tools, land mines, nitrocellulose cotton, leather goods, and steel. Small-scale experiments ranged from photography to sugar refining. At its peak the complex had a fifty-ton (48,000 kg) reverberatory furnace and employed over a thousand workers.[5]

Nariaki and Nariakira shared several key traits despite their political differences. Both were esteemed, if not revered, by their supporters, which made them valuable to Abe. Both were politically ambitious but, by convention, excluded from shogunal office. The Shimazu were *tozama* daimyo and were therefore traditionally excluded from shogunal offices. The Tokugawa of Mito were a *gosanke* family, one of the three houses descended from Tokugawa Ieyasu's younger sons. As such they could supply a shogunal heir if the main line failed. At the same time, the Tokugawa of Mito were barred from key shogunal offices, much like the Shimazu. Finally, both Nariaki and Nariakira needed help from Abe. In Satsuma, Nariakira was embroiled in a bitter succession dispute with his half-brother, Hisamitsu. In Mito, Tokugawa Nariaki needed political rehabilitation: he had been forced to retire as daimyo and confined to his residence in 1844 because of his radical policies during the Tenpō reforms.

Abe advanced the political careers of both men. He had Nariaki released from house arrest and then arranged the marriage of one of Nariaki's sons to a daughter of the shogun.[6] In Satsuma, Abe intervened in local politics, forcing Shimazu Nariakira's father, Narioki, to step down and yield the domain to Nariakira.[7] These actions made Shimazu Nariakira and Tokugawa Nariaki figures of national importance. Unfortunately, neither lord repaid Abe with steadfast support. Nariakira made a few shows of deference and cooperation. In 1854, for example, Satsuma completed work on Japan's first Western-style warship. In a show of respect and support, Nariakira offered the ship to the shogunate, which used it as a training vessel.[8] But on crucial questions such as trade in Ryukyu, Nariakira continued to favor Shimazu interests over Tokugawa. In Mito, Nariaki was still more difficult. Restored to national prominence, he became an outspoken critic of shogunal policy. With his prestigious bloodlines, Nariaki envisioned himself as Abe's partner rather than his supporter.

Abe faced different but equally frustrating challenges with traditional power holders, such as the *hatamoto* and *fudai* daimyo. The *fudai* domains of Oshi and Hikone, for example, were eager to accept shogunal largess but less interested in expending their own funds on coastal defense. In general, the shogunal administration was unenthusiastic about military reform. The shogun's coastal defense office (*kaibō-gakari*), for example, argued that it was pointless to build a Western-style sloop, since a Japanese copy "could in no way compete in combat with foreign warships."[9] Even proponents of reform were daunted by the cost. The Uraga magistrates, Toda Ujiyoshi and Asano Nagayoshi, knew that Japan needed Western warships and favored extensive military preparations. But they were dismayed by the cost of a comprehensive military modernization. Developing a new navy would take many years, and in the interim, the shogunate could only hope that Western warships did not come. Toda and Asano's combination of urgency and resignation illustrates elegantly the internal contradictions of shogunal rule. The costs of rebuilding Japan's military were the "duty of the shogun's house," but the shogun, with a regional income base, could not provide for national defense.[10]

Until 1852, the hope that the foreigners could be easily rebuffed was plausible, if optimistic. Those who opposed expensive new weapons could point to a series of recent skirmishes. In 1837, a US merchant ship, the *Morrison*, entered Uraga Bay with the goals of repatriating Japanese castaways, opening trade relations, and spreading Christianity. The ship fled after Japanese coastal batteries opened fire. In 1846, US Commodore James Biddle anchored two warships at the mouth of Edo harbor and requested a trade treaty. His letter was received, but when the shogunate refused both trade and diplomatic relations, Biddle left quickly and peacefully. Those events made it possible to discount news of the Opium War. Perhaps the "Western barbarians" were focused on China and uninterested in Japan.

In 1852, however, the Nagasaki magsitrate received an alarming report from the Dutch: the United States was sending a large squadron to Edo to demand a treaty.[11] The Dutch warning was explicit: "The United States of North America can stand with the mightiest nations of Europe. This means the fleet consists of exceptional steam and sailing ships!" The United States would not go away quietly: "If the question [of opening ports] must be decided with weapons, a long and bloody conflict is a foregone conclusion."[12]

Even this report could not break the logjam in Edo. Abe relayed the warning to select daimyo, but to little effect. Skeptics argued that the

Dutch were merely spreading wild rumors in the hope of improving their own position. As a result, preparations for Perry's mission were more administrative than military. Abe secretly approved Satsuma's request to build a Western-style warship. He promoted Kawaji Toshiakira, a samurai official of humble origins but great talent, to the lofty position of magsi-trate of the exchequer. Toda Ujiyoshi, the Uraga magistrate, was given a more honorable seat in Edo Castle, symbolically emphasizing the defense of Edo Bay. But more substantive changes were beyond Abe's grasp. His strategy of compromise had deepened rather than resolved a domestic political impasse.[13]

Perry's arrival in Uraga Bay on 1853/6/3 (July 8) dismayed the shogunate and startled many ordinary Japanese. American accounts, however, often mischaracterize the event, exaggerating Japanese amazement at Western technology. "Martians landing in spaceships with gamma ray guns could not have caused more of an uproar," reads one popular history.[14] These descriptions of shock and awe reflect how Perry hoped to overwhelm the Japanese with Western technology. But in Japan, many were more curi-ous than astonished by Perry's machines. Having examined translations of gunnery manuals, for example, Japanese military experts were eager to see American cannon firsthand and they exhausted Perry's staff with detailed and exacting questions.[15] Perry's two steamships made a striking impression as they billowed smoke and sailed into the wind. But local mil-itary experts had been studying steam engines for years, so the technology was well known, if only in the abstract.[16] Similarly, ordinary samurai were more curious than terrified by the foreigners and their weapons. After the formal reception of President Millard Fillmore's letter of state on 1853/6/9 (July 14), both Japanese and American soldiers broke ranks to mingle and examine each other's weapons.[17] Edo townsmen did not flee in panic but gathered on the shore and rented sightseeing boats to observe the foreign-ers more closely.[18]

Perry's mission to Japan was momentous, but not for its immediate shock value. Indeed, when Perry departed peacefully on July 15 (1853/6/10), Abe seemed to have averted a crisis. But Perry's mission sparked a race among the Western powers to conclude treaties with Japan. The Russian envoy, Admiral Putiatin, reached Nagasaki in late August 1853. He had hoped to beat Perry to Japan but was delayed by technical problems. A British squadron arrived the following year. The scope of Western demands also steadily increased. When Perry returned to Edo in 1854, the shogunate

北亞墨利加人物

ペルリ像

FIGURE 3.1 Japanese Depiction of Perry. Library of Congress.

agreed to the Convention of Kanagawa. It provided for the resupply of US ships and opened two ports, Shimoda and Hakodate, to minimal trade. Russia was allowed similar terms in Hakodate, Shimoda, and Nagasaki. But the Western powers wanted more: extensive trade (with tariffs set by the Western power), diplomatic recognition, and treaty ports with extraterritoriality. Beginning in 1856, the United States began demanding an unequal treaty with Japan similar to its treaty with Siam. Like China, Japan directly confronted the contradiction between the ideals of Western international law and the practice of imperialism: all states were equal, except for those in the vast "uncivilized" reaches of the non-European world.[19]

FIGURE 3.2 Photograph of Perry, c. 1855. Library of Congress.

The crisis of imperialism was most clear at Japan's periphery. Under the Northeast Asian international system, the Tokugawa had left Japan's borderlands lightly defended and underdeveloped, with a loose sense of boundaries and territoriality. That approach had ensured peace with the Shō, the Qing, and the Yi. But under the European international order, such vague borders invited the use of force. In Ryukyu, for example, Perry was openly belligerent. In late July 1853, he demanded that Ryukyu provide land for a coal depot. When the king's regent refused, Perry threatened to send troops and occupy the Ryukyuan royal palace. The king promptly complied. Perry's threat of force exceeded his official instructions but not the broader logic of his mission. An influential supporter of his mission,

Aaron Haight Palmer, had explicitly advocated the seizure of either Ezo or Ryukyu.[20] Perry himself defended the possible seizure of Ryukyu as an "act of humanity . . . to protect these miserable people against the oppression of their tyrannical rulers." US intervention in Ryukyu would also force the government of Japan "to some sort of reason."[21]

Perry's actions the following year were still more destabilizing. In July 1854, he negotiated a treaty between the United States and Ryukyu providing for "unrestricted travel and free trade for American citizens throughout all Ryukyu." This was vastly more intrusive than the US treaty with the shogunate, the Convention of Kanagawa.[22] Even more disturbing, the treaty opened up the question of the sovereign status of the Ryukyu. Under the Tokugawa-Qing implicit entente cordial, the Tokugawa had concealed their control over Ryukyu from the Qing, and the Qing, in return, had ignored evidence of Japanese influence. Could Perry's treaty with Ryukyu be reconciled with this arrangement?

Ryukyuan officials desperately sought to maintain the Tokugawa-Qing status quo. The US-Ryukyu treaty was drafted in English and Chinese, but not Japanese, and dated according to the Gregorian and Qing calendars. Thus, the Shō continued to conceal Japanese influence. But Perry understood that Ryukyu was under de facto Japanese control. This situation was potentially explosive under the European international system. If the Tokugawa allowed the Shō to conclude treaties independently, then the Western powers could cite the logic of European international law and claim that Japan had ceded sovereignty over Ryukyu.[23] If, instead, Edo insisted that treaties involving Ryukyu required shogunal approval, then they would be offending the Qing and rupturing a centuries-old multi-lateral arrangement. European notions of international law and territoriality thus required conflict between the Tokugawa, the Shō, and the Qing. The shogunate now had to conform to the European world system, either as aggressor or as victim.

There was a nearly simultaneous crisis at the shogunate's northern border. On 1853/8/30 (October 2), news reached Edo that Russia was building a fortress on the southern end of Sakhalin.[24] Putiatin, the Russian envoy to Japan, had not approved that action, but it dramatized the need for an explicitly defined Japanese-Russian border. Putiatin suggested that all of Sakhalin and the Kuriles down to Urup were Russian. The Japanese representative, Kawaji Toshiakira, countered that the Kuriles should be divided in half and that Sakhalin was entirely Japanese. The two sides could not agree so the 1855 treaty divided the Kuriles at Urup and left the question of Sakhalin unresolved. As soon as the treaty was concluded, however, British

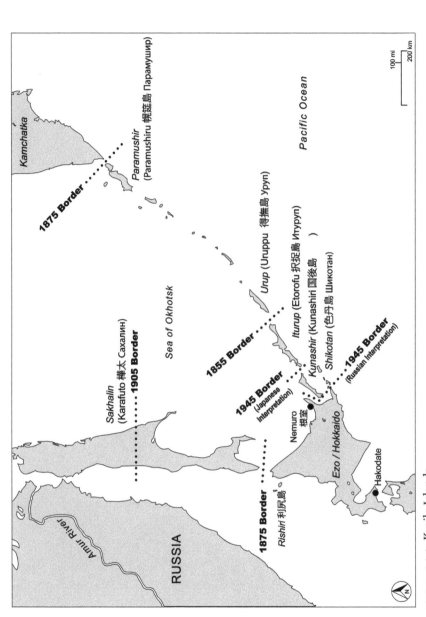

FIGURE 3.3 Kurile Islands.

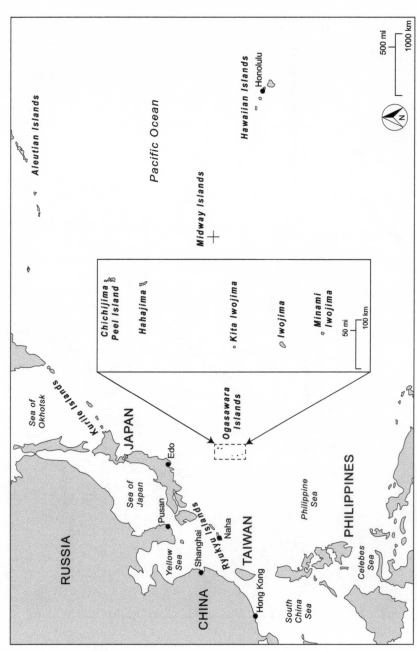

FIGURE 3.4 Ogasawara Islands.

and French forces seized Urup as part of their action against Russia in the Crimean War. These events made clear the need to adopt a European form of territoriality. A porous and lightly defended northern frontier had long served shogunal interests, but it was now a geopolitical liability. More broadly, Japan was now fully embroiled in the British-Russian contest for control of Asia and the Pacific. In 1861, for example, Russian warships entered Aso Bay on Tsushima and refused to leave until pressured by the British navy.

The most explicit challenge to Tokugawa territoriality came on the Ogasawara Islands (or Bonin Islands), an archipelago roughly 1,000 kilometers south of Edo. The Tokugawa shogunate surveyed the islands in 1675 but left them uninhabited. In 1823, a US whaling ship visited the islands, and in 1827 a British officer claimed them as British territory. In the 1830s, the islands were settled by a handful of Western men and their Pacific island wives. When Perry arrived in 1853, the island had a population of around thirty.[25]

Perry had no territorial designs on Edo or the Japanese main islands, but he explicitly favored turning the Ogasawara Islands into an American colony. Perry acknowledged Japan's sovereignty over the islands but insisted that "the present settlers have unquestionably [*sic*] priority of right of jurisdiction." Perry began establishing an American base on the archipelago before his arrival in Uraga, purchasing land for a coal depot in June 1853. He was explicit that the islands should become a commercial and ethnic outpost of the United States. "My plan is to establish a colony at Port Lloyd, Peel Island, the principal of the Bonin group, leaving the question of sovereignty to be discussed hereafter."[26] Practically, Perry thought that the islands would make an ideal refueling point for steamers traveling between Shanghai and Honolulu. More expansively, he considered the islands as key to American expansion: "to me it seems that the people of America will, in some form or other, extend their dominion and their power, until they shall have brought within their mighty embrace multitudes of the Islands of the great Pacific, and placed the Saxon race upon the eastern shores of Asia."[27] Perry envisioned a coming race war between Saxons and Slavs, but his concern with the Ogasawara Islands was eerily prescient in that the archipelago is best known for the Battle of Iwo Jima in World War II.

These skirmishes and crises on Japan's periphery highlighted the weakness of Abe's strategy. An evolving coalition of daimyo could not establish unitary sovereignty over a clearly demarcated Japanese nation. But Abe was loath to alienate even the most feckless daimyo. In Ezo, for example, the shogunate took direct control of Hakodate in 1853 and then, in 1855, claimed direct authority over the entire island. But Abe was disinclined to punish the Matsumae house, and he gave them new landholdings and a cash allowance. Despite clear evidence of Matsumae misconduct and negligence, Abe was unwilling to antagonize a fellow daimyo.[28]

In Ryukyu, the problems of the early modern order were still more striking. Under the Tokugawa system, Ryukyu was embedded in a web of relationships: the Shō swore fealty to the Shimazu, the Shimazu swore fealty to the Tokugawa, and the Shō directly paid homage to the shogunate. But that did not establish clear sovereignty under European international law. Indeed, despite cordial relations between Abe and Nariakira, the interests of the shogunate and Satsuma often diverged. The Shimazu wanted to develop Naha (the Ryukyuan capital) as an international port, possibly as a rival to Nagasaki, and they pursued bilateral ties with Britain and France independent of the shogunate. The divergence of Tokugawa and Shimazu interests was starkly revealed in 1867 when the Satsuma delegation to the Paris Centennial Exposition described themselves as representatives of the "Kingdoms of Satsuma and Ryukyu."[29] That gesture was incompatible with the idea of Japan as a unified state.

Shogunal Decline and Daimyo Ascendance

Between 1854 and 1868, the shogunate gradually lost control over national affairs. That decline was punctuated by two moments of shogunal resurgence, one under Ii Naosuke from 1858 to 1860, and the second from 1866 to 1868 under Tokugawa Yoshinobu. The details of shogunal decline are complex, but it was driven by two major trends. First, the shogunate lost control over the imperial house. Certain that the court would not oppose the shogunate, the Tokugawa house embraced the notion that the shogun ruled at the emperor's behest. Starting in the 1850s, that strategy proved toxic. Radical loyalists began to use the court to extract concessions from Edo, and by the 1860s the imperial court itself became a site of violent conflicts, with coups and counter-coups to control the palace gates. The last shogun, Tokugawa Yoshinobu, was able to regain the court's support, but by then the damage was done. The violence and turmoil of the 1850s and 1860s had changed the political landscape, shattering the illusion of shogunal supremacy. The shogun was no longer Japan's paramount military leader but just one contender for imperial support.

The second trend was a resurgence of daimyo autonomy. In seeking the support of daimyo, Abe unwittingly whetted their appetite for power: powerful daimyo came to expect that the shogunate would respond to their demands. That problem was exacerbated by changes to domestic controls. Daimyo had always maintained independent armies, but the Tokugawa had held their autonomy in check with institutions such as sankin kōtai, the system of daimyo attendance in Edo. The reforms of the 1850s and 1860s changed this balance of power. Beginning in 1862, mandatory time in Edo was drastically reduced to three months every three years. Yoshimune had relaxed sankin kōtai in the 1720s but demanded direct contributions to the shogun's treasury. The reforms of the 1860s, by contrast, were intended to give daimyo increased resources for military reform. The result was more powerful daimyo who were less fearful of Edo. The shogunate realized too late that it had strengthened its own rivals: when the regime attempted to reinstate the sankin kōtai schedule in early 1864, many powerful daimyo simply ignored the order.[30]

These two trends, daimyo ambition and imperial ascendance, complicated a range of issues, from treaty negotiation to shogunal succession. In negotiating with the Western powers, the shogunate wanted the support of daimyo and the imperial court. Accordingly, it engaged in intricate multi-party consultations. But those negotiations produced grandstanding and posturing more than sober deliberation. Tokugawa Nariaki, for example, viewed the 1854 Convention of Kanagawa as a means to buy time: Japan should refuse any further concessions and mobilize for war. Xenophobes in the imperial court and radical imperial loyalists believed that Japan could somehow easily reject Western demands. But by the 1860s, it was clear to most informed observers that the "barbarians" could not simply be "expelled." Japan, like China, would face a decades-long struggle against imperialism. The debate over "expulsion" became increasingly cynical, as both the shogunate and key daimyo opportunistically endorsed "expulsion" plans even when they privately considered those goals absurd.

The problem of shogunal succession also became embroiled in a broader struggle. From 1853 to 1866, the shogunate endured infirm and childless rulers. The twelfth shogun, Ieyoshi, died less than two weeks after Perry's departure, on 1853/6/22 (July 27, 1853). His heir, Iesada, was childless and sickly. It was widely (and correctly) assumed that Iesada would not father a son, so his succession triggered a struggle to decide his adoptive heir. Under normal circumstances, this contest would have been contained within the Tokugawa house. In the 1850s, however, the succession dispute became enmeshed in daimyo and imperial ambition. Like the debate over the treaties, the debate over succession became a proxy war for other issues, making the struggle both more volatile and more convoluted. Here, too, Abe's strategy of national consensus had the unexpected consequence of inflaming domestic tensions.

Abe himself resigned as chair of the council of elders in 1855, but his successor, Hotta Masayoshi, continued his approach of broad consultation. In 1858, based on the advice of several daimyo, Hotta sought the assent of the imperial court for a second round of treaties. Hotta envisioned imperial approval as a simple and pro forma matter. The imperial court had never contested Tokugawa authority over foreign affairs. Even on matters pertaining to the imperial house, the court had grudgingly deferred to Edo. Hotta was thus certain that the court would approve the treaties, allowing him to quell dissenting daimyo. Hotta's strategy was a disaster. Rather than support the treaties, the court rebuked the shogun for placing the nation in peril. Hotta's plan to win approval for the treaties had, instead, made ratification more difficult. Humiliated, Hotta resigned in June 1858.

Why did Hotta miscalculate so badly? It is tempting to agree with Townsend Harris, the US consul, who found Hotta's approach bizarre. If imperial assent was automatic, he wondered, what could Hotta gain by an official request? If assent was not automatic, then what would Hotta do if the emperor said no? Harris criticized his Japanese counterparts for "trifling with a serious matter." Their actions were "like the acts of children and unworthy of wise statesmen like those who rule Japan."[31] Upon reflection, however, Hotta's desire to combine the emperor's sacerdotal authority with the shogun's temporal legitimacy was not strange at all. Napoleon, for example, had relied on Pope Pius VII for his coronation as Emperor of France in 1804. But Hotta had mistakenly assumed that the imperial court would comply with a shogunal request. What had gone wrong?

The court's rebuff to Hotta came from two distinct sources. First were radical imperial loyalists, true believers in the slogan *sonnō jōi*. Radical loyalism was inspired by Mito Studies, but in the 1850s it emerged as a diffuse radical movement: advocates included court nobles, daimyo, schoolteachers, and masterless samurai (*rōnin*). Loyalists considered the very presence of Westerners in Japan an insult to the emperor and opposed the treaties with furious indignation. While their enmity toward the West was clear, their vision for the future was less so. Much as European utopian Marxists expected that a proletarian revolution would lead to a withering away of the state, so too radical loyalists imagined that imperial rule would bring an end to politics in the conventional sense. The state would disappear, replaced by organic communities connected through Shinto ritual.[32] This was a glorious and intoxicating vision, and, combined with xenophobia, it inspired years of terroristic violence. Starting in 1858 and lasting into the early Meiji era, loyalist partisans, commonly called *shishi*, maimed and murdered their enemies, cutting down court nobles, samurai, and foreigners—anyone who challenged their vision of a "pure" Japan. Although *shishi* often organized along domain lines, they also forged alliances across domain boundaries and were largely beyond daimyo control. Hotta, underestimating the fervor of *shishi* and the power of *sonnō jōi* thought, had stirred a hornet's nest.[33]

Hotta's failure also had a second source. Imperial assent to the treaties had become entangled in the question of shogunal succession. The succession dispute focused on two candidates. The inside candidate was Tokugawa Yoshitomi, the eldest son of the daimyo of Wakayama (or Kii). He was supported by much of the shogunal administration, which viewed him as young and pliant. The rival candidate was Tokugawa Yoshinobu, the seventh son of Tokugawa Nariaki of Mito. His candidacy was promoted by a broad coalition of daimyo, including the lords of Satsuma, Fukui, and Uwajima. They argued that difficult times called for a bold choice: primogeniture favored Yoshitomi, but Yoshinobu was more intelligent and mature. In terms of practical politics, Yoshinobu was the candidate of reformers and outsiders while Yoshitomi was favored by the shogunal establishment. These clashing agendas produced a bizarre coincidence of interests. Many of Yoshinobu's advocates were pragmatically prepared to accept the treaties, but, ironically, their arguments in favor of Yoshinobu appealed to advocates of "expulsion." If Yoshinobu were indeed more vital and capable, could he perhaps drive the barbarians back into the sea? As Yoshinobu's proponents lobbied the court, they unwittingly raised the expectation that the barbarians could indeed be "expelled." That hope, in turn, stoked the court's xenophobia, intensified resistance to the treaties, and undermined Hotta's request for imperial assent.[34]

The result of these clashing agendas was disastrous for Hotta. In May 1858 (3/20) emperor Kōmei stridently declared that the treaties would

FIGURE 3.5 An Imperial Courtier. Tojō Rekishikan (Tojō Museum of History), Matsudo. Reprinted with permission.

FIGURE 3.6 Shogun and Head of the Tokugawa House. From Reed, *Japan*, 1:238.

The Four Faces of the Last Shogun: Tokugawa Yoshinobu employed his remarkable political acumen to master four distinct public personae (Figures 3.5–3.8).

FIGURE 3.7 Western-oriented Military Reformer. Tojō Rekishikan (Tojō Museum of History), Matsudo. Reprinted with permission.

FIGURE 3.8 Distinguished Gentleman. Tojō Rekishikan (Tojō Museum of History), Matsudo. Reprinted with permission.

be "a disaster for the land of the gods and precipitate a national crisis." The concessions demanded by the United States would endanger the Japanese body politic itself (*kokutai*).³⁵ The emperor directed Hotta to consult again with the daimyo in order to restore "national honor." The directive made no mention of the shogunal succession dispute, frustrating Yoshinobu's supporters. It was a stunning rebuke to Hotta and ended his political career.

This humiliation prompted a furious response. Hotta's successor, Ii Naosuke, abandoned Abe's strategy of broad consultation in favor of naked shogunal power. He moved rapidly on both foreign and domestic affairs, approving the US treaty and deciding shogunal succession in favor of Yoshitomi. Ii responded to his critics with overwhelming force. He jailed his challengers on the shogunal council of elders. He forced a dozen key imperial courtiers to resign. He had major daimyo, including the lords of Mito, Owari, and Fukui, confined to quarters or banned from Edo. He ordered the execution or *seppuku* (ritual suicide) of men ranging from senior Mito samurai to abbots in Kyoto. Ii was roundly criticized for authorizing the so-called Harris Treaty, the 1858 United States-Japan Treaty of Amity and Commerce. But Ii himself was more concerned with the question of succession: it was untoward for outsiders to press their opinions on an internal matter of the Tokugawa house. On the question of the treaties, Ii followed the letter of the imperial edict while subverting imperial intent. He consulted with the daimyo, as instructed. He then pragmatically concluded that resisting the treaties would bring ruin to Japan.³⁶

Ii succeeded, temporarily, in stemming shogunal decline, but he had no political vision for the future. He hoped that some new weapons, combined with samurai spirit, would resolve the foreign crisis. Ii wrote with greater engagement and insight on the tea ceremony than on domestic politics or foreign affairs. At heart, he was merely a defender of shogunal primacy within the status quo. In Ezo, for example, he divided the island among the six domains entrusted with northern defense: Sendai, Nanbu, Akita, Aizu, Shōnai, and Tsugaru. This situation recalled the vigor of the early Tokugawa shoguns, who rewarded their allies but brooked no dissent. But this revitalized feudalism did little to address the deeper structural problems of the regime: the shogunate remained a regional regime in terms of resources but a national government in terms of its responsibilities.³⁷

This shogunal resurgence ended with Ii's assassination. On March 24 (1860/3/3), seventeen *rōnin* from Mito and a samurai from Satsuma ambushed Ii's cortege just outside Edo Castle. Aided by a snowstorm, they murdered Ii's bodyguards, shot Ii himself, then severed and stole his head. In their manifesto, the assassins blamed Ii for staining the national honor by allowing foreigners to live in Japan and practice Christianity. Ii's murder stunned the shogunate. Not only had the loyalists killed the government's chief officer, but they had done so in broad daylight at the foot of the shogun's castle. The shogunate did not announce Ii's death until May 20 (1860/i3/30), insisting in the interim that he was merely "ill." Such rituals were part of local practice: the death of a daimyo was announced only after the details of succession had been established. In the case of Ii, however, these formalities seemed absurd. The shogunate had closed the ward gates of Edo to conduct a manhunt for the assassins, so it was difficult to sustain official reports of Ii's "illness." The British consul, Rutherford Alcock, wondered why the shogunate refused to announce Ii's death even after news of his murder became "public property, as it were, and the common gossip of the bath-houses—an institution of Japan, corresponding to the cafe in France."[38]

Ii's assassination prompted a return to the politics of consensus and conciliation. In order to defuse the threat of radical loyalism, the shogunate proposed a marriage between the imperial house and the Tokugawa. The underlying logic was straightforward: marrying the young shogun Iemochi (formerly Yoshitomi) to Kazunomiya, the emperor's half-sister, would create national unity. In practice, the Kazunomiya marriage became a source of renewed discord. The imnperial court presumed that the shogunate would expel the "barbarians" from Japan as a precondition of the marriage. Instead, the shogunate proceeded to conclude commercial treaties with Belgium, Prussia, and Switzerland. The emperor was furious at this insubordination. After extended negotiations, the imperial court agreed to allow the marriage, but the emperor denounced the leaders of the shogunal council of elders, Andō Nobumasa and Kuze Hirochika. That sparked rumors of a shogunal coup in retaliation against the emperor, and those rumors prompted an assassination attempt against Andō, leaving him badly wounded. Although the Kazunomiya marriage was concluded in March 1862 (1862/2/11), the strategy backfired. Rather than create national unity, the marriage had intensified radical loyalism and stoked anti-shogunal fury.[39] Battered and demoralized, the shogunal administration turned on its own, censuring Andō and Kuse for their "iniquitous" actions and dismissing them from office.[40]

Also in the name of national unity, the shogunate revived broad consultation with the daimyo. In 1862, Matsudaira Yoshinaga (also called Keiei, Shungaku, 1828–1890), the lord of Fukui, was given the new title "minister of political affairs" (seiji sōsai). Tokugawa Yoshinobu, loser of the shogunal succession dispute, was named guardian (kōken) to the shogun Iemochi. The shogunate named several other daimyo as "councilors" (san'yo), and from 1864 those lords met in Kyoto with select court nobles to form a national council.

These reforms reflected Matsudaira Yoshinaga's belief that broad consultation would resolve the Tokugawa foreign crisis. Rather than acting unilaterally on foreign affairs, the Tokugawa needed to consult with the imperial house and the daimyo, and then speak on behalf of all of Japan. Further, Yoshinaga recommended that the shogunate and the domains all establish bicameral parliaments (harurimon comonsu) as in England and France. Each regional parliament would consist of samurai as well some farmers and townsmen. Through public debate (kōkyō no ron), the Tokugawa house could foster national unity and thereby reclaim its ancient glory.[41]

Contrary to Yoshinaga's grand hopes, consultation did not create national unity but instead fostered new rivalries. The most serious rift was between Tokugawa Yoshinobu and his former supporters. In the 1850s, several of the greatest tozama lords had supported Yoshinobu's candidacy as heir to the shogun: his allies included the Shimazu of Satsuma, the Yamauchi of Tosa, the Date of Uwajima, the Hachisuka of Tokushima, and the Nabeshima of Saga. They had promoted Yoshinobu based on his reputation as a capable and intelligent reformer. In the 1860s, however, those allies came to loathe Yoshinobu for those very virtues. Yoshinobu was determined to strengthen the shogunate and was unwilling to sacrifice Tokugawa authority in the name of national unity. He continued to promote broad consultation but on terms that served shogunal power. By 1868, Yoshinobu's determination and political savvy had turned his former allies into open enemies.

Yoshinobu proved particularly adept at manipulating the imperial house. Loyalist radicals had won imperial support by appealing to the court's xenophobia, but Kyoto also wanted stability. The court became disenchanted with sonnō jōi loyalists after 1864, when radicals from Chōshū fought with troops from Aizu and Satsuma in the streets of Kyoto. During the fighting, large sections of Kyoto burned. Yoshinobu knew that "expelling the barbarian" was impossible, but he convinced the court that he could get rid of the foreigners while maintaining domestic peace. He thus stole the "expulsion" issue from loyalist radicals and then marginalized

Chōshū loyalists as "enemies of the court." Those were great but toxic victories. Divide and conquer was a cornerstone of Tokugawa control, but those tactics could not be reconciled with the discourse of national unity. Yoshinobu deftly manipulated the most powerful daimyo, but in doing so he raised suspicions about his own motives and antagonized former allies. Yoshinobu also faced trouble from within the shogunate, where many viewed him as an ambitious outsider.[42]

While Yoshinobu sought to reassert Tokugawa power, Satsuma and Chōshū were gradually moving toward an anti-shogunal alliance. As late as 1864, Satsuma and Chōshū were bitter antagonists, struggling for control of the imperial court. When Chōshū loyalists controlled the gates to the imperial palace in the early 1860s, they snubbed Satsuma. In 1863, Satsuma and Aizu together staged a palace coup and expelled Chōshū forces from Kyoto. The following year, Chōshū forces attempted a counter-coup, which, as noted above, failed and angered the imperial court. The shogunate, together with Aizu and Satsuma, then embarked on a military campaign to "punish" Chōshū, now branded an enemy of the throne. At the last moment, however, Satsuma realized that destroying Chōshū was not to its advantage. Saigō Takamori, the Satsuma commander, offered moderate terms of surrender and disbanded the expeditionary force.[43]

That gesture began a shift in the domestic balance of power, as the two rivals explored cooperation and then alliance. Satsuma agreed to help Chōshū obtain Western weapons and to work for its pardon by the imperial court. By 1865/8, Satsuma had helped Chōshū purchase a warship and 7,300 rifles.[44] The resurgence of Chōshū and the nascent Satsuma-Chōshū alliance posed a dilemma for the shogunate. The shogunate wanted a clear sign of submission from Chōshū, ideally a direct apology from the daimyo himself. But Chōshū's leaders refused to negotiate. The shogunate felt compelled to respond to this indignity, but how? Military action had little support. Satsuma, a leader in the previous campaign, openly refused to support the shogunate. Chōshū's neighbors, including Hiroshima, Okayama, and Tatsuno, opposed another attack. The shogunate saw its isolation but felt compelled to defend its honor. Yoshinobu himself thought that Chōshū's disobedience threatened shogunal authority. For months, the shogunate sought some concession that might demonstrate Edo's supremacy, but Chōshū was defiant.[45]

By the summer of 1866, the shogunate was ensnared in a trap of its own making. Because it had publicly insisted on concessions from Chōshū, its legitimacy rested on the domain's compliance. But the shogunate could not force compliance without mobilizing the daimyo, and that support was not forthcoming. Shogunal power assumed daimyo malleability: lords would each fight on behalf of the shogunate in order to gain reward, or simply to avoid shogunal retribution. Once that aura of authority faded, the shogunal system was dysfunctional. The Tokugawa had national responsibility without national authority.

On 1866/6/7 the shogunate launched an ill-fated campaign to "punish" Chōshū. On paper, the Tokugawa had assembled a large army, but it was a feckless force, poorly suited for an unpopular war against a spirited enemy. The campaign was a disaster. The planned invasion of Chōshū turned into Chōshū's invasion of neighboring domains. Hiroshima promptly sued for peace, freeing Chōshū to concentrate on other fronts. In 1866/8, Chōshū crossed the Straits of Shimonoseki to invade Kokura. The "punishment" of Chōshū had instead given the rebels control of a major shipping lane. Amid this debacle, the shogun Iemochi died on August 29 (7/20), giving the shogunate a dignified pretext to request a ceasefire.

By late 1866, the shogunate was in near collapse. A single rebellious domain had defeated Japan's supreme warlord. The shogunate's campaign to punish its enemies had instead punished its allies. The shogun was dead, reopening the ongoing succession crisis. By rights, the Tokugawa shogunate should have imploded in late 1866. Instead, the crisis of 1866 prompted one of the most remarkable reform efforts in Japanese history. Defeat by Chōshū had discredited defenders of the shogunal status quo. Yoshinobu seized this chance to push through the most radical Japanese reform project in a millennium. Yoshinobu sought nothing less than the complete reorganization of the shogunate "from a feudally organized suzerain regime into a unified national regime organized along the bureaucratic lines of Napoleonic France."[46] This effort shaped the course of the Meiji Restoration. Yoshinobu's reforms meant that Chōshū and Satsuma could not wait for the Tokugawa to quietly collapse. Instead, they needed to topple the shogunate before it created a successful, modern state.

The Shogunal Phoenix and Anglo-French Rivalry

Following the death of Iemochi, Yoshinobu became the effective leader of the shogunate. He was formally invested in January 1867 (1866/12/5), but he had taken control months earlier. Yoshinobu began dismantling the most basic structures of Tokugawa military and civil organization, replacing them with modern, centralized systems of administration. He replaced the shogunal council of elders with a cabinet system of five ministers: foreign affairs, home affairs, army, navy, and finance. Rather than a system of broad and general consultation, this new cabinet system emphasized distinct spheres of authority. The reforms combined multiple heritable and non-heritable stipends and allowances into a single salary system. These changes were part of a broader, long-range plan for revitalized national control. The shogunate would reassess the tax yield for all of Japan and use the revenue to support its new ministries. The government would establish a national university to train samurai and commoners from across Japan in agriculture, commerce, and industry.[47]

In military affairs, Yoshinobu moved to dismantle independent battalions led by Tokugawa liege vassals. Instead of providing troops, Yoshinobu ordered his vassals to pay into the shogunal treasury. With these funds, Yoshinobu began creating modern infantry, artillery, and cavalry units, all responsible to a single shogunal command. Casting aside centuries of precedent, the shogunate began recruiting commoners from across its territories. The most capable commoners were trained, paid, and promoted as non-commissioned officers, much like the structure of European forces.[48]

In economic development, the shogunate hired foreign specialists to explore potential iron and coal resources. It lifted the long-standing ban on horse-drawn wheeled vehicles, permitting their use on the national highway system. It promoted regular steamship service between Edo and Osaka. In its final days, the shogunate authorized construction of a railroad between Edo and Yokohama. In social and cultural affairs, the government lifted a range of restrictions on foreigners and foreign customs. It began promoting cattle ranching and the consumption of beef and dairy products. It allowed foreigners to enter restaurants in Edo and Osaka, leading to Edo's first Western-style restaurant in late 1867. It lifted restrictions on marriages between Japanese and foreigners. In places, these changes suggest the desperation of a regime in collapse, concerned more with symbolism than the long-term consequences of reform. Overall, however, the reforms represent a serious, if protean, plan for a new Japan. Shogunal plans for a new railroad, for example, included the details of financing, controls on cost overruns, access rights for foreigners and Japanese subjects, and purchase rights for the Japanese government.[49] For his part, Yoshinobu described his reforms as a root and branch change in Tokugawa policy, designed to restore shogunal authority after 300 years of incompetence and sloth. He envisioned a complete "revolution in military strategy" and the creation of a "wealthy nation and a powerful military" (*fukoku kyōhei*).[50]

As a result of these changes, by late 1867, the shogunate was more "modern" than the imperial alliance. The shogunate had, in embryonic form, anticipated many early Meiji reforms: a European-style cabinet system with nationwide financial and economic authority, economic development informed by the advice of Western technical specialists, the abolition of hereditary status distinctions and obligations, and national conscription for a new, modern army and navy. By contrast, many imperial loyalist samurai advocated a national government centered on the emperor, but they also remained bound to daimyo authority. While loyalists envisioned a new imperial government, their plans also assumed a daimyo council and the continuation of daimyo authority. In both Satsuma and Chōshū, reformers had begun to dismantle key parts of the old regime. New military units, for example, cut across old heredity hierarchies. But Satsuma and Chōshū could not organize a coalition of domains while simultaneously preparing to dissolve the domains themselves. Indeed, that tension between central authority and daimyo autonomy would not be resolved until 1871.

The shogunate's reform efforts relied on French support. Beginning in early 1865, France supplied the shogunate with advanced cannons and agreed to dispatch a military training mission. The mission arrived in January 1867 and began training roughly 230 officers. This was less than the 2,000 men sought by the shogun, but the French promised to train Japanese officers, who would in turn train their own men.[51] French efforts were eagerly promoted by the resident consul, Léon Roches. Although France was officially neutral in Japanese domestic affairs, Roches hoped to help fashion a new Japan, reshaped by French ideals and modern technology.[52]

Roches understood Japan in terms of his previous postings in North Africa, where, according to his memoirs, he had "gone native": speaking Arabic, wearing native dress, hunting, and socializing with locals. According to Roches, his ability to bridge cultures, and his personal ties to local rulers, were critical to French success. In Algeria, for example, he imagined that his relationship with the emir resulted in a fatwa allowing for treaties with Christians. Roches explicitly compared Japan to North

Africa, insisting that "in reading the memoranda of the Japanese government or in listening to the objections formulated by its ministers, one could imagine oneself in Morocco." Roches presumably saw in Yoshinobu a Japanese counterpart to Aḥmad Ibn Muṣṭafa, the Bey of Tunis, who abolished slavery, instituted secular education, and developed a new French-style military. By extension, Roches viewed Japan as a potential French client state like Tunis, tied to Paris not through direct conquest but through economic, political, and cultural dependence.[53]

Yoshinobu, for his part, carefully cultivated Roches's support. He appealed both to Roches's pride in *la mission civilisatrice* and to French animus toward Britain. Yoshinobu wrote to Roches that he hoped to "place my country among the nations of the civilized world" and asked for Roches's support in this "work of civilization."[54] At a meeting with Roches in March 1867, Yoshinobu highlighted their joint fear of Britain. What would happen, he asked Roches, if Britain, with support from Satsuma and Chōshū, seized ports in the Japanese southwest and turned them into bases similar to Hong Kong? Roches insisted that was unlikely, partly because the other foreign powers would not allow it. Yoshinobu thus won a French commitment to check British interests.[55]

British intervention was less overt than French but no less influential. Harry Parkes, the British consul, was committed to neutrality but also to Anglo-French rivalry. After learning of the French military mission, Parkes hastily approved a British naval mission largely to "be even with" Roches.[56] Aside from such gestures, Britain quietly supported anti-shogunal forces. In 1866/6, Parkes had a formal meeting in Satsuma with Shimazu Hisamitsu and his retainers. Parkes did not broach the topic of British support, but when asked, he hinted that Britain would welcome a challenge to Yoshinobu. Parkes's subordinates and associates were more explicit.[57] Ernest Satow, translator for the British legation, actively supported Satsuma and Chōshū. In a series of editorials in the *Japan Times* he argued that Britain needed to give up the "worn-out pretense of acknowledging the Tycoon [shogun] to be the sole ruler of Japan, and take into consideration the existence of other co-ordinate powers." Britain should consider negotiating treaties directly with the major daimyo since the shogunate was a national government in name only. While the original editorials were anonymous, Satow also prepared a Japanese translation and sent it to the daimyo of Tokushima, the lord of his Japanese tutor. The translation was promptly published, listing Satow as author and describing him as an English officer. It sold well and was widely understood as official British policy.[58] Satow was also candid in his meetings with Satsuma samurai, openly encouraging them to oppose the shogunate and offering British support.[59]

The British legation also overlooked the activities of Thomas Glover, a Scottish merchant. Glover became a major arms supplier to Satsuma and Chōshū and helped send young samurai from those domains on study trips to London. Those visits had a marked impact on Japanese politics. The future prime minister, Itō Hirobumi, for example, was transformed by his time in England. As late as 1862, Itō was a *sonnō jōi* loyalist, joining other Chōshū samurai in an attack on the British legation. In 1863, he was smuggled to London with Glover's help and was amazed by the impact of the Industrial Revolution and the sophistication of British institutions. He became convinced that the violent expulsion of foreigners was futile and hurried back to Japan to dissuade his colleagues from further attacks on British subjects. As a member of the Meiji government, he advocated the adoption of Anglo-American institutions, such as the US national bank system. He became celebrated in the Anglo-American world as an exemplar of the "new Nippon": diligent, progressive, and cosmopolitan.[60] Itō's transformation was extreme, but by 1867 many in Satsuma and Chōshū had come to a cosmopolitan understanding of Japanese politics.

Envisioning a New Japan

These events were part of a broader transformation of Japanese political discourse. In the late Tokugawa era, the discourses of cosmopolitan chauvinism and revolutionary nostalgia provided the basis for an intense engagement with Western political and socioeconomic practices. It is common to refer to the early Meiji era as a period of "civilization and enlightenment" (*bunmei kaika*), marking an influx of Western influences ranging from Darwinian theory to beef stew. But this conventional account obscures important continuities with late Tokugawa thought. By the 1860s, a striking range of thinkers had begun arguing that Western political practices were fully consonant with Japanese culture.

The discourse of cosmopolitan chauvinism suffused Japanese thought both in depth and in breadth. As early as 1862, for example, Katō Hiroyuki, a samurai from Tajima, began a careful survey of world politics. He concluded that constitutional monarchies and republics were part of a global trend. Japan needed to adopt these political forms

because it was "an inevitable trend of the times." For Katō, republicanism and constitutionalism were not foreign or Western political forms
but best practices based on universal norms. Even within the West, he
argued, countries with constitutional systems were thriving but autocracies were crumbling. To reject global best practice as foreign, he insisted,
was to condemn Japan to decline. Katō implicitly grafted these new universal standards onto older Confucian norms. The ancient sage kings of
China, he noted, had ruled with impartial justice (*kōmei seidai*), but more
recent rulers lacked such virtue. Constitutional systems and the division
of powers, however, could help ensure virtuous rule. These systems were
not only in tune with "popular sentiment (*sejō*)," but were also based on
"the will of heaven."[61]

The theme of global norms is also prominent in the work of Yokoi
Shōnan, an influential advisor to Matsudaira Yoshinaga, the daimyo
of Fukui. Through Yoshinaga, Yokoi had a direct impact on shogunal
reforms, including the suspension of sankin kōtai. Yokoi argued that Japan
needed to embrace emerging world standards of governance. The world
had entered an era of increased international contact, and Japanese isolation was both unsustainable and unnatural. Yokoi was greatly optimistic
about this new world, which he envisioned as peaceful and prosperous.
He referred to this international system as "the nations of the world as
one, a brotherhood of the four seas" (*bankoku ittai shikai kyōdai*), a phrase
that loosely quoted the Analects of Confucius while at the same time suggesting a European-style "family of nations." This familial order was based
on the principles of heaven (*tenri*) and reflected underlying universal principles (*shizen no risei*).[62]

For Yokoi, the rise of this new international environment mandated
radical changes in Japanese politics. The sankin kōtai system, for example, was designed to weaken the daimyo rather than to build a strong and
prosperous nation. Japan needed instead to emulate international best
practice. Such emulation was not mimicry but a core element of good
governance. The United States, Yokoi argued, had grown strong and prosperous by seeking knowledge around the world and copying everything
from politics to technology. Yokoi was especially impressed by the power
of open deliberation: the United States and Britain and had elevated public morals by basing political decisions on public discussion. This had
the unexpected result of making their countries stronger during wartime.
Once the populace understood the reason to go to war, it did not shrink
from hardship.[63]

Because Western best practices were rooted in universal principles, they were neither new nor foreign. On the contrary, Western practices that encouraged morality, prosperity, and peace were merely continuations of governance by the sage kings of antiquity. Thus, for Yokoi, George Washington was the equivalent of the sage kings of ancient Chinese dynasties such as the Xia (c. 2070–c. 1600 BCE), the Shang/Yin (c. 1766 to c. 1122 BCE), and the Zhou (c. 1122–256 BCE). Like Katō, Yokoi saw recent history in terms of a decline in Chinese civilization and a rise of the West.[64] But he also emphasized the complementarity and continuity of Chinese and Western thought. Song-era Confucian thought, for example, had discerned universal principles of human conduct, but it neglected practical observation. Western learning was now the essential complement to classical Chinese thought. Yokoi insisted that such syncretism was authentically Japanese. "Since ancient times our country has had not one fixed school of thought, but Shinto, Buddhism, and Confucianism. Now we should also adopt the successes of the West."[65] Yokoi thus naturalized Western political thought by invoking both radical nostalgia and cosmopolitan chauvinism. Japan needed to adopt the universal aspects of foreign practices, just as it had in the ancient past.

Parallel developments existed in formal reform proposals. In 1867/5 Akamatsu Kosaburō, a samurai from Ueda domain, proposed an elected national legislature. The upper house would consist of thirty lords and the lower house of 130 men elected "without regard to pedigree." The legislature would primarily make recommendations to the throne, but in extreme cases the legislature could override an imperial veto. These reforms would ensure the power and virtue of the throne and restore the national polity (kokutai). Akamatsu also called for a new legal system, conforming to international standards, and extensive military reform to employ the abilities of all able-bodied men and women.[66] Akamatsu did not cite either Yokoi or Katō, but his proposal is rooted in an appreciation of Western political forms similar to theirs. Akamatsu thought that a strong legislature would enhance rather than undermine imperial authority, a notion he shared with Yokoi and Katō. Further, he appealed not to Western models but to universal norms (bankoku futsū).

These works reflect a new depth of engagement with Western political thought and institutions. Equally important, however, was a less sustained but broader interest in foreign practices. Beginning in the mid-1800s, for example, Napoleon Bonaparte began to appear in Japanese discourse as an exemplary national hero. Tokugawa-era discourse on Napoleon was, in many ways, empirically flawed and confused. Japanese commentators had no way to contextualize key issues in Napoleon's life such as the Corsican independence movement or French republican thought. But they were intrigued by the more accessible aspects of his biography: his heroic rise from a petty noble family to national leadership, his establishment of a great empire, his interest in science and technology, his widespread popularity and support among ordinary Frenchmen. Reworked by Japanese intermediaries, Napoleon came to resemble an exemplary Confucian scholar-official: studious, wise, loyal, and self-sacrificing. Abstracted out of a European context, Napoleon's life resonated with that of many future Meiji leaders, ambitious and determined men from the bottom of the samurai estate.

The first detailed account of Napoleon in Japan was an 1818 poem by Rai San'yō, an eccentric historian, painter, poet, and calligrapher. In "Ode of the King of France" ("Furaō no uta"), he described Napoleon as a military hero who, on the verge of completing a long campaign of conquest, was defeated by deep snow and freezing cold.[67] Rai's poem inspired a biography of Napoleon by the Dutch Studies scholar Koseki San'ei. Koseki worked as a shogunal astronomer and translated texts ranging from geography to medicine, including a tract on cowpox vaccination.[68] Koseki's biography of Napoleon is sometimes described as a translation of Joannes van der Linden's *Het leven van Bonaparte* (1802), but it is better understood as an adaptation, reinterpreting Napoleon's life in terms of Confucian political thought. According to Koseki, the French Revolution was in accord with "the mandate of heaven" because Louis XVI impoverished his country and oppressed his people, making a revolution both just and inevitable. The French Revolution was a revolt against tyranny (*gyakusei*) in which valiant heroes established enlightened and just (*seimei*) rule for the people.[69]

Koseki's work made Napoleon accessible to loyalist samurai. The translation avoided problematic political concepts, such as republicanism, and focused instead on more familiar notions, such as national defense. For example, Koseki rendered the word "freedom" (*fureiheido*, from Dutch "vrijheid") with a long gloss, explaining that it is "a word celebrating a victory over an enemy country, and [thus] becoming a free and independent (*fuki*) country." This idiosyncratic translation meant that Napoleon's life was immediately relevant to samurai seeking to repel Western encroachment and Napoleon became a hero to Japanese political activists, including Saigō Takamori, Yoshida Shōin, and Sakuma Shōzan.[70] Koseki also stressed Napoleon's interest in science and technology as a complement to his civil and military triumphs. He thus harmonized the promotion of advanced technology with older notions of universal virtue.

Koseki's influence is evident in the writings of Yoshida Shōin, the charismatic Chōshū scholar and activist. In 1859, while in prison for criticizing the shogunate, Yoshida lamented the fecklessness of the Japanese political elite. The shogunate and the daimyo had failed to "repel the barbarian" and defend the "land of the gods" (shinshū). They had neglected the wise and far-sighted policies of ancient Japan. After 3,000 years of independence, Japan was now under foreign control, and the shame of this subjugation was unbearable. Then, with no sense of irony, Yoshida remarked that Napoleon himself would be anguished by such a loss of "freedom" (furēhēdo). In this context, Napoleon was not a "barbarian," but, on the contrary, an inspiration for loyalists in the "land of the gods." Yoshida linked Napoleon to the great heroes of the Eastern Jin (265–420) and Southern Song (1127–1279). Greater than any single era or region, they were universal exemplars of virtue. This meant, paradoxically, that Japan could repel the Western "barbarians" by emulating Napoleon. Defending the land of the gods and restoring the sage rule of ancient Japanese emperors required Napoleonic courage, resourcefulness, and loyalty.[71]

Yoshida's embrace of Napoleon was part of a broader, transnational response to France and French ideals. The influential Italian nationalist Giuseppe Mazzini, for example, embraced the 1789 French Revolution as the start of an international tide of nationalist revolutions. For Mazzini, the defeat of Napoleon Bonaparte at Waterloo marked a temporary triumph of despotism over democracy and national self-determination. The French Revolution had started a movement that "told the different peoples: *you are the true masters of your native soil; you are the sole interpreters of your own law of life.*"[72] In 1849, when Louis Napoleon intervened to crush the Italian nationalist movement, Mazzini invoked French republican ideals to criticize France itself. For Mazzini, nationalism and cosmopolitanism were inherently complementary, and French republican principles were the common heritage of all humanity.[73] Yoshida Shōin's understanding of the French Revolution was fragmentary and confused, but he arrived at a similarly cosmopolitan appreciation of France, despite having never left Japan. For Shōin, the French Revolution, the American War of Independence, and the Song dynasty's battles against the Khitan were all battles of national independence, and all were worthy of respect and emulation.

Yoshida's thinking is of particular import because several of his disciples, including Itō Hirobumi, Kido Takayoshi, and Yamagata Aritomo, were instrumental in creating the Meiji government. But Yoshida's approach to Napoleon reveals a broader current in late Tokugawa thought. The tropes of radical nostalgia and cosmopolitan chauvinism allowed Japanese thinkers to integrate modern European culture with the ancient Japanese past. Supremely moral conduct was universal, and Japanese patriots were obliged to venerate and emulate such conduct. If the West produced moral exemplars, then they could be abstracted out of their "barbarian" origins. That reinterpretation of the "barbarian" legitimized the Meiji government's promotion of Western practices.

End Game: The 1867/12/9 Coup

In the last days of 1867, the contours of the post-shogunal state emerged. The shogunate would be replaced by new national institutions, uniting the daimyo under the sovereign authority of the emperor. Japan would create a new army and a new navy, mobilizing people and resources from the entire realm. The new government would be both more centralized and more inclusive.

That common ground attenuated the violence of the Meiji Restoration. Nonetheless, the last days of the old regime saw a frenzied struggle for political control. Activists from Satsuma and Chōshū were eager for a military confrontation with the shogunate, but other key daimyo were more cautious. Representatives of Tosa, in particular, hoped to arrange a peaceful settlement, and they won the backing of the lord of Fukui, Matsudaira Yoshinaga. On 1867/10/3, Tosa retainers presented a formal proposal to the shogunate in the form of a petition by Yamauchi Yōdō, the daimyo of Tosa. Based on radical nostalgia and cosmopolitan chauvinism, the petition described revolutionary political change as a return to ancient ways. It advocated the "revival of ancient kingly rule" (*ōsei fukko*). Practically, this meant the surrender of all political power to the imperial court and the establishment in Kyoto of a bicameral assembly (*giseisho*). The legislators would range from court nobles to commoners, selected for their virtue and integrity. The court would establish new schools and research centers, reform the army and navy, and dispatch envoys to renegotiate the unequal treaties. The result of this "revolutionary reform" (*isshin kaikaku*) would be a new government, capable of maintaining "independence in the world."[74]

Yoshinobu eagerly embraced the Tosa proposal. In light of the "global situation," he declared, the Tosa proposal was reasonable. To that end, he agreed to return "political authority" (*seiken*) to the imperial court and pledged to work with the new national council. Yoshinobu's move was tactically brilliant. By agreeing to restore political power to the court, he stole the issue from Chōshū and Satsuma. At the same time, his "surrender" allowed Yoshinobu to reposition himself in the emerging political order. The imperial court accepted Yoshinobu's "return of political authority" on 10/15 but also called for a meeting of the daimyo to decide the course of reform. Since Yoshinobu had deftly manipulated daimyo councils before, he had every reason to expect substantial power in any national assembly. Furthemore, Yoshinobu was directed to maintain his foreign and domestic political power until the council convened.[75] Finally, Yoshinobu confounded the hopes of imperial loyalists by retaining his high-ranking titles in the ancient imperial order, such as General of the Right Imperial Guards (*ukon'e no taishō*) and Inner Palace Minister (*naidaijin*). For centuries, those titles had served primarily as imperial recognition of Tokugawa hegemony. Shoguns received the title of General of the Right Imperial Guards because they were powerful; they did not become powerful upon receiving the title. But many imperial loyalists hoped to reverse that relationship and to infuse ancient titles with true power as part of an imperial restoration. By holding on to his imperial titles, Yoshinobu confounded that goal. If imperial loyalists restored Nara-era administrative structures, they would make Yoshinobu the highest-ranking warlord in the imperial cabinet.[76]

Yoshinobu's tactical surrender infuriated both his enemies and his allies. Shogunal retainers, such as *hatamaoto* and *fudai* daimyo, were both outraged and confused. What was their role in the new political order? Had the last shogun abandoned long-standing shogunal allies? It seemed as if Yoshinobu had sacrificed the Tokugawa shogunate to save the Tokugawa house. Loyalists in Satsuma and Chōshū were equally incensed. Yoshinobu had turned a seemingly disastrous situation to his advantage. By dodging a confrontation, Yoshinobu had again positioned himself as the voice of reason and compromise. To the dismay of Satsuma and Chōshū, Yoshinobu remained in good favor with the imperial court. Emperor Kōmei had repeatedly inveighed against foreign "barbarians" despoiling the "land of the gods," but he was equally disturbed by the recklessness of anti-foreign radicals.[77] Yoshinobu seemed like a reasonable and reliable compromise, and imperial loyalists found it difficult to outmaneuver an imperial favorite.

Yoshinobu's hold on the court had been weakened on 1866/12/15 by Kōmei's death. The emperor's sudden demise was widely attributed to poison, and historians continue to debate whether the monarch was poisoned or intentionally infected with smallpox.[78] Kōmei was succeeded by his son Mutsuhito, better known as the Meiji emperor. The new monarch was only fourteen and unlike his father, had never known a world without Western warships in Japanese ports. Accordingly, unlike his father, the Meiji emperor had no expectation that Japan could return to relative cultural and political isolation. This change of sovereign thus helped dissipate the court's xenophobia. But many powerful courtiers remained leery of Satsuma and Chōshū, and Yoshinobu retained enough influence at court to blunt his rivals from the southwest. When Chōshū began sending troops to Kyōto in early 1867/12, for example, Yoshinobu arranged for an imperial order redirecting them to Osaka.[79]

In order to turn the court against Yoshinobu, Satsuma resorted to a palace coup. On 1867/12/8, the imperial court convened a meeting of daimyo, court nobles, and samurai to discuss the pardon of Chōshū, lifting its designation as an "enemy of the court." Yoshinobu was not opposed to the pardon and declined to attend. The council agreed, as expected, to pardon Chōshū, but then, in the late evening, moved on to a Satsuma-backed proposal. In addition to Chōshū, the conference agreed to pardon several influential court nobles (including Iwakura Tomomi and Sanjō Sanetomi) who had been censured for their radical, pro-Chōshū activities. Iwakura had been confined to a village in north Kyoto, but once pardoned, he quickly joined the meeting. In the early hours of 12/9 the conference broke for recess and the imperial regent Nijō Nariyuki returned home. In his absence, Iwakura seized control. He called in troops, primarily from Satsuma, to seize the gates of the imperial palace. Satsuma troops were girded for battle, and the standing guard from Aizu and Kuwana was intimidated and withdrew. Iwakura then summoned the assembly to hear the decree of the new emperor. Seated behind a bamboo screen on a high platform, the young monarch read an edict declaring the "revival of ancient kingly rule."

This imperial edict was revolutionary but it invoked radical nostalgia, citing a return to ancient ways to justify radical change. The decree abolished the shogunate, including the office of shogun as well as lower posts such as Kyoto Protector (*Kyōto shugo*), held by the daimyo of Aizu. Key offices of the imperial court were also eliminated: Nijō's post of imperial regent (*sesshō*), a center of power since the seventh century, was no more. The edict instituted a new political structure to replace the shogunate and conventional imperial court positions. Prince Arisugawa, descendant of a seventeenth-century emperor, would be prime minister (*sōsai*); high-ranking courtiers and major daimyo were named legislators (*gijō*), including the lords of Satsuma, Tosa, Owari, and Fukui; lower courtiers were named councilors (*san'yo*). This bicameral assembly was markedly less inclusive than Tosa's proposal, with no mention of ordinary samurai or commoners. These innovations were described as part of the "revival of ancient kingly rule" rather than a radical break with tradition.

The new government convened on the evening of 12/9 and, over the objections of Tosa and Fukui, moved to change the terms of Yoshinobu's surrender. He would now surrender not just his post as shogun but his imperial titles and lands as well.[80] Even in the face of this provocation, Yoshinobu maintained his equanimity. Rather than fight in the streets of Kyoto, he withdrew his forces to Osaka. On 12/16, he summoned representatives of the United States, Britain, France, Holland, Italy, and Prussia to inform them that he remained the effective ruler of Japan.[81] From Osaka, he exploited divisions in the new imperial government, particularly the ambivalence of Tosa and Owari. By the end of the month his efforts were yielding fruit: the new government agreed that the details of Yoshinobu's surrender would have to be part of future deliberations over the new government's finances.[82]

Yoshinobu's resilience drove Satsuma to extreme measures. Since they could not outmaneuver him in deliberations, Satsuma used street violence to provoke a crisis. Beginning in late 1867/11, Satsuma samurai and loyalist *rōnin* began a campaign of targeted mayhem in Edo, ransacking merchant warehouses, setting fire to shogunal property, and attacking police officers. On 12/23, after weeks of rumors, a suspicious fire broke out and destroyed the shogunal castle's women's quarters. That same evening, assailants attacked the villa of Shōnai domain, a close shogunal ally, and fled through the city to the Satsuma compound. Edo officials were outraged and sought retribution: on 12/25 they attacked and burned the Satsuma compound, killing several men.[83]

In Osaka, Yoshinobu had been struggling to hold back his supporters, but when news of the fighting in Edo reached Osaka, he could restrain his men no longer. On the first day of the Japanese New Year, he issued a fiery decree, denouncing the imperial council of 12/9 as nothing more than a coup by Satsuma. Those villains had deceived the young emperor, dismissed his trusted advisors, and burned and pillaged in Edo. Yoshinobu demanded that these traitors be handed over so that he might avenge this affront to the imperial house. In the first days of the New Year, the shogunate sent troops north from Osaka to Kyoto, in a desperate attempt to "punish" its rivals. The battle was joined.

In less than a week, Tokugawa forces were defeated. This swift collapse was unexpected. The shogunal army was nearly 13,000 men strong and included 900 French-trained infantry, some of the best troops in Japan. They were supported by samurai from Aizu, Kuwana, and other allied domains. Many troops on the shogunal side fought with great courage. Forces from Aizu showed how effective traditional samurai tactics could be: on at least two occasions they routed Satsuma and Chōshū riflemen with swords and pikes by charging before the enemy could reload. But shogunal forces were undermined by feckless leadership, disorganization, and chronic disunity. Lacking a coherent strategy, their troops were consistently in the wrong place at the wrong time and unable to take advantage of their numerical superiority. Shogunal forces did not advance after victories and reinforcements did not deploy as ordered. As the shogun's army faltered, its allies began to hedge their bets. Yodo domain, nominally a Tokugawa ally, refused to allow shogunal troops to take refuge in Yodo Castle. A final blow came on 1/6 when Tsu domain switched sides and began shelling Aizu troops rather than the enemy. Battered from without and eroded from within, the armies of the shogunate imploded.[84] Yoshinobu ordered a retreat to Edo. There was scattered talk of a valiant last stand, but Yoshinobu had lost the will to fight. In 1868/4, the last shogun surrendered Edo Castle without a fight.

Meiji leaders would later insist that they overthrew a backward, hidebound, and insular regime. Western observers saw nothing of the sort. On the contrary, they held Yoshinobu in uniquely high regard. The US Consul Robert Bruce Van Valkenburgh, for example, described him as "the most progressive and liberal in his ideas of any Japanese official." The nascent Meiji government had won the support of Kyoto, but that endorsement was tainted by the court's legacy of insularity and xenophobia. Despite a change in monarch, the imperial decree of 12/9 still lamented how foreigners had brought turmoil to Japan: "The unprecedented national crisis that began in 1853 endlessly troubled the heart of the previous emperor, and this became known to the masses." Accordingly, most foreign officials were suspicious of the new regime. In the words of US Secretary of State

William Henry Seward, "the Tycoon's resignation of his powers into the hands of the Mikado would seem to be occasion for regret."[85]

Despite these gloomy predictions, the Meiji government would achieve revolutionary change. But it would do so in alliance with its erstwhile enemies. In the battles of 1868, anti-Tokugawa forces and Tokugawa loyalists were divided more by factional animosities and rancor than by ideology. Both sides included stodgy conservatives and xenophobes, and reformers on the imperial side resembled their Tokugawa counterparts more than their own conservatives. Reformers on both sides were influenced by cosmopolitan chauvinism and radical nostalgia, looking both to Western models and ancient local precedents. In the short term, the Meiji government needed to defeat the Tokugawa in battle in order to assert its own legitimacy. But as passions cooled, it became clear that many Tokugawa vassals could be valuable servants of the new state. That rapprochement allowed the Meiji state to achieve revolutionary change without revolutionary violence.

4

A Newly Ancient Japan

BEGINNING IN 1868, the self-described imperial government transformed the formal political structure of Japan. It toppled the Tokugawa shogunate, dissolved the domains, and created a new centralized state. Those changes were remarkably peaceful. The new government removed an entire ruling elite without provoking a protracted civil war. On the contrary, the early years of the Meiji state were characterized by a surprising aversion to conflict. On the Tokugawa side, advocates of a dignified surrender proved more influential than hardliners. As a result, the last Tokugawa shogun died not in battle in 1868 but of old age in 1913, wealthy and respected. Despite Yoshinobu's surrender, some Tokugawa allies refused to capitulate. Aizu domain, in particular, was adamantly opposed to the ascendance of Satsuma and Chōshū, and that struggle split Japan along regional lines: the northeast versus the southwest. Both Japanese and foreign observers wondered whether rebels in the northeast would secede, precipitating a long and bloody conflict like the US Civil War. But even for diehards in Aizu, open sucession was a bridge too far. The rebels stopped short of seceding and the fighting was over after a few pitched battles.

Between 1869 and 1871, the new government peacefully dissolved the entire daimyo class. Initially, the new Meiji government approached the daimyo with great caution. The Meiji leadership, which was overwhelmingly samurai, believed that loyalty to one's lord was a cardinal virtue, and they were loath to destroy the institutions to which they themselves had sworn fealty. Instead, they continued Tokugawa-era efforts to work through the daimyo, establishing daimyo advisory councils and encouraging daimyo to modernize their armies and balance their budgets. Rather than move directly toward a powerful central government, they hoped that dozens of regional reform efforts might add up to a Japanese nation-state.

That hope was in vain, but the restraint with which the Meiji government approached the daimyo had an unexpected outcome. It undermined rather than encouraged the continuance of daimyo rule. Over these years, as they struggled with domain reform, some of Japan's most astute and capable daimyo emerged as advocates of central control. They argued that domain reform was not only difficult but also unproductive: dozens of regional reform efforts would not create a Japanese nation-state. Rather than fight in defense of noble privilege, many of the last generation of daimyo were eager to be coopted: a handful received positions in the new Meiji government, but most simply accepted lavish pensions and disappeared from political life. That quiet surrender of the old regime reveals how local understandings of Japan had been transformed. It was difficult to be an advocate for Japan without supporting a Japanese nation-state, and that required the dissolution of the domains. A new cosmopolitan chauvinist vision of Japan thus undermined the old regime.

The Boshin War (1868–1869)

The war that destroyed the Tokugawa is known as the Boshin War, a name derived from the Chinese zodiac signs for the year 1868. Although some partisans held out until 1869/5/18 (June 27), the fate of the shogunate was decided in the first few days of 1868. By 1869/1/17, Yoshinobu was convinced that his best option was a dignified surrender. Instead of defending the Tokugawa shogunate, he shifted his attention to something smaller, the Tokugawa house. He petitioned the imperial court to recognize his adopted heir, a four-year-old named Kamenosuke. Yoshinobu began dismantling the shogunate from within, dismissing key *fudai* lords and liege vassals from shogunal service and ordering them to obey imperial decrees. Those decrees anticipated the demands of the Meiji government and blunted its appetite for a punitive campaign against the Tokugawa.[1]

International concerns also heightened the new government's desire to avoid a protracted civil war. The nascent Meiji government understood that it needed to protect the life and property of foreigners to secure its legitimacy. But the imperial alliance included xenophobic radicals, who were emboldened by the collapse of the shogunate, and the new government found it difficult to restrain its own troops. When imperial troops entered Kobe on 1868/1/11 (February 4), for example, they injured diplomatic personnel and killed several soldiers in the foreign concession, a zone administered by the foreign powers under the unequal treaties.

The consuls of Britain, the United States, France, Prussia, Italy, and the Netherlands issued a joint letter, demanding reparations and the punishment of those responsible. Only by such actions, they warned, could "future and friendly relations be preserved between the government of the undersigned and that of his Majesty the Mikado."[2] Within a few years, the Meiji government had repaired its image, declaring its commitment to, in Itō's words, "that strong feeling of brotherly love which so unites distant peoples."[3] But establishing that new public image required a quick peace rather than a long civil war.

The imperial government was also concerned with civil unrest. Popular protest surged in the 1860s, sparked largely by inflation and poor harvests. Eager to placate the populace, the new imperial army promised tax relief, a commitment it would soon regret. The tenor of the protests revealed a frayed social fabric. Rather than follow convention, and appeal to the government for mercy and compassion, protestors began to employ the phrase "world renewal" (*yonaoshi*), invoking a utopian, quasi-religious vision of the future. Moving beyond simple economic demands, they envisioned a new age of enlightenment, abundance, and equality. Then, in mid-1867, broad swathes of Japan erupted in carnivalesque revelry. Townsmen and villagers created impromptu festivals. Prompted by the "mysterious" appearance of religious amulets, they left home for pilgrimage sites or indulged in raucous public dancing, wearing wild costumes, cross dressing, or simply stripping naked. Since most commoners could not travel or hold festivals without permission, these spontaneous celebrations were an open snub to authority. These protests had no overt political content: participants sang bawdy but fatalistic songs ending with the refrain "ee ja nai ka," or "what the hell!" but they made no direct references to shogunal misrule or imperial virtue. But beneath this merriment was clear evidence of social unrest: revelers targeted the wealthy, wrecking their homes with frenzied dancing.[4] For Japan's political elite, this was yet more evidence of popular discontent and the deterioration of conventional social controls.[5]

These domestic and international pressures weighed against a protracted punitive campaign. Although the new government blustered about the "crimes" of the shogunate, it wanted peace and cooperation more than vengeance. Thus, while complaining that Yoshinobu had "deceived the imperial court," the new government allowed him to retire to Mito domain. His chief officers, despite their "grave crimes," were also granted imperial clemency and allowed to retire from public life. Edo Castle was to be surrendered to the lord of Owari, a collateral Tokugawa house. The

Tokugawa promised to hand over all war materiel. On 1868/4/11 imperial troops peacefully entered the city. The fall of the shogunate was complete.[6]

With his surrender, Yoshinobu abandoned the Tokugawa shogunate but saved the Tokugawa lineage. Indeed, the new Meiji government would reward Kamenosuke, Yoshinobu's five-year-old heir, with a massive fief. Ironically, Yoshinobu's surrender agreement prompted the most dogged resistance of the Boshin War. The surrender terms ignored both Tokugawa-allied domains such Aizu and ordinary Tokugawa vassals. Those parties felt betrayed and abandoned. They ignored Yoshinobu's decision to surrender and elected to fight the new imperial government on their own. The main resistance movement was the Northern Alliance (Ōuetsu reppan dōmei), a regional coalition of domains. At its core, the fighting was a contest between the new government and Aizu domain, whose samurai had fought tenaciously at Fushimi-Toba. But the struggle expanded into a broader regional conflict, between the northeast and the southwest. The leaders of the new Meiji government were overwhelmingly from the southwest, Satsuma and Chōshū in particular. Aizu, by contrast, was in the northeast. When the imperial army insisted that Aizu be "punished," the lords of neighboring domains instead appealed for leniency on Aizu's behalf. The Meiji government interpreted this regional solidarity as sedition, and the struggle became a civil war.

The Northern Alliance aspired to sustain the Tokugawa order without Tokugawa support. Yoshinobu had resigned as shogun, but the Alliance re-created the old regime with a new shogunate and its own imperial court. The daimyo of Sendai was declared the new shogun and an imperial prince, Kitashirakawa Yoshihisa (1847–95), was quietly enthroned as an alternative emperor.[7] Intriguingly, this creation of a separate eastern throne recalled a contingency plan developed by the Tokugawa more than 250 years earlier. In 1616, the Tokugawa began the tradition of having an imperial prince serve as the chief abbot of Kan'ei-ji, a shogunal temple in Edo. The plan was that if anti-Tokugawa forces ever gained control of Kyoto and began issuing orders in the name of the emperor, the Tokugawa could respond with its own emperor. It would enthrone the abbot of Kan'ei-ji, thereby creating a new "emperor" in Edo, who was conveniently the head of a Tokugawa temple. In 1868, more than 250 years later, the Northern Alliance acted on this plan, referring to chief abbot Kitashirakawa with terms normally reserved for a reigning emperor. Rumors of Kitashirakawa's enthronement were so widespread that foreign diplomats and newspapers wrote of a second "Northern

Mikado." There was Japanese precedent for a civil war between rival emperors: from 1336 to 1392 two lineages of distant cousins each claimed the throne. But in 1868, the Northern Alliance chose not to publicly declare Kitashirakawa the sole true monarch of Japan.[8] Even while fighting against Satsuma and Chōshū, the rebels stopped short of provoking an irreparable schism.

Aizu and its allies fought with ferocity and courage, but they could not hold back the imperial army. The Northern Alliance surrendered in 1868/9 after two months of intense combat. In their last days, they were joined by a rump of the shogunal navy, led by Enomoto Takeaki. Enomoto was outraged by Yoshinobu's surrender but did not defect until 1868/8/19 when he felt certain that Kamenosuke, the Tokugawa heir, was safe. Then he left Edo with some 2,000 retainers, several French advisors, and the shogunate's best warships. After stopping in Sendai, they proceeded to Ezo and quickly overwhelmed government forces, capturing the city of Hakodate on 10/26.[9] The government chose not to attack in winter, and Enomoto's rebels held out until 1869/5 (June).

Had Enomoto defected four months earlier, he might well have embraced the goals of the Northern Alliance and sought to reconstruct the old regime.[10] But by late 1868 that goal lay in ashes, and instead, Enomoto and his supporters created a new regime, known in English as the "Republic of Ezo." The term "republic" was a misnomer, but it reflects how progressive and Western-oriented the Ezo rebellion appeared to foreign observers. The US Consul Van Valkenburgh, for example, praised Enomoto for "consistently advocat[ing] progress, and a liberal foreign intercourse."[11] Enomoto's core grievance was that Yoshinobu's surrender had ignored many Tokugawa vassals, leaving them as *rōnin*, former samurai without income or support. He requested control over Ezo as compensation for those lost stipends and holdings. But when addressing foreigners, Enomoto situated this grievance in the context of global political change. The governments of Asia, he declared, suffered from a chasm between ruler and ruled, leading to anger and resentment. The situation in Japan was merely an example of that pervasive problem, and it would be resolved once the new government allowed the rebels to communicate directly with their sovereign. Foreign arbitration, Enomoto declared, could give the rebels access to their emperor, prevent an internecine war, and allow Japan to establish a "civilized government" (*bunmei no seifu*).[12] Unlike the leaders of the Northern Alliance, Enomoto was able to recast his grievances within cosmopolitan discourse.

Because of its international engagement, the Ezo rebellion anticipated aspects of the Meiji government. The "Republic of Ezo" was deeply
concerned with international legitimacy and was led by Western-trained
Japanese and foreign advisors. Enomoto had studied naval science in
Holland for five years and was a staunch proponent of military modernization. He was comfortable around Westerners and could meet privately
with the British consul without a translator since both men were fluent in
Dutch. Assisting Enomoto were several French military officers, members
of a mission to the shogunate who had ignored their home government's
orders to remain neutral. Lieutenant Jules Brunet became the rebellion's de facto foreign minister; he drafted the rebels' French-language
announcements, arranged meetings with foreign consuls, and handled
preliminary negotiations with foreign powers. [13] Brunet deftly recast the
rebels' grievances in terms of natural rights: the rebels wanted peace but
they had "legitimate rights to live honorably in the land of their fathers
and [they] are ready to defend those rights, arms in hand."[14] Working
together, Enomoto and Brunet convinced the foreign consuls in Hakodate

FIGURE 4.1 Jules Brunet and Tokugawa Military Officers, c. 1868. Brunet is in the
front row, second from the left, turning towards Tokugawa army officer Matsudaira
Tarō. Hakodate City Central Library (Hakodate-shi Chūō Toshokan).

to mediate between the rebels and the imperial government.[15] The Meiji government rejected such mediation, since it would have constituted indirect recognition of the rebel cause. But the offers to mediate reveal how the Ezo rebels had impressed the foreign powers.

The misnomer "Republic of Ezo" also reflects how deftly Enomoto appealed to foreign opinion. There was nothing "republican" about the Ezo rebellion. The rebels believed in imperial rather than popular sovereignty, and they never described their own government as a republic. The phrase "Republic of Ezo" likely emerged from a promise by Brunet that the rebel government would choose its leaders according to "universal suffrage."[16] The rebels did indeed hold an election on 1868/12/15. Enomoto was elected president, winning 156 of 856 ballots cast. But suffrage in that election was far from "universal." Only one-third of the rebels cast ballots: voting was restricted to those who held the position of squadron commander and higher rank. Ordinary soldiers and the general population were excluded and largely unaware of the proceedings. The account of one soldier refers to the election as a "great banquet" for senior officers.[17] In English-language accounts, however, this election was understood as an imitation of Western democracy. This garbled, but positive, assessment of the Ezo rebellion reflects how highly Enomoto was regarded in foreign circles.

Resistance to the nascent Meiji government thus took two distinct forms. The Northern Alliance attempted to resurrect shogunal rule even after Yoshinobu had dissolved the Tokugawa shogunate. The "Republic of Ezo," by contrast, anticipated some of the most progressive aspects of the Meiji government. It held elections, albeit with a limited franchise. It embraced advanced technology and employed foreign advisors. It was deeply concerned with international legitimacy. In 1869, the nascent Meiji government saw these accomplishments as a threat. After defeating the "Republic of Ezo" in June 1869, it imprisoned Enomoto and his supporters. But ideological affinities proved more important than wartime animosities, and the government soon rehabilitated and embraced the rebels. In 1872, it pardoned Enomoto and two years later appointed him minister plenipotentiary to Russia. The Ezo government's army minister, Ōtori Keisuke, was pardoned and appointed minister plenipotentiary to both China and Korea. The Ezo navy minister, Arai Ikunosuke, became head of the Meiji government's meteorological agency.

The Meiji government's treatment of Brunet was similarly forgiving. Brunet escaped back to France and the Meiji government initially demanded his punishment, but it soon granted full pardons to Brunet and his fellow French officers. Brunet was eventually transformed into a hero, decorated with both the Order of the Rising Sun and the Order of the Sacred Treasure. Brunet returned the compliment by writing a book on modern Japanese "orders of chivalry," complete with a glowing account of the Meiji emperor.[18] This rehabilitation of the rebels of the "Republic of Ezo" reflects how ideology cut across factional lines: the Meiji government found eager allies among its old foes.

By contrast, the leaders of the Northern Alliance disappeared from public life. The daimyo of Sendai and Yonezawa had little to offer the new government and sank into genteel obscurity.[19] They could not legitimize Japan in a new international environment, explain the imperial state to European observers, disseminate new social or material technologies, or even converse comfortably with foreigners. On the contrary, they embraced exactly what the new government sought to discard. Resistance to the Meiji government in the Boshin War thus took two distinct forms: the Northern Alliance reflected the Meiji government's past while the "Republic of Ezo" resembled its future.

The Dissolution of the Domains

In order to create a nation-state, the Meiji government needed to replace the daimyo. It could not establish national authority while maintaining hundreds of independent armies, navies, and tax systems. Radical nostalgia offered ample reason to dissolve the domains swiftly and completely. The abrogation of tradition could be justified by older precedents. The daimyo had emerged only in the 1400s and 1500s to fill a power vacuum caused by the collapse of older institutions: imperial authority and the Ashikaga shogunate. As a symptom of imperial decline, the daimyo would logically disappear under a newly powerful imperial state

In practice, however, replacing the domains was a fraught process. The leaders of the Restoration were primarily samurai, men for whom loyalty was a defining virtue. How could they advocate the elimination of their own lords? And, after centuries of daimyo rule, what would the new government put in its place? The Meiji government could not remove the daimyo until it had a new system of regional control. Accordingly, the new government was extremely cautious in confronting daimyo rule, moving gradually and incrementally for nearly two years.

In its early days, the government gave no sign that it would dissolve the domains. On the contrary, it rewarded its allies with hereditary land grants, creating new domains. In that way it was more like a Meiji shogunate than a radically new imperial government. The largest new domain was a fief created for the Tokugawa heir, Kamenosuke. At 700,000 *koku* it was larger than Chōshū or Tosa, and it made Kamenosuke (now formally Tokugawa Iesato) one of the wealthiest daimyo in the realm. The government also established an attendance schedule in Tokyo for daimyo, a policy reminiscent of sankin kōtai, the Tokugawa-era system of daimyo attendance in Edo. The daimyo of Tokushima, Hachisuka Mochiaki, for example, was supposed to be in his Tokyo villa in the winters of 1872, 1875, 1878, and 1881. Tokugawa Kamenosuke was scheduled for the winters of 1871, 1874, 1877, and 1880.[20] The government also punished its enemies by reducing their holdings, much like the Tokugawa had in the early 1600s. The Matsudaira of Aizu, for example, were stripped of their holdings but then reinvested as the lords of Tonami domain, a holding one-eighth the size and more than 300 miles away from their original territory.[21] The Meiji government also created new domains to compensate daimyo displaced by the creation of Kamenosuke's new fief. Nagao domain, for example, was created in 1868/7 for Honda Masamori, formerly the daimyo of Tanaka domain.

The government's deference to traditional authority was revealed in the famous "Charter Oath" of April 1868. That five-article oath was sworn by Sanjō Sanetomi to the ancient gods on behalf of the Meiji emperor. The first article declared, "We shall determine all matters of state by public discussion, after assemblies have been convoked far and wide." Advocates of Japanese democracy would later insist that those words promised the creation of an elected assembly. But the drafters of the oath were thinking more modestly of daimyo councils. The oath was designed largely to pull daimyo away from individual local agendas and into the new national government.[22] Indeed, the early national councils of the Meiji government, the *kōgisho* and *shūgiin*, were both based on old domain lines and reproduced hereditary status distinctions. In that sense, they closely resembled the ruling council of the Northern Alliance. Such institutions suggested that daimyo status still mattered, and samurai acted accordingly. The Tokugawa vassal Ōsawa Mototoshi, for example, falsified a report of his holdings so that he would be classified as a daimyo rather than a hatamoto: he described a large lake in his territory as land under reclamation.

The Meiji leadership sustained daimyo authority partly because they were unsure of how to replace it. In 1869/1, in a first step toward central control, the government began reappointing the daimyo as "domain governors" (han chiji), leaving them in power while redefining them as agents of Tokyo. The first daimyo to "return" their investitures were the lords of Chōshū, Satsuma, Tosa, and Hizen, the powerful southwestern domains that had defeated the Tokugawa. Pressed by their own retainers, they offered their investitures to the emperor in a formal ceremony on 1869/1/20. Many daimyo understood that this precedent was a veiled order and began voluntarily "returning" their holdings as well. A mere fourteen holdouts were ordered to "return" their holdings on 1869/6/24. This process was described as the "return" of daimyo investitures to the emperor (hanseki hōkan) because, according to imperial ideology, all sovereignty derived from the emperor. The daimyo were already imperial vassals, so the formal gesture of "returning" their investitures merely confirmed that the daimyo themselves recognized the emperor as their lord. The emperor responded to this gesture by reinvesting the daimyo with the new status of "governor," marking them as imperial servants rather than shogunal vassals.

Rhetorically, these rituals of "return" drew on cosmopolitan chauvinism and radical nostalgia, connecting the ancient past to modern challenges. The announcement of the first "return" declared that Japan had been under imperial rule since the days of Amaterasu. The return of domain investitures recognized this ancient truth, but it would also help Japan "stand equal with foreign countries." A return to ancient principles was thus completely compatible with the establishment of Japanese sovereign authority in a new international order.[23]

As domain governors, daimyo were simultaneously regional lords and agents of central authority. The governors' high-ranking officers were, similarly, both samurai retainers and also central government officials, now bound by new civil service regulations (shokuinrei). That hybrid, interim system had the unexpected effect of turning the daimyo themselves against daimyo rule. The government gave daimyo authority over their holdings but ordered them to reduce samurai stipends, to retire their debts, and to begin purchasing new arms. That process was both demanding and humiliating. Daimyo needed to reduce their own expenses, to make cuts in their retainers' stipends, and to institute complicated reforms. For many daimyo, the demands of reform began to overweigh the perquisites of power.[24]

Hachisuka Mochiaki, the daimyo of Tokushima, epitomized how daimyo came to reject their own status. In 1867, as heir apparent, Mochiaki had suggested to the British diplomat Ernest Satow that he wanted to abdicate and study in England.[25] When his father died suddenly in 1868/1, Mochiaki became daimyo and immediately began clashing with his own vassals. Mochiaki wanted to join the Boshin War on the imperial side, but the domain establishment was more cautious. The Hachisuka had long enjoyed Tokugawa favor, and Mochiaki's father had been adopted from the Tokugawa house. After his appointment as domain governor, Mochiaki confronted a new crisis. He was required to reduce samurai stipends on the orders of the central government, but who exactly were his samurai? In Tokushima, that was a divisive question. One of Tokushima's elite samurai families, the Inada, had their own castle and vassals. According to new national standards, the Inada were samurai, but the vassals of the Inada were not. As vassals of vassals, Inada samurai were to be classified as soldiers (*sotsu*) rather than samurai (*shi*), resulting in a reduction in both income and status. The Inada vassals were determined to avoid this demotion and in 1869/8 they appealed to the Meiji government for a special accommodation. [26]

Rather than engage this dispute, Mochiaki hoped to avoid it. In 1870/1, he recommended dissolving all domains in favor of smaller administrative units. The government, he wrote, needed to fulfill its promise to abolish old customs and to create a powerful, centralized imperial state. It needed to break up domains into prefectures and to place all samurai under the command of a national army minister. The very word domain (*han*), he argued, was pernicious and should be decisively abolished.[27] A full nineteen months before the Meiji government dissolved the domains, Mochiaki was advocating the end of daimyo rule.

In the interim, the Tokushima-Inada dispute exploded in violence. The Meiji government hoped to accommodate the Inada vassals by resettling them in Ezo. In Tokushima, however, both factions continued to fight over conventional samurai status. The Inada vassals proposed the creation of a new Inada domain. That would make them direct vassals of a daimyo and therefore true samurai rather than sub-vassals. That proposal infuriated a group of Tokushima samurai, including the head of the domain academy, who viewed the Inada appeal as insulting and disloyal.[28] Determined to defend the honor of their lord, on 1870/5/13 nearly a thousand Hachisuka retainers attacked the Inada villa in Tokushima, murdered the occupants, and burned it to the ground. Mochiaki was dismayed and humiliated: in

1868 his vassals had failed to rally to the imperial cause, and then in 1870 they had embarrassed him in front of the new imperial government. Their understanding of samurai honor had served only to bring Tokushima under suspicion of treason (*muhon*) against the central government.[29]

For Mochiaki, the end of daimyo rule in 1871 was more a relief than a defeat. Like all daimyo, he was granted a generous severance package in government bonds. Free to leave Japan, he went to England and studied at Oxford. Upon his return he proved himself a capable if unexceptional administrator and was eventually appointed ambassador to France and then minister of education. Financially savvy and politically well connected, Mochiaki found capitalism as appealing as feudalism. His investments in railroads, insurance, and textiles provided him with ample income, and his status as a Meiji government official maintained his prestige.[30]

The case of Tokushima domain was remarkable for its explosive violence and for the intensity of Mochiaki's disaffection, but the underlying tensions were common to many domains. Many lords shared Mochiaki's sense that daimyo rule was a fool's errand, and daimyo such as Ikeda Yoshinori of Tottori and Tokugawa Yoshikatsu of Nagoya recommended dissolving the

FIGURE 4.2 Satsuma Military Officers. Note the combination of Western military uniforms and traditional samurai haircuts in this studio portrait of Satsuma officers. J. Paul Getty Museum, 84.XO.613.7.

domains in favor of a more powerful central government.[31] One of the few vocal defenders of traditional power structures was Shimazu Hisamitsu, father of the young daimyo of Satsuma. Hisamitsu regularly upbraided the new government for weakening daimyo authority and undermining traditional status distinctions. He fulminated against the adoption of Western dress, which failed to distinguish adequately between high- and low-born individuals; against the education of women, which he deemed contrary to orthodoxy; and against the intermarriage of commoners and samurai.[32] Given the size and military might of Satsuma, Hisamitsu's disaffection was intimidating, but his was a lonely voice. Rather than rally other daimyo to a common cause, he reveled in his own pugnacious denunciations of change.

While daimyo resistance to reform faded, the new government in Tokyo became increasingly aware of the need for centralized control. Military leaders, such as Yamagata Aritomo and Saigō Takamori, wanted troops that were loyal to the emperor, not individual domains. Diplomatically, the continuation of daimyo rule undermined the international reputation of the Meiji state. It was impossible to convince foreigners that Japan was becoming a respectable nation-state while Hisamitsu paraded through the capital with a samurai retinue in traditional dress. Financially, the central government could not control its budget without stipend reform and the direct collection of taxes. In civil affairs, the reform of samurai stipends was chaotic, with different strategies in each domain.

By mid-1871, the divisive question was not whether to dissolve the domains but what form of government to establish in their place. A few general objectives were widely shared: the Meiji state would need to combine ancient imperial sovereignty with international best practice. That meant some form of monarchy with a clear separation of powers. But the Meiji leadership struggled with the details. Should the state have a strong legislature? An independent judiciary? How many ministries and which would be the most powerful?[33] In 1871/7, the Meiji leadership finally agreed on the outlines of the new state. The formal structures were a fusion of ancient Japanese and modern Western forms. The upper-level institutions recalled the institutions of the ancient Japanese state. The supreme agency was the Council of State (*dajōkan*), which held paramount legislative, executive, judicial, and administrative power. The Council of State consisted of three chambers. The most powerful was the Grand Chamber (*sei'in*), with seven members: the Grand Minister (Sanjō Sanetomi), the Minister of the Right (Iwakura Tomomi), the Minister of the Left (vacant, but later held by Shimazu Hisamitsu) and four grand councilors (*sangi*). The Council also included two lesser chambers: the Chamber of the Left (*sa'in*) and the Chamber of the Right (*u'in*). These titles drew heavily on classical East Asian models. The terms "Council of State," "Grand Minister," and "Minister of the Right" were based on the ancient Nara-Heian court. In that way, the "new" government echoed the institutions of Tang China.

Beneath the Tang-style council was a cabinet system inspired by European models. The new cabinet structure had eight ministries: foreign, finance, military, education, industry, justice, imperial household, and religious affairs, or literally the Ministry of Shinto Deities (*jingishō*). The inclusion of a foreign ministry was the most striking example of European practice. In the ancient Tang and Nara governments, diplomatic affairs were handled by the Ministry of Rites (*reibushō*).

These two structures fit together imperfectly and reflected ongoing tensions within the Meiji settlement. Positions in the Council of State were held primarily by the old elite: court nobles and daimyo. The cabinet, by contrast, was staffed largely by low-ranking samurai. It was left unclear how the two sectors would interact. How closely would the Grand Chamber oversee the operation of the ministries? In practice, would the finance minister or the grand minister determine the budget? These were nettlesome questions, but even an imperfect centralized structure was deemed better than hundreds of regional authorities. With much trepidation, the government prepared to dismiss Japan's regional rulers. [34]

On 1871/7/14, the government announced that domains would be replaced with prefectures. The language of the decree once again reflected the tropes of cosmopolitan chauvinism and radical nostalgia. The decree abrogated daimyo tradition in the name of more ancient tradition. The emperor could not protect his subjects and make Japan "stand with the nations of the world" while relying on the conventions of daimyo rule. It was necessary, therefore, to secure a true return of authority to the emperor.[35] Daimyo would be well compensated for their lost income, but they would no longer rule. The Meiji government braced itself for violent reaction, but there was none. Demoralized, disorganized, and seduced by generous pensions, the last generation of daimyo quietly faded from the scene.

The dissolution of the domains marked the birth of the modern Japanese state. Samurai revolutionaries had swept aside the old regime and established, in its place, a new centralized government. That transition was peaceful largely because the daimyo themselves had lost faith in the institutions of the old regime. But the Meiji government had also ensured peace by deferring many challenges. The new government had hinted at radical change, but its reforms had not yet touched the lives of most Japanese. Farmers still paid taxes in much the same manner as their grandparents had done. The samurai still proudly wore two swords, as a public symbol of their superiority to commoners. Military and government appointments were still based primarily on hereditary privilege. The Meiji government had created a Japanese state but not yet a Japanese nation. That second stage of the Meiji revolution would produce a second wave of conflict and turmoil.

5

The Impatient Nation

THE DISSOLUTION OF the domains made the Meiji regime a centralized state, but more in name than in practice. The government had direct authority over all Japanese subjects and, in theory, it could reach every village in Japan. The remaining task was to use that power to turn Japanese subjects into Japanese nationals and to create a Japanese nation-state. For all its grand pronouncements, in 1871, the Meiji state barely touched the daily lives of most Japanese. There was no national taxation: the state received revenue from across Japan, but it was collected through thousands of different local systems. There was no national army, only an Imperial Guard cobbled together from the samurai troops of a few great domains. There was no national legal code. Education was still conducted primarily by local monks or in private academies. The government spoke in grand terms of the equality of all Japanese subjects, but in practice, daily life was still governed by conventional hierarchies. Samurai still lorded over commoners and wore two swords, their hereditary emblems of superior status. Pariah castes, such as *eta* and *hinin* (lit. "non-persons"), were still bound by long-standing restrictions on work and residence. As in the Tokugawa era, the Japanese people were united largely by a shared sense of difference, a common code of distinctions by status and region. The great project of creating a single Japanese nation remained to be done.

At the same time, the government hoped to secure its international legitimacy and revise the unequal treaties. Key provisions of the treaties symbolically marked Japan as a subjugated nation. Under the provision of extraterritoriality, for example, Westerners who committed crimes in Japan were tried in their own courts under their own laws. Such arrangements were common in treaties between the great powers and "uncivilized" nations, so the treaties implicitly marked Japan as culturally inferior.

More practically, under the unequal treaties, Japan could not set its own import or export tariffs. That limited the government's ability to raise revenue and to shape economic development. Finally, the treaties were an ever-present reminder of Japan's defeat. The Western powers had imposed the treaties through gunboat diplomacy, and that humiliation had undermined the Tokugawa shogunate. While the new Meiji government no longer sought to "expel the barbarian," it was eager to cleanse itself of that disgrace. The government therefore embarked on a diplomatic offensive to revise the treaties.

In pursuit of these goals, the Meiji leadership made a remarkable decision: it would split in half. Key officials would leave Japan and travel to the United States and Europe, explaining the Restoration to foreign leaders, learning about the West, and laying the groundwork for treaty revision. Meanwhile, a "caretaker government" (*rusu seifu*) would remain in Japan and carry on the domestic revolution. Thus, for almost two years, from November 1871 until September 1873, the story of the Japanese state is twofold. On the one hand, it is the story of the caretaker government in Tokyo, led by veterans of the Restoration such as Saigō Takamori, Itagaki Taisuke, and Etō Shinpei. On the other, it is the story of the Iwakura Mission, a massive embassy, named after its nominal leader, the court noble Iwakura Tomomi.

The distinct experiences of those two governments led to a political crisis. Under the best of circumstances, it would have been challenging to reintegrate the two halves of the government. But the two groups had developed starkly different understandings of how to build a powerful Japanese nation-state. The Iwakura Mission was stunned to witness the impact of the Industrial Revolution in America and Europe. In England, for example, railroads and factories had transformed daily life, creating astonishing levels of poverty and pollution, but also great wealth and national power. While the mission members were familiar with technological achievements such as the steam engine, they were amazed by the depth and breadth of England's industrial transformation. Massive modern factories seemed to be everywhere, and that raised a new set of questions. How could Japan to develop a comparable depth of infrastructure? How could the Meiji state create a new Japan, similarly crisscrossed by railroads and telegraph lines, with skies darkened by factory smoke? The idea that the Japanese state would need to promote specific technologies was not new. Even before the Meiji Restoration, domains such as Saga and Satsuma had promoted high-tech capital-intensive projects such as blast furnaces and shipyards. But the Ōkubo administration became convinced that the state would need to lead all aspects of Japanese industrialization, not just capital-intensive factories or infrastructure projects, such as railroads and telegraphs, but also the production of ordinary consumer goods such as ceramics and lacquer ware. That approach to economic development stemmed from a new perception that Japan was economically underdeveloped. It was poor in entrepreneurship as well as poor in capital. For all their samurai pride, members of the Iwakura Mission were struck by Japan's economic inferiority compared to what they were seeing. The caretaker government, by contrast, experienced no such shock. Accordingly, men like Etō imagined that economic parity with the West was close at hand. Japanese entrepreneurial energy merely needed to be unleashed by a new legal code.

The Iwakura Mission was also astonished by the decline of France and the rise of Germany. It toured Paris and Berlin after the 1870–71 Franco-Prussian War, in which Bismarck had diplomatically and militarily humiliated the most powerful state in continental Europe. That defeat sparked a steady Japanese reappraisal of France, which had supplied military and legal advisors to Japan in the 1870s. By the 1880s, however, Japanese advisors were increasingly German. Like the Industrial Revolution, the Franco-Prussian War was interpreted differently by the Iwakura Mission and the caretaker government. From Japan, the communards of the 1871 Paris Commune could be envisioned as a glorious fusion of republican ideals and samurai valor. Even after the French army had surrendered to Prussia, the proud men of Paris had fought on, concerned more with honor and love of country than with their lack of supplies. Was this not the apotheosis of patriotism? If ordinary shopkeepers and craftsmen fought with the valor of great warriors, clearly France was an ideal nation-state. Even in defeat, France was worthy of emulation. The Iwakura Mission, however, saw something much less glorious. The Third Republic was dysfunctional and struggling to pay reparations to Germany. Meanwhile, in Berlin, Otto von Bismarck was building a modern German army with French monies. The Iwakura Mission returned as converts of Prussian realpolitik. Wars were not about honor or high principle, however useful those ideas might be as propaganda. Nor were wars about scrambling for territory. Rather, war was a tool to be employed cautiously and judiciously in the expansion and consolidation of state power.

The political crisis of 1873 was thus a clash between two different visions of how to build a powerful Japanese nation-state. Did Japan need a strong state to lead its backward people? Or were the Japanese people, as members of a proud and powerful nation, ready to lead their state? Did the state need to emancipate its people or to guide them? This debate over the nature of government built on older tensions within classical Chinese thought. Were commoners fundamentally ignorant (*gumin*) and incapable of self-governance? Should the state, in its role as "parents of the people," uplift and reform their behavior? Or was it essential for the state to hear and respond to popular grievances? Was Confucius right when he asserted that a ruler defending his realm needed the confidence of his people more than either weapons or food?[1] Overlaid on these ancient questions were samurai notions of virtue and loyalty. Was a samurai's loyalty to his lord's person or to his lord's house? Could a loyal samurai disobey his lord's command in the name of higher abstract principles? And how could these traditions be carried forward in a world without daimyo or a shogun? Was a samurai's loyalty to the nation, the state, or the government? Japanese thinkers wrestled with these questions while integrating newer, Western notions of state sovereignty, human rights, and the equality of man. That intellectual struggle produced a syncretic but compelling body of thought drawing on the Confucian classics, samurai ethics, and European political thought.

Because of this hybridity, the 1873 Political Crisis does not map neatly onto conventional political distinctions. In much historical writing, the caretaker government is described as deeply conservative. Two key members of the caretaker government, Saigō Takamori and Etō Shinpei, were later involved in uprisings by tradition-minded samurai, and the caretaker government is therefore often associated with "reactionary opposition to modernization."[2] But contemporary observers saw something starkly different. The English-language *Japan Gazette*, for example, described the caretaker government as "republicans" and the Iwakura Mission as "monarchists."[3] That description would have startled members of both the Iwakura Mission and the caretaker government, who were united in their support for imperial sovereignty. But the *Gazette's* account stemmed from partisanship, not confusion or ignorance. The editor, John Reddie Black, was on close personal terms with the leaders of the caretaker government, and his son, Henry Black, became something of a fellow traveler in Japanese opposition politics. In using the term "republican," the *Gazette* was applauding the caretaker government's embrace of terms such as "rights" and "liberty."[4]

The Japan Weekly Mail, by contrast, opposed the caretaker government and took an opposite stance. It faulted them for recklessness. In an extended reference to Paul Bunyan's *Pilgrim's Progress,* it likened the government's impatience to the temptations of Satan. The Japanese government had imagined that some shortcut "would lead it abreast of the nations who have not only been centuries toiling along the path" but had also developed "increasing moral and intellectual force." The tempting illusion that Japan could rapidly catch up to the West was merely "the net of the Flatterer," the trickery of the devil.[5]

These contrasting accounts highlight different facets of the caretaker government. It was committed to republican ideals, arguing that a core duty of the state was to defend the rights and liberties of its people. It pursued radical egalitarian goals, attacking status, class, and gender distinctions. At the same time, its sense of rights was infused with the samurai sense of honor. Defending the "rights of the people" thus encompassed avenging slights to samurai honor. That expansive sense of "rights" led to a reckless foreign policy. By the time the Iwakura Mission returned in late summer 1873, the caretaker government was ready to start wars with both China and Korea. The caretaker government was equally impatient and reckless in domestic policy. Convinced that it could rapidly transform Japan into a world power, it pressed ahead at breakneck speed on military conscription, the abolition of status distinctions, religious indoctrination, and compulsory primary school education. Like other revolutionary regimes (French, Russian, and Chinese), it associated moderation and patience with cowardice and treason.

The members of the Iwakura Mission, by contrast, were committed to the steady and deliberate consolidation of state power. It would take generations, not months or years, for Japan to rival Western economic power and, in the interim, the Japanese people needed guidance more than liberation. How could Japanese commoners lead the state when they lacked an appreciation of the Industrial Revolution? The transformation of Japan into a great power would require not liberation but state leadership, especially in the economy. The Japanese people could enjoy civil rights but only under the aegis of a powerful, developmental state. In foreign policy, Japan would fight wars, but only as part of a coherent geopolitical strategy, not to avenge slights. In emulation of Prussia, the Iwakura Mission favored war only when the outcome was certain and a defeated enemy could be saddled with the bill.

The principal forces in modern Japanese politics emerged from the 1873 Political Crisis. In January 1874, soon after resigning from the government, key former officials issued a public call for an elected assembly, insisting that a strong Japan required broad participation in public affairs. That document marks the beginning of Japan's democracy movement. But those same men were also passionate supporters of wars against China and Korea, eager to build a Japanese empire. The 1873 Political Crisis thus birthed two entangled popular movements: democratic calls for representation and inclusion, and populist calls for mobilization and war. The victorious faction, led primarily by Ōkubo Toshimichi, was focused instead on state power over popular support. It created a powerful bureaucracy dedicated to industrial development, a forerunner of the Japanese developmental state. The antecedents of "Japan Inc.," the post–World War II growth-oriented alliance of business and government, emerged from the aftermath of the 1873 Political Crisis.

The Iwakura Mission

The Iwakura Mission had three overlapping mandates. First was to differentiate the Meiji government from the Tokugawa regime.[6] Second was to declare the Japanese government's eagerness to renegotiate the unequal treaties. Third was to learn firsthand about Western institutions. Those goals were complementary: by learning about Western institutions, the Mission hoped to convince Western governments that it was serious about domestic reform and thus different from the Tokugawa shogunate.

That triple agenda was first suggested by Guido Verbeck, a Dutch-born advisor to the Meiji government. When Verbeck learned that the new government was planning to dispatch a diplomatic mission to the West, he sent a detailed set of recommendations to Ōkuma Shigenobu, a Meiji official from Saga. Verbeck suggested that the embassy convey to Western diplomats Japan's desire to be "fully received and admitted to the society of nations as contemplated by International Law" and to achieve "a perfect political equality with the States of the West." But the embassy should also expect Western diplomats to reject those requests, insisting that Japan did not yet merit equal treatment. Western officials would argue that Japanese culture was simply too different and too insular. Japan's civil and criminal court system did not correspond to "western standards of justice," and Japanese law still prohibited Christianity and freedom of movement by foreigners. Verbeck proposed that the Mission engage these objections in earnest. It should request a written "enumeration of these supposed essential measures to be taken by his [Majesty's] Government for the establishment of political equality." It should be accompanied by several large study committees tasked with examining Western institutions. Those committees would compile exacting reports so the government could then have an informed debate on the course of domestic reform.[7]

Verbeck emphasized the importance of learning about the West from direct observation rather than texts. "There is something in the civilization of the West," he wrote, "that must be seen and felt in order to be fully appreciated." While the study of texts was valuable for understanding theories and principles, Western institutions were the result of "practice and experience," not just "abstract reason." Furthermore, the West abounded in both positive and negative examples, offering "in the greatest variety, excellences to be studied and imitated, as well as defects to be known and avoided." Verbeck's emphasis on direct observation is especially remarkable since he himself had served as a teacher in Saga domain's academy of foreign studies, where he taught English to several future Meiji leaders. He was thus directly familiar with the limits of a classroom education.[8] His emphasis on the impact of personal observation was prescient: the Iwakura Mission members were indeed transformed by their experiences abroad.

The Meiji government followed many of Verbeck's recommendations. The embassy was led by a high-ranking member of the government, Iwakura Tomomi, minister of the right and the most capable court noble in Japan. To mark the seriousness of the mission, Iwakura was given the formal appointment of envoy extraordinary-ambassador plenipotentiary (tokumei zenken taishi), while four other government leaders were named vice-ambassadors: Ōkubo Toshimichi, Kido Takayoshi, Itō Hirobumi, and Yamaguchi Naoyoshi.[9] Those appointments reflected the coalition of domains that toppled the shogunate: Ōkubo was from Satsuma, Kido and Itō from Chōshū, and Yamaguchi from Saga. The mission also included a large number of researchers and students: officials, staff, and students totaled more than 100 persons. Remarkably, Ōkuma, to whom Verbeck had addressed his recommendations, was excluded from the mission, squeezed out by more powerful figures.

The Iwakura Mission left Tokyo in late December 1871 (1871/11/23) and after two weeks in San Francisco crossed the United States on the newly completed transcontinental railroad. The Mission faced its first diplomatic challenge soon after arriving in Washington, DC. Secretary of State Hamilton Fish surprised the delegation with his willingness to consider several key Japanese requests, including tariff autonomy and the modification of extraterritoriality. Fish's conciliatory position was strategic. The United States was eager to distinguish its own ambitions in the Pacific from European colonialism, and Fish hoped to dramatize that point by making concessions to Japan in advance of the European powers. The United States was also eager to reassert its primacy in Japan's relations with the West. It had "opened" Japan in 1853 but then lost ground during the Civil War. Now, post-bellum, President Grant again wanted the reunited nation to "be the pioneer in the trade & commerce between Japan, China and the balance of the world."[10] Fish's spirit of conciliation stemmed from that ambition.

At the same time, Fish confounded the delegation with questions about their credentials. Were they authorized to sign a treaty or merely to begin initial consultation? Could they commit to a draft treaty, with the assumption that ratification would be a mere formality? The Japanese delegation was both delighted and confused. Fish seemed to be hinting at major treaty revisions, but such negotiations were beyond their mandate. In response to Fish's queries, the Iwakura Mission decided to request an enhanced mandate from Tokyo. In late March 1872 (1872/5/2) Ōkubo and Itō left Washington, DC, for Tokyo, to confer with the caretaker government and request authorization to negotiate new treaties. The caretaker government agreed to elevate Iwakura's credentials, and Ōkubo and Itō returned to Washington in late July (1872/6/17).[11] The Iwakura Mission seemed poised to bring home a diplomatic triumph: concessions on the unequal treaties.

Instead, the negotiations collapsed in acrimony. Full of optimism, but ignorant of Western diplomatic culture, the Iwakura Mission proposed to Fish a general conference in Europe on treaty reform. Fish was dismayed. His goal was to strengthen US-Japanese bilateral relations, not to send a US delegate to an international conference. A large multi-lateral conference would eclipse any special US-Japan relationship, so Fish read the Japanese proposal as a rejection of his earlier overtures. He became angry and distrustful. "It was not consistent with the dignity and self-respect" of the United States, he declared, to negotiate a treaty with Japan in Europe. Writing confidentially to Grant, he accused Iwakura of "prevarication" and "Oriental cunning." Through its ambition and inexperience, the Iwakura Mission had snatched defeat from the jaws of victory and irritated, rather than persuaded, US diplomats.[12] In his diary, Kido Takayoshi expressed utter despair: "Even though we have worked diligently for more than a hundred days . . . and two of our men have made a special trip to our country and back over 5000 *ri* of ocean and 3000 *ri* of plains and mountains . . . all of our effort have come to naught. . . . I can ill-endure my regret that after arriving here, through our haste, we brought things to this end."[13]

The failure of negotiations in Washington, DC, transformed the Iwakura Mission. Overreaching on treaty revision had actually worked against Japanese interests, so thereafter the mission erred on the side of caution. Indeed, the mission abandoned not only plans for a general conference in Europe but also any hope of prompt treaty revision. Instead, the Mission focused on its third goal: the detailed observation of Western institutions. Those observations reinforced the Mission's new focus on long-term strategy rather than quick results: it would take decades, not years, for Japan to rival Western economic power.

In letters back to Japan, Ōkubo explained how the firsthand observation of Europe had changed his understanding of Japan's place in the world. On the surface, it seemed that Japan was approaching a Western standard of "civilization." The Meiji government had begun universal education and established a new court system. There was telegraph service from Tokyo to Nagasaki and a railroad from Tokyo to Yokohama. But after months in Europe and America, all this now seemed superficial and insubstantial.[14] The extent of Western economic development was astonishing. In England, railways, roads, bridges, and canals stretched to remote corners of the country. There were enormous factories for every possible industry: shipbuilding, textiles, sugar refining, even a brewery in Birmingham that Ōkubo described as thirty miles long. That massive industrial base was beyond anything he imagined, but it was the key to Britain's wealth and power.[15] Building a strong Japanese nation-state would require building a similar industrial base.

Ōkubo's second discovery was the rise of Prussia and the relative decline of France. In the nascent German Empire, Bismarck was flush with victory over France and near the peak of his powers. In Ōkubo's account, the chancellor could propose legislation to the Reichstag fully confident that

FIGURE 5.1 Railroad from Shinbashi to Shinagawa from an 1875 guide to "famous places" by Hiroshige III. LACMA (16.16.5). Reprinted with permission.

it would be readily passed. When the Kaiser addressed the Reichstag, he was greeted with rapturous applause. Prussia had thus combined the dignity and stability of a monarchy with a popular assembly. Better still, the Reichstag could expand the Prussian military by spending an indemnity won from France. The principles of the Paris Commune might be noble, but Bismarck's realpolitik paid cold hard cash. Prussia, Ōkubo noted, was unlike anything he expected: vastly more advanced and impressive but still "simple and honest."[16]

France, by contrast, was in turmoil. Both the left and the right distrusted the provisional president Adolphe Thiers. Monarchists found him insufficiently conservative, while leftists blamed him for crushing the Paris Commune, so the assembly was united only in its contempt for Thiers. It voted to bar Thiers from speaking before the assembly and then passed a vote of no confidence. Ōkubo found these maneuvers absurd. How could a nation's president be banned from speaking to its parliament? If this was democracy in action, Ōkubo wanted none of it.[17] These experiences confirmed Ōkubo's older preferences for rule of law over popular assemblies.[18] Indeed, Ōkubo concluded that French, English, and American political models were inappropriate for Japan's level of development. It would be better to look to Russia and Prussia, which more closely matched Japan's level of "enlightenment" (kaika).[19]

Kido was similarly impressed by the virtues of order and stability. Upon his return, he authored an essay in the Japan Weekly Mail asserting that the French themselves were envious of the English. "Englishmen," he insisted, "make full use of those rights granted by the state." The French, by contrast, "make use of only half the rights bestowed upon them, while illicitly seeking to seize the rights they do not have." The result was chaos and a decline in national power.[20] Kido was also troubled by how Russia, Austria, and France had devoured Poland, exploiting its internal dissension. Both Poland and China, he observed, were wealthy and civilized, but domestic squabbling had led both to ruin.[21]

While the Mission was in Berlin on March 19, orders arrived from Tokyo requesting that Kido and Ōkubo return to Japan.[22] Sanjō Sanetomi, the nominal head of the caretaker government, was desperate for help. Sanjō was ostensibly the leader of the caretaker government, and within the rarified world of the imperial court nobility he outranked even Iwakura. But he lacked the practical political skills needed to contain factionalism within his own cabinet. After much discussion, the Mission decided to send Ōkubo back immediately; he arrived in Tokyo in early May. Kido, however, continued on to Russia as planned and did not return to Japan until July. When Iwakura and the rest of the mission reached Tokyo in September, after a leisurely passage through Southeast Asia, they arrived to find Japan in exuberant revolutionary turmoil.

The Caretaker Government

Like the Iwakura Mission, the members of the caretaker government came from the coalition of domains that had toppled the shogunate. The grand councilors of the Grand Chamber were Saigō Takamori (Satsuma), Itagaki Taisuke (Tosa), Ōkuma Shigenobu (Saga), and Etō Shinpei (Saga). Chōshū was represented by the acting heads of two powerful ministries: finance (Inoue Kaoru) and the army (Yamagata Aritomo). Unlike the Iwakura Mission, however, the caretaker government was committed to the rapid revolutionary transformation of Japan. Blissfully unaware of Western Europe's technological and material superiority, they anticipated Japan's swift rise to world power status. Ideologically, the caretaker government advocated individual liberty and equality but also the samurai virtues of duty and self-cultivation. While actively dismantling the hereditary privileges of the samurai estate, the caretaker government sought to create a Japanese nation that embodied the best of samurai tradition. For the men of the caretaker government, these goals were in harmony. The pursuit of self-interest and self-cultivation was fully compatible with duty, honor, and service to the greater good. That syncretic vision of politics and society, labeled "republicanism" by the *Japan Gazette*, might instead be termed "samurai populism": its vision of "rights" and "liberty" was suffused with a samurai sense of service. A samurai's greatness lay in both his individual talent and his selfless loyalty, and that became the basis of a new vision of self-reliance and patriotic self-sacrifice. Convinced that their policies would unleash the greatness of the Japanese people, the caretaker government had no fear of foreign wars, and in the fall of 1873 it was preparing to attack both Korea and Taiwan. Idealistic, passionate, and impatient, "samurai populism" was the opposite of the deliberate realpolitik now esteemed by the Iwakura Mission. That clash of visions fractured the Japanese government.

The force of "samurai populism" was most evident in the conscription of commoners. The imperial proclamation announcing conscription (1872/11/28) boldly declared that all Japanese were now equal in their rights and duties. This was described as a return to the ancient national armies of the Nara period, in which the emperor himself had purportedly led conscripted commoners. The samurai estate's long-standing monopoly on military service was faulted as an evil transgression of this ancient practice. Samurai themselves were denounced as arrogant idlers inclined to senseless violence. But this overt criticism of samurai tradition was balanced by a more quiet celebration of samurai culture: all Japanese would now "repay their country in blood."[23] That phrase resonated with the samurai sense that a vassal was obliged to repay his lord's munificence. Conscription would bring that noble sense of purpose to the masses. For many Japanese, however, the phrase was not ennobling but terrifying, since it suggested that the new national government was literally intent on taking their blood.[24]

The legal reforms of the caretaker government focused on rights, liberty, and individual autonomy. Etō Shinpei, justice minister and grand councilor, wrote that the primary purpose of a state was to defend the rights of its people. Patriotism stemmed from this principle: people would voluntarily defend the state in order to defend their own rights. Etō's policies reflected this belief in the power of a self-actualized Japanese people. In legal reform, he advocated the rapid adoption of the Napoleonic Code. The Japanese people, he reasoned, were ready to explode with entrepreneurial energy and could propel Japan to unprecedented wealth and power. But this popular energy was stifled by the Tokugawa legal system. Because Japan lacked a public legal code, rights and duties were unclear, and it was impossible for its people to avoid protracted litigation. Under a Western legal code, the people would know, clearly and definitively, how to do business. What were their rights to buy and sell property? To lease and to rent land? To issue and receive loans? Liberated from legal confusion, Japan's farmers and merchants could drive the nation forward.[25]

The caretaker government's policies on education were similarly radical. When the government announced compulsory primary education in 1872, it declared the primacy of the people over the state. It rejected the "evil" notion that the purpose of education was to help samurai directly serve the government. On the contrary, the purpose of education was individual self-improvement: to help individuals become prosperous and wise. Therefore, education would henceforth focus on law, politics, science, medicine, and practical matters in farming, public administration, business, and engineering rather than the memorization of classical texts.[26] Implicit in these reforms was the assumption that a wealthy and intelligent public would naturally strengthen the nation-state, so self-improvement constituted its own form of loyal service. Furthermore, education was for all, irrespective of gender or status, and the reforms vehemently denounced gender bias in education. In a statement to the Grand Chamber, education minister Ōki Takatō insisted that men and women were identical in their essential humanity and that boys and girls therefore deserved equal educational opportunities.[27] Similarly, education should be extended to all without regard to income. Japan's new educational system would uplift all children, and their knowledge would become the foundation of the Japanese state.[28] Filled with this sense of revolutionary potential, a majority of the caretaker government imagined that they could rapidly transform Japan. Catching up with the great powers merely involved unleashing the energy of the Japanese people.

The caretaker government saw individual rights and self-interest as fully compatible with a stable and harmonious social order. Etō, for example, carried over from Confucianism the conviction that distinct social positions were essential to social harmony: all people might be equal, but they were not the same. The problem, for Etō, was that in Tokugawa Japan, distinction had become mired in hereditary ascriptive status, so the social order was based on ancestry rather than ability or function. Samurai inherited distinctive rights and duties, irrespective of their ability to fight or govern. For Etō, a comprehensive civil code such as the Napoleonic Code would match legal distinctions to ability and achievement. Lenders and debtors, renters and tenants, minor children and propertied adults, would each have different rights and duties based on their social roles rather than on their birth status. Legally clarifying the rights of all Japanese subjects would thus lead to order rather than disorder.

Etō compared such legal clarity to an effective military command structure, likening unmarried men to new recruits and married men to trained soldiers. By contrast, traditional Japanese society was like a motley gang of soldiers whose appointments were unrelated to duties and responsibilities. This militarized vision of liberty was part of "samurai populism." In Etō's conception, ending hereditary samurai status would actual help realize samurai values by creating a society of loyal, self-actualized but dutiful national subjects. Samurai values could be redeemed, paradoxically, through the egalitarian elimination of samurai status.[29]

Even before the return of the Iwakura Mission, dissenting members of the caretaker government criticized this focus on liberty and equality. Inoue Kaoru, for example, rejected the notion that Japan's future lay in the emancipation of its people. He argued instead that there were two elements to national progress: the government and the people. The great nations of Europe relied on the resourcefulness of their people, and the caretaker government was trying to emulate that approach. But the Japanese people were simply not that sophisticated. Japanese merchants haggled over petty profits instead of engaging in world trade. Japanese craftsmen were ignorant of modern machinery, and Japanese farmers relied on the local gentry for their knowledge of agriculture. The samurai were supposedly the "parents of the people," but they were, in fact, ignorant of both warfare and public administration. It would take years to raise the Japanese people to Western standards. In the interim, the rashness of the caretaker government's reforms was toxic, like a too-potent medicine that kills rather than cures the patient. The government needed to move cautiously and to emphasize state power over popular support.[30]

Terashima Munenori, vice-minister of foreign affairs (*gaimu daibu*), was also dismayed by his colleagues' radical views. He explicitly denigrated their pronouncements on the "so-called right to freedom" and "natural liberty." Like Inoue, he argued that the government needed first to build state power. True liberty was possible only under the aegis of a strong state that "collects taxes fairly and equitably, runs impartial courts, and governs everyone fairly and equitably so as to calm the hearts of the people." Terashima was especially alarmed that the caretaker government had connected military conscription with equality and liberty. All Japanese were now, supposedly, equal in both their rights and their obligations to the state. But Terashima doubted that Japanese farm boys and shop clerks were ready to become soldiers. Prussia, he noted, had a conscript army, but those recruits had learned patriotism and military drill in school. In order to have a conscript army, Japan needed to emulate Prussia and produce loyal and dutiful subjects instead of confusing the populace with vapid talk of "rights" and "freedoms."[31]

This clash of visions was paralleled by a clash of budget priorities. Men like Inoue demanded that the government stay on budget and they viewed fiscal stability as key to national strength. Transforming Japan through education was well and good, but where was the money? The ministry of education wanted roughly 3 million yen to provide free and compulsory primary schooling, but Inoue argued that the treasury could afford perhaps 1 million. Inoue fought a similar battle with the justice ministry over the costs of a new court system. These struggles were complicated by confusion over administrative jurisdiction. It was unclear, for example, which agency had final say over the budget. In theory, the Grand Chamber was superior to all the ministries, but some of its most powerful members, including Saigō and Itagaki, had no interest in finance. In that power vacuum, the finance ministry asserted authority over the general budget, but other agencies contested that claim. Unable to resolve its budget

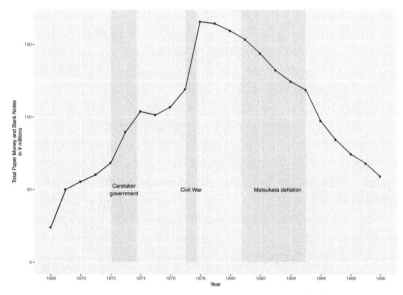

FIGURE 5.2 Growth of the Paper Money Supply in early Meiji-era Japan. Data from Matsukata, *Report on the Adoption of the Gold Standard in Japan*, 29, 97–98.

priorities, the government employed the stopgap measure of printing more money. Between 1872 and 1874, the Japanese paper money supply increased by almost 50 percent.[32] Various ministries battled over other issues as well. The finance ministry claimed authority over all regional civil servants, but the justice ministry insisted on authority over judges and judicial officers. The two ministries both asserted the right to collect court fines. The ministry of industry was entrusted with the development of railroads and telegraph, but it fought with the finance ministry over basic roads and bridges.[33]

In addition to internal dissension, the caretaker government also faced popular opposition. In particular, military conscription provoked fierce resistance throughout Japan. The initial impact of conscription on most households was minor because of extensive exemptions for family hardship. But the government's radical language was inflammatory. It referred to conscription as a "blood tax." That was intended as a boldly egalitarian, patriotic turn of phrase. All Japanese were now equal in their rights and freedoms, and they were therefore also equal in their duty to pay taxes. Military service was also a tax, paid by risking one's own lifeblood.[34] Such language resonated with samurai notions of duty and courage, but villagers interpreted the term literally and concluded that army recruiters were collecting blood from young men.

Rural communities were also outraged by reforms that overturned traditional status distinctions and taboos: new hairstyles, new regulations on cattle slaughter, and the elimination of distinctions between commoners and lower castes such as *eta*. The promotion of new Western hairstyles for men, for example, seemed to invert the conventional social order. In the Tokugawa era, most adult men shaved the front and crown of their heads, grew their hair longer on the sides and back, and then gathered that longer hair into a bundle, which was dressed and flipped forward toward the crown. The Western hairstyle promoted by the Meiji government, by contrast, featured short hair, commonly with a part. But that "new" style resembled the hairstyle of the *hinin*, an outcaste group. The seemingly minor issue of men's hairstyles was thus connected to a deeper struggle over status and privilege. From the perspective of the Meiji elite, abolishing status distinctions was part of creating a single, unified Japanese nation. Hinin were no longer "outcastes" but equally Japanese subjects and part of the new Japanese nation-state. But for tens of thousands of villagers, these reforms were an assault on the fabric of society.[35] Tokyo was wiping away distinctions between the ritually clean and unclean. In several locations, anger over conscription, new schools, and cultural changes coalesced to produce massive protests. In the summer of 1873, over 60,000 people were arrested in massive protests in western Japan.[36]

Education reform provoked dissent both within the government and without. Although the finance ministry reduced the education budget by more than 50 percent, the education ministry refused to scale back its plans. Instead, it began education reform without sufficient revenue, shifting the cost to localities.[37] Across Japan, villagers were required to pay for an educational system they did not like or understand. In more prosperous rural communities, local Confucian educators were a source of pride, but new regulations required the abolition of all existing schools. In its desire to "liberate" the population, the government antagonized many local elites. By forcing the population to be "free," they were attacking respected local leaders and institutions. The response was a wave of attacks on new schools.[38]

The government's radical urgency extended to textbooks. Conventional education focused largely on basic literacy and the memorization of classical texts, so there were no appropriate local materials in other fields. The government scrambled to translate foreign, largely American, primary school texts, such as the popular *Wilson Reader*. The strange result was that Japanese primary school texts featured stories of children playing baseball, stories about George Washington, and awkward adaptations of Christian prayers, but relatively little about Japan. The Meiji emperor received only one line in Japan's first modern history textbook. The ministry of education also recommended works written for adult audiences, such as Fukuzawa Yukichi's *Conditions in the West* (*Seiyō jijō*) and *An Encouragement of Learning* (*Gakumon no susume*). These were influential, widely read books, and *An Encouragement of Learning* distilled many of the ideals behind the 1872 reforms. Its famous opening line declared the fundamental equality of man: "It is said that heaven creates no man above other men and creates no man below other men." Any distinctions not based on educational accomplishments were thus illegitimate. Further, individuals could best serve the nation and common good by pursuing their own advancement through education. But while the text eloquently expressed the goals of education reform, it was written for adults and was likely baffling to most children seeking basic literacy.[39]

There was similar turmoil in jurisprudence. Japanese courts began issuing bold rulings, although the justice ministry was struggling with two incompatible legal codes: French and Chinese. In criminal law, judges worked from the "New Legal Compendium" (*Shinritsu kōryō*) of 1871, which was based on a synthesis of Ming and Qing Chinese law. But in civil law, the Justice Ministry was working on a translation of the Napoleonic Code. That split reflected the dual nature of Restoration ideology: it was both a return to the ancient Japanese past and an embrace of state-of-the-art Western models. Japan's oldest law code, the Taihō Code of 701, was based on Tang-era law, so a return to the past meant a reevaluation of Chinese models. Beginning in 1869, the Meiji government charged specialists in Chinese law with "updating" criminal law based on Ming and Qing codes. But in civil law, reformers looked instead to European models of reason and justice.

These two approaches were irreconcilable. Chinese law conflicted not only with European law but also with the Meiji government's own decrees. The Meiji government had eliminated status distinctions, but the New Legal Compendium provided for different punishments based on class. For the same crime, a noble would be confined to his home while a commoner would be beaten with a small cane. As justice minister, Etō attempted to resolve these discrepancies, but his reforms created further turmoil. He ordered a draft revision of the criminal code, replacing beatings with imprisonment, but the revised code still linked punishments to hereditary status.[40] At the same time, Etō pushed ahead with plans for the rapid implementation of the Napoleonic Code, despite the warnings of his own staff. They were struggling to develop consistent Japanese translations of terms such as "civil rights" (*droit civil*).[41] The process was so rushed that even the government's French legal advisor, Georges Hilaire Bousquet, lamented the "inanity" of the project.[42] In the absence of a fully revised civil code, Etō nonetheless pushed ahead with an edict allowing Japanese subjects to sue their own government. This infuriated other officials, who viewed it as both reckless and as an assault on their administrative prerogatives.[43]

The government's religious reforms also provoked turmoil. The Meiji government gave official support to the anti-Buddhist sentiments of nativist ideologues, who insisted on Shinto purity. But many Japanese religious sites, including the famous Tokugawa mausoleum at Nikkō, had long featured both Buddhist and Shinto icons. For laypeople, that syncretism was familiar and unproblematic. By analogy, few Americans today think of Christmas trees as a Christian perversion of an ancient and "pure" Celtic Yule tradition, or of Easter eggs as a corruption of Mediterranean fertility rites. Japanese nativists, however, sought just such a "return" to a "pure" Shinto, purged of Buddhist influence. In Mito domain, attacks on Buddhist temples began in the 1840s, and under the Meiji government this briefly became a national policy. Thousands of Buddhist temples were either destroyed completely or ransacked, "cleansed" of Buddhist influence, and recategorized as Shinto shrines.[44]

The caretaker government added to this turmoil with a campaign to promote a new, syncretic state religion. Although largely Shinto in orientation, the campaign employed a diverse group of evangelists, including Buddhist priests, itinerant storytellers, actors, and lay preachers. Like the Cult of the Supreme Being in revolutionary France, the new religion was designed to synthesize existing practices with reason and patriotism. In Japan, the campaign focused on "Three Great Teachings": respect for the gods and love of country; the principles of "Heaven and the Way of Man"; and reverence for the emperor. While the campaign invoked the sun goddess Amaterasu, well known and revered throughout Japan, it also emphasized obscure Shinto gods, familiar only to religious scholars and philologists. Chapbooks issued to official evangelists thus insisted on reverence for the obscure Shinto diety Amenominakanushi no kami and also the patriotic duty of compliance with military conscription, public education, and national taxation. Japanese commoners were alternately bemused, bored, and alarmed by this new government creed. The syncretism was so radical and strange that in northeastern Japan, locals attacked a group of government evangelists after mistaking them for Christians. Paralyzed by the incoherence and complexity of its mandate, the government's Great Teaching Institute earned the ignominious nickname "bureau of indecision."[45]

The turmoil provoked by the caretaker government extended to quotidian issues such as the measurement of time. In late 1872, the government announced that Japan would abandon the traditional lunar-solar calendar in favor of the Gregorian calendar. The government acted with customary frenzy. Less than a month before the change, on 1872/11/9, the government decreed that the second day of the twelfth month (1872/12/2) would be followed by New Year's Day of the following year, rather than the third day of the twelfth month. The reform thus eliminated almost an entire month at the end of 1872. In its public decree, the government appealed to lofty ideals: the complexity of the older calendar was decried as an impediment to the "advancement of human understanding." But calendar reform also reflected the caretaker government's financial distress. By ending the year early in the twelfth lunar month, the government shaved one month of salaries from its 1872 budget.[46]

Still more disturbing, the government was unsure whether it had also adopted the Western workweek along with the Gregorian month and year. In the traditional Japanese urban work schedule, every fifth day was dedicated to the settling of outstanding accounts and the following day was treated as a day off. Thus the 1st, 6th, 11th, 16th, 21st, and 26th of each month were holidays. This was commonly known as a "one-six holiday" schedule. By contrast, the Western division of time into seven-day units was rooted in the biblical story of creation: God created the world in six days and then rested on the seventh. Nonetheless, several Japanese ministries advocated adopting the six-day Western workweek so as to better coordinate with Western advisors. As early as 1871 the military had requested making Sunday a holiday to match its foreign employees' schedules.[47] The justice ministry and the finance ministry agreed, but the foreign ministry wanted consistent schedules across all government agencies.[48] The ministry of education itself was internally divided. It adopted Sunday as a holiday in 1872 and instituted a new curriculum based on weeks, although it was unclear how many days were in a "week."[49] But it then reversed itself and returned to the conventional "one six" schedule.[50]

In April 1873, the ministry of education attempted to reconcile the foreign nature of the seven-day week with Japanese tradition. According to the ministry's calculations, Emperor Jinmu had founded the Japanese empire 2,533 years earlier, on a Saturday. The ministry therefore argued that a seven-day week with Saturdays off would be both practical and reflect the eternal virtues of the imperial line.[51] Unfortunately, the ministry's suggestions were inconsistent. While they advocated making Saturday a holiday based on the original date of Jinmu's ascension to the throne, they also advocated making February 11 a national holiday, Empire Day (*Kigensetsu*), based on the same calculations. Under the Gregorian calendar, however, February 11 could fall on any day of the week. In 1874, *Kigensetsu* would fall on a Wednesday; in 1875, on Thursday; in 1876, on a Friday; and in 1877, on a Sunday. *Kigensetsu* would not, in fact, fall on a Saturday until 1882. Nor did ministry officials consider the problem of having foreign employees, who were overwhelmingly Christian, take Saturday, rather than Sunday, as a holiday. The result of these reforms was widespread confusion, contained only by the still-limited reach of the government.[52]

The caretaker government sought to legitimize this maelstrom of reform through unprecedented public displays of the emperor. For centuries, imperial authority had rested on an aura of remoteness and inaccessibility, but the Meiji leadership now sought the opposite. Instead of keeping the monarch removed from his people behind a "jeweled curtain," the Meiji government wanted to glorify him through public rituals, making the young sovereign an emblem of progress and reform.[53] From June (1872/5/23) to August 1872 (1872/7/12), the Meiji emperor did a grand tour of western Japan, visiting Osaka, Kobe, Nagasaki, Kumamoto, and Kagoshima. His itinerary reflected the caretaker government's vision of a modern monarch. He left the palace on horseback rather than being carried in a palanquin, and he wore a new Western-style swallowtail uniform. He boarded a steam, ironclad warship flying the Japanese national flag and was saluted by a Japanese navy band. He toured factories and observed the manufacture of new products, such as Western-style umbrellas. He visited a new middle school, heard the students practice arithmetic and foreign languages, and met with foreign teachers. For traditionalists, such a public display of the emperor was both dangerous and unseemly, but that break with convention was one goal of the tour. In an address to out-of-office court nobles in Kyoto, the emperor declared the need for radical change. In order for Japan to stand with the Great Powers, the Japanese people needed to be united and embrace knowledge from around the world. The court nobility could advance that cause by discarding outdated customs, assiduously studying "the world's enlightenment" (*udai kaika*), and thereby becoming role models for the people. That decree turned the nobility's self-image upside down. The emperor no longer valued them as repositories of convention but as trailblazers of new knowledge.[54]

The imperial grand tour was a great success, but such public rituals could not contain either popular opposition to reform or dissent within the government itself. When the Iwakura Mission members returned in mid to late 1873, they were alarmed by what they saw as reckless and misdirected reforms. The caretaker government, in its eagerness to transform Japan, had seemingly abandoned any sense of long-term planning or coordination. Different ministries were fighting each other. When the finance ministry cut the justice ministry's budget, the justice ministry retaliated with corruption charges against the finance minister. A flood of contradictory edicts was undermining the government's credibility, and the pursuit of radical change was stoking open popular rebellion. For the caretaker government, this was the normal tumult of a great revolution. From the perspective of the Iwakura Mission, however, Japan was careening toward national ruin. Still more alarming than the caretaker government's domestic policies was its foreign policy. The Iwakura Mission returned to find the government preparing for war.

The Foreign Crisis

While the Iwakura Mission was abroad, focusing on Japanese relations with the Western powers, the caretaker government sought to recast Japanese relations with its East Asian neighbors. How would the new Meiji government replace the long-standing network of Tokugawa-Chosŏn-Qing diplomatic relations? Korea, Japan, and China had remained at peace by ignoring and evading questions of sovereignty and territoriality. But those early-modern arrangements, the early-modern Northeast Asian international order, could not be reconciled with the Western international order. European international politics allowed for both equally sovereign states and colonial empires, but it was hostile toward ill-defined spheres of state power. How would the Meiji state, the Chosŏn dynasty, and the Qing Empire define their relationships in that new world order? In foreign policy, as in domestic policy, the caretaker government sought a swift radical transformation. They would quickly settle all of Japan's outstanding diplomatic and territorial disputes, even at the risk of war.

The belligerence of the early Meiji state was driven by multiple forces. In part, it was an emulation of Western imperialism, which provided ample precedent for attacking China and Korea on the thinnest of pretenses. In 1856, for example, Great Britain began a four-year war in China over a purported insult to the Union Jack. In 1866, France attacked Korea in retaliation for the execution of Catholic missionaries, who had entered Korea in violation of local law. In 1871, the United States provoked a confrontation by entering Korean territorial waters without authorization. Early Meiji policy was thoroughly informed by these precedents, prompting the historian Robert Eskildsen to describe Japanese policy as "mimetic imperialism."[55] Beyond this inspiration, the caretaker government was also driven by samurai populism. Within that discourse, insults to the Japanese state were also insults to samurai honor, attacks on the rights of Japanese subjects, and affronts to the majesty of the imperial house. That heady mix of revolutionary ardor and samurai bravado inspired a reckless approach to foreign affairs. Convinced of the righteousness of their cause, the caretaker government could not imagine how attacking China and Korea might weaken the new Meiji state. When the returning Iwakura Mission members counseled prudence and caution, the caretaker government mocked them for weakness and cowardice.

Key issues in Japan-Chinese relations had been partly resolved by the Sino-Japanese Friendship and Trade Accord (*Nisshin shūkō jōki*), negotiated in 1871.[56] But many in Japan viewed that agreement as an embarrassing blunder. Japanese diplomats had embarked for Beijing confident that they could impose on China a Western-style unequal treaty. They used, as a model for their draft, the treaty between Prussia and the Qing, which provided for extraterritoriality, access to the Chinese interior, and most-favored nation status. But in Beijing, the Japanese delegation was thoroughly outmaneuvered by their Chinese counterparts.

The Qing delegation, led by Li Hongzhang, dismissed the Japanese draft entirely. Li was not only a seasoned diplomat but also an accomplished scholar and battle-hardened general. He convinced the Japanese envoys to embrace a new framework for East Asian relations. Neither Japan nor China would seek special privileges. Instead, they would act as equals and defend each other against "injustice and insults." Outmaneuvered by Li, Japanese representatives returned to Tokyo with an agreement contrary to their original instructions: rather than imposing Western-style imperialism on China, they had agreed to a vague Sino-Japanese alliance against unnamed third parties. China, rather than Japan, had dictated how Sino-Japanese relations would be reconciled with new, Western diplomatic norms. The words "mutual assistance" against "injustice and insults" were especially troublesome and prompted the British consul to ask if Tokyo had concluded a military alliance with Beijing. The Sino-Japanese treaty thus threatened to disrupt Japanese relations with the Great Powers. Japanese officials wanted to renegotiate the accord, but Li refused. Japan agreed to confirm the accord, but only after receiving assurances that China would not interpret "mutual assistance" as a military alliance.[57]

Although the caretaker government was prepared to ratify the treaty, it wanted to win concessions on other issues. The first was symbolic: how would China receive representatives of the Meiji state? The second was territorial. How would Japan and China reconcile their overlapping claims on the Ryukyu archipelago? The caretaker government's foreign minister, Soejima Taneomi, was determined to press China on both these fronts. Contrary to the spirit of the Friendship and Trade Accord, he sought to impress the Qing with Japanese military prowess. Soejima planned to arrive in Tianjin for the official treaty ratification aboard Japan's most fearsome warship, the *Kōtetsu*, a French-built ironclad.[58] To Soejima's chagrin, the *Kōtetsu* could not navigate the shallow channels near Tianjin and he was forced to arrive aboard an American steamer.

Despite this failed attempt at a dramatic entrance, Soejima pressed ahead on other powerful symbols, such as diplomatic protocol. Soejima insisted that his credentials as foreign minister made him superior to the Western diplomats in Beijing, who were merely ambassadors or envoys.[59] Soejima therefore insisted on precedence in any joint meeting with the Qing emperor. At the same time, Soejima made himself an ally of the Western powers in their objections to Chinese protocol. For centuries, the Western powers had objected to the Chinese tradition of the kowtow, which required that foreign envoys kneel and prostrate themselves before the emperor. That ritual marked the supremacy of the Chinese monarch to all other sovereigns.[60] The Qing court had officially abandoned the kowtow in 1860, but the recently ascended Tongzhi emperor had not yet held his first audience. Western diplomats in Beijing were therefore anxious to see if the Qing court would fulfill its promise to comply with European diplomatic norms. On these questions of protocol, Soejima won a resounding success. When the Tongzhi emperor received foreign representatives on June 29, 1873, Soejima was the first to present his credentials. He entered the Qing imperial reception alone and was followed by the European representatives, who entered as a group.[61] That ceremony symbolically reversed Li Hongzhang's diplomatic triumph in the Sino-Japanese Friendship and Trade Accord. Li had specified the textual terms of the first Western-style

Sino-Japanese treaty, but Soejima had triumphed in a spectacle before a Western audience. Japan had led the Western powers in forcing the Qing to abandon its ritual superiority. Soejima's triumph was acclaimed by the world press. The *New York Herald*, for example, wrote that while Western countries had long sought to be received by the Qing emperor, "Japan has held the key of this *sesame* and . . . has just applied it to the lock of Chinese diplomacy."[62]

Soejima also tried to advance Japanese territorial claims to Ryukyu and Taiwan. Japan's claim to Ryukyu stemmed from Satsuma's 1609 conquest of the Shō kingdom, but its claim to Taiwan was new. The two claims were connected by an 1871 incident in which Taiwanese aboriginals, members of the Paiwan tribe, killed fifty-four Ryukyuans after they were shipwrecked near the village of Mudan.[63] Soejima planned to press the Chinese state for redress on the Ryukyuans' behalf, insisting that the Ryukyuans were Japanese subjects. If China agreed to punish the Paiwan, it could be read as an acknowledgment that the victims of the Mudan Incident were Japanese. If China declined, then Japan would have cause to attack Taiwan in order to "punish" the "savage" Paiwan on behalf of Japan. If China disavowed legal responsibility for the Paiwan, then Japan could stake its own territorial claim to the island.[64]

Soejima's expansionist strategy combined Satsuma samurai bravado with the logic of Western imperialism. His plan to colonize Taiwan was inspired by an American advisor, Charles W. Le Gendre (1830–1899), a decorated Civil War officer and former American consul in Amoy.[65] Le Gendre had become concerned with the east Taiwan coast in 1866, when aboriginals killed American shipwreck survivors. Le Gendre then led a joint Chinese-American military expedition into aboriginal territory and successfully negotiated a treaty with Tokitok, chief of the Paiwan tribe. The agreement provided refuge to any future shipwreck survivors who waited on shore and raised a red flag. [66] The Paiwanese had followed that accord in 1869 and 1870, but in 1871, the Ryukyuans had unwittingly violated the treaty by wandering into the hills.[67]

The Mudan Incident convinced Le Gendre that a foreign power needed to seize and "civilize" Taiwan in order to guarantee maritime safety. Remarkably, Le Gendre did not question the kindness or the integrity of the Paiwan chief Tokitok. Rather, he doubted the aging chief's ability to rein in younger rivals, for whom headhunting was a rite of manhood. He had still less faith in the Qing.[68] The Chinese government claimed suzerainty over Taiwan, but it could not guarantee the safety of shipwreck survivors, or even erect a lighthouse in aboriginal territory. If China's claim to Taiwan was empty, then some civilized power needed to seize control of the region to ensure safe navigation in the western Pacific. "Humanity," Le Gendre wrote, "makes it a law to civilized nations to see that that portion of Formosa is kept clear of any of the inhospitable hordes that infest it." If China "has not the ability or the power to perform the task, the foreign powers will have to take the case in hand."[69] Since his career in the US diplomatic service seemed stalled and the United States had explicitly rejected action in Taiwan, Le Gendre offered his services to the Meiji state in late 1872.[70]

Le Gendre convinced Soejima that Japan had a legitimate claim to Taiwan under international law. Soejima, in turn, convinced the caretaker government that the Qing had given Japan a freehand not only in Taiwan but also in Korea. But the basis for Soejima's claims was astonishingly thin. The Qing did not renounce control over either Ryukyu or Taiwan and did not even recognize the victims of the Mudan Incident as Japanese. The Ryukyuans were Chinese, according to the Qing. In Soejima's account, however, Qing representatives referred in passing to some aboriginals in eastern Taiwan as "not yet subjugated" and "uncivilized." In Soejima's reading, this became a declaration that the Qing had renounced effective control over the Pacific coast of Taiwan.[71] Soejima offered an equally strained interpretation of Chinese-Korean relations. Qing representatives expressed a desire to maintain Korea's traditional position as a tributary state. In Soejima's reading, this became a Qing renunciation of Chinese interest in Korean affairs. In neither case were these remarks documented in an official transcript. Nonetheless, Soejima returned to Japan in late July 1873 convinced that the Qing had given Japan a free hand in both Korea and Taiwan.[72]

The caretaker government accepted Soejima's account of his mission with remarkable credulity. Ōkuma Shigenobu questioned whether it was wise, in the absence of a written record, to act on Soejima's interpretation of Chinese statements.[73] But most of the caretaker government was eager to contrast Soejima's accomplishments with the struggles of the Iwakura Mission. While the Iwakura Mission was foundering, the caretaker government was building a Japanese empire. Soejima's account also fed a growing hunger among samurai for some sort of foreign military action. Such feelings were especially strong in Satsuma, where the memory of foreign conquests was a part of local political culture.[74] Most Satsuma samurai learned to read and write by transcribing "Tale of a Tiger Hunt" (*Toragari monogatari*), an account of how brave warriors from Satsuma brought back a live tiger from Korea as tribute for Hideyoshi in 1594.[75] Satsuma also remained deeply invested in its 1609 conquest of Ryukyu. In 1867, for example, Satsuma sent emissaries to France with credentials that referenced Ryukyu but not the Tokugawa or Japan: "His Highness Matsudaira Shuri no Daibu, Minamoto Shigehisa, Ruler of Ryukyu." For the Paris Exposition Universelle, the Satsuma delegation struck medals reading "the Kingdoms of Satsuma and Ryukyu."[76]

Soejima's account also catalyzed a growing hostility toward Korea. Japanese-Korean tensions had been growing since the last days of the Tokugawa shogunate and intensified under the new Meiji government.[77] The Yi court wanted to maintain the status quo wherein intermediaries, such as officials from Tsushima, handled Japanese-Korean relations. Under that arrangement, the Japanese trading post in Pusan, the *waegwan* (J. *wakan*), was administered not by the Tokugawa shoguns but by the daimyo of Tsushima, and Japanese-Korean relations avoided the Japanese imperial house entirely. The Meiji state, however, insisted that Korea accept diplomatic correspondence from the Japanese emperor. That demand made no sense in Pusan or Seoul. Who was this emperor and why hadn't the Tokugawa or the Sō mentioned him before? After two centuries of peaceful relations why was Japan demanding recognition of a different sovereign? In Japan, however, Korea's refusal to recognize the emperor was interpreted as an affront to the imperial house and a challenge to the Meiji state's legitimacy, and there was broad support for some sort of punitive action. At the extreme, some argued that international turmoil warranted a Japanese conquest of Korea. The Russian occupation of Aso Bay on Tsushima in 1861, the defeat of China in the "Arrow War" of 1856–60, and the belligerence of the Western powers in Korean waters all suggested a collapse of the Northeast Asian international system. As early as 1861, scattered voices argued that Japan should confront that power vacuum by building its own empire starting with Korea.[78]

Japanese-Korean tensions came to a head in May 1873, when Meiji officials arrived in Pusan in Western-style military uniforms. Korean officials took insult at this violation of tradition, described the changes as "shameless," and stopped supplying *waegwan*. The caretaker government began discussing a punitive strike against Korea to avenge these insults.[79] The caretaker government approached the Korean standoff with a dangerous mix of samurai bravado, nationalist cant, and revolutionary ardor. A vocal faction of samurai hoped for a chance to redeem their lost honor. They had failed to repel the "Western barbarians," but perhaps they could smite a disrespectful neighbor. There were even private plans for war against Korea from disgruntled samurai in the southwest.[80] This bellicose samurai rhetoric dovetailed with the logic of gunboat diplomacy. In 1856, for example, the British had attacked China on the thinnest of pretexts: a purported insult to the Union Jack. By that standard, Japan had ample cause for war: Korean officials had insulted representatives of the Japanese government and refused to provide supplies to the *waegwan*. Examining Western precedent, foreign ministry officials determined that military retaliation was justified under international law.[81]

Driven forward by such arguments, in August 1873 the government approved a plan to send Saigō Takamori to Korea as a special emissary. Saigō was a paradoxical figure, who straddled seemingly irreconcilable political positions. He was widely respected as an icon of traditional samurai virtues: loyalty, courage, and frugality. But as a leader of the caretaker government he had endorsed the conscription of commoners. Saigō was acutely pained by how the Restoration had brought into conflict his multiple commitments and loyalties: to his comrades; to Satsuma, his homeland; to his daimyo, Shimazu Tadayoshi; to his daimyo's father, the dyspeptic Hisamitsu; to the young Japanese emperor; and to the Japanese empire. He viewed the embassy to Korea as a chance to reconcile these conflicts in a final act of glory. He would try to convince the Yi court to recognize the Japanese imperial government. If Korean officials agreed, he would return in triumph, bringing glory to the imperial throne. If Korean officials refused, he would press his case until they killed him, giving Japan a just cause for war. In either case, he would have acquitted his duties as both a Satsuma samurai and an imperial servant.

Kido and Ōkubo, recently returned from Europe, were appalled by the recklessness of this plan. Ōkubo criticized the government's lack of strategy and foresight. Had anyone considered the consequences of war? Had anyone tallied the costs? Would the government raise taxes, issue bonds, or just print money? Had the government prepared war materiel? And did the caretaker government imagine that an invasion of Korea would not draw in the great powers? Were they prepared to fight China, Russia, or Great Britain? More broadly, Ōkubo criticized the caretaker government's vision of national strength. While Japan needed to defend its national honor, it could only do so if it were wealthy and powerful. True national strength required promoting industrialization, increasing exports, and reducing the debt. That would take years, and a precipitous attack on

Korea would only weaken Japan. Rather than securing Japan's sovereignty, a war would invite foreign meddling in Japanese affairs.[82]

The 1873 crisis was thus a clash of worldviews. Those pressing for an attack on Korea saw war as a tool of national mobilization. What better way to unite the Japanese people than a war in the name of Japanese honor? Such arguments fused samurai swagger with the newer language of imperialist jingoism. The opponents of a Korean campaign were not pacifists but cautious statists. War could be a tool of statecraft, but only if the outcome was certain before the conflict. Japan was diplomatically and materially unprepared for war, and no measure of popular passion could overcome those hard facts. The recent Franco-Prussian War had been just such a battle between Prussian realpolitik and French revolutionary passion. Realpolitik had won and the Iwakura Mission had seen the results in Paris and Berlin. Japan's choice was clear.

This standoff over Korea lasted until October. Demoralized and exhausted by the long struggle, Sanjō Sanetomi resigned, claiming illness. That left Iwakura as the highest-ranking court noble in the government and tipped the balance of power. Although the two factions remained roughly equal, Iwakura became the government's representative to the emperor, and he secured an imperial decision canceling Saigō's mission.[83] For supporters of a confrontation with Korea, this was skullduggery of the lowest order, but they could not oppose an imperial command. Outraged and outflanked, Saigō, Itagaki, Etō, Gotō Shōjirō, and Soejima Taneomi resigned in protest. They were followed by dozens of sympathetic high-ranking officials and military officers.

After these resignations, Ōkubo dominated Japanese politics until his death in 1878. Historians refer to these five years as the "Ōkubo administration" (Ōkubo seiken). His administration differed from the preceding caretaker government in both substance and style. The caretaker government produced a whirlwind of reform decrees, but it struggled with practical issues of implementation and enforcement. Its goal was transforming Japan by unleashing the energies of its people. Only with an enthusiastic populace could Japan become a powerful nation-state. The Ōkubo administration, by contrast, was less interested in the popular will, either as a part of political legitimacy or as a tool for advancing national interests. Successful governance required careful, long-range planning. Popular support was helpful but secondary. The Ōkubo administration aspired to transform Japan, but that transformation would be driven by bureaucratic deliberations, not by popular zeal. Further, in contrast to the caretaker government's sense of urgency, the new government emphasized patience. Establishing Japan as a world power would take years or decades rather than months, and the government would need to focus on sustainable long-term change. That ran counter to popular expectations for faster change, such as the prompt revision of the unequal treaties, so the government needed to be insulated from popular demands. Ōkubo had seen how popular resentment of the unequal treaties had undermined the Tokugawa shogunate. Indeed, as an anti-shogunal activist, he had once stoked that impatience. Having himself failed to revise the treaties, he saw popular expectations as unrealistic and therefore dangerous.

The losers of the 1873 Political Crisis, now out of power, insisted that the state heed popular grievances. In January 1874, key members of the now-defunct caretaker government published a petition denouncing the Ōkubo administration as autocratic (*dokuyūshi*) and declaring the people's right to participate in government affairs. They invoked both Western principles, such as "no taxation without representation," and older Confucian-style critiques of the government for its failure to acknowledge respectful dissent (*genro yōhei*). That demand for a representative assembly (*minsen giin setsuritsu kenpakusho*) birthed modern Japanese mass politics, inviting into the public sphere thousands of farmers and townspeople. For centuries, samurai had delegated the details of urban and rural administration to commoners while simultaneously excluding them from higher levels of political discourse. The 1874 petition shattered that divide. It legitimized public criticism of the government and sparked an explosion of public dissent in newspaper editorials, petitions, and public rallies. The leaders of the caretaker government had publicly declared that the Japanese nation-state could only be as strong as its people's voice in government. Beginning in 1874, thousands of Japanese commoners rushed forward to provide that strength.

The 1873 Political Crisis thus birthed Japanese democracy but also its less appealing fraternal twin, populist militarism. Many who quit the government in 1873 continued to agitate for war with Korea. Like Japanese democracy, populist militarism was a potent fusion of old and new ideas. Samurai bluster about avenging foreign insults was old. In the 1860s, such discourse had undermined the shogunate and driven many samurai to xenophobic violence. But Western ideas gave this old invective a new appeal. War could now be justified under international law and as part of an international scramble for empire. Saigō's loyal lieutenant Kirino Toshiaki, for example, argued that Japan needed to take over East Asia in order to maintain its own national independence. The great powers of Britain, France, Prussia, and Russia were planning to seize Korea, Manchuria, and China. Japan needed to strike first in order to "stand equal with the nations of the world" (*udai bankoku ni heiritsu*). Not only were samurai compelled to defend the honor of the Japanese emperor, but they also needed to protect the Japanese nation in a dangerous and predatory international environment.[84] After the 1873 Political Crisis, such demands for war and empire, like calls for elections and democracy, occurred in an expanding public sphere of print media and public events. That vibrant and volatile public debate collided with the Ōkubo administration's vision of state-directed change.

6

The Prudent Empire

LIKE THE CARETAKER GOVERNMENT, the Ōkubo administration sought to establish Japan as a sovereign power within the nineteenth-century European international system. Unlike the caretaker government, however, the Ōkubo administration was convinced that this project would take decades. Those who had seen Europe and America firsthand on the Iwakura mission were deeply aware of Japan's material and technological inferiority. Only after decades of economic development and technological modernization could Japan overcome that inferiority and negotiate with the Great Powers from a position of strength. Accordingly, the government focused on consolidating state power and promoting economic growth. It reformed the land tax, creating the most uniform national tax system in roughly a millennium. It dismantled the samurai class and began building a modern army and navy based on commoner conscripts. It poured funds into a range of infrastructure and industrial projects, including mines, railroads, telegraph lines, iron and steel foundries, shipyards, and textile mills as well as factories for glass, lacquer ware, ceramics, and soap.[1] The new government fully believed that it could raise Japan to great power status, but it knew that such a transformation would require mastering the Industrial Revolution, not stoking revolutionary passions. Former samurai might clamor for a war of honor in Korea or Taiwan, but Japanese diplomacy needed to be grounded in prudent realpolitik. Popular sentiment was something to be tamed rather than mobilized. Historian Banno Junji has described this face of Meiji politics as "developmental despotism" (kaihatsu dokusai).[2]

The Ōkubo government confronted two main forms of opposition: reactionary opposition to reform and burgeoning demands for popular representation. Despite their differences, those two movements were united in their opposition to the autocracy of the Ōkubo cabinet. In response, the administration tried both to placate and to suppress its challengers. In 1874, it staged a punitive attack on Taiwan to appease demands for a more aggressive foreign policy, specifically from disgruntled samurai in the southwest. But when small groups of disaffected samurai launched violent attacks, the state responded with overwhelming force. In January 1877, such confrontations exploded into a full civil war after followers of Saigō Takamori raided an armory in Kagoshima and began marching north to Tokyo. The Meiji state mobilized nearly 60,000 soldiers and sailors against a rebel army of roughly 30,000, and by March the rebels were in retreat. The fighting dragged on until late September as the rebels managed to evade the advancing Imperial Army. The Meiji state won the War of the Southwest, also known as the "Satsuma Rebellion," but at enormous financial and human cost. At least 10,000 combatants died in the fighting and the Meiji government's direct military costs were over 40 million yen, roughly a half-year's revenue. The financial implications of the war lasted well beyond the nine months of combat. The government covered its expenses largely by printing money, causing the value of the yen to plummet. Prices soared for basic commodities such as rice, charcoal, and salt.[3]

The government also faced non-violent demands for greater political inclusion, most pointedly, calls for the creation of an elected national assembly. The Meiji state confronted this aspect of the opposition, known as the "Freedom and Popular Rights Movement" (*Jiyū minken undō*) with both oppression and accommodation. Beginning in late 1873, the government steadily tightened its control of the press and public assembly. The Meiji state had initially encouraged a free press as a necessary part of an "enlightened" society, but the Ōkubo administration moved to restrict publications critical of the government. It imposed increasingly tough regulations on the press, restricted public gatherings, and eventually required a police presence at all political meetings. At the same time, the Meiji state made some concessions to public opinion. An 1875 imperial decree promised to respond to "popular sentiment" with a "constitutional polity," and in 1879 the government introduced prefectural assemblies, albeit with limited powers and only some elected members.[4] In 1881, the government granted a major opposition demand, promising to introduce by 1890 not only a constitution but also a national assembly. But that constitution would be written by the Meiji oligarchy and bestowed upon the people as a gift from their emperor. The people would get as much self-rule as the state would allow. The struggle for a greater popular voice would continue, but within structures established by the Meiji state.

Meiji State and Meiji Empire

Like the early Tokugawa shoguns, the Ōkubo government did not reject war, only wars with unpredictable outcomes. The Ōkubo administration was willing to support military action so long as it seemed manageable, inexpensive, and contained. The most striking example is the 1874 Taiwan Expedition, a punitive raid against Taiwanese aboriginals, nominally in response to the 1871 Mudan Incident. Based on the advice of Le Gendre, the Meiji government assumed that the Great Powers would recognize its claim to Taiwan. Under those circumstances, the expedition seemed like a low-risk, high-yield proposition, and in early April the government authorized a colonial expedition. To the surprise and dismay of the Meiji leadership, the UK objected vociferously to the impending attack and Washington disavowed Le Gendre's actions.[5] In response, the Meiji leadership tried to postpone the expedition, but the commander, Saigō Tsugumichi, had already received an imperial edict, and he ignored Tokyo's last-minute vacillation.[6] The clash created a chasm between Japan's internal and external accounts of the expedition. To avoid antagonizing the United States and Britain, the Meiji government disavowed its territorial ambitions, insisting that its punitive raid was merely an investigatory mission.[7] Internally, however, the Taiwan Expedition was described as a colonial venture: Saigō Tsugumichi, among others, hoped to seize parts of eastern Taiwan and send disaffected Satsuma samurai there as settlers.[8]

As a colonial enterprise, the Taiwan expedition was a failure. Japanese troops eventually "pacified" parts of eastern Taiwan, but they suffered heavy losses from disease and struggled against aboriginal guerilla tactics. The army's samurai volunteers proved particularly ineffective, since they ignored directives on malaria prophylaxis and general hygiene.[9] On the diplomatic front, Beijing refused to cede Taiwan, and Tokyo was not prepared to meet Chinese resistance with open war. As a means of winning international recognition for Japan's claim to Ryukyu, however, the expedition was a success. Beijing agreed to pay a large indemnity of 500,000 silver taels (roughly 37,000 lbs.): 100,000 for the murder of the Ryukyuans and 400,000 to cover Japan's costs in attacking China. The death indemnity amounted to indirect recognition of Ryukyu as Japanese territory since it was paid to the Japanese government rather than the families of the victims. The remainder of the indemnity, payment for war costs, reflected a Japanese emulation of Western practice; in 1858, for example, Britain had received 4 million taels as repayment for the burden of attacking and defeating China in the Opium Wars. British observers were not flattered by Japan's "mimetic imperialism." On the contrary, Harry Parkes, the British consul to Japan, lamented without a trace of irony that China was "willing to pay for being invaded."[10] But American observers were more laudatory. The *New York Times*, for example, praised Japan for resolving the "irremediable nuisance of Formosa." The Meiji state had combined "Oriental cunning and Western bluntness" for "a triumph of which the youngest member of the family of civilized nations—reckoning by years of formal acknowledgment—may well be proud." Aggression against China was thus, for this newspaper at least, evidence that Japan was "civilized" and had joined the "comity of nations."[11]

The Meiji state's approach to Korea was also based on Western models, but it was more cautious than policy towards Taiwan. In the 1873 Political Crisis, the government had fractured over whether to risk war with Korea, and Ōkubo had then warned against an expensive, open-ended conflict. Along those lines, the Ōkubo cabinet avoided an overt invasion of Korea and focused instead on undermining Sino-Korean ties. In September 1875, the Japanese warship *Unyō* provoked a firefight near Kanghwa Island and then destroyed Korean coastal fortifications. In the ensuing negotiations, Japan threatened war, but its key demand was Chinese recognition of Korea and Japan as equally sovereign states. The resulting Treaty of Kanghwa (1876) therefore encapsulated many of the tensions within nineteenth-century Western international law: Japan established itself as Korea's equal but also as its quasi-colonial superior.[12] In accordance with the declaration that Japan and Korea were equal, Korea agreed to exchange ambassadors directly with the Meiji state rather than through Tsushima domain. But the agreement also echoed the treaties imposed on Japan in the 1850s. Korea was forced to open three ports to foreign trade and to allow Japanese merchants to trade and live throughout Korea. Korea also granted Japan extraterritorial rights: Japanese subjects in Korea could be tried only in consular courts.[13] Overall, the declaration that Korea was sovereign implied an end to Qing claims that the Korean king was a vassal of the Qing emperor. As with the Taiwan Expedition, the Meiji state's repudiation of East Asian protocols in favor of gunboat diplomacy won acclaim in Western newspapers. The *Pall Mall Gazette* in London observed that Japan, "the smallest of the Eastern States, only just emerged from absolute seclusion" had succeeded in "opening" Korea "where two of the great Western Powers failed, and had to retreat with serious loss, both in ships and credit. This is a diplomatic achievement of which the Japanese may well be proud."[14]

The Meiji state used these foreign engagements to consolidate and define its national territory. The conclusion of the Taiwan Expedition, for example, galvanized Japanese efforts to remake Ryukyu into a domestic prefecture rather than a foreign tributary land. The caretaker government had begun that process in 1872, but its decrees were a messy combination of early modern and modern notions of sovereignty and territorial power. In 1872/9, for example, the government summoned a Ryukyuan delegation to Tokyo and informed them that Ryukyu was under the control of the Meiji emperor. The official decree insisted that Ryukyu was culturally part of Japan, identical in language and custom. That emphasis on cultural similarity was consonant with Western models of the nation-state. But the ceremony was replete with words and gestures that replicated older notions of Ryukyu as a culturally distinct tributary state. The delegation's gifts to the Meiji emperor included Chinese goods (Chinese writing brushes, ink stones, and ink), reflecting Ryukyu's status as a contact point with China. The embassy also offered uniquely Ryukyuan products, such as "island cloth" (*shima-tsumugi*) and, in return, the king of Ryukyu received "Japanese brocade" (*Yamato nishiki*). That gift exchange emphasized Ryukyuan cultural difference rather than the integration of Ryukyu into a Japanese nation-state. Ryukyu was accordingly described as the southern part of a sprawling Japanese empire, which encompassed the "four seas" and "eight corners of the earth." Further complicating the situation, the caretaker government bestowed on the Ryukyuan king the unique title of "domain king" (*han'ō*). By resurrecting the word "domain," the Meiji government actually reversed one of its key centralizing reforms: just the year before, the government had dissolved the domains (*han*) and replaced them with prefectures. Domains were now officially part of a defunct political system. But the title "domain king" suggested that Ryukyu's unique place within the Japanese polity would continue under the Meiji government. Those odd word choices and the selection of official gifts revealed confusion within the Japanese government: were Japan's interests best served by the diplomatic ambiguities of the status quo or by a bold new assertion of sovereign power?[15]

After the Taiwan Expedition, the Ōkubo administration moved aggressively against the Tokugawa legacy of coincident sovereignties. It sought to define Ryukyu as both culturally and politically Japanese and to terminate Ryukyu's traditional ties with China. Ōkubo considered the Shō court to be "stubborn, bigoted, and narrow-minded," but he hoped to win them over with a combination of traditional Confucian benevolence and modern Western technology. In 1874, he proposed using the indemnity from China to purchase thirty steamships for Ryukyu. Those new ships would improve the lives of ordinary Ryukyuans by replacing the traditional, shipwreck-prone, shallow-keel boats used to travel to both China and Japan. Providing new ships thus combined modern technology with the tropes of Confucian benevolence, and Ōkubo imagined that such gestures would win over the Ryukyuan political elite.[16]

To Ōkubo's dismay, the Shō court was unmoved. Shuri Castle rejected Japanese "benevolence" and refused to implement Japanese-style reforms. Tokyo then dispatched troops and demanded that Ryukyu accept both the steamships and the relief rice. Facing military force, the Shō court conceded, but it continued to appeal to China and other foreign powers for help in resisting Japan. Tokyo was alarmed but it delayed further action because of domestic concerns: violent samurai rebellions in late 1876, escalating into full civil war in 1877, and then the assassination of Ōkubo in May 1878.[17]

Tokyo returned to the Ryukyu problem again in late 1878, largely to preempt foreign intervention. Former American president Ulysses S. Grant was scheduled to visit East Asia in 1879 as part of a round-the-world tour, and Beijing was planning to request his arbitration of the Ryukyu dispute. The Meiji government wanted to appear reasonable and amicable when hosting Grant, but it was unwilling to negotiate sovereign control of Ryukyu. To preclude any discussion of sovereignty, Tokyo moved to assert direct control before Grant's visit. In March 1879, Japanese troops seized control of Shuri Castle, deposed King Shō Tai, and announced the creation of Okinawa Prefecture. In May, the former king was shipped to Tokyo, where the Meiji emperor denounced his insolence, but then, in his abundant mercy, pardoned his crimes and granted him a peerage.[18]

The creation of Okinawa Prefecture was a direct rebuke to Beijing, which had warned Tokyo against unilateral action. But having seized Ryukyu, Tokyo could afford to appear reasonable, gracious, and conciliatory. When Grant proposed concessions in the spirit of "magnanimity and justice," Tokyo offered to cede to China the southwestern end of the archipelago in return for most favored nation status in relations with China. Beijing's representatives accepted this proposal, but the Chinese foreign ministry refused to sign. This turmoil within the Chinese government allowed Tokyo to reject further negotiations without appearing belligerent. On January 5, 1881, Japan's minister to Beijing notified China that Tokyo considered the matter of Ryukyu closed. China protested, but to no avail.[19]

In these new assertions of sovereignty, the Meiji government emphasized Ryukyu's cultural similarity to Japan. It insisted that the Ryukyuan language was merely a dialect of Japanese, that Ryukyuan etiquette was identical to that of Japan, and that the Ryukyuan religion was none other than Shinto.[20] These claims were not only untrue, they also constituted a complete reversal of Tokugawa-era policy, which had focused on the cultural distinctiveness of Ryukyu. But these falsehoods were politically effective and, combined with adept diplomacy and military force, secured international recognition of Ryukyu as Japanese. Nonetheless, Meiji policy continued to reflect the liminal status of Ryukyu as a quasi-colony within the Japanese "homeland." Although Ryukyu was now internationally recognized as part of Japan, the Meiji state delayed the implementation of key reforms, wary of sparking unrest. Conscription, for example, was not extended to Okinawa until 1898, twenty-five years after it was implemented in the home islands. Land reform, including the abolition of communal farmlands, was not begun until 1899. While delaying those major reforms, the government made some limited attempts to mark ordinary Ryukyuans as Japanese subjects. Ryukyuans were required, for example, to adopt family names and register under the Meiji household registration system (*koseki*).[21] But having won international recognition of Ryukyu as Japanese, Tokyo postponed the challenges of assimilation. When Japan renewed its efforts to assimilate Ryukyu in the late 1890s, it was as part of a new stage of imperial conquest. China ceded Taiwan to Japan in 1895 under the Treaty of Shimonoseki. After claiming Taiwan as a Japanese colony, the Meiji state moved to assimilate Ryukyu as part of the Japanese "homeland" (*naichi*) rather than part of its empire. The expansion of the Japanese empire thus included a redefinition of the Japanese "homeland."

A parallel process of consolidation unfolded in the far northeast, where the Ōkubo administration sought to incorporate Ezo into a Japanese nation-state. As a contact zone between the Tokugawa regime and the Russian Empire, Ezo once lay in a gray zone between homeland, frontier, and colony. In 1875, Enomoto Takeaki, rehabilitated and released from prison, negotiated a clear international border between Japan and Russia, ending the ambiguous joint possession of Sakhalin. Under the Treaty of St. Petersburg, Japan renounced its claims to Sakhalin in exchange for complete control of the Kuriles up to the Kamchatka peninsula. The establishment of a clear international border galvanized efforts to redefine the Ainu as Japanese imperial subjects. The government redoubled earlier efforts to impose Japanese hairstyle and clothing on the Ainu. It banned poison arrows, instead encouraging hunting with firearms. It sought to impose sedentary agriculture, issuing title deeds and banning the practice of burning homes after the death of an occupant.[22] Nonetheless, Ezo retained a liminal status as a quasi-colony within a Japanese nation-state. The Meiji administrative agency for Ezo, for example, was known in English as the Hokkaido Colonization Office (1869–82) (*Hokkaidō kaitakushi*).

Radical nostalgia shaped these efforts to make Ezo an integral part of Japan, and Meiji-era terms were replete with ancient references. The Hokkaido Colonization Office used an anachronistic term for "office" (*shi*), recalling the Azechi or Ansatsu-shi, an eighth-century agency that administered northeastern Honshū.[23] The Meiji government's program of settling former samurai on military outposts in Hokkaido, the *tondenhei*, was named after an ancient Chinese institution.[24] The toponym "Hokkaidō" itself, coined in 1869, recalled the ancient division of Japan into five inner provinces (*ki*) in the greater Kyoto-Nara area, and seven outer "circuits" or dō (*goki shichidō*). Renaming Ezo as Hokkaido, the "Northern sea circuit," created an eighth "circuit" and implied that Ezo had been a part of the ancient imperial state. Intriguingly, the term Hokkaido is now a linguistic fossil. It remains the official name for the prefecture, even though the broader attempt to revive the ancient "five province seven circuit" system collapsed when the Meiji government designated Tokyo, rather than Kyoto, as its capital. Moving the capital to Tokyo, in the ancient Tōkaidō, or "Eastern sea circuit," destroyed the logic of that system since the new center of Japan was at its ancient periphery. Today Hokkaido is the only prefecture with the suffix "dō": Japan's newest territory has its most ancient name.[25]

Renaming Ezo as Hokkaido also domesticated the territory by removing an etymological association with savagery. The second character in the toponym Ezo meant savage or barbarian, reflecting a Tokugawa-era distinction between barbarians (*iteki*) and humans (*ningen*). Meiji discourse rejected these distinctions, emphasizing instead the transformation of the Ainu into Japanese imperial subjects as "aboriginals" (*dojin*) and later as "former aboriginals" (*kyūdojin*).[26]

While linking Hokkaido to the ancient imperial state, the Hokkaido Colonial Office also embraced transnational notions of economic development. The office relied heavily on American advisors, most prominently

Horace Capron (1804–55), a former United States commissioner of agriculture. These advisors explicitly cited the settlement of the American West as a model for Hokkaido. Japan, they declared, needed land grant colleges, like those created by the Morrill Act of 1862. It needed to encourage the migration of farmers by copying the Homestead Act of 1862. It needed cattle ranches, dairy farms, and apple orchards, all ideally with American-style organization and architecture.[27] The Japanese government eagerly embraced this vision of Hokkaido as parallel to the American West, but its discourse on Hokkaido was also suffused with a sense of overseas expansion and settlement. The inaugural issue of the official publication, the *Hokkaido Development Journal* (*Hokkaidō kaitaku zasshi*), compared Japanese settlers in Hokkaido to the Mayflower Pilgrims, pioneers in a new land.[28] More broadly, the discourse of encouraging migration to Hokkaido anticipated later arguments about both emigration and colonization. Fukuzawa Yukichi, for example, urged former samurai to settle in Hokkaido but then shifted his focus to emigration to the Americas. Tsuda Sen, editor of the *Hokkaido Development Journal*, later advocated settlement in Korea and North China, while his son and daughter both emigrated to California.[29]

The impact of Meiji policy in Hokkaido was decidedly mixed. Sapporo Agricultural College, now Hokkaido University, emerged as a respected and influential institution of higher education. But many of the Colonial Office's other enterprises were poorly conceived and badly run. The government's settler promotion policy was fraught with contradictions. It subsidized immigration to Hokkaido but assigned to the original settlers the poorest lands, on the periphery of the fertile lowlands. Better lands were reserved for later settlers, or held back by officials, who then arranged to sell them to speculators. Poor transportation and underdeveloped markets meant high prices for basic commodities, and many settlers found Hokkaido winters unbearably cold. Few migrants became permanent settlers.[30] Beyond farming, the Colonial Office's diverse portfolio of ranches, canneries, breweries, mines, mills, and foundries tended to bleed money. Capron, in particular, seems to have disregarded labor costs, capital costs, culture, and climate in his advice to the Meiji government.[31] Tragically, one of the most enduring aspects of Meiji policy was contagion: the Ainu population was decimated as settlers spread measles, influenza, and tuberculosis.[32] Another legacy was scandal. When the government began selling its assets in Hokkaido after 1881, reports of corruption caused a political crisis.

Similarly to Ryukyu and Ezo, the Ogasawara Islands were traditionally a liminal space in terms of race, ethnicity, and international law. In 1875, according to a report by a British consul, the inhabitants were a creole society of thirty-seven men and thirty-two women. The British report described five of the male settlers as "whites," referring to the European-born men, but the islanders themselves were pointedly unconcerned with either racial classification or national identity. They self-identified as Bonin Islanders and, in the estimation of the British consul, "they wished to be left alone in undisturbed possession of their holdings, and the less that was said about nationality or protection of any kind the better."[33] Unfortunately for the islanders, nineteenth-century international politics did not allow for such undisturbed places. Commodore Perry himself had suggested turning the islands into a US colony, and the Meiji state scrambled to redefine the territory as an integral part of the Japanese "homeland."

The incorporation of Ogasawara was broadly similar to that of Ezo and Ryukyu, but the presence of "whites" presented unique problems. Under extraterritoriality, the European-born settlers on the Ogasawara Islands were potentially subject to the legal jurisdiction of their "home" countries. In order to have an effective legal control over the islands, the Meiji government needed to transform those "white" settlers and their families into subjects of the Japanese emperor. The incorporation of the Ogasawara Islands thus prompted the creation of a new legal category, "naturalized foreigner" (kika gaikokujin), a term specifically designed to accommodate the islanders' special status. As part of the naturalization process, the islanders were registered under the koseki household registration system and thereby became Japanese imperial subjects. To emphasize the incorporation of Ogasawara as part of the homeland, in 1880 the islands were placed under the administrative jurisdiction of Tokyo, more than 600 miles away. Nonetheless, the islands retained a marginal, semi-colonial status. In 1878, the government barred "naturalized foreigners" from resettling on Japanese main islands (naichi), confirming the settlers' status as simultaneously in and out of Japan. That ban was lifted in 1897, in conformity the 1889 Meiji constitution, but by that time the original settlers were a small minority on the island. The Meiji government encouraged the emigration of main-island Japanese, and the Ogasawara population soared from fewer than 100 in 1875 to over 3,000 by 1894.[34]

The Domestic Transformation

In domestic policy, the Ōkubo administration rejected a key tenet of the caretaker government: that the success of the Japanese nation-state required the urgent mobilization of popular energies. Ōkubo did not disparage the importance of liberty (*jiyū*) and popular rights (*minken*) as did his colleagues Inoue Kaoru and Terashima Munenori. But he insisted that the relative underdevelopment of the Japanese people constrained their ability to enjoy rights and freedoms. The populace, he opined, was "accustomed to years of feudal oppression and has long embraced warped and wicked practices," so the Japanese people were simply not ready to govern themselves. Ōkubo advocated a gradual expansion of political rights, steering a cautious middle course between the turmoil of the French republic and Russian despotism. But Japan, he insisted, could never be a democracy (*minshu*), which was a rare and unstable form of government. The United States was barely 100 years old, so the world's only lasting democracy was Switzerland. For Ōkubo, the 1789 French Revolution suggested that precipitous moves toward popular rights could create tyranny instead of liberty. Long term, England seemed like an ideal model for Japan: a prosperous island with a limited monarchy and a massive empire. But given the backwardness of the Japanese people, Ōkubo could not yet see entrusting them with political responsibility. Japan needed first to raise their intelligence (*sairyoku*) and foster their patriotism.[35]

One of the Ōkubo administration's first acts was to reverse earlier policy and tighten controls on the press. The early Meiji state had been broadly supportive of newspapers as "essential to enlightenment." It had warned against slander, incitement to criminal conduct, and news that was "injurious to public sentiment," but it had encouraged reporting on domestic and international affairs as part of the "broadening of human knowledge."[36] In October 1873, however, the Dajōkan announced new laws banning any "irresponsibly critical comments" on politics or national law. The edict also prohibited any news that might "interfere with national law through the vilification of the national polity (*kokutai*), the discussion of national laws, or advocacy of foreign laws."[37] In 1875, the government tightened these restrictions with harsh new penalties of up to three years in jail for a range of offenses including "defaming national edicts and undermining obedience to national law."[38] Foreign governments collaborated with this crackdown. When the Meiji government complained about publications by British subjects, the British consul forbade its subjects from printing or publishing newspapers in Japan. The target of this ban was likely the dissident journalist John Reddie Black who had supported the losing faction in the 1873 Political Crisis.[39] The Meiji state also imposed new restrictions on public assembly. Beginning in July 1878, all public lectures involving political affairs were monitored by the police and could be disbanded for statements that might "instigate popular discontent." After 1880, the organizers of all political meetings were required to obtain prior approval from the police.[40]

In education policy, the Meiji state also moved to emphasize obedience and loyalty to the state. Initially, the government focused on placating local opposition by restoring some local control and by reducing tuition. In 1879, however, the government explicitly repudiated central elements of the 1872 system. In an imperial declaration, the government lamented that recent reforms had neglected loyalty and filial piety in favor of the acquisition of knowledge and skills. That excessive emphasis on "civilization and enlightenment" was pernicious and contrary to the true purpose of Japanese education. Japan needed to reemphasize virtues such as loyalty to one's lord and parents in order to secure national independence. Those explicit references to Confucian hierarchy were a stark contrast to the government's earlier emphasis on individual self-actualization. Whereas the 1872 reforms had emphasized the obligation of parents to educate their children, the 1879 declaration focused on children's deference to their parents. The new policy also emphasized conventional gender roles such as the "virtuous wife" (seppu), in contrast to the caretaker government's moves toward gender neutrality.[41]

The Ōkubo administration's low estimation of the Japanese people shaped its economic policy. After 1873, the government began working directly with private enterprises to promote the adoption of advanced technologies. It sold or leased plants and equipment to private entrepreneurs for a range of products, including cloth, thread, printing type-blocks, ceramics, lacquer ware, soap, and tinplate. That direct collaboration with private enterprise marked a shift in state policy.[42] There was a consensus within the Meiji government that the state needed to help build the infrastructure of a modern economy, such as railroad and telegraph lines. To that end the government opened a railroad line from Shinbashi (central Tokyo) to Yokohama in 1872, and then one from Osaka to Kobe in 1874, and from Osaka to Kyoto in 1877. The telegraph system expanded rapidly, beginning with a short line from Tokyo to Yokohama in 1869, but then extending over 700 miles southwest from Tokyo to Nagasaki in 1873 and over 600 miles northeast to Otaru (Hokkaido) in 1875. There was also a consensus that the state needed to support capital-intensive, high-technology enterprises. The Yokosuka shipyard, for example, was begun by the Tokugawa shogunate in 1866 and expanded by the Meiji government, eventually becoming a major naval base and arsenal. The government also opened the Tomioka silk reeling plant in 1872, a huge factory with more than 300 kettles, completed at a cost of nearly ¥200,000.[43]

While continuing these industrial promotion policies, the Ōkubo administration also began direct government support for private enterprises. In 1874, for example, the government leased a textile mill to a group of private investors for ¥650 per year. In 1877 it leased a kiln for ¥40 per year and a tin plate machine for ¥65 per year. It sold soap-making equipment to a private group for 15 percent below cost.[44] Behind these various subventions was a dim view of Japanese entrepreneurship. Ōkubo was convinced that the Japanese people were ignorant and of "weak disposition." Since the people lacked "diligence and perseverance," it was the responsibility of the state to "press and induce" them to undertake new enterprises. While laissez-faire policies might work in advanced Western economies, Japan would need to protect, promote, and nurture key industries until its people were more economically mature.[45] That attitude was strikingly unlike Etō's conviction that Japan needed to liberate rather than protect its entrepreneurs. For Etō, Japan's merchants were fully capable of leading the economy so long as the state provided them with the proper framework, an efficient and transparent legal system.

Perhaps the greatest accomplishment of the Ōkubo administration was land tax reform, which stabilized the state's major source of revenue. The dual goals of tax reform were to create a reliable stream of revenue and to equalize the tax burden across Japan by replacing regional tax systems with a single standardized cash payment. To stabilize revenue, the government moved from taxing the harvest to taxing the land itself. That change formally committed the Meiji state to capitalist principles of ownership. Under Tokugawa-era law, it was difficult to sell farmland since, in theory, it could not be owned: the local daimyo, samurai, and farmers all had interlocking claims to different aspects of the land. Local communities also had diverse traditions of holding lands in common. The Meiji land tax reform formally replaced these practices with clear title deeds, and the landholder now owed taxes based on the value of the land. Finally, by collecting taxes in cash rather than in kind, the government could secure a steadier stream of revenue. The Meiji land tax reforms were thus central to the creation of a strong, centralized state.[46]

The government implemented tax reform with great trepidation, anticipating massive resistance. Remarkably, although some regions experienced double-digit increases in taxation, there were few protests when the tax was introduced in 1874. In 1876, however, there were large, widespread protests because of a fall in rice prices. Since taxes were based on the previous year's rice price, a ¥10 tax bill required 1.37 bushels of rice in 1875, but two bushels in 1876. Alarmed by the scale and intensity of the protests, in January 1877, the government reduced the tax rate from 3 percent to 2.5 percent of land value. The protests abated, but simmering anti-government sentiment generated popular support for the rebels in the War of the Southwest. The lower tax rate also exacerbated the state's fiscal problems, particularly since it coincided with the massive costs of civil war.[47] Despite these problems, land tax reform achieved a new level of state power and centralization. By 1878, all Japanese landowners paid taxes to Tokyo at the same rate and at the same time across the archipelago. The ancient imperial state had attempted a similarly centralized system some 1,100 years before, but the Meiji regime enforced its claims with modern bureaucratic efficiency.

The government approached conscription with a similar combination of resolve and caution. The caretaker government announced conscription in late 1872, but the actual draft did not begin until August 1873. In the wake of the "blood tax" anti-conscription protests and riots, the government was careful to minimize the impact of conscription on rural families. The regulations provided multiple exemptions: for the ill or disabled; those under five *shaku* one *sun* in height (roughly 5 ft./154.5 cm.); potential household heads; those with a brother already in the military; those convicted of a crime; government officials; students in higher-level public schools, medical school, or military schools; and those studying abroad. The wealthy could also receive a draft exemption by paying ¥270. Many of these exemptions were exploited to avoid service, and the early Meiji army was comparatively small because over 80 percent of draft-age men received exemptions from service. In 1878, the army was only 41,000 compared to over 1.3 million in Germany. The government moved slowly to close off exemptions. In 1878, for example, it prohibited men twenty years old and younger from claiming the head of household exemption. That stopped families from setting up largely fictive "branch households" for their sons. Only in 1889 did the government limit draft exemptions to illness and disability. As with the land tax, conscription marked a new level of systematic and centralized state power. In trying to evade the draft, young men throughout Japan were seeking exemptions from the same rules. Thus, even opposition to the state was marked by a new level of national uniformity.[48]

One of the most fraught issues for the Ōkubo administration was the dissolution of the samurai estate. The early Meiji state and the caretaker government had made tentative moves to replace stipends and abolish hereditary privileges. In early 1872, the caretaker government approved a plan, proposed by Inoue Kaoru, which closely resembled the eventual 1876 program. Samurai stipends were to be reduced sharply and replaced by income-bearing bonds, with cuts falling most heavily on the wealthiest retainers. But the consensus behind the project was fragile. Saigō and other men from Satsuma were worried about opposition from their lord, Shimazu Hisamitsu, who was vociferously criticizing the new government for its radicalism. Writing back from overseas, Iwakura and Kido also cautioned against precipitous action. In the absence of a stable consensus, the government moved more modestly to simplify the stipend system. It eliminated the distinct rank of "sotsu" for lower samurai and classified all retainers with heritable income as "shizoku," a neologism for "former samurai."[49]

The Ōkubo cabinet continued the caretaker government's incrementalism. It made stipends subject to progressive taxation, ranging from 2 percent to 35.5 percent. It began a program of voluntary stipend conversion, urging ex-samurai to take payment in a combination of bonds and cash and to use those proceeds to buy a farm or business. Those initial conversions ended badly, in part because a poor rice harvest in 1873 raised the price of rice, penalizing those who had elected to take their stipends in cash.[50]

The government moved decisively against samurai perquisites in March 1876, stripping samurai of their long-standing right to wear swords in public. Thereafter, swords were restricted to active-duty military personnel and police officers.[51] In August, the government moved to eliminate stipends. All hereditary stipends were replaced with bonds, ranging in value from five to fourteen years' income, and with annual yields ranging from 5 percent to 7 percent. The overall reduction in annual payments was roughly 45 percent, but the conversion schedule was highly progressive, favoring samurai with the smallest stipends. For example, samurai with an annual stipend of 15 *koku* or less (the lowest bracket) received bonds worth fourteen years of income paying 7 percent per annum. The resulting annual income loss was only 2 percent. At 250 *koku*, however, the bonds were only worth ten years' income and paid only 6 percent, reducing annual income by 40 percent. Samurai in the highest bracket, 7000 *koku* and above, incurred income losses of 75 percent or more.[52]

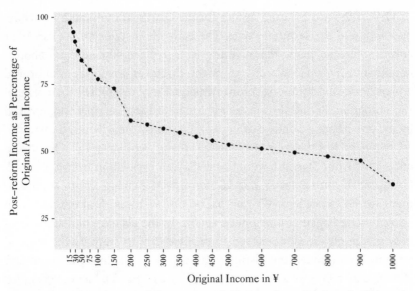

FIGURE 6.1 Stipend to Bond Conversion, 1876. Data from Kondō, ed., *Chitsuroku shobunhō*, esp. 17–24.

As an administrative project, the conversion of stipends was a remarkable achievement. In only its ninth year, the new government managed a massive domestic bond issue without wild swings in prices or interest rates. Anticipating that many samurai might quickly sell their bonds, causing a precipitous drop in prices, the government instructed its nascent banking system to buy the bonds. To finance cash payments on the bonds, the government floated a large loan in England.[53] The end of stipends effectively dissolved the samurai as a privileged class, but the economic impact varied widely. For some samurai, the bonds represented a sudden infusion of capital, providing new business opportunities. In Yonezawa domain, for example, many samurai households had begun weaving in late 1700s, renting looms and thread from brokers, and selling back finished cloth. That extra income supplemented their meager stipends. The conversion of stipends into bonds allowed those families to buy their own tools and supplies and become independent producers.[54] Similarly, the majority of samurai in Gifu successfully adapted to new lives in farming or small business. For others, however, the conversion program represented a daunting challenge. Many samurai considered ignorance of business and finance a mark of elite status, so managing their bonds required precisely the skills and knowledge they both lacked and disdained. The inability of samurai to understand their finances was so striking that period observers coined the phrase "doing business like a former samurai" (*shizoku no shōhō*), meaning a complete lack of business sense. Period tabloids reveled in lurid stories of once-powerful samurai pulling rickshaws or selling their wives and daughters into prostitution. But those anecdotes are not representative of the overall impact of stipend reform. The strongly progressive conversion schedule meant that the most severe cuts in income were concentrated on a relatively small elite. Most former samurai met their loss of hereditary privilege with a combination of steely resolve and quiet resignation.[55]

A vocal minority attacked the stipend conversion program with both words and weapons. But by 1876 it was difficult to muster a straightforward defense of hereditary privilege. Rather than defend "tradition," opponents of stipend reform invoked "samurai populism." A letter in the anti-government *Hyōron Shinbun*, for example, criticized the government's unilateral action as "despotic" (*assei*) and called for its overthrow. A Tosa-based political group, the Risshisha, cited the unfair treatment of samurai, but in the context of a call for an elected assembly. Rather than block reform, such activism sought to turn former samurai into leaders in a new political landscape.[56]

In judicial reform, the Ōkubo administration believed that the rights of the individual could only be secured by a strong state, so it focused on consolidating state power through the military, the bureaucracy, the police, and a new criminal code (1882). Postponing the creation of a Japanese civil code allowed the Meiji state to consolidate its power, and only in 1899 did the Meiji government decree a comprehensive civil code. That approach was the opposite of the caretaker government's insistence on swift and comprehensive legal reform. Without a new civil code, judges struggled with ongoing mundane questions such as how to confirm the validity of a contract, adjudicate a divorce, or divide an estate. Judges could not rely on Tokugawa-era law because it did not offer uniform national precedents. On the contrary, Tokugawa-era law emphasized the differences between Japanese status groups, such as samurai and commoners, distinctions the Meiji government had abolished. Relying on Tokugawa precedent would thus undermine a core principle of the new nation-state: the unity of the Japanese people. Instead, Meiji administrators and judges developed an ad hoc body of national case law that fused samurai notions of the family with Western legal norms.

That evolving legal code gradually overruled many regional and status-based variations in marriage and inheritance laws. In the Tokugawa era, samurai and commoners were governed by different laws and norms.

Samurai households, for example, favored primogeniture and impartible inheritance. That reflected the nature of samurai patrimony: a household's primary asset was the father's hereditary position as a servant of his lord, which was essentially impartible. Commoners, however, were more flexible both in dividing a family's assets and in choosing an heir, with considerable regional variation. While some commoner households also favored primogeniture, in the southwest, commoners tended toward a more egalitarian division of assets among sons. In Shikoku, some villages favored ultimogeniture, succession of the youngest son, over primogeniture. Areas with high levels of labor migration also had traditions of proxy headship in which wives were recognized as household heads in their husband's absence.[57] In family relations, commoner households were more concerned with spousal compatibility than with gender hierarchy. For samurai households, a wife's unquestioning obedience to her husband was analogous to a vassal's undying loyalty to his lord. But that parallelism was meaningless for farm households, since male farmers had no tradition of vassalage. Instead, farm households celebrated spousal harmony as essential to economic prosperity.[58]

Since most Meiji-era officials were former samurai, they looked to samurai family customs when issuing rulings and decrees. Under the 1872 Meiji household registration system (*koseki*), for example, Japan was made up of patriarchal households (*ie*), rather than individuals, thereby codifying a samurai view of society. Under *koseki*, each household had a unique head, commonly an adult man, who was the legal representative of his wife, children, and younger siblings. Adult children needed the permission of their household head to marry or to form an independent household. The government recognized that some aspects of samurai patriarchy were ill-suited to commoner households and made allowances for commoner practices, such as partible inheritance. But the overall impact was to create uniformity across the archipelago.[59] On paper, if not in practice, an Ainu household on Kunashiri Island, a Ryukyuan household on Yaeyama Island, a Japanese farming household in Tosa, and a creole household on Iwojima Island were all structurally identical to a former samurai household in Tokyo.[60]

The koseki system thus invented an artificially uniform family system based on Japanese "tradition," but making Japan look "civilized" required reconciling that "tradition" with Western legal frameworks. That process was especially difficult because the Meiji government's 1871 criminal code was based on Chinese law, while reformers of the civil code focused on

French and later German law. The Chinese criminal code defined five levels of family relations. At the first level for a man were his parents, his children, his adoptive parents, and his adoptive children. For a woman, that first level consisted solely of her husband. At the second level for a man were his grandparents, his father's wives, his father's siblings (paternal uncles and aunts), his own siblings, his wives and concubines, his nieces and nephews, and his daughters-in-law. For a woman, that second level included her husband's parents, but not her own.[61] The criminal code thus assumed not only formalized patriarchy but also polygamy, and so it clashed with European notions of infidelity. Under the Napoleonic Code, for example, a husband's taking of a mistress was grounds for divorce. The government's pronouncements on civil law were thus routinely in conflict with its own criminal code.

The struggle to reconcile those conflicting traditions was one of the defining features of Meiji legal reform. As early as 1872/11, Fukuoka Takachika and Etō Shinpei urged that concubines be excluded from household registers as family members. Monogamy, they declared, was in accordance with "the laws of nature" (*tenri shizen no dōri*), while treating a concubine as a family member contravened "natural law." Because monogamy was mandated by "heaven's law," the abolition of concubines was not a rupture with tradition but a return to ancient principles. Rather than describe the issue as a conflict between Chinese and Western law, they appealed to universal values and natural law. While others in the government were sympathetic to these arguments, they noted that since even the imperial house had concubines, the issue would require careful deliberation.[62] Undeterred, Fukuoka and Etō suggested, also unsuccessfully, that concubines be reclassified as family servants.[63] The status of concubines was partly resolved by the 1882 criminal code, which omitted concubines as relatives, but only in 1884 did the Council of State confirm that concubines were no longer relatives and should therefore be removed from household registers.[64]

Entangled with the distinction between wives and concubines was the distinction between "legitimate" and "illegitimate" children. That contrast was critical in European family law, but almost irrelevant in early modern Japan. In Tokugawa-era law, the most common distinction among children was between a household's designated heir (*chakushi*) and other siblings or half-siblings (*shoshi*). Children by concubines, rather than wives, were legally unremarkable and not precluded from succession. In 1873, however, the Council of State established a new distinction: a child born to a "wife or concubine" (*saishō*) was henceforth a "*kōseishi*," literally a "public child," whereas others were "*shiseishi*," literally "private child." That terminology was an amalgam of the European distinction between "legitimate" and "illegitimate" children with the classical Chinese practice of treating concubines as family members. Only after 1884, when concubines were removed from household registries, did the neologism "shiseishi" begin to correspond to the European notion of "illegitimacy": "legitimate" children were those born to a woman registered as a member of her husband's household. In the absence of a comprehensive civil code, however, "legitimacy" remained ill defined, evolving slowly through case law. Most children born to a married couple were "legitimate" since, upon marriage, a woman normally entered her husband's household. As late as the 1890s, however, the government was still ruling on problematic situations, such as children born to couples who were legally married but where the woman had not officially registered as a member of her husband's house.[65]

These tensions between different legal traditions played out at all levels of society. The Meiji emperor and empress, for example, were publicly depicted as a monogamous couple, and the empress began performing duties appropriate for a Victorian lady of high station. She hosted state dinners and appeared beside the emperor when he visited schools, factories, and military installations.[66] But, more quietly, the emperor fathered nineteen children by five different imperial concubines. Since the empress herself was childless, in 1887 the emperor's son by a lady-in-waiting (*tenji/ naishi no suke*) was designated his heir. According to the traditions of the Japanese imperial house, this was unproblematic. Indeed, the Meiji emperor himself was the child of a lady-in-waiting. Internationally, however, the Japanese government wanted to depict the Meiji emperor as a modern monarch, so Western media were told that the empress had "adopted as her own child the Emperor's son by one of his deputy wives."[67] Monogamy became an imperial tradition only in the twentieth century, beginning with the marriage in 1900 of the future Taishō emperor.

The personal lives of Meiji leaders also reflected these shifting and fluid attitudes toward wives and concubines. In the 1870s, for example, Katsu Kaishū's Tokyo household included children by at least three women: his wife and two mistresses. This was unremarkable to Katsu's Japanese contemporaries, but it was shocking to Americans such as Clara Whitney, the teenage daughter of missionary educators. Katsu had provided extensive financial support for the Whitneys' school, and Clara regularly played and studied with Katsu's children. She was dismayed to learn that two of Katsu's sons, Umetarō and Shichirō, had different mothers, and she lamented that "the Empire is undermined by such practices." Despite her initial dismay, in 1886, Clara chose to marry Katsu's "illegitimate" son Umetarō, possibly because she was already pregnant. In 1900, however, Clara and Umetarō ended their marriage, and she returned to the United States and settled in Pennsylvania with their five children. Clara and Umetarō's relationship covered a range of evolving family structures. When Umetarō was born in 1864, the concept of "illegitimacy" did not exist in Japan. In her diary, Clara wrote that Umetarō confessed to her his "secret," but Umetarō was not legally illegitimate until years later. His shame at his "illegitimacy" likely reflected a new sense of family structure stemming from his conversion to Christianity. As for Clara, according to an 1873 Dajōkan edict, she became a Japanese subject through her marriage to Umetarō, and their children were accordingly Japanese nationals. Thus, Clara and Umetarō's children were members of his household and would remain his wards upon dissolution of the marriage. The 1899 civil code, however, allowed for custody to be decided by mutual consent of parents, permitting Clara to move the children out of the country.[68]

The Meiji's government's decision to delay a civil code left unresolved these many questions of women and the family, but that confusion could be emancipatory. The fluidity of social norms and laws in the 1860s and 1870s provided unique opportunities to cross gender and status boundaries. A compelling example is the case of Kusumoto Ine, who rose from humble origins to serve as midwife to the imperial house. Kusumoto was born in Nagasaki in 1827 to Philipp Franz von Siebold, a physician in the Dutch factory, and his Japanese concubine, Taki.[69] Siebold was expelled from Japan in 1829 on charges of espionage, having exchanged detailed maps with several Japanese scholars. In keeping with Nagasaki local practice, Siebold provided financially for his daughter in advance of his departure. But Siebold also took the unusual step of asking his Japanese medical students to look after Ine's education. She was a capable and determined student. Ine's medical career was unimpeded by her status as "illegitimate" and "mixed race." On the contrary, as a practitioner of "Dutch" or Western medicine, she entered a circle of physicians who served Date Munenari, the lord of Uwajima domain. A renowned patron of Western learning, Munenari retained Ine as a physician for the Uwajima Castle women's quarters, granting her an official stipend. Her status in Uwajima Castle was so high that William Willis, physician for the British legation, mistakenly described her as "Chief Physician of the Uwajima Family," noting that she and her family "seem to be upper class retainers."

Ine's family was fluid and crossed national and status boundaries. Her father returned to Japan in 1859, and he supported her education and career, but she continued to live with her mother, daughter, and son-in-law, Mise Shūzō, also a prominent physician in the service of the Uwajima house. She also maintained ties with her half-brothers, Alexander and Heinrich, Siebold's sons by his German wife. Ine did not marry, although she gave birth to a daughter after one of her mentors, Ishii Sōken, raped her. She rejected Sōken's offers of marriage, but she accepted career support from Ishii Kendō, Sōken's son by another woman.

Ine's medical career reached its apex around 1873 when she was called to attend the emperor's concubine Mitsuko in childbirth. Although that pregnancy tragically ended in the death of both mother and child, Ine was awarded ¥100 for her services, a sum equivalent to several years' income for many samurai or skilled craftsmen. That moment was emblematic of the emancipatory power of the Meiji Restoration: an "illegitimate," "mixed-race," single mother and rape survivor was commended for her service as personal physician to the imperial house. Ine thrived, both personally and professionally, in a window between the collapse of the Tokugawa order and the consolidation of the Meiji state. Had she been born earlier, she likely would have lived an unremarkable life in Nagasaki. Had she been born later, her gender and lack of formal education would have held her back. Indeed, the modernization of the Meiji state steadily reduced Ine's professional authority. In 1874, the Meiji state began to regulate medicine as a profession rather than a craft, and it required physicians to pass a series of examinations in order to receive government certification. Ine's medical experience was extensive, but she had learned through apprenticeship rather than formal education and was unprepared for this new exam-based regulatory regime. She was eventually certified to practice medicine, but only in the limited capacity of "old midwife," rather than as an obstetrician or "new midwife." The Midwives' Ordinance of 1899 eliminated Ine's "old midwife" option and would have ended her career, but she seems to have voluntarily stopped practicing beforehand.[70] The trajectory of Ine's life was characteristic of a broader phenomenon. The "modernization" of the Meiji state, with its expanding regulatory reach, brought to a close an era of opportunities.

The Meiji Opposition

A sprawling range of opposition groups contested the Ōkubo administration's expansion of state power. Those groups were distinct at their extremes but united by a distrust of the government's autocracy and its foreign policy. Many former samurai were incensed by the government's Korea policy. Saigō Takamori, for example, declared that Ōkubo's strategy of tricking the Chosŏn dynasty into a conflict was beneath the honor of samurai. Japan should have explicitly fought for its honor rather than emulating the vilest deceits of Western diplomacy. For many ex-samurai, the imagined glory of conquering Korea and Taiwan was a substitute for their lost privilege and prestige. That emphasis on samurai honor fused surprisingly well with demands for popular governance. Insisting that there was a popular mandate for war, activists recast samurai belligerence as a democratic value. If the "people" demanded an aggressive foreign policy, then the government needed to follow the "popular will." The opposition movement thus fused new and foreign democratic ideas with samurai notions of justice and rectitude.

The Saga Rebellion of 1874 is emblematic of that ideological syncretism. After resigning from office, Etō assembled a group of like-minded partisans and together they resolved to attack Korea and complete the work of the Restoration. Their group, the "Attack Korea Party" (Seikantō), grounded its militarism in a theory of civil rights and natural law. They insisted that the rights of the state and the rights of the people were fundamentally interdependent. The state could properly exercise its national rights only in accordance with the rights of the people (*minken*). Further, if the state lost its national rights, the people would also lose their civil rights. For Etō and his allies, that connection logically required an invasion of Korea. By insulting Japanese officials, Korea had impugned Japan's national honor, and that had diminished Japan's national rights. It was thus the duty of all Japanese men to avenge that insult in defense of their own individual rights and honor. Writing in passionate if stilted English, Etō insisted that war with Korea was something to which "any man, as rational being, must adhere with full impulse."[71] Thoroughly informed by Western legal theory, but true to Japanese warrior values, the Seikantō manifesto reads like a samurai gloss on the *Federalist Papers*.

Etō's actions in Saga terrified the Tokyo government, and Ōkubo mobilized the army in anticipation of trouble. Etō then forged an alliance of convenience with the Saga Patriot Party (Yūkokutō), a group of conservative, xenophobic ex-samurai committed to cleansing Japan of foreign influence. The Saga Patriot Party was critical of those who "idolized the foul ways of the barbarian," so it had little in common with Etō's Seikantō, many of whose members had traveled and studied abroad. But the two groups found common cause in their contempt for the Ōkubo administration's autocracy and in the need for "equitable and impartial public discussion" (kōhei shūgi). On the evening of February 15, 1874, the rebels attacked Saga Castle and routed government forces. But the government mobilized more troops, which broke and scattered the rebels on February 27. Etō escaped and traveled 150 miles south to Kagoshima to appeal to Saigō for help, but he was captured and executed together with twelve other leaders of the rebellion.

The rebels' demand for "equitable and impartial public discussion" was part of a transformation of political culture. Under the Tokugawa, the open discussion of national politics was prohibited, but by the 1870s, high politics was a regular part of public discourse. A broad range of print media, from high-minded policy journals to rumor mongering tabloids reported all aspects of politics, including foreign affairs, domestic regulations, economic policy, and corruption scandals. These new media built on earlier forms of public discourse, such as broadsides (kawaraban) and colorful woodblock prints (nishikie), but those were highly coded to evade Tokugawa-era censorship. For example, an 1853 print by the famous artist Utagawa Kuniyoshi depicted a physician visiting a sick princess, who was surrounded by concerned family and attendants. Superficially the print depicts a scene from the popular story Chikusai, but it was actually a wry commentary on the question of shogunal succession. The "princess" corresponded to the dying shogun Ieyoshi, and the doctor represented shogunal advisor Mizuno Tadakuni. Using period diaries and letters, historians have reconstructed the way readers in 1853 decoded the print as a sly parody of shogunal politics. Beginning in the late 1860s, this coded political journalism broke out into the open, and prints began "reporting" a heady mix of news, gossip, rumor, scandal, and pure fantasy.[72]

The early Meiji period produced range of journalistic media. Some publishers combined the woodblock print tradition with aspects of Western newspapers to create colorful tabloids. Others emulated the structure and format of more staid Western-language newspapers, with clear distinctions between news, editorials, and reader correspondence.[73] Highly literate and hungry for news, the Japanese public drove a steady expansion in Western-style newspapers. By the early 1880s, hundreds of different newspaper companies were printing more than 60 million copies per year for a population of roughly 30 million. By 1890, circulation had soared to over 180 million copies. These newspapers ran the gamut from semi-official government

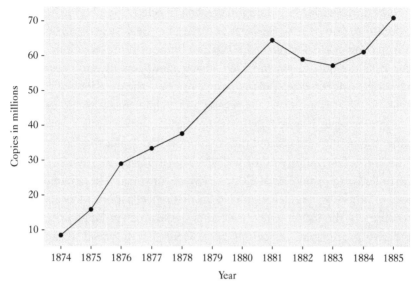

FIGURE 6.2 Japanese Newspaper Circulation. Data from Matsumoto and Yamamuro, ed., *Genron to media*, 490.

publications to vehemently anti-government journals.[74] The Ōkubo administration was alarmed by the stridency of the opposition press, but it struggled to mute dissent without lapsing into despotism. One problem was that the government's own actions had legitimized public dissent. Amid the 1873 Political Crisis, both sides had voiced their views in newspaper articles and public statements. Those precedents produced a boisterous public sphere that pushed back against surveillance, censorship, and arrests.

Political activists also confronted the government through direct petitions (*kenpakusho*). The Meiji government initially encouraged petitions in the name of "opening paths of speech" (*genro dōkai*), a phrase that suggested respectful dissent by high-ranking officials.[75] Beginning in 1872, however, commoners became increasingly willing to submit written grievances directly to the national government, and they offered exacting recommendations on a broad range of topics including foreign affairs, industrial promotion policy, education reform, the postal system, and religion. The petition gained increased legitimacy as a form of dissent in January 1874, when recently resigned members of the caretaker government, including Itagaki, Etō, and Soejima Taneomi, used it to criticize the Ōkubo administration. Their petition accused the government of autocracy and demanded the swift establishment of an elected national assembly (*minsen giin*).

Like much early Meiji thought, the 1874 "elected assembly" petition was a vibrant fusion of new Western and familiar local ideas. It insisted, for example, on the principle of no taxation without representation: "People who have the duty to pay taxes to a government concurrently possess the right to be informed of, and to approve or reject the decisions of that government. That is a universally accepted principle, and it would be superfluous to explain it here." By insisting that democracy was a "universal" value, the petitioners refuted the contention that Japan was not ready for democracy. Telegraphs worked perfectly well in Japan, they noted, because the underlying principles of electricity were universal. There had been no need to carefully adapt telegraphy to the distinctive aspects of local culture. Accordingly, the technology of elections would work in Japan because the underlying principles of natural rights were also universal. If Japan was ready for electricity and steam engines, then it was also ready for national elections. The petition thus voiced the trope of cosmopolitan chauvinism: it was patriotic to insist that Japan conform to universal principles and embrace international best practice.[76]

The authors reinforced this claim to universality by invoking older East Asian notions of political legitimacy and propriety. They criticized the government's autocracy with the classical Chinese phrase *"genro yōhei,"* literally "blocking paths of speech." That phrase referred to the government's own promise to open "paths of speech," while also invoking centuries of Chinese political thought. In Song-era Chinese thought, the phrase *"genro yōhei"* commonly referred to interference with the ability of government ministers to voice respectful dissent. It was the obligation of a minister to point his lord toward virtuous behavior, even when that meant criticizing the lord's wishes. In that classical sense, *"genro yōhei"* referred to the actions of a thin stratum of advisors to the throne, but it reflected the idea that principled dissent was a sign of loyalty rather than disloyalty.[77] The 1874 petition expanded this notion of "opening paths of speech," connecting demands for elections with East Asian concepts of legitimate rule. Within that logic, the mechanism of elections was new and Western, but the underlying principles of freedom of speech and consent of the governed were ancient and familiar.

The 1874 "elected assembly petition" catalyzed the transformation of Japanese political discourse. Published in the *Nisshin shinjishi* newspaper, the document reached a broad audience and changed the nature of dissent. Petitioners became increasingly bold, challenging the administration on the very nature of governance. The number of petitions soared, with over 520 submitted in 1874. The drafters of the 1874 petition also changed Japanese politics by openly banding together and forming a political party to advance their ideals. That group, the Public Patriot Party (Aikoko kōtō), inspired the formation of similar groups across Japan, and by the early 1880s there were hundreds of political societies in Japan, debating and contesting high politics in unprecedented fashion.[78] While the Public Patriot Party itself was ephemeral, it transformed Japanese politics by insisting that dissent could be patriotic rather than seditious.

Participation in this new world of politics varied by region. In broad sections of central Japan, many of the new activists were commoners. Rural commoners had long been engaged in local politics as village leaders; indeed, samurai rule relied on a high degree of village-level self-governance. Tokugawa-era samurai commonly left village affairs in the hands of competent commoners, intervening only when disputes could not be resolved locally or crossed village lines. In many regions, that commoner leadership leaped from the village level onto the prefectural and national stage in the early Meiji era. Thus in 1882 in Shiga Prefecture, fifty of fifty-two elected prefectural assemblymen were commoners. Voters in Saitama and Gifu elected no former samurai at all. Police surveillance reports on political activity are similar: in 1882, thirty-eight out of forty-eight political speakers in Saitama were commoners. At the periphery, however, samurai continued to dominate politics, especially in the southwest. Thus, ex-samurai held twenty-two of twenty-seven elected seats in Kōchi (formerly Tosa domain), thirty-six of forty-two in Kumamoto, and forty-three of forty-seven in Kagoshima (Satsuma domain).

That difference in the impact of ex-samurai was partly a legacy of Tokugawa-era politics. In the early Tokugawa period, domains with smaller samurai populations moved the majority of their retainers to central castle towns, leaving the countryside in the hands of commoners. Domains with larger samurai populations left more samurai in rural areas, where they displaced commoners as local leaders. Large samurai populations thus had a multiplier effect: in Kōchi, samurai were roughly 10 percent of voters but 80 percent of the assembly. These regional differences created a hybrid national movement. The early leadership of the opposition was largely former samurai like Itagaki, often from the southwest, but the membership increasingly comprised commoners across the archipelago.[79]

The Meiji government moved quickly both to suppress and coopt this growing opposition movement. Invoking new press laws, it fined and arrested journalists for criticizing the government: at least eleven were jailed in 1875, eighty-six in 1876, and forty-seven in 1877.[80] The editors of Japan's leading journal of ideas, *Meiroku Zasshi*, chose to close their publication rather than self-censor to avoid arrest.[81] But the government also moved to mollify the opposition, especially Itagaki. Kido, in particular, was eager to appease Itagaki and somehow mend the 1873 fracture. In early 1875, the oligarchy and Itagaki agreed to a compromise: the government would allow broader, popular participation in politics, and, in return, Itagaki would rejoin the government. The emperor issued a decree promising "gradual" moves toward constitutional government and the government promptly convened two deliberative assemblies: an Assembly of Local Officials (*chihōkan kaigi*) and a Senate (*genrōin*).[82] But the limited mandates of those two bodies caused discord rather harmony. Could either of these councils overturn government decrees? Draft laws of their own? Or were they limited to submitting non-binding recommendations? How would the two chambers interact? And how would the members of these councils be chosen? Meetings of the Assembly of Local Officials were consumed by fractious debate over how future members should be elected, and the government dissolved the assembly after less than a month (June 20 to July 17, 1875). The Senate lasted longer but was equally discordant. The Senate members were nominally imperial appointments, but many were Itagaki allies, the price of Itagaki's agreement to rejoin the government. They promptly began insisting that the Senate had investigatory powers and could act on petitions accusing government officials of malfeasance. That was not the gradualist, consultative body envisioned by Kido. In September 1875, Itō Hirobumi and Kido moved to sharply curtail the power of the Senate. In response, Itagaki and his allies resigned.[83]

Despite its brevity, Itagaki's rapprochement with the government generated several powerful precedents. The government committed itself publicly to both a constitution and a national assembly. Those declarations linked the Restoration to an emerging trend toward constitutionalism and electoral mandates, especially among rising global powers such as the United States, Britain, and Prussia.[84] Within Japan, public debate now assumed that Japan would become a constitutional monarchy and focused on what sort of constitution was best suited to the empire. In that environment, Itagaki expanded his political base beyond former samurai from Tosa, drawing commoner support and establishing affiliate political societies across Japan. Those groups were the antecedents of Japan's peaceful democratic resistance to government autocracy.

The collapse of the 1875 settlement also set the stage for anti-government violence. From 1875 to 1877 the government faced a series of increasingly fierce armed insurrections. That explosive discontent had three main causes: a surge in the effective tax rate (due to a fall in rice prices), the commutation of samurai stipends, and the ban on ordinary ex-samurai wearing swords. The government placated resistance to the land tax by lowering the tax rate, but it was more difficult to appease former samurai who rejected almost all Meiji reforms. In the Shinpūren Rebellion of October 1876, for example, the participants consulted a Shinto oracle for the timing of their attack and used only traditional weapons, such as swords and spears. They criticized the government for banning swords and for its slavish imitation of "foreign barbarians" (*iteki*). In coordinated attacks on October 24, the rebels killed the Kumamoto governor, the commander of the Kumamoto garrison, and the garrison chief of staff, and they seized control of the garrison itself. The rebels were routed the following day, but their attack inspired similar revolts in Akizuki and Hagi. Those uprisings were quickly suppressed as well, but the government was alarmed by the potential for a large-scale rebellion in Satsuma and, to preempt rebellion, it dispatched troops to take control of the Kagoshima armory. That move triggered the rebellion it was designed to forestall. The unannounced arrival of central government troops infuriated local partisans, who seized the armory themselves on January 29, 1877. Satsuma was now effectively at war with the government it had helped to create.[85]

The War of the Southwest (*Seinan sensō*), more commonly known in English as the Satsuma Rebellion, was unprecedented in its scale and intensity. In contrast to the Saga Rebellion of 1874, which ended as a regional skirmish, the War of the Southwest was a civil war. It drew nationwide interest and support from all levels of society. Suppressing the rebellion took nine months and required the mobilization of tens of thousands of government troops. The tide of battle tipped decisively toward the government in April 1877, but the ultimate defeat of the rebels took an additional five months, as they repeatedly escaped encirclement. That long retreat generated public sympathy for the rebels, and colorful broadsheets depicted them as brave and stalwart heroes. In order to comply with censorship laws, the text of the broadsheets dutifully described the rebels as traitors, but the illustrations celebrated their steadfast courage and loyalty. After looking at Japanese print shops and their customers, the American zoologist Edward Morse described Saigō as "the rebel chief, beloved by all Japanese."[86]

A primary cause of the 1877 rebellion was the government's attack on samurai privilege. In Satsuma, however, resistance was intensified by unique local factors. The core of the rebel movement was the Shigakkō, a network of private military academies in Satsuma established after the 1873 Political Crisis. Most Shigakkō leaders were army and navy officers who had quit the Meiji government in support of Saigō Takamori, and many also held powerful positions in local government. The Shigakkō was therefore not just a school system but also a network of political societies, and its member were influential enough to constitute a shadow government. That power was still further amplified by the unique status of Kagoshima within the Meiji settlement. The prefectural governor, Ōyama Tsunayoshi, was himself a Satsuma native who was closely affiliated with the Shigakkō, and he worked to blunt the local impact of national programs such as land tax reform.[87] By late 1876, the Meiji state had already appointed non-native governors in such powerful domains as Chōshū (Yamaguchi Prefecture) and Tosa (Kōchi Prefecture), but not in Satsuma. On the contrary, the Tokyo government was so concerned with samurai resentment in Satsuma that it allowed a unique modification in the stipend reform program. On December 11, 1876, in response to a direct appeal from the Ōyama, Tokyo announced a generous additional tier of bonds for low-income Satsuma retainers.[88] That failed to stop the revolt, but it reflects the Meiji state's reluctance to confront Satsuma exceptionalism. In that sense, the War of the Southwest was a necessary final step in the consolidation of the Meiji state. The *Tokio Times* accordingly compared the victory of the Meiji government over Satsuma to the victory of the Union over the Confederacy: "Widespread throughout the empire it is accepted and appreciated, as never before, that this is one country;—not a bundle of semi-sovereign and jealous powers, but a nation. . . . That this, an inevitable crisis, here as in America, has been fairly met and satisfactorily adjusted is matter for congratulation."[89]

But the War of the Southwest was far more than a single domain's reactionary defense of samurai privilege. It drew widespread support from proponents of "samurai populism." In Kumamoto, for example, the rebels were supported by a group of activists called the "Popular Rights Party" (Minkentō). The group began in 1874 as a school with an eclectic curriculum. Readings included translations of Jean-Jacques Rousseau's *Social Contract* and Montesquieu's *The Spirit of the Laws*, but in the evening, students focused on military drills, such as fencing and the evacuation of wounded comrades. When the Minkentō leaders learned of the uprising in

Kagoshima, they gathered secretly and began making their own ammunition out of fishing weights and kitchenware. They renamed their group the "Communal Action Brigade" (Kyōdōtai) and described their aims in a group oath: "Above, we will purge [the government] of villainous officials, below, we will ease the suffering of the farmers, at home we will preserve the people's rights (*minken*), and abroad we will expand the nation's rights (*kokken*)."[90] That oath was a succinct distillation of "samurai populism," an impassioned fusion of samurai pride, noblesse oblige, and natural rights doctrine.

In Tosa, some members of Itagaki's Risshisha, planned to overthrow the Tokyo government in support of the rebellion. Their conspiracy was discovered in August and over forty men were sent to prison. The leaders of the plot were "modernizers" and proponents of key Meiji government reforms, not simple samurai reactionaries. Mutsu Munemitsu, for example, had worked on land tax reform before quitting the government in 1873. During his five-year prison sentence for treason, he worked on translating Jeremy Bentham's *Utilitarianism* into Japanese.[91] Rehabilitated after prison, he served as ambassador to the United States and foreign minister. Ōe Taku was a judge before his arrest and imprisonment. After a twelve-year prison sentence, he reentered politics and won election to the new Diet in 1890, and today he is best known for his opposition to bonded labor and his advocacy on behalf of the *eta* and *hinin*. He was also active in business and served as president of the Tokyo Stock Exchange. Hayashi Yūzō was sentenced to ten years in prison, but he also reentered politics and eventually served as minister of communications and as minister of agriculture and commerce.

These men had little in common with the sword-wielding, oracle-consulting samurai of the Shinpūren, so what drove them to attempt an armed insurrection? They did not draft a manifesto, but an 1890 biography of Ōe declared that he hoped to fulfill the imperial Charter Oath and to "establish constitutional government." They resorted to force only because the autocracy of the Ōkubo administration foreclosed other forms of political change.[92] The *Japan Daily Herald* voiced that same sentiment when it described the War of the Southwest as a move toward democracy: "There is now such an almost universal feeling throughout the country in favor of popular representation, that any further attempt to crush it would probably only result in future troubles." If the government were to "relax the bonds which now bind the people, to lay the foundation of liberty of the press, and to give the populace some share, however slight, in the government of the country, the late outbreak—much as it is to be deplored—will have worked for good."[93]

The disparate anti-government movements of 1877 were also connected by the larger than life persona of Saigō Takamori. Saigō had long enjoyed an almost religious following among Satsuma samurai, especially imperial loyalists. Tradition-minded samurai considered him to be a paragon of warrior virtue: frugal, incorruptible, honorable, and unquestionably loyal. He rejected Western dress except for his military uniform and favored simple cotton kimonos over frock coats. But Saigō's vision of Japan went well beyond a defense of tradition. His approach to the Shigakkō, for example, suggests that he was hoping to transform the samurai estate into a self-reliant yeomanry. At the school directly patronized by Saigō, the Yoshino Kaikonsha, students read Chinese classical texts and practiced military drills, but they also raised their own food crops, such as millet and Japanese sweet potatoes. While many of the Shigakkō were fiercely xenophobic, Saigō recruited foreign language teachers and invited a British physician to Kagoshima, the Satsuma castle town, to teach medicine. Scattered in Saigō's aphorisms and poems was a vision of the samurai as frugal, courageous, self-reliant young patriots who could thrive even when stripped of their hereditary income and authority. That vision was capacious enough to enthrall both advocates of constitutional government and defenders of the samurai tradition. Woodblock tabloids conveyed that ethos by creating the phrase "a new government, rich in virtue" (*shinsei kōtoku*) and depicting it on rebel banners. In point of fact, there were no such pennants, but the phrase captured the duality of Saigō's appeal. For his supporters, Saigō represented the best of the old and the new: the opportunities and freedoms of the Meiji era with the comforts of Confucian noblesse oblige.[94]

The War of the Southwest ended on September 24, 1877, when Saigō and several of his loyal lieutenants died in a suicide march into enemy fire. The defeat of the rebels marked the end of domestic military challenges to the Meiji state. For men like Itagaki, the choice was abundantly clear: challenging the government through words might be futile, but challenging it through arms was fatal. Victory on the battlefield was a triumph for the Ōkubo administration, and it left Ōkubo as the single most powerful member of the government. But Ōkubo himself had less than a year to steer the Meiji state: on May 17, 1878, he was assassinated by six former samurai. The assassins are sometimes described as "disgruntled *shizoku*," a phrase that is woefully incomplete.[95] Their manifesto was replete with reference to popular rights and democratic principles as well as samurai valor. They criticized the government for obstructing public debate and for suppressing the people's rights. Since securing civil rights was essential to national honor, the Ōkubo administration's autocracy was leading the nation to ruin. By murdering a villain such as Ōkubo, and then surrendering to the police, the assassins claimed to be offering their own lives in the name of the 1868 Oath and 1875 imperial edict.[96] Rather than simply look to the past, the assassins repositioned a traditional samurai vendetta in the new language of popular rights. Such radical nostalgia was central to the Meiji Restoration, invoked both by political leaders and their assassins.

The End of the Revolution

The assassination of Ōkubo created a power vacuum within the Meiji government. On a personal level, the three giants of the Restoration (Kido, Saigō, and Ōkubo) were now all gone. Kido had died in May 1877 after a long decline from tuberculosis, Saigō in the War of the Southwest, and then Ōkubo by assassination. Those deaths created a bitter struggle for power within the Meiji elite. Ōkubo's death, in particular, raised the question of who would steer Japanese civil affairs. Ōkubo had arrogated enormous power to himself as head of the Home Ministry. That agency, created after the 1873 Political Crisis, had broad authority over domestic policy, including economic development, public works, communications, policing, local government, and the household registration system. Its sprawling portfolio thus encroached on the authority of the ministries of finance, justice, and industry. With Ōkubo's death, the home ministry portfolio passed to Itō Hirobumi, consolidating his rising position within the government.

Itō's rise was particularly threatening to Ōkuma Shigenobu, who found both his policies and his person under threat. As a former samurai from Saga, Ōkuma felt isolated by the growing exclusiveness of the Satsuma-Chōshū clique, and he was besieged on policy questions as well. Ōkuma had eagerly promoted the Ōkubo administration's economic development policies, but those came under challenge after the War of the Southwest. Military expenses had swelled the government's budget deficit and begun to undermine the value of the yen. Basic commodity prices began surging in 1879, and by 1880 the cost of rice was double its 1877 price. Key finance officials, such as Inoue Kaoru and Matsukata Masayoshi, insisted that a balanced budget was the answer. Ōkuma acknowledged the problem of inflation, but he insisted that it was due to a trade deficit and a shortage of specie: the government had printed ¥20 million in unconvertible currency to finance the war. He suggested that Japan borrow specie internationally

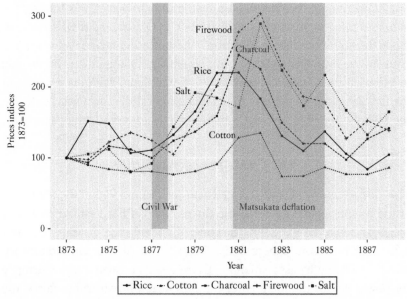

FIGURE 6.3 Wholesale Commodity Prices in early Meiji-era Japan. Data from Matsukata, *Report on the Adoption of the Gold Standard in Japan*, 36, 103.

in order to buy back its unconvertible currency and that it repay the loan with the proceeds from increased taxes. Although Ōkuma held the portfolio of finance minister, he was nonetheless forced into a compromise. In late 1880, he agreed to a plan to reduce expenditures by selling off government assets. That compromise effectively reversed Ōkuma's policy of directly promoting industrial development.[97]

The government was also divided over the looming question of a constitution and a national assembly. It had promised the "gradual" development of constitutional government in 1875, and that process was accelerated by popular pressure. After the failure of armed resistance in 1877, the Risshisha focused on extending its membership beyond Kōchi and creating a national organization. At two large national meetings in March and October 1880, the party voted to initiate a mass movement for constitutional government. They created a new organization, the Association for a National Assembly, which would coordinate with local political societies: arranging speaking tours, disseminating news, and helping local groups draft their own constitutions. The Association scheduled a follow-up meeting for October 1881, which would serve as a national constitutional convention. Those moves generated an explosion of popular political activity, including scores of constitutions drafted by local activists.[98]

The government responded by trying to coopt Fukuzawa Yukichi, a prominent intellectual. Fukuzawa had been seeking government support for his school, the Keiō Gijuku (now Keiō University), and jobs for his graduates. Many of his students had, in fact, been employed by the finance minister under the patronage of Inoue and Ōkuma. In early 1881, the government proposed that Fukuzawa run a new government-sponsored newspaper, the precursor to the *Jiji Shinpō*, and use his influence to promote the oligarchy's vision of constitutional government. Fukuzawa initially demurred, but agreed once he was assured that the government's plans included an elected assembly.[99]

The government also tried to agree internally on a constitution, but those discussions intensified tensions within the oligarchy. Itō and Inoue Kaoru both acknowledged the need for an elected assembly but thought that its powers should be primarily passive. Itō hoped that the assembly would assuage popular discontent by allowing the people to "observe and confirm the exactness of national finance." Through observation, the people would gain "maturity and experience" and they might "gradually" be allowed to participate more substantively in public affairs. Initially, however, no elected assembly should "interfere" with governmental affairs.[100] Ōkuma, by contrast, suggested the early creation of a powerful elected assembly that would form a government and determine national policy. Instead of lofty notions of national unity, he insisted on the benefits of open rivalry between political parties. Instead of "gradual" progress toward an assembly, he suggested that elections be held by 1882. Itō was stunned by this proposal and attacked it as reckless, radical, and unsuited to Japan.[101]

Tensions within the oligarchy were further inflamed by a corruption scandal. As part of its anti-inflationary policies, the government decided to sell the Hokkaido Colonial Bureau's sprawling portfolio of investments. Since the bureau's business projects were running large deficits, selling off the bureau's assets would help balance the budget, but the terms of the sale reeked of collusion and malfeasance. Kuroda Kiyotaka, the bureau head, arranged to sell its properties to a friend and fellow ex-samurai from Satsuma, Godai Tomoatsu, for only ¥300,000, although the government had spent over ¥14 million purchasing and developing the properties. The deal even included a thirty-year zero-interest loan. When the terms of the sale were announced in July 1881, the press seized on the story as evidence of the government's contempt for its own people. To the dismay of the government, criticism was not limited to opposition newspapers. Normally pro-government dailies such as the *Yūbin Hōchi Shinbun* and the *Tōkyō Nichi Nichi Shinbun* faulted the government for its "oligarchic" ways. The opposition seized on the scandal as tangible evidence of government misconduct and began holding large public protests. In August 1881, for example, the *Tōkyō Yokohama Mainichi Shinbun* staged a rally at a major kabuki theater and sold thousands of tickets. Despite the sweltering summer heat, people stood in line for hours for a chance to hear famous political activists denounce the government. Amid this storm of criticism, Ōkuma's objection to the sale made him an opposition hero. Editorial cartoons depicted the debate over the sale as a battle between Kuroda and Ōkuma, with Ōkuma as an advocate of "the people's rights." Ōkuma's rivals were already disturbed by his radical proposal for a constitution, so this surge in public acclaim deepened their suspicion and animosity.[102]

The 1881 Political Crisis was a distinctly modern political struggle, involving the mass media and corporations as well as a clash of powerful personalities. The exact details remain murky, but one theory is that Ōkuma hoped to use his popularity to enhance his position within the oligarchy, perhaps forcing out rivals such as Itō. An alternative theory is that Itō, Kuroda, Inoue Kaoru, and Inoue Kowashi saw Ōkuma's popularity as a threat and chose to force him from the government. Inoue Kowashi, an Ōkubo protégé and chief secretary of the Council of State (*dajōkan daishokikan*), seems to have spread rumors that Ōkuma was part of a vast conspiracy involving opposition newspapers, Fukuzawa Yukichi, and the Mitsubishi Company. Those accusations lacked solid evidence but had the virtue of plausibility. Mitsubishi would logically have opposed the sale of government assets to a potential rival, Godai's Kansai Trading Company (Kansai bōekisha). And many of Fukuzawa's students and supporters worked for opposition newspapers and for Mitsubishi, which was in turn subsidizing opposition newspapers. Further, because Mitsubishi was based in Tosa, while Godai was from Satsuma, the rivalry between the two companies intensified lingering suspicions that the government was narrowing to a Satsuma-Chōshū clique. In this instance, new business rivalries coincided with old domain rivalries. Even more than a century later it remains unclear whether Ōkuma was hoping to oust Itō or whether such rumors were actually part of Itō's campaign against Ōkuma.[103] What is certain is that the conflict drew in new and newly politicized forces: newspapers, political societies, public intellectuals, and business interests. As such, the conflict was Japan's first modern political crisis.

Ōkuma's opponents in the government moved decisively to block his ambitions. On October 11 they met to demand his resignation, and he stepped down the following day, citing poor health. Dozens of his supporters resigned in solidarity, including the minister of agriculture and commerce (Kōno Togawa) and the director of the railway bureau (Maejima Hisoka).[104] The government also canceled the sale of the Hokkaidō Colonization Bureau's assets to the Kansai Trading Company. Finally, the government released an imperial decree, promising a constitution and an elected assembly by 1890. That decree served both to placate the opposition and to reassert government control over the nature of the constitution. Japan's constitution would be drafted by the oligarchy, not by dissidents like Ōkuma and his allies.

Those actions marked the end of the Meiji Revolution. The foreign crisis of the 1850s and 1860s had produced a fierce contest over how to defend and legitimize the Japanese state. That clash of visions and ideals had generated the ebullient revolutionary turmoil of the early Meiji era transformation. The 1881 Political Crisis, however, marked a decisive narrowing of political choices. Instead of rapid and radical change, the Meiji state was now decisively committed to gradualism. Japan would challenge the unequal treaties and build its own colonial empire, but only after decades of economic development and domestic reform. The people would have a voice in their government, but that, too, would be part of a gradual state-directed process. The government would fulfill its 1881 promise of a constitution, but that document would be drafted in secret by Itō Hirobumi and presented to the Japanese people in 1889 as a gift from the emperor. While cognizant of popular discontent, the state officially treated popular constitutional drafts as irrelevant and illegitimate. Once promulgated, the 1889 constitution remained, unaltered and unamended, as Japan's supreme national law until 1947. Further, the government codified key elements of state power, such as civil service regulations, the national police, and the cabinet system before presenting the constitution and convening the first Diet. Prewar Japanese democracy thus developed within the structures of state power established in the 1880s.

At the same time, the crisis helped solidify the two most effective and durable forms of opposition. First, the crisis confirmed the power of an activist press and mass mobilization. Through editorials, lectures, and rallies, the Japanese people had forced a decisive shift in the nature of the state. That was unprecedented. Popular protests had long forced minor changes in government policy, such as tax reductions. But the 1881 Political

Crisis produced a new ambit of legitimate dissent: the people could pub-licly contest the very structures of the state. The Japanese oligarchy could have deployed the army or the police to crush the protests, but it was constrained by both Confucian and Western notions of tyranny. Having faulted the shogunate for despotism, the Meiji oligarchy was loath to rep-licate that vice by eliminating opposition voices. The desire to look "civi-lized" in Western eyes also inveighed against the massive and arbitrary arrest of dissidents. The Japanese government's quest to wield authoritar-ian power, without an overt reliance on state violence, would become a defining feature of Meiji politics.

Second, the crisis produced political parties as an effective and durable force. Galvanized by the success of opposition rallies, Itagaki recast his political organization as the Liberal Party (Jiyūtō) while Ōkuma and his allies formed the Constitutional Progressive Party (Rikken Kaishintō). Japan now had two former government officials leading opposition groups, which lent political parties a new air of legitimacy. Activist news-papers and political parties would have been unthinkable, as well as illegal, a mere fifteen years before. Parties would have been crushed as cabals and newspapers smothered by censorship. By the 1880s, however, the partisan denunciation of government policy, complete with detailed counterpro-posals, had become a normal part of political life.

Beyond these continuities with later Japanese history, the Crisis of 1881 is a striking example of global isomorphism. Increasingly embedded in a new international order, the Japanese polity came to resemble its for-eign partners and rivals. In 1860, for example, it would have been absurd to compare the Meiji emperor to his approximate contemporary Queen Victoria. Until the late 1860s, the Japanese emperor was essentially invis-ible to his people, and Japan was a relatively isolated agrarian economy. Britain was a major imperial power, while Japan was besieged by impe-rialism. By end of their reigns, however, the comparison seemed sensi-ble. Both monarchs reigned over constitutional monarchies with overseas empires. The two sovereigns had presided over massive expansions of the popular franchise while at the same time enjoying increases in monarchi-cal prestige. Queen Victoria had become empress of India while also over-seeing an expansion of suffrage through the Reform Act of 1867. The Meiji emperor opened the first European-style parliament in Asia and oversaw the colonization of Taiwan and Korea. Both monarchs presided over mas-sive and rapid industrialization and the ensuing social dislocations. Both monarchs served, to an unprecedented degree, as national symbols and their anniversaries and funerals became moments of national commemoration. In both countries, a new level of loyalty to the throne helped dissipate social tensions.

Japan and Britain became similar because they were part of common global processes and developed similar answers to similar questions. Practically, how did a modern monarch mobilize his or her subjects? How much was by emancipation and how much by indoctrination? Conceptually, what made a specific group of people a nation? What types of racial, cultural, or linguistic similarities constituted the British or Japanese nation? And what constituted a legitimate empire? How could one nation-state justify its control over another people? Japan's confrontation with those global questions is often described as "modernization" or "modernity," but that approach fails to acknowledge that global isomorphism was not a uniquely modern process. In the 600s and 700s, Japan, Tang China, and the kingdoms of the Korean peninsula grew more alike as they fought for and against each other. That ancient process of isomorphism was most certainly not "modernization," but it anticipated modern patterns of global isomorphism. Nor can the Meiji-era adaptation of global best practice be summarized as "Westernization." By the end of the Meiji era it seemed as though global isomorphism might require a reverse importation of models back from Japan. Advocates of "national efficiency" argued that Britain should emulate Japan in order to stem its decline.[105] One of the most imaginative examples of that new assessment of Japan was H. G. Wells's *Modern Utopia*, in which a "voluntary nobility," known as "samurai," rule a utopian society on a distant planet.[106] In similar fashion, Robert Baden-Powell, founder of the Boy Scout movement, extolled the Japanese as models of modern patriotism and self-sacrifice.[107] Japan, it seemed, had built a nation-state worthy of British esteem and emulation.

Participants in Meiji politics did not describe their experience as global isomorphism, but they did make sense of their world through the tropes of cosmopolitan chauvinism and radical nostalgia. After 1881, for example, national political debate was no longer over whether to base a Japanese constitution on Western models but over which Western model to adapt: Prussian, English, or French. But that debate built on a robust discourse in which desirable Western norms were understood as universal values. As Itō observed in his 1881 discussion of a constitution, "the current political crisis" is driven by "global trends" (*udai no fūki*) and is not unique to any single country or land.[108] As part of that global discourse on sovereign power, Japan would naturally look to international best practice.

How did the most successful countries in the world become economically rich and militarily strong? How did they balance monarchical authority with civil rights?

At the same time, the 1881 Political Crisis highlighted the power of radical nostalgia to legitimize political reforms. The October 12 imperial decree announcing a national assembly looked to the future by invoking the ancient past. The creation of a constitutional monarchy (*rikken seitai*) was described both as the emperor's legacy for future generations and a continuation of twenty-five centuries of imperial rule. Gradual progress toward a constitution was, according to the edict, part of a well-considered plan that included the creation of the Senate in 1875 and prefectural assemblies in 1878. While a national assembly was a new form of government, adaptability was one of the many august traditions of the imperial rule, so an assembly was fully consonant with imperial tradition. Under radical nostalgia, nothing was more traditional than this new form of government. But since the emperor himself had committed to this grand project, it was essential that his people avoid destructive chatter and idle speculation. Closing with a reference to the ancient Chinese *Book of Documents* (Ch. Shujing), the emperor ordered his subjects to be patient while he clarified for posterity illustrious principles of governance. That was a thinly veiled command to stop submitting draft constitutions while the government pondered how best to explain constitutional monarchy in terms of ancient imperial practice.[109] For decades, such radical nostalgia had been invoked to stoke the fires of the Meiji Revolution. The revolutionaries of the 1860s had called upon tradition to undermine the shogunate and create a boldly new regime. In 1881, however, those same tropes were deployed to bring that revolution to a close.

Conclusion

WHERE DOES THE Meiji Restoration fit in the broad sweep of Japanese history? The common adjectives of "Westernizing" and "modernizing" capture one face of the Restoration. Meiji-era reformers remade Japanese institutions based largely on Western models, transforming everything from haircuts to criminal law. The goal was to legitimize Japan in a new and challenging international order. But a focus on "Westernization" and "modernization" misses how the Restoration was, both implicitly and explicitly, a recapitulation of ancient policies. Threatened by the Tang Empire, the ancient Japanese imperial court sought to situate itself as a legitimate power within the Chinese interstate system. That goal involved not only military defense but also a broader cultural and philosophical project: creating a Japanese polity that would be recognized as "civilized" across the region. To that end, the ancient Japanese state borrowed ideas, technologies, and rituals from the continent. Even while borrowing ideas from China, the Nara and Heian courts insisted on Japanese distinctiveness, but they did so within a political and philosophical framework that originated in China.

The Meiji Restoration, over a millennium later, was a parallel process. In "restoring" the emperor to his ancient glory, Meiji leaders sought to win broad international recognition for the Japanese state. As in the 600s and 700s, statesmen were concerned with a military threat: how could Japan resist a powerful and expansionist empire? In the 1800s, however, that foreign threat was not Tang China but Western imperialism. Nonetheless, the Japanese response again fused cultural borrowing with an emphasis on local distinctiveness. The Japanese emperor was restyled both as a counterpart to European monarchs and as a descendant of the Sun Goddess, and thereby cosmopolitan but also unique in the world. The construction of the Meiji state explicitly harkened back to ancient precedents while embracing modern Western social and political practices.

Considered in this long sweep of millennia rather than decades, Japanese political history reveals some unexpected continuities. There are strange parallels, for example, between Japanese political involvements on the Korean peninsula in the seventh and twenty-first centuries. In the 660s, Japan and China backed rival polities on the Korean peninsula: the nascent Yamato state was allied with Paekche and Tang China supported Silla. Some thirteen centuries later, Japan and China are again backing rival Korean states: the People's Republic of China (PRC) is allied with the Democratic People's Republic of Korea (DPRK) while Japan supports the Republic of Korea (ROK). Both alliances are strained. Cooperation between the ROK and Japan is painful and politically fraught because of Japan's colonial control over Korea from 1905 to 1945. In 2012, for example, the formal ratification of an agreement on intelligence sharing was postponed because of a long-standing dispute over so-called "comfort women." The two governments disagree over whether and how many Korean women were forced into prostitution by the Japanese Army. As a result, Japanese-ROK cooperation is officially conducted through the United States as a common ally. Thus, the Japanese military has "observer" status when the United States and the ROK conduct military exercises, and Japan and the ROK share military intelligence through the United States. ROK and Japanese military forces also train together, but on neutral ground, like Alaska.[1] Since 2014, the three parties have referred to their cooperation as the "US-Japan-ROK Trilateral." On the other side, the PRC-DPRK alliance was once united by a communist vision of human progress, but since the 1980s the two sides have diverged. The PRC is now a market-oriented one-party state, while the DPRK has created a distinctive combination of Confucian monarchy, economic autarky, and neo-Stalinist surveillance. The DPRK routinely resists PRC prodding to de-escalate its confrontation with the ROK and to introduce economic reforms. North Korea is thus as troublesome an ally as was Silla, which unified the peninsula with Tang help but then attacked and drove out Chinese forces.

At the same time, there are stark differences in these parallel geopolitical struggles. In the twenty-first century, political alliances are described in language that originated in modern Europe. Thus, press releases from the Japanese Ministry of Self-Defense refer to United Nations resolutions, "international society" (*kokusai shakai*), "collective security" (*kyōtsū no anzen hoshō*), and "objectivity."[2] Such language was not, of course, a part of

Yamato-Paekche cooperation in the 600s. Seventh-century discourse was a thoroughly Chinese in origin, even as Paekche and Yamato jointly opposed Tang China. In period discourse, joint military operations were not based on an alliance of equals but on a hierarchy of monarchs bound by tributary ties. Ancient Japanese and Korean sources agree on that conceptual framework even as they disagree on which ancient monarchs were superior.[3]

That shift in language is both an artifact of global isomorphism and a legacy of Western imperialism. The modern international system originated in a European discourse of international relations. It became a global language of politics through European conquest and colonization. Thus, the ubiquity of phrases such as "international cooperation" in modern discourse reflects a legacy of Western political dominance. The United Nations, for example, is nominally made up of equally sovereign nation-states, and public discussion among these distinct but equal states is supposed to lead to cooperation and then peace.[4] Prior to Western imperialism, diplomats in Beijing, Edo, or Seoul would have scoffed at this emphasis on equality and discussion, either as an ideal or a conceit. For them, a hierarchy of sovereigns was part of a moral order. Western imperialism crushed those East Asian norms of international conduct.

Modern "universal" institutions like the United Nations are actually part of a long Western tradition of maintaining international order, beginning with the Peace of Westphalia and running through the Congress of Vienna and the League of Nations. All these institutions and agreements were shaped by a series of tensions. First is a tension between equality and difference: all nation-states are equally sovereign polities, but as separate nation-states they must also be ethnically distinct from each other. Second is a tension between equality and hierarchy: the modern international system extols both the equality of all nation-states and the superiority of great powers.

Many of these tensions are made visible in public rituals, such as the display of flags. According to UN regulations, national flags are all of identical size and shape, although the UN flag flies above the rest. This display reflects a central principle of the modern international order: the equal sovereignty of all states. All states are, at least in theory, equal in their rights, and their flags are, therefore, equal in size and shape. The common shape of world flags is a vivid example of the normative and symbolic force of global isomorphism. There is no military or technological advantage to a rectangular flag, but it marks membership in an international community. But equal size and shape does not mean the same. On the contrary, the flags serve to differentiate countries through their different emblems. The iconography of each flag purportedly reveals its country's distinct national history and culture. Thus the fifty stars and thirteen stripes of the United States flag reflect the growth of the union, while the British Union Jack is a blend of the Cross of St. George (England), the Cross of St. Andrew (Scotland), and the Cross of St. Patrick (Ireland). The Japanese "sun-mark" flag (Nisshōki) echoes the literal meaning of the word Nihon (Japanese for Japan) as the "origin of the sun," or "land of the rising sun."[5] On the UN's supposedly neutral field of flags, Koranic verse (Saudi Arabia) can co-exist with the Star of David (Israel), Daoist trigrams (ROK), and the communist star (China). The flags are thus all different but in a strictly regulated way.[6]

The structure of the United Nations also reveals a tension between equality and hierarchy. With its emphasis on the equality of nation-states, the United Nations is superficially hostile to empires. At the same time, it accords special status to five current and former empires as permanent members of the Security Council. Those five nations represent the victorious coalition in World War II, but also five great imperial powers: the United States, the United Kingdom, the USSR/Russia, France, and China. That special elite status reflects a long-standing belief that the maintenance of international order requires the intervention of great powers and empires. Thus, to paraphrase George Orwell, all nations are equal, but some are more equal than others.[7]

The global dominance of this Western vision of political power reflects, on the one hand, the "Rise of the West." For millennia, Japan, China, and Korea made war and peace within a common discourse based on classical Chinese texts, Confucian norms of conduct, and Buddhist visions of virtue. Those ideas and values now seem part of a remote past. The triumph of the Western international system is so thorough that Chinese, Japanese, and Korean officials discuss their own past in Western terms. Consider, for example, the current dispute between Japan, Taiwan, and China over the Senkaku/Diaoyu Islands. The Japanese government insists that the islands were first discovered by a Japanese survey in 1885. There were no overt markers of sovereignty on the islands before 1885, so the Roman legal principle of *terra nullius* or "nobody's land" applied: the islands were free for the taking. In order to stake an official claim to the islands, the Japanese government erected a monument on one of the islands in 1895. This approach to sovereignty marks how thoroughly the Meiji state had adapted to European notions of law and territoriality. Under the Tokugawa order it would have been absurd to suggest that state sovereignty required dispatching government agents to place markers on uninhabited peripheral islands.[8]

Chinese counter-arguments are equally anachronistic. The Chinese government insists that navigational records and log books from as early as the 1300s denote the islands as Chinese. But such readings assume a level of clarity and exactitude foreign to those documents. As Peter Bol has observed, prior to Western influence, Chinese cartographers were largely unconcerned with the exact depiction of uninhabited, peripheral territories. Detailed Chinese maps and gazetteers go back to at least the third century BCE, but they were designed to mark zones of jurisdiction rather than exact spatial boundaries. Government maps told local officials "which settlements fell under [their] jurisdiction and what property was held by the inhabitants of those settlements."[9] The absolute boundaries of territories without people were unimportant. As in Japan, exact maps depicting frontiers were imperialist projects, created largely in competition with modern European empires.[10]

These disputes thus reveal a complete triumph of a "modern," "Western" sense of space and power over East Asian "tradition." As such, it has displaced one of the great diplomatic achievements of early-modern Northeast Asia: how the Qing, Tokugawa, and Shō avoided an explicit contest over sovereignty. Rather than trumpet their conquest of Ryukyu in 1609, the Tokugawa chose an opposite strategy. They concealed evidence of Japanese control lest China stop its trade missions to Ryukyu. The Ming and Qing chose to indulge this conceit. Today, however, Chinese and Japanese state agents actively ignore this legacy in order to find, in early modern documents, explicit and exclusive claims to sovereign power.

In similar fashion, Japan and South Korea are locked in a sovereignty dispute over a cluster of barely habitable rocks. The "islands" are known in Japanese as Takeshima, in Korean as Tokto, and somewhat neutrally as the Liancourt Rocks. Although the islands have only two permanent residents (subsidized by the Republic of Korea to support its territorial claim), and total less than 0.2 square kilometers (0.07 sq. miles), the question of sovereignty has become a source of public friction between Tokyo and Seoul. In the mass media, the dispute has become entangled with the legacy of the Japanese colonial empire in Korea, and nationalists on both sides have pushed their claims with increasingly bellicose rhetoric. Like the Senkaku/Diaoyu Islands dispute, the Takeshima/Tokto dispute breaks with an early modern East Asian practice of looking past such questions. The Tokugawa and Chosŏn governments tolerated each other's differing opinions on the sovereignty of Tsushima, an island more than 3,500 times larger than Takeshima/Tokto. The two governments had no interest in arguing over barren rocks. The rules of modern, Western, "international society," however, hinge on exact borders and connect control over rocks to economic and military power. According to the 1994 UN Convention on the Law of the Sea, sovereignty over the islands will determine the extent of the two countries' Exclusive Economic Zones, so political control over the rocks will affect fishing rights and access to possible undersea fields of gas hydrate, a potential source of natural gas.[11]

This conceptual hegemony of the Western international order continues despite predictions to the contrary. In the 1990s, the political scientist Samuel Huntington confidently predicted that a relative decline in Western military and economic power would lead to a concomitant retreat of Western political ideas. That, in turn, would lead to a "Clash of Civilizations," most markedly a clash between "the West and the rest." With the end of the Cold War, he observed, "the great divisions among humankind and the dominating source of conflict will be cultural." Thus, cultural differences between the United States and Japan would weaken the US-Japan military alliance, while East Asia would grow more unified under its common Confucian heritage. China would emerge as the leader of a Confucian alliance and, more broadly, the leader of a massive Confucian-Islamic alliance against the West. That alliance would challenge "Western interests, values and power" as part of a struggle between "the West and the rest."[12]

These proclamations were debated in earnest, but they now seem almost comically wrong. China is not allied with Islam against the "West"; on the contrary, it is fighting against an Islamic movement in Xinjiang. The PRC is desperately attempting to create a vision of Uighur ethnic identity that is supportive of Beijing rather than affiliated with pan-Islamic ideals. The PRC describes that fight not as a rejection of the "Western" value of religious liberty but as cooperation in the equally Western "war on terror." The US-Japanese alliance has grown stronger, not weaker, in the face of Chinese military and economic growth. There is no evidence of regional solidarity, against the West or anything else. The resurgence of Chinese economic and military power has not led China, Japan, and Korea to renegotiate their international relations in terms of Confucian kingship or to describe trade treaties as part of imperial tribute missions. East Asia has grown rich and powerful within the European international order.

Reflecting on the long sweep of Japanese history, this is unsurprising. There is no reason to assume that Western values should overlap with Western power or Western interests. Put simply, imperial ideologies can long outlive empires. For many centuries, before modern imperialism, the hegemony of the Chinese international order thrived independently of the vicissitudes of Chinese imperial power.[13] The collapse of the Tang in 907 did not result in a widespread rejection across East Asia of Chinese attitudes toward political power and legitimacy. On the contrary, those ideas were reproduced in the absence of Chinese power. In the 1200s, for example, when the Mongol empire threatened to invade Japan, it conveyed its intentions through classical Chinese discourse. The Mongols were not ethnically Chinese but Central Asian nomads, and they explicitly declared their ethnic difference. Their invasion fleet was not Chinese but comprised Mongol horsemen and impressed Korea sailors. But the Mongols did not think to assert a distinctly Mongol view of empire or to write in Japanese, Mongol, or Korean. Rather, they described their ascendant empire in classical Chinese terms, with references to the ancient sages, the "mandate of heaven," and the duties of loyal subjects to legitimate sovereigns.[14] Similarly, when Toyotomi Hideyoshi aspired to conquer the Ming in the 1590s, he did not reject Chinese conceptions of power. In his official epistle to the Chosŏn throne, he couched his megalomania in terms of classical Confucian and Buddhist virtues. In Japan, he had "nurtured the farmers," shown compassion for the bereaved, and brought his people prosperity. He was thus morally entitled to dominate the world. These Chinese "values" were so abstracted from Chinese imperial power that Hideyoshi could invoke them when challenging the Ming.[15] In this way, for centuries, Chinese attitudes toward empire were dissociated from Chinese imperial power.[16]

The Meiji Restoration is a stark instance of this process of reproduction and cooptation, but in the face of Western imperialism. Restoration leaders and activists embraced "Western" ideas precisely because they could be disembodied from their Western origins and adopted as universal values. Rather than struggle with a stark choice between "the West" and "Japan," they refashioned Japan as a distinct and legitimate polity within the Western world order. That process required a rediscovery of Japanese uniqueness. To celebrate Japan as a nation-state, writers and activists looked to the glories of the ancient imperial court. Becoming "modern" thus meant extolling Japanese "tradition." Much

historical writing effaces this process by invoking the dual dichotomies of "Japan" versus "the West" and "modern"/"modernity" versus
"tradition." The revolutionary force of the Meiji Revolution came from
an opposite set of convictions: the resolute sense that the ancient past
could guide the future and that universal truths could enhance and
advance local virtues.

Notes

INTRODUCTION

1. Kenchō Suematsu [Suyematsu], *A Fantasy of Far Japan or Summer Dream Dialogues* (London: Archibald Constable, 1905), 287–293; "Brief History of the Government Troubles and Their Result—Our Intercourse with the Country—Remarks of Gov. Ito of Jeddo," *New York Times*, May 14, 1871.

2. For an example of this false dichotomy, see Niall Ferguson, *Civilization: The West and the Rest* (London: Allen Lane, 2011), 221–222.

3. Comparing the Qing to the Romanov and Ottoman empires, Rowe observes that "viewing the Qing as a fairly typical example of an early modern land-based Eurasian empire, we could argue that its final expiration in 1911 arrived just about on time." William T. Rowe, *China's Last Empire: The Great Qing* (Cambridge, MA: Harvard University Press, 2009), 285.

4. Stephen Howe, *Empire: A Very Short Introduction* (Oxford: Oxford University Press, 2002), 85–86.

5. Jürgen Osterhammel succinctly summarizes the intersection of racial discourse and great power rivalries in late nineteenth-century empires: "a 'might is right' ideology, mostly suffused with racism; the supposed incapacity of native peoples to govern themselves in an orderly manner; and an (often preventive) protection of national interests in the contest with rival European powers." See Jürgen Osterhammel, *The Transformation of the World: A Global History of the Nineteenth Century* (Princeton, NJ: Princeton University Press, 2014), 401. See also Prasenjit Duara, "Civilizations and Nations in a Globalizing World," in *Reflections on Multiple Modernities: European, Chinese, and Other Interpretations*, ed. Dominic Sachsenmaier and S. N. Eisenstadt (Leiden: Brill, 2002), 79–99; Prasenjit Duara, *Sovereignty and Authenticity: Manchukuo and the East Asian Modern* (Lanham: Rowman & Littlefield, 2003), esp. 9–40; Prasenjit Duara, *Rescuing History from the Nation: Questioning Narratives of Modern China* (Chicago: University of Chicago Press, 1995), esp. 17–50; and James Louis Hevia,

English Lessons: The Pedagogy of Imperialism in Nineteenth-Century China (Durham, NC: Duke University Press, 2003).

6. Mahmood Mamdani, *Citizen and Subject: Contemporary Africa and the Legacy of Late Colonialism* (Princeton, NJ: Princeton University Press, 1996), 3–5.

7. My interpretation of the Meiji Restoration as the construction of a nation-state is influenced by the Japanese "kokumin kokka" thesis. See, in particular, Nishikawa Nagao 西川長夫, *Kokkyō no koekata: kokumin kokka ron josetsu* 国境の越え方: 国民国家論序説, 2nd ed. (Tokyo: Heibonsha, 2001); Nishikawa Nagao 西川長夫 and Matsumiya Hideharu 松宮秀治, eds., *Bakumatsu Meiji-ki no kokumin kokka keisei to bunka hen'yō* 幕末・明治期の国民国家の形成と文化変容 (Tokyo: Shin'yōsha, 1995). Nishikawa explicitly draws on the Japanese translation of Benedict Anderson's *Imagined Communities: Reflection on the Origins and Spread of Nationalism*, 2nd ed. (London: Verso, 1991). For the question of Japanese nationalism and the Restoration see Mitani Hiroshi 三谷博, *Meiji ishin to nashonarizumu: bakumatsu no gaikō to seiji hendō* 明治維新とナショナリズム: 幕末の外交と政治変動 (Tokyo: Yamakawa Shuppansha, 1997); Mitani Hiroshi 三谷博, *Meiji ishin o kangaeru* 明治維新を考える (Tokyo: Yūshiya, 2006).

This new focus on nationalism addresses a long-standing weakness in the historiography. The idea of the Meiji Restoration as a "nationalist revolution" was put forward by W. G. Beasely over fifty years ago, but he saw no need to investigate nationalism itself. Rather, Beasely invoked nationalism as a means of dodging the period debate over whether the Restoration was a bourgeois revolution or a process of "modernization." Therefore, as Marlene Mayo observed, "we arrive at nationalist revolution, almost by default, after everything else has been ruled out." In similar fashion, Albert Craig explained the Restoration in terms of "han nationalism" without exploring nationalism as a historically contingent phenomenon. Both "han nationalism" and ordinary "nationalism" were treated as natural, almost inevitable expressions of local pride. By contrast, this book emphasizes how nation-states and nationalism are part of a specific international order. The Meiji Restoration makes sense as a "nationalist revolution" primarily in the context of other nineteenth-century nationalist revolutions rather than as an organic outcome of long-standing cultural forces and biases. As Giddens has observed, while nation-states celebrate their uniqueness, they "exist only in systemic relationship with other nation-states. The internal administrative coordination of nation-states from their beginnings depends upon reflexively monitored conditions of an international nature. 'International relations' is coeval with the origins of nation-states." Marlene J. Mayo, "Nationalist Revolution in Japan," review of *The Meiji Restoration* by W. G. Beasley, *Monumenta Nipponica* 29 (1974): 83–91; W. G. Beasley, *The Meiji Restoration* (Stanford, CA: Stanford University Press, 1972); Albert M. Craig, *Chōshū in the Meiji Restoration* (Cambridge, MA: Harvard University Press, 1961), esp. 149; Anthony Giddens, *A Contemporary Critique of Historical Materialism*, Vol. 2: *The Nation-State and Violence* (Berkeley: University of California Press, 1985), 4.

Totman's encyclopedic study of the fall of the Tokugawa bakufu recognizes the importance of this global context: "The regime fell because the imperialist intrusion of the mid-nineteenth century presented it with a set of political tasks that it could handle neither then nor at any time in its past." What Totman neglects is how the nineteenth-century international order presented Japanese leaders with both a threat and a model for political action. The "imperialist intrusion" was part of an international order that conditioned both the fall of the shogunate and the creation of a Japanese nation-state as the metropole of a Japanese empire. Conrad Totman, *The Collapse of the Tokugawa Bakufu, 1862–1868* (Honolulu: University of Hawai'i Press, 1980), esp. xiii.

8. Duara neatly notes how this "tension between nationalism and transnationalism within civilization reflects the tension between universalism and particularism underlying the world system of nation-states." See Duara, "Civilizations and Nations in a Globalizing World," 89, 95.

9. There are diverse and somewhat contradictory accounts of the origins of the first version of "Kimigayo." I have here on a relied primarily on a 1912 essay by Wada Shinjirō containing an interview with Ōyama, reprinted in Shigeshita Kazuo 繁下和雄, Satō Tetsuo 佐藤徹夫, and Oyama Sakunosuke 小山作之助, eds., *Kimigayo shiryō shūsei* 君が代史料集成 (Tokyo: Ōzorasha, 1991), 5: 19–27; and an interview with Nishi Kensō published in the *Kagoshima Shinbun* in 1919, reprinted in Shigeshita and Satō, eds., *Kimigayo shiryō shūsei*, 5: 38–44. The two accounts are in general agreement, although Ōyama describes Fenton simply as an English bandmaster and places his meeting with the soldier, Egawa Yogorō, in late 1870 or early 1871, when Ōyama himself was already in Europe. See Ōyama Genshi Den Hensan Iin 大山元帥伝編纂委員, ed., *Genshi kōshaku Ōyama Iwao* 元帥公爵大山巌 (Tokyo: Ōyama Genshi Den Kankōkai, 1935), 319. The imperial review is also documented in Kunaichō rinji teishitsu henshūkyoku 宮内省臨時帝室編修局, ed., *Meiji tennō ki* 明治天皇記 (Tokyo: Yoshikawa Kōbunkan, 1968–1977), 2:332–335.

10. Shisō mondai kenkyūjo 思想問題研究所, *Kokugō kokki kokka no yurai to seishin* 国号国旗国歌の由来と精神 (Tokyo: Higashiyama Shobō, 1937), 66–96.

11. A full critique of "modernization" and "modernity" is well beyond the purpose of this study, but my general avoidance of those terms is informed by the work of Frederick Cooper. In particular, I am troubled by the teleology implicit in the term "modernity" and the sense that, as Cooper suggests, it recapitulates many of the problems of modernization theory: "Has all the work that has gone into critical theory merely reproduced American sociology of the 1950s, reversing modernity's valence from positive to negative, while leaving it intact?" I am also sympathetic to the critique that invocations of "modernity" can obscure more tangible processes, such as capitalism and imperialism. Frederick Cooper, *Colonialism in Question: Theory, Knowledge, History* (Berkeley: University of California Press, 2005), 113–149, quote from 118. In Japanese history, Julia

Thomas has explored how conventional notions of "modernity" often rest on implicit dichotomies of East versus West, nature versus culture, and nature versus human society. Such approaches inevitably reduce Japanese history to a "deformed" or "belated" modernity, and she argues instead for a reconfigured modernity that can encompass multiple historical experiences. Julia Adeney Thomas, *Reconfiguring Modernity: Concepts of Nature in Japanese Political Ideology* (Berkeley: University of California Press, 2001), esp. 15–31. See also Harry Harootunian, "Remembering the Historical Present," *Critical Inquiry* 33, no. 3 (2007): esp. 471–475. For a robust defense of modernity in Meiji history, see Carol Gluck, "The End of Elsewhere: Writing Modernity Now," *American Historical Review* 116, no. 3 (2011): 676–687.

12. My account of "global isomorphism" draws heavily on John Meyer's "world society" approach. See, for example, John W. Meyer, "World Society, Institutional Theories, and the Actor," *Annual Review of Sociology* 36 (2010): 1–20; for transnational systems as ontological phenomena, see John W. Meyer, John Boli, and George M. Thomas, "Ontology and Rationalization in the Western Cultural Account," in *Institutional Structure: Constituting State, Society, and the Individual*, ed. George M. Thomas (Newbury Park, CA: Sage, 1987), 11–37; John W. Meyer et al., "World Society and the Nation-State," *American Journal of Sociology* 103, no. 1 (1997): 144–181. For an examination of different forms of isomorphism, see Mark S. Mizruchi and Lisa C. Fein, "The Social Construction of Organizational Knowledge: A Study of the Uses of Coercive, Mimetic, and Normative Isomorphism," *Administrative Science Quarterly* 44, no. 4 (1999): 653–683.

13. In Meiji discourse, the tensions of radical nostalgia appeared in the coincidence of two phrases: *ōsei fukko* 王政復古 and *isshin* 一新. *Ōsei fukko* or "revival of ancient kingly rule" described the Meiji Restoration in terms of a return to local practices of the early Heian era and before. Another popular period description was "revolution" (*isshin* 一新), referring not to the ancient past but to change and innovation. These phrases highlight the tension encompassed by radical nostalgia: the reconciliation of the ancient and the new.

14. My term "radical nostalgia" overlaps in many ways with Hobsbawn and Ranger's famous "invention of tradition." I use the neologism "radical nostalgia" to emphasize first, the recovery of long-lost institutions and practices, rather than the maintenance or defense of ongoing "traditions." Second, rather than the nebulous celebration of a glorious Japanese past, "radical nostalgia" involved the recovery of specific institutions as solutions to contemporary political challenges. For considerations of the invention of tradition and the Japanese case, see Takagi Hiroshi 高木博志, "Nihon no kindaika to 'dentō' no sōshutsu 日本の近代化と「伝統」の創出," in *'Dentō' no sōzō to bunka hen'yō* 「伝統」の創造と文化変容, ed. Parutenon Tama パルテノン多摩 (Tama: Parutenon Tama, 2001), 81–122; Nishikawa Nagao 西川長夫, "Nihongata kokumin kokka no keisei: hikakushiteki kanten kara 日本型国民国家の形勢ー比較史的観点から," in

Bakumatsu Meiji-ki no kokumin kokka keisei no bunka hen'yō 幕末・明治期の国家形成と文化変容, ed. Nishikawa Nagao 西川長夫 and Matsumiya Hideharu 松宮秀治 (Tokyo: Shin'yōsha, 1995), 3–42; and Stephen Vlastos, ed., *Mirror of Modernity: Invented Traditions of Modern Japan* (Berkeley: University of California Press, 1998). For the intriguing case of the invocation of ancient Rome and Israel in the early American Republic, see Eran Shalev, *Rome Reborn on Western Shores: Historical Imagination and the Creation of the American Republic* (Charlottesville: University of Virginia Press, 2009).

15. My term "cosmopolitan chauvinism" is partly an expansion of Benedict Anderson's notion of the nation-state as a "modular form." The same notion of modularity, I would argue, can be applied to other transnational systems, such as the classical Chinese tribute system. In each case, local political identities and institutions were shaped both by local conditions and the norms and strictures of a transnational system. Thus, as discussed throughout this study, classical East Asian states such as the Japanese ritsu-ryō state were "modular" instances of Tang institutions. For a recent summary of the Chinese tribute system, see David C. Kang, *East Asia before the West: Five Centuries of Trade and Tribute* (New York: Columbia University Press, 2010). For discussions of Anderson and nationalism, see Manu Goswami, "Rethinking the Modular Nation Form: Toward a Sociohistorical Conception of Nationalism," *Comparative Studies in Society and History* 44, no. 4 (2002): 770–799; Dipesh Chakrabarty, "Towards a Discourse on Nationalism," review of *Nationalist Thought and the Colonial World: A Derivative Discourse* by Partha Chatterjee, *Economic and Political Weekly* 22 (1987): 1137–1138; Ernst Gellner, *Nations and Nationalism* (Ithaca, NY: Cornell University Press, 1983); Benedict Anderson, *The Spectre of Comparisons: Nationalism, Southeast Asia, and the World* (London: Verso, 1998); Anderson, *Imagined Communities*; Anderson, *The Spectre of Comparisons: Nationalism, Southeast Asia, and the World*; Antony Anghie, *Imperialism, Sovereignty, and the Making of International Law* (Cambridge: Cambridge University Press, 2004); Partha Chatterjee, *Nationalist Thought and the Colonial World: A Derivative Discourse* (London: Zed Books, 1986); Andreas Osiander, "Sovereignty, International Relations, and the Westphalian Myth," *International Organization* 55, no. 2 (2001): 251–287.

16. See Katō Hiroyuki's 1862 essay "Newest Theses" (*Saishinron* 最新論), also known as Tonarigusa 隣草, translated variously as "Neighboring Grasses" and "Essays on a Neighboring Land." I rely here on the annotated text in Emura Eiichi 江村栄一, ed., *Nihon kindai shisō taikei 9: Kenpō kōsō* 日本近代思想体系9:憲法構想 (Tokyo: Iwanami Shoten, 1989), 2–25. For interpretations, see Thomas, *Reconfiguring Modernity*, 84–110; Winston Davis, *The Moral and Political Naturalism of Baron Katō Hiroyuki* (Berkeley: Institute of East Asian Studies, University of California, 1996); and Bob Tadashi Wakabayashi, "Katō Hiroyuki and Confucian Natural Rights, 1861–1870," *Harvard Journal of*

Asiatic Studies 44, no. 2 (1984): 469–492. My argument for "cosmopolitan chau-vinism" dovetails in many ways with Thomas's focus on the trope of "nature" in Meiji thought. For Katō, if political principles were rooted in "natural principles" (*tenri*) or "nature" (*shizen*), then political institutions should be similar around the world.

17. See Satō's *The Pillar of Heaven* (*Tenchūki* 天柱記, 1825), in Bitō Masahide 尾藤正英 and Shimazaki Takao 島崎隆夫, eds., *Nihon shisō taikei 45: Andō Shōeki, Satō Nobuhiro* 日本思想体系45:安藤昌益, 佐藤信淵 (Tokyo: Iwanami Shoten, 1977), 361–423. See also Jason Ānanda Josephson, *The Invention of Religion in Japan* (Chicago: University of Chicago Press, 2012), 116–118.

18. For a survey of this syncretism, known as *honji suijaku* 本地垂迹, see Mark Teeuwen and Fabio Rambelli, *Buddhas and Kami in Japan: Honji suijaku as a Combinatory Paradigm* (London: RoutledgeCurzon, 2003).

19. Ryusaku Tsunoda, William Theodore De Bary, and Donald Keene, eds., *Sources of Japanese Tradition*, 2 vols. (New York: Columbia University Press, 1958), 1:369–370. For the original text see Hara Nensai 原念斎, Minamoto Ryōen 源了圓, and Maeda Tsutomu 前田勉, eds., *Sentetsu sōdan* 先哲叢談 (Tokyo: Heibonsha, 1994).

20. For the general question of Chinese thought as both specific and universal see Thomas, *Reconfiguring Modernity*, 40–42; and Ronald P. Toby, *State and Diplomacy in Early Modern Japan* (Princeton, NJ: Princeton University Press, 1984), 211–230.

21. See *Gyōsō tsuiroku* 暁窗追録 in Joun (Hōan) 栗本鋤雲 (匏庵) *Hōan jisshu* 匏菴十種, 2 vols. (Tokyo: Kyūsenkan, 1869), 2:5.

22. For the details of Katō's intellectual development, see Thomas, *Reconfiguring Modernity*, 87–100. She aptly described the fluid but vibrant intellectual environ-ment of the 1860s and 1870s as a "sprawling free-for-all" rather than a "focused sporting event."

23. For considerations of the cultural contexts of linear and nonlinear time, see Duara, *Sovereignty and Authenticity: Manchukuo and the East Asian Modern*, 26–28; and Duara, *Rescuing History from the Nation: Questioning Narratives of Modern China*, 17–50.

CHAPTER 1

1. Charles Tilly, "Reflection on the History of European State-making," in *The Formation of National States in Western Europe*, ed. Charles Tilly and Gabriel Ardant (Princeton, NJ: Princeton University Press, 1975), quote from 42. The bibliography on this question is extensive. For Tilly's definitive development of his own thesis see Charles Tilly, *Coercion, Capital, and European States, AD 990–1992*, rev. pbk. ed. (Cambridge, MA: Blackwell, 1992). For a vigorous critique, see Brian D. Taylor and Roxana Botea, "Tilly Tally: War-Making and State-Making in the Contemporary Third World," *International Studies Review* 10, no. 1 (2008).

Victoria Tin-bor Hui, *War and State Formation in Ancient China and Early Modern Europe* (Cambridge: Cambridge University Press, 2005) examines the case of war and state-formation in ancient China. Tilly focused on Europe but Victor Lieberman has looked beyond Europe, examining not only the origins of the European state but also the role of interstate contact in world history, exploring how interstate contact and conflict drove state-formation in Eurasia over the period 1300 to 1830. Lieberman found major commonalities in the development of regimes as disparate as Russia, Vietnam, France, and Burma. Rather than contrast European vitality with Asian "stagnation," Lieberman focused on "strange parallels" across the Eurasian region: between 1300 and 1830 nascent polities underwent territorial consolidation, administrative centralization, and cultural integration. Like Tilly, Lieberman saw military competition as central to this process of state-building, although his thesis also emphasizes peaceful interactions, such as rivalries in trade and ideas. See Victor Lieberman, "Transcending East-West Dichotomies: State and Culture Formation in Six Ostensibly Disparate Areas," in *Beyond Binary Histories: Re-imagining Eurasia to c.1830*, ed. Victor Lieberman (Ann Arbor: University of Michigan Press, 1999), 19–102, and Victor Lieberman, *Strange Parallels: Southeast Asia in Global Context, c. 800–1830*, Vol. 2: *Mainland Mirrors: Europe, Japan, China, South Asia, and the Islands* (Cambridge: Cambridge University Press, 2009), 1–122, esp. 131–148. For a powerful dissent to focus on universal models of state-building, see Roy Bin Wong, *China Transformed: Historical Change and the Limits of European Experience* (Ithaca, NY: Cornell University Press, 1997).

2. What I here describe as Japan's first era of globalization is sometimes described as "ancient" or "archaic" globalization in contrast to modern globalization. My approach here follows Jennings, who notes that although many scholars argue "that globalization is unique to the modern era, their definition of globalization paradoxically provides us with a straightforward criterion that we can use to identify earlier periods of globalization." He describes the idea of globalization as a quintessentially modern phenomenon as "modernity's greatest theft" and calls for a "pluralization" of "globalization." See Justin Jennings, *Globalizations and the Ancient World* (Cambridge: Cambridge University Press, 2011), esp. 1–3, 19–21. Bayly uses the modifiers "archaic" and "early modern" to mark earlier forms of globalization. See C. A. Bayly, *The Birth of the Modern World, 1780–1914: Global Connections and Comparisons* (Malden, MA: Blackwell, 2004), 41–44. For a counter-argument and a defense of globalization as a singular phenomenon, see Jürgen Osterhammel, "Globalizations," in *The Oxford Handbook of World History*, ed. Jerry H. Bentley (Oxford: Oxford University Press, 2011). In the Japanese-language literature, the notion of an "ancient East Asian world" is well established. See, for example, Nishijima Sadao 西嶋定生 and Yi Sŏng-si [Ri Sonshi] 李成市, eds., *Kodai higashi Ajia sekai to Nihon* 古代東アジア世界と日本 (Tokyo: Iwanami Shoten, 2000).

3. There were diplomatic exchanges between Japanese polities and the Asian mainland from at least 57 CE, but the intensity of trade and cultural exchange surged in the sixth century. For the historiography of early contacts, see Joshua A. Fogel, *Articulating the Sinosphere: Sino-Japanese Relations in Space and Time* (Cambridge, MA: Harvard University Press, 2009), 7–13; Joshua A. Fogel, "2011 Arthur O. Lovejoy Lecture "The Gold Seal of 57 CE and the Afterlife of an Inanimate Object," *Journal of the History of Ideas* 73, no. 3 (2012).

4. Bruce L. Batten, "Foreign Threat and Domestic Reform: The Emergence of the Ritsuryō State," *Monumenta Nipponica* 41, no. 2 (1986).

5. Fogel, *Articulating the Sinosphere*, 22–26.

6. The standard study of Hideyoshi in English is Mary Elizabeth Berry, *Hideyoshi* (Cambridge, MA: Harvard University Press, 1982). For the limits of Hideyoshi's land surveys, see Phillip C. Brown, *Central Authority and Local Autonomy in the Formation of Early Modern Japan: The Case of Kaga Domain* (Stanford, CA: Stanford University Press, 1993).

7. Richard von Glahn, "Myth and Reality of China's Seventeenth-Century Monetary Crisis," *Journal of Economic History* 56, no. 2 (1996): 432–436; Dennis O. Flynn and Arturo Giráldez, "Cycles of Silver: Global Economic Unity through the Mid-Eighteenth Century," *Journal of World History* 13, no. 2 (2002). Quote from John E. Wills, "Relations with Maritime Europeans, 1514–1662," in *The Cambridge History of China*, Part 2, Vol., 8: *The Ming Dynasty, 1368–1644*, ed. Denis Twitchett and Frederick W. Mote (Cambridge: Cambridge University Press, 1998), 333.

8. Dennis O. Flynn and Arturo Giráldez, "Arbitrage, China, and World Trade in the Early Modern Period," *Journal of the Economic and Social History of the Orient* 38, no. 4 (1995); Dennis O. Flynn and Arturo Giráldez, "Born with a 'Silver Spoon': The Origin of World Trade in 1571," *Journal of World History* 6, no. 2 (1995); Flynn and Giráldez, "Cycles of Silver: Global Economic Unity through the Mid-Eighteenth Century," 398–399. See also William S. Atwell, "Another Look at Silver Imports into China, ca. 1635–1644," *Journal of World History* 16, no. 4 (2005).

9. Ōishi Manabu 大石学, *Edo no gaikō senryaku* 江戸の外交戦略 (Tokyo: Kadokawa Gakugei Shuppan, 2009), 17, 19, 24.

10. The Chinese communities were somewhat illicit because of the Ming ban on direct trade between China and Japan, but they thrived on indirect trade and smuggling. The expatriate Korean communities were largely hostages, both of pirates and Hideyoshi's invasion. See Yasunori Arano, "The Formation of a Japanocentric World Order," *International Journal of Asian Studies* 2, no. 2 (2005): 194; Adam Clulow, "From Global Entrepôt to Early Modern Domain: Hirado, 1609–1641," *Monumenta Nipponica* 65, no. 1 (2010): 1–35. For the possibility of continued smuggling and the survival of Chinese communities such as Bōnotsu, see Robert I. Hellyer, "The Missing Pirate and the Pervasive Smuggler: Regional Agency in Coastal Defence, Trade, and Foreign Relations

in Nineteenth-Century Japan," *International History Review* 27, no. 1 (2005). The Korean community of Satsuma is the subject of Shiba Ryōtarō's historical novel *The Heart Remembers Home.*

11. For an overview of Japanese expatriate communities, see Robert LeRoy Innes, "The Door Ajar: Japan's Foreign Trade in the Seventeenth Century" (Ph.D. diss., University of Michigan, 1980), 57–66.

12. Arano, "The Formation of a Japanocentric World Order," 195–196.

13. Fogel, *Articulating the Sinosphere*, 30–31. Zhu is also known as Zhu Zhiyu (朱之瑜) and Zhu Luyu (魯璵).

14. Ōishi, *Edo no gaikō senryaku*, 148–160.

15. Luís Fróis, *Historia de Japam*, ed. Josef Wicki, 5 vols. (1583–1587; reprint, Lisbon: Biblioteca Nacional de Lisboa, 1976), 5: 238. I am thankful to Yūko Shimizu for bringing my attention to this source.

16. Estimates of the size of the Japanese Christian population vary, as do estimates of the size of the total population, which range from 12 million to 16 million for the early 1600s. The estimate of 700,000 Christians is from Ōishi, *Edo no gaikō senryaku*, 64. This would be 5.83 percent of a population of 12 million.

17. Kenneth M. Swope, "Crouching Tigers, Secret Weapons: Military Technology Employed during the Sino-Japanese-Korean War, 1592–1598," *Journal of Military History* 69, no. 1 (2005): 20; Thomas Conlan, *Weapons & Fighting Techniques of the Samurai Warrior, 1200–1877 AD* (London: Amber Books, 2008), 143–153.

18. Conlan, *Weapons*, 153–165.

19. Ibid., 165–205.

20. Kenneth M. Swope, "Deceit, Disguise, and Dependence: China, Japan, and the Future of the Tributary System, 1592–1596," *International History Review* 24, no. 4 (2002).

21. For details on the envoy, Harada Kiemon, see Gakushō Nakajima, "The Invasion of Korea and Trade with Luzon: Katō Kiyomasa's Scheme of the Luzon Trade in the Late Sixteenth Century," in *The East Asian Mediterranean: Maritime Crossroads of Culture, Commerce and Human Migration*, ed. Angela Schottenhammer (Wiesbaden: Harrassowitz, 2008).

22. Jurgis Elisonias, "Christianity and the Daimyo," in *The Cambridge History of Japan*, Vol. 4: *Early Modern Japan*, ed. John Whitney Hall (Cambridge: Cambridge University Press, 1991), 366–368; Arano, "The Formation of a Japanocentric World Order," 192.

23. Arano, "The Formation of a Japanocentric World Order," 193, 213.

24. Iwao Seiichi 岩生成一, "Nanyō Nihonmachi no kenkyū 南洋日本町の研究," in *Yamada Nagamasa shiryō shūsei* 山田長政資料集成, ed. Yamada Nagamasa Kenshōkai 山田長政顕彰会 (Shizuoka: Yamada Nagamasa Kenshōkai, 1974), 294–296

25. For the original edict, see Ishii Ryōsuke 石井良助, ed., *Tokugawa kinreikō* 徳川禁令考 (Tokyo: Sōbunsha, 1959-1961), 6:565–567.

26. For Japanese silver and world markets, see Innes, "The Door Ajar," 378; Flynn and Giráldez, "Arbitrage, China, and World Trade in the Early Modern Period"; Flynn and Giráldez, "Born with a 'Silver Spoon,'" 201–221. For early Tokugawa policy on precious metals, see Robert I. Hellyer, *Defining Engagement: Japan and Global Contexts, 1640–1868* (Cambridge, MA: Harvard University Asia Center, 2009), 48–60. For an opposing view see Atwell, "Another Look at Silver Imports into China, ca. 1635–1644," 467–489.

27. Gregory Smits, *Visions of Ryukyu: Identity and Ideology in Early-modern Thought and Politics* (Honolulu: University of Hawaiʻi Press, 1999), 15–16; Hellyer, *Defining Engagement*, 34–36.

28. For a chronology of missions, see Arano Yasunori 荒野泰典, *"Sakoku" o minaosu* 「鎖国」を見直す (Kawasaki: Kawasaki Shimin Akademī Shuppanbu, 2003), 75; Toby, *State and Diplomacy in Early Modern Japan*, 48–49

29. Hellyer, *Defining Engagement*, 45. Later Tokugawa protocols specified Ming-style clothing.

30. Ibid., 38–39. For a good summary of attempts to conceal Japanese influence, see Smits, *Visions*, esp. 44–46. Because Satsuma actively sought to hide Japanese customs from Chinese envoys, the 1609 Japanese political domination of Ryukyu coincided with an increase in Chinese cultural influence. This coincidence of Chinese cultural domination and Japanese political domination was noted even by a member of Perry's 1853–54 mission, who observed that Ryukyu was "*de facto* and *de jure* a part of Japan" despite the "the similarity, if not the identity, of their religion, literature, and many of their manners and customs" with China. See Francis L. Hawks, ed., *Narrative of the Expedition of an American Squadron to the China Seas and Japan, performed in the years 1852, 1853, and 1854, under the command of Commodore M.C. Perry, United States Navy, by order of the government of the United States. Compiled from the original notes and journals of Commodore Perry and his officers at his request, and under his supervision* (Washington, DC: A.O.P. Nicholson, 1856), 222, and Smits, *Visions*, 43–44, 71–132.

31. Kamiya Nobuyuki 紙屋敦之, *Ryūkyū to Nihon, Chūgoku* 琉球と日本・中国 (Tokyo: Yamakawa Shuppansha, 2003), 78–80; Smits, *Visions*, 46. See also Higashionna Kanjun 東恩納寛惇, *Higashionna Kanjun zenshū* 東恩納寛惇全集, ed. Ryūkyū Shinpōsha 琉球新報社 (Tokyo: Daiichi Shobō, 1978), 1:70–71.

32. Uehara Kenzen 上原兼善, "Chūgoku ni taisuru Ryūnichi kankei no inpei seisaku to 'michi no shima' 中国に対する琉日関係の隠蔽政策と「道之島」," in *Rettōshi no minami to kita* 列島史の南と北, ed. Isao Kikuchi 菊池勇夫 and Maehira Fusaaki 真栄平房昭 (Tokyo: Yoshikawa Kōbunkan, 2006), 35–41.

33. Kamiya traces the appearance of Takarashima/Tokara in official histories to Sai On's 1725 edition of *Chūzan seifu* (Kamiya, *Ryūkyū to Nihon, Chūgoku*, 85–86) while Smits gives a discussion of the later official history *Kyūyō* (Smits, *Visions*, 44–45). For a good overview of the imaginary country issue, see Uehara, "Chūgoku ni taisuru Ryūnichi kankei," and Kamiya, *Ryūkyū to Nihon, Chūgoku*, 78–91.

34. George Smith, *Lewchew and the Lewchewans; Being a Narrative of a Visit to Lewchew, or Loo Choo, in October, 1850* (London: T. Hatchard, 1853), 36–37; George Smith, *Ten Weeks in Japan* (London: Longman, Green, Longman, and Roberts, 1861), 345–346.

35. For details, see Etsuko Hae-jin Kang, *Diplomacy and Ideology in Japanese-Korean Relations: From the Fifteenth to the Eighteenth Century* (London: Macmillan Press, 1997), 136–166.

36. In the early 1600s, Korean diplomats wanted to date correspondence according to the Ming calendar while shogunal officials wanted to use the Japanese imperial calendar. Japanese letters to Chosŏn from 1607, 1617, and 1624 used the neutral zodiac calendar, and shogunal officials argued that Korea should reciprocate by abandoning the Ming calendar. Chosŏn diplomats abandoned Chinese era names in correspondence with Japan after the fall of the Ming (1644). See Toby, *State and Diplomacy in Early Modern Japan*, 90–97.

37. James Bryant Lewis, *Frontier Contact between Chosŏn Korea and Tokugawa Japan* (London: Routledge Curzon, 2003), 24–26; Kang, *Diplomacy and Ideology*, 138–146, 154–166; Toby, *State and Diplomacy in Early Modern Japan*, 76–83.

38. Japan used the title "king" for diplomatic correspondence only in 1711, based on the reforms of Arai Hakuseki. For that debate, see Kang, *Diplomacy and Ideology*, 197–222; Kate Wildman Nakai, *Shogunal Politics: Arai Hakuseki and the Premises of Tokugawa Rule* (Cambridge, MA: Council on East Asian Studies, Harvard University, 1988), 190–202; Ōishi, *Edo no gaikō senryaku*, 109–112. There is a sizable body of scholarship arguing that the usage of the term "taikun" represents a break with the Sinocentric international order, and a move toward a "Japan-as-central-kingdom" view or a distinctly Japanese worldview (*Nihongata ka-i chitsujo* or *Nihongata ka-i ishiki*). See Toby, *State and Diplomacy in Early Modern Japan*; Ronald P. Toby, "Contesting the Centre: International Sources of Japanese National Identity," *International History Review* 7, no. 3 (1985); Arano, "The Formation of a Japanocentric World Order," 185–216; Arano Yasunori 荒野泰典, *Kinsei Nihon to Higashi Ajia* 近世日本と東アジア (Tokyo: Tōkyō Daigaku Shuppankai, 1988). While I do not reject that view, I am more interested in how terms such as "taikun" represented the shared diplomatic interests of both parties and allowed for the maintenance of peaceful relations. For such a reconsideration, see Lewis, *Frontier Contact between Chosŏn Korea and Tokugawa Japan*, 9–10. For a useful historiographic survey, see Ikeuchi Satoshi 池内敏, *Taikun gaikō to "bui": kinsei Nihon no kokusai chitsujo to Chōsen-kan* 大君外交と「武威」— 近世日本の国際秩序と朝鮮観 (Nagoya: Nagoya Daigaku Shuppankai, 2006).

39. Hoon Lee, "The Repatriation of Castaways in Chosŏn Korea-Japan Relations, 1599–1888," *Korean Studies* 30, no. 1 (2006): 80–85; James Bryant Lewis, "The Pusan Japan House (Waegwan) and Chosŏn Korea: Early Modern Korean Views of Japan through Economic, Political, and Social Connections" (Ph.D. diss., University of Hawai'i at Manoa, 1994), 42–44, 72–73.

40. Bruce Cumings, *Korea's Place in the Sun: A Modern History* (New York: Norton, 1997), 78; JaHyun Kim Haboush, *A Heritage of Kings: One Man's Monarchy in the Confucian World* (New York: Columbia University Press, 1988), 23–26, 39–47.

41. For Ming investiture and the founding of the Chosŏn Yi dynasty, see Kang, *Diplomacy and Ideology*, 53–54; Philip de Heer, "Three Embassies to Seoul: Sino-Korean Relations in the 15th Century," in *Conflict and Accommodation in Early Modern East Asia: Essays in Honour of Erik Zurcher*, ed. Leonard Blussé and Harriet T. Zurndorfer (Leiden: E. J. Brill, 1993), 240–253; Donald N. Clark, "Sino-Korean Tributary Relations under the Ming," in *The Cambridge History of China Vol. 8 Part I*, (Cambridge: Cambridge University Press, 1998), 272–300

42. Kang, *Diplomacy and Ideology*, 167–168, 173–194.

43. Iwai Shigeki 岩井茂樹, "Shindai no goshi to 'chinmoku gaikō' 清代の互市と「沈黙外交」," in *Chūgoku Higashi Ajia gaikō kōryū-shi no kenkyū* 中国東アジア外交交流史の研究, edited by Fuma Susumu 夫馬進 (Kyoto: Kyōto Daigaku Gakujutsu Shuppankai, 2007).

44. For a survey of Japanese scholarship, see Peng Hao [Hō Kō] 彭浩, "Nagasaki bōeki ni okeru shinpai seido to Shinchō no taiō 長崎貿易における信牌制度と清朝の對應," *Tōhōgaku* 東方学 119 (2010): 73–90. In English, see Norihito Mizuno, "China in Tokugawa Foreign Relations: The Tokugawa Bakufu's Perception of and Attitudes toward Ming-Qing China," *Sino-Japanese Studies* 15 (2003): esp. 140–144; Anthony Reid, "The Unthreatening Alternative: Chinese Shipping to Southeast Asia, 1567–1842," *Review of Indonesian and Malaysian Affairs* 27 (1993): 13–32; Angela Schottenhammer, "Japan—The Tiny Dwarf? Sino-Japanese Relations from the *Kangxi* to the *Qianlong* Reigns," in *The East Asian Mediterranean*, ed. Angela Schottenhammer (Wiesbaden: Harrassowitz, 2008), 331–388. For diplomatic approaches to the Ming, see Miki Watanabe, "An International Maritime Trader—Torihara Sōan: The Agent for Tokugawa Ieyasu's First Negotiations with Ming China, 1600," in *The East Asian Mediterranean*, ed. Angela Schottenhammer (Wiesbaden: Harrassowitz, 2008), 169–176. For translated primary sources on the *shinpai* system and trade with Southeast Asia, see Yoneo Ishii, *The Junk Trade from Southeast Asia: Translations from the Tōsen fusetsu-gaki, 1674–1723* (Singapore: Institute of Southeast Asian Studies, 1998).

45. See Arai's "Gaikoku tsūshin jiryaku 外国通信事略," in Arai Hakuseki 新井白石, *Gojiryaku* 五事略, ed. Takenaka Kunika 竹中邦香, 2 vols. (Tokyo: Hakusekisha, 1883), 1:36–37, written c. 1716. See also Imaizumi Teisuke 今泉定介 and Ichishima Kenkichi 市島謙吉, eds., *Arai Hakuseki zenshū* 新井白石全集 (Tokyo: Yoshikawa Hanshichi, 1905-1907), 3:642.

46. Namikawa Kenji 浪川健治, *Ainu minzoku no kiseki* アイヌ民族の軌跡 (Tokyo: Yamakawa Shuppansha, 2004), 17–26. On the broader question of trade in Pacific Northeast Asia (the *Santan* trade), see Brett L. Walker, *The Conquest of Ainu*

Lands: Ecology and Culture in Japanese Expansion, 1590–1800 (Berkeley: University of California Press, 2001), 128–176; and Sasaki Shirō 佐々木史郎, *Hoppō kara kita kōekimin: kinu to kegawa to Santanjin* 北方から来た交易民: 絹と毛皮とサンタン人 (Tokyo: Nihon Hōsō Shuppan Kyōkai, 1996).

47. Until 1559, the Matsumae house was known as the Kakizaki.

48. Walker, *The Conquest of Ainu Lands,* 27–43; Namikawa, *Ainu minzoku no kiseki,* 32–49.

49. Walker, *The Conquest of Ainu Lands,* 48–72.

50. Ibid., 133–135. Inagaki Reiko 稲垣令子, "Kinsei Ezochi ni okeru girei shihai no tokushitsu: uimamu, omusha no hensen o tōshite 近世蝦夷地における儀礼支配の特質-ウイマム・オムシャの変遷を通して," in *Minshū seikatsu to shinkō shisō* 民衆生活と信仰・思想, ed. Minshūshi Kenkyūkai 民衆史研究会 (Tokyo: Yūzankaku, 1985), 113–116. For the transformation of Ainu rituals of submission, see Walker, *The Conquest of Ainu Lands,* 217–218

51. Walker, *The Conquest of Ainu Lands,* 85–87, 156–161.

52. Ronald P. Toby, "Mapping the Margins of Japan," in *Cartographic Japan,* ed. Kären Wigen, Fumiko Sugimoto, and Cary Karacas (Chicago: University of Chicago Press, 2016).

53. For the "compound state," see Mark Ravina, *Land and Lordship in Early Modern Japan* (Stanford, CA: Stanford University Press, 1999), 27–45, 195–210.

54. The definitive study of attainder (*kaieki*) and daimyo relocation (*tenpō*) is Fujino Tamotsu 藤野保, *Shintei bakuhan taiseishi no kenkyū* 新訂幕藩体制史の研究 (Tokyo: Yoshikawa Kōbunkan, 1975). See also Harold Bolitho, *Treasures among Men: The Fudai Daimyo in Tokugawa Japan* (New Haven, CT: Yale University Press, 1974)

55. Lee A. Butler, "Tokugawa Ieyasu's Regulations for the Court: A Reappraisal," *Harvard Journal of Asiatic Studies* 54, no. 2 (1994): 532–533.

56. The Shimazu submitted to residence in Kyoto only after Hideyoshi pushed them back to a fraction of their former lands. Yamamoto Hirofumi 山本博文, *Sankin kōtai* 参勤交代 (Tokyo: Kodansha, 1998), 28–31.

57. Ibid., 31–32

58. Kuwahata Hajime 桑波田興, *Kokushi daijiten* 国史大事典, s.v. "Shimazu Yoshihiro 島津義弘." Yoshikawa Kōbunkan, 1979–1997.

59. Fudai daimyo with holdings in the Kantō region were allowed an abbreviated schedule, arriving in the second month and leaving in the eighth month.

60. Conrad Totman, *Early Modern Japan* (Berkeley: University of California Press, 1993), 140.

61. Anne Walthall, "Village Networks. Sodai and the Sale of Edo Nightsoil," *Monumenta Nipponica* 43, no. 3 (1988): 293–303; Susan B. Hanley, "A High Standard of Living in Nineteenth-Century Japan: Fact or Fantasy?" *Journal of Economic History* 43, no. 1 (1983): 293.

62. Chie Nakane and Shinzaburō Ōishi, eds., *Tokugawa Japan: The Social and Economic Antecedents of Modern Japan*, translation edited by Conrad D. Totman (Tokyo: University of Tokyo Press, 1990); Totman, *Early Modern Japan*, 260–268.

63. Tsuneo Satō, "Tokugawa Villages and Agriculture," in *Tokugawa Japan*, ed. Chie Nakane and Shinzaburō Ōishi (Tokyo: University of Tokyo Press, 1990); David L. Howell, "Hard Times in the Kantō: Economic Change and Village Life in Late Tokugawa Japan," *Modern Asian Studies* 23, no. 2 (1989); Edward E. Pratt, *Japan's Protoindustrial Elite: The Economic Foundations of the Gōnō* (Cambridge, MA: Harvard University Asia Center, 1999), 15–77; Thomas C. Smith, *The Agrarian Origins of Modern Japan* (Stanford, CA: Stanford University Press, 1959).

64. Totman, *Early Modern Japan*, 667–667, 153.

65. James L. McClain, John M. Merriman, and Kaoru Ugawa, eds., *Edo and Paris: Urban Life and the State in the Early Modern Era* (Ithaca, NY: Cornell University Press, 1994), 13, 218–219, 346–247; Harada Nobuo 原田信男, *Edo no ryōrishi: ryōribon to ryōri bunka* 江戸の料理史: 料理本と料理文化 (Tokyo: Chūō Kōron Sha, 1989), 145. For the dissemination of cultural trends through *sankin kōtai*, see Constantine Nomikos Vaporis, *Tour of Duty: Samurai, Military Service in Edo, and the Culture of Early Modern Japan* (Honolulu: University of Hawaiʻi Press, 2008).

66. Kanbashi Norimasa 芳即正, *Shimazu Shigehide* 島津重豪 (Tokyo: Yoshikawa Kōbunkan, 1980), 42–45. The delicacy was 糟醃九年母冬瓜.

67. John Whitney Hall, *Tanuma Okitsugu, 1719–1788: Forerunner of Modern Japan* (Cambridge, MA: Harvard University Press, 1955), 108–109

68. Maruyama Yasunari 丸山雍成, *Sankin kōtai* 参勤交代 (Tokyo: Yoshikawa Kōbunkan, 2007), 209–220.

69. Miyamoto Mataji 宮本又次, *Kōnoike Zen'emon* 鴻池善右衛門 (Tokyo: Yoshikawa Kōbunkan, 1958). For the details of Kōnoike finances, see Miyamoto Mataji 宮本又次, *Ōsaka no kenkyū* 大阪の研究, 5 vols. (Osaka: Seibundō Shuppan, 1967), 4:195–698; 5: 481–732.

70. Ravina, *Land and Lordship in Early Modern Japan*, 155–157. For the transformation of the Japanese economy in comparative perspective, see Angus Maddison, *Contours of the World Economy, 1–2030 AD: Essays in Macro-economic History* (New York: Oxford University Press, 2007), esp. 139–157; and Julia Adeney Thomas, "Reclaiming Ground: Japan's Great Convergence," *Japanese Studies* 34, no. 3 (2014).

71. Ravina, *Land and Lordship in Early Modern Japan*, 168–186.

72. This process of separating samurai from farmers is known in Japanese scholarship as *heinō bunri*. For a discussion in Japanese, see Asao Naohiro 朝尾直弘, *Nihon kinseishi no jiritsu* 日本近世史の自立 (Tokyo: Azekura Shobō, 1988), 189–213, and Yamaguchi Keiji 山口啓二 and Sasaki Junnosuke 佐々木潤之介, *Taikei Nihon rekishi 4: Bakuhan taisei* 体系・日本歴史4:幕藩体制 (Tokyo: Nihon hyōronsha, 1971), 25–30. In English, see Michael P. Birt, "Samurai in Passage: The

Transformation of the Sixteenth-Century Kanto," *Journal of Japanese Studies* 11, no. 2 (1985).

73. Constantine N. Vaporis, "Samurai and Merchant in Mid-Tokugawa Japan: Tani Tannai's Record of Daily Necessities (1748–54)," *Harvard Journal of Asiatic Studies* 60, no. 1 (2000): quote from 211–212. See also Kozo Yamamura, "The Increasing Poverty of the Samurai in Tokugawa Japan, 1600–1868," *Journal of Economic History* 31, no. 2 (1971).

74. For an overview of the Kyōho reforms, see Fujita Satoru 藤田覚, *Kinsei no san dai-kaikaku* 近世の三大改革 (Tokyo: Yamakawa Shuppansha, 2002), 17–29, and Totman, *Early Modern Japan*, 208–315. For an extended study, see Kasaya Kazuhiko 笠谷和比古, *Tokugawa Yoshimune* 徳川吉宗 (Tokyo: Chikuma Shobō, 1995).

75. Fujita, *Kinsei no san dai-kaikaku*, 19–20.

76. Maruyama, *Sankin kōtai*, 241–244; Yamamoto, *Sankin kōtai*, 60–61.

77. The 1720 edict was the *kuniyaku fushin rei* 国役普請令. For a list of major projects, see Kasaya, *Tokugawa Yoshimune*, 123–125

78. Totman, *Early Modern Japan*, 300, 314; Kasaya, *Tokugawa Yoshimune*, 123–125. Unlike *agemai*, *kuniyaku fushin* was not a boon for the shogunal fisc, and several large projects proved costly for the shogunate.

79. The bibliography on annual (*kemi*) and fixed assesment (*jōmen*) systems is extensive. In English, see Philip C. Brown, "The Mismeasure of Land. Land Surveying in the Tokugawa Period," *Monumenta Nipponica* 42, no. 2 (1987); Philip C. Brown, "Practical Constraints on Early Tokugawa Land Taxation: Annual Versus Fixed Assessments in Kaga Domain," *Journal of Japanese Studies* 14, no. Summer (1988); Patricia Sippel, "Abandoned Fields. Negotiating Taxes in the Bakufu Domain," *Monumenta Nipponica* 53, no. 2 (1998); and Kozo Yamamura, "Toward a Reexamination of the Economic History of Tokugawa Japan, 1600–1867," *Journal of Economic History* 33, no. 3 (1973). For an overview in Japanese, see Fujita, *Kinsei no san dai-kaikaku*, 23–25.

80. For Yoshimune as a patron of the sciences, see Federico Marcon, "Inventorying Nature: Tokugawa Yoshimune and the Sponsorship of Honzōgaku in Eighteenth-Century Japan," in *Japan at Nature's Edge: The Environmental Context of a Global Power*, ed. Brett L. Walker, Julia Adeney Thomas, and Ian Jared Miller (Honolulu: University of Hawai'i Press, 2013); Federico Marcon, *The Knowledge of Nature and the Nature of Knowledge in Early Modern Japan* (Chicago: University of Chicago Press, 2015), 115–139.

81. John Lee, "Trade and Economy in Preindustrial East Asia, c. 1500–c. 1800: East Asia in the Age of Global Integration," *Journal of Asian Studies* 58, no. 1 (1999): 9–10; Hellyer, *Defining Engagement*, 59–68.

82. Totman, *Early Modern Japan*, 302–303; Tasaburō Itō, "The Book Banning Policy of the Tokugawa Shogunate," *Acta Asiatica* 22 (1972). For greater detail, see Nakamura Kunimitsu 中村邦光, "Kyōho kaikaku no okeru 'kinsho kanwa': Nihon

kagaku-shi jō no gokai 享保改革における<禁書緩和>—日本科学史上の誤解," *Butsurigaku-shi nōto* 物理学史ノート 9; Ōishi Manabu 大石学, "Nihon kinsei kokka no yakusō seisaku: Kyōho kaikaku o chūshin ni 日本近世国家の薬草政策—享保改革期を中心に" *Reikishigaku kenkyū* 歴史学研究 639; Nakamura Yasuhiro 中村安宏, "Muro Kyūsō to Shushigaku: Kyōho kaikaku, kagaku dōnyū hantairon o chūshin ni 室鳩巣と朱子学・享保改革—科学導入反対論を中心に," *Nihon shisōshi kenkyū* 日本思想史研究 31; F. B. Verwayen, "Tokugawa Translations of Dutch Legal Texts," *Monumenta Nipponica* 53, no. 3.

83. Hellyer, *Defining Engagement*, 70–71, 136; Lee, "Trade and Economy," 10; Totman, *Early Modern Japan*, 312–313. The spread of sugar production benefited Japan's overall balance of trade but at the expense of Satsuma, which had a near monopoly on domestic sugar production before the 1720s.

84. Totman, *Early Modern Japan*, 312.

85. For a summary of Yoshimune and sweet potatoes, see Sakai Kenkichi 坂井健吉, *Satsumaimo* さつまいも (Tokyo: Hōsei Daigaku Shuppankyoku, 1999), 292–296.

86. Kasaya, *Tokugawa Yoshimune*, 174–188; Hellyer, *Defining Engagement*, 68–70.

87. Kasaya, *Tokugawa Yoshimune*, 136–166; Izui Asako 泉井朝子, "Tashidaka-sei ni kansuru ichi kōsatsu 足高制に関する一考察," *Gakushūin shigaku* 学習院史学, no. 2 (1965).

88. Sorai had a personal audience with Yoshimune in 1727 and wrote a long policy proposal (*Discourse on Government* or *Seidan* 政談) for that occasion. The audience is evidence that the shogun thought highly of Sorai, but the exact nature of Sorai's influence before 1727 is unclear.

89. Olaf G. Lidin, ed., *Ogyū Sorai's Discourse on Government (Seidan): An Annotated Translation* (Wiesbaden: Harrassowitz Verlag, 1999), 124–125, 138, and Yoshikawa Kōjirō 吉川幸次郎 et al., eds., *Nihon shisō taikei 36: Ogyū Sorai* 日本思想体系 36: 荻生徂徠 (Tokyo: Iwanami Shoten, 1973), 295, 305. See also J. R. McEwan, *The Political Writings of Ogyū Sorai* (Cambridge: Cambridge University Press, 1962), 36–37.

90. Lidin, ed., *Ogyū Sorai's Discourse on Government*, 128–130; Yoshikawa et al., eds., *Nihon shisō taikei 36: Ogyū Sorai*, 298–300, 343–345. See also McEwan, *The Political Writings of Ogyū Sorai*, 60–63.

91. Lidin, ed., *Ogyū Sorai's Discourse on Government*, 218–245; Yoshikawa et al., eds., *Nihon shisō taikei 36: Ogyū Sorai*, 365–389. See also McEwan, *The Political Writings of Ogyū Sorai*, 79–80.

92. Roald Kristiansen, "Western Science and Japanese Neo-Confucianism: A History of Their Interaction and Transformation," *Japanese Religions* 21, no. 2 (1996); Josephson, *The Invention of Religion in Japan*, 106–107. The Nishikawa texts are "A Townsman's Companion" (Chōnin bukuro 町人袋, 1719) and "A Farmer's Companion" (Hyakushō bukuro 百姓袋, 1731) in volumes 7 and 8 of Nishikawa Joken 西川如見, *Nishikawa Joken isho* 西川如見遺書, ed. Nishikawa Tadasuke 西川忠亮, 18 vols. (Tokyo: Nishikawa Tadasuke, 1898–1907). Nishikawa

recommended that farmers read *Hydraulic Machinery of the West* (Saisei suihō, Ch. Taixi shuifa 泰西水法, 1612), a treatise by the Jesuit Sabbathinus de Ursis and Xu Guangqi 徐光啓.

93. The bibliography on Sorai is enormous. For two contrasting but complementary views of Sorai, see Tetsuo Najita, ed., *Tokugawa Political Writings* (Cambridge: Cambridge University Press, 1998), and John Allen Tucker, *Ogyū Sorai's Philosophical Masterworks: The Bendō and Benmei* (Honolulu: University of Hawai'i Press, 2006). For Sorai and Yoshimune, see Kasaya, *Tokugawa Yoshimune*, 57–59. Maruyama's famous interpretation is in Masao Maruyama, *Studies in the Intellectual History of Tokugawa Japan*, trans. Mikiso Hane (Princeton, NJ: Princeton University Press, 1974).

94. The decision was also a response to falling rice prices. Attempts to stop inflation had proven too successful, and a larger Edo population would drive prices back up. See Totman, *Early Modern Japan*, 307.

95. For a summary of the historiography on territoriality, see Charles S. Maier, "Consigning the Twentieth Century to History: Alternative Narratives for the Modern Era," *American Historical Review* 105, no. 3 (2000). Lauren Benton has convincingly argued that the notions of exclusive territoriality attributed to the Peace of Westphalia became widely accepted only in the 1800s. See Lauren A. Benton, *A Search for Sovereignty: Law and Geography in European Empires, 1400–1900* (Cambridge: Cambridge University Press, 2010), esp. 1–39, 279–300.

96. Legal scholars have begun to use the term "Eastphalian" to describe the East Asian international system as an alternative to the "Westphalian" order. See Tom Ginsburg, "Eastphalia and East Asian Regionalism," *University of California Davis Law Review* 44, no. 3 (2010), and Saeyoung Park, "Reordering the Universe: The Unyō Crisis of 1875 and the Death of Eastphalia," unpublished manuscript, 2015.

CHAPTER 2

1. For an overview of these events, see Hirakawa Arata 平川新, *Kaikoku e no michi* 開国への道 (Shōgakkan, 2008), 70–121.

2. Donald Keene, *The Japanese Discovery of Europe, 1720–1830*, rev. ed. (Stanford, CA: Stanford University Press, 1969), 31–35. Kudō's report was "A Study of Hearsay about Ezo" (Akaezo fūsetsu kō 赤蝦夷風説考) (1783). Benyowsky was a remarkable figure, although his memoir is as fanciful as his reports of a Russian invasion. See Maurice Auguste Benyowsky, comte de, *Memoirs and travels of Mauritius Augustus Count de Benyowsky; magnate of the kingdoms of Hungary and Poland, one of the chiefs of the confederation of Poland, &c. &c. Consisting of his military operations in Poland, his exile into Kamchatka, his escape and voyage . . . through the northern Pacific Ocean, . . . Written by himself. Translated from the original manuscript. In two volumes,* 2 vols. (London: G. G. J. and J. Robinson,

1790). For a brief biography, see Karel Fiala, "First Contacts of Czechs and Slovaks with Japanese Culture (Up to World War I): The Major Publications and Personalities," *Japan Review: Journal of the International Research Center for Japan Studies* 3 (1992). Benyowsky's name is rendered in various forms, including Morice August Benyowsky and Móric Ágost Count de Benyovszky.

3. Keene, *Japanese Discovery of Europe,* 37–39, 108–109; Walker, *The Conquest of Ainu Lands,* 164.

4. Walker, *The Conquest of Ainu Lands,* 165–172; Keene, *Japanese Discovery of Europe,* 38, 128–134. For additional examples of the Matsumae house deceiving the shogunate, see Ōishi Shinzaburō 大石慎三郎, *Tanuma Okitsugu no jidai* 田沼意次の時代 (Tokyo: Iwanami Shoten, 1991), 135.

5. Fujita Satoru 藤田覚, *Kinsei kōki seijishi to taigai kankei* 近世後期政治史と対外関係 (Tokyo: Tōkyō Daigaku Shuppankai, 2005), 4–6; Fujita Satoru 藤田覚, "Bakufu Ezo-chi seisaku no tenkan to Kunashiri-Menashi jiken 幕府蝦夷地政策の転換とクナシリ・メナシ事件," in *Jūhasseiki Nihon no seiji to gaikō* 十八世紀日本の政治と外交, edited by Fujita Satoru 藤田覚 (Tokyo: Yamakawa Shuppansha, 2010), 218–220; Mark Ravina, "Tokugawa, Romanov, and Khmer: The Politics of Trade and Diplomacy in Eighteenth-Century East Asia," *Journal of World History* 26, no. 2 (2016): 285–286.

6. Walker, *The Conquest of Ainu Lands,* 172–176.

7. For a useful overview of Anglo-Russian relations, see David Fromkin, "The Great Game in Asia," *Foreign Affairs* 58, no. 4 (1980). Or for greater detail, see Enno E. Kraehe, "A Bipolar Balance of Power," *American Historical Review* 97, no. 3 (1992), and Paul W. Schroeder, "Did the Vienna Settlement Rest on a Balance of Power?" *American Historical Review* 97, no. 3 (1992). For British interest in the castaways and parallels between the Laxman and Macartney missions, see J. L. Cranmer-Byng, "Russian and British Interests in the Far East 1791–1793," *Canadian Slavonic Papers / Revue Canadienne des Slavistes* 10, no. 3 (1968): esp. 359–365.

8. Vasilii Mikhailovich Golovnin and Petr Ivanovich Rikord, *Narrative of My Captivity in Japan, during the Years 1811, 1812 & 1813,* 2 vols. (London: Henry Colburn, 1818), 1:14–15; Ravina, "Tokugawa, Romanov, and Khmer," 284–285.

9. George Alexander Lensen, *The Russian Push toward Japan: Russo-Japanese Relations, 1697–1875* (Princeton, NJ: Princeton University Press, 1959), 96–120; Ravina, "Tokugawa, Romanov, and Khmer," 286–287.

10. Matsudaira Sadanobu's account of the senior council deliberations ("Roshiajin toriatsukai tedome" 魯西亜人取扱手留) is reproduced in Yamashita Tsuneo 山下恒夫, ed., *Daikokuya Kōdayū shiryōshū* 大黒屋光太夫史料集 (Tokyo: Nihon hyōronsha, 2003), 1:147–308. See, in particular 1:149–158, 193–195. Also Fujita, *Kinsei kōki seijishi,* 4–13; Ravina, "Tokugawa, Romanov, and Khmer," 287–290.

11. Ravina, "Tokugawa, Romanov, and Khmer," 287–292. The difference between Japanese and Russian perceptions of the Dutch likely stems from the uniqueness

of VOC-Tokugawa relations. Within the Tokugawa system, the Dutch were foreign but were also Tokugawa vassals. For that foreign-domestic duality, see Adam Clulow, *The Company and the Shogun: The Dutch Encounter with Tokugawa Japan* (New York: Columbia University Press, 2014), esp. 95–131.

12. Ravina, "Tokugawa, Romanov, and Khmer," 291–292.
13. Ibid., 292–293.
14. Lensen, *The Russian Push toward Japan*, 143–145.
15. Ibid., 144–159; Inobe Shigeo 井野邊茂雄, *Ishin zenshi no kenkyū* 維新前史の研究, rev. ed. (Tokyo: Chūbunkan, 1942), 191–201.
16. Lensen, *The Russian Push toward Japan*, 158–174.
17. Hiroshi Mitani, *Escape from Impasse: The Decision to Open Japan*, trans. David Noble (Tokyo: International House of Japan, 2006), 14–16; David N. Wells, *Russian Views of Japan, 1792–1913: An Anthology of Travel Writing* (New York: RoutledgeCurzon, 2004), 7–8.
18. Ravina, "Tokugawa, Romanov, and Khmer," 292–294.
19. Noell Wilson, "Tokugawa Defense Redux: Organizational Failure in the *Phaeton* Incident of 1808," *Journal of Japanese Studies* 36, no. 1 (2010): 1–17; Noell Wilson, *Defensive Positions: The Politics of Maritime Security in Tokugawa Japan* (Cambridge, MA: Harvard University Asia Center, 2015), 113–121.
20. For details, see John Jason Stephan, "Ezo under the Tokugawa Bakufu 1799–1821: An Aspect of Japan's Frontier History" (Ph.D. diss., University of London, 1969), 75–141, 225–250. The Hakodate magistrate was called the Ezo magistrate from 1799 to 1802.
21. David L. Howell, *Geographies of Identity in Nineteenth-century Japan* (Berkeley: University of California Press, 2005), 131–153; Stephan, "Ezo under the Tokugawa bakufu," 70–74.
22. Brett L. Walker, "The Early Modern Japanese State and Ainu Vaccinations: Redefining the Body Politic 1799–1868," *Past & Present*, no. 163 (1999): esp. 129–135.
23. Hokkaidō chō 北海道庁, ed., *Shinsen Hokkaidō shi* 新撰北海道史 (Sapporo: Hokkaidō chō, 1936–37), 2: 412; Hirakawa, *Kaikoku e no michi*, 67–68. The signpost text is recorded as both 天長地久大日本国 and 天長地久大日本属島. For a consideration of various accounts, see Kōno Tsunekichi 河野常吉, "Kunashiri Etorofu no kenpyō ni kansuru dan'an 国後択捉の建標に関する断案," *Sapporo Hakubutsu Gakkai Kaihō* 札幌博物学会会報 4, no. 1 (1912). For the explorer Kondō Jūzō's account, see Kondō Jūzō 近藤重蔵, "Zoku Ezo sōshi 続蝦夷草紙," 210.08, Sapporo Municipal Central Library 札幌市中央図書館.
24. Kikuchi Isao 菊地勇夫, *Bakuhan taisei to Ezochi* 幕藩体制と蝦夷地 (Tokyo: Yūzankaku, 1984), 89–115; Mitani, *Escape from Impasse*, 15.
25. Hakodate Shishi Hensanshitsu 函館市史編さん室, ed., *Hakodate shishi: tsūsetsu hen* 函館市史 通説編 (Hakodate: Hakodate-shi, 1980), 1:496–498.
26. Wilson, "Tokugawa Defense Redux," 16–27.

27. Ibid., 27–32.

28. The edict is formally known as the Order for the Repelling of Foreign Ships (Gaikokusen uchiharai rei 外国船打払令).

29. Tōyama Kagemichi 遠山景晋, "Chūkai injun roku 籌海因循録," in *Nihon kaibō shiryō sōsho* 日本海防史料叢書, ed. Sumita Shōichi 住田正一 (Tokyo: Kaibō Shiryō Kankōkai, 1932; originally published 1824), 4: 114; Mitani, *Escape from Impasse*, 17–18.

30. Katō Yūzō 加藤祐三, "Kurobune zengo no seikai 7: 'keiken to fūsetsu' Morison-gō jiken to Ahen sensō jōhō 黒船前後の世界 (7) <経験と風説>モリソン号事件とアヘン戦争情報," *Shisō* 思想, no. 719 (1984); Mitani, *Escape from Impasse*, 45–46, 49.

31. The exact motivations behind this purge, known as Bansha no goku 蛮社の獄, remain unclear. For an overview, see Donald Keene, *Frog in the Well: Portraits of Japan by Watanabe Kazan, 1793–1841* (New York: Columbia University Press, 2006), and Mitani, *Escape from Impasse*, 47–49.

32. Bob Tadashi Wakabayashi, "Opium, Expulsion, Sovereignty: China's Lessons for Bakumatsu Japan," *Monumenta Nipponica* 47, no. 1 (1992). Mineta was later rehabilitated as an expert on coastal defense.

33. R. H. van Gulik, "Kakkaron 隔鞾論: A Japanese Echo of the Opium War," *Monumenta Serica* 4, no. 2 (1940).

34. Mitani, *Escape from Impasse*, 49–50. The position of Shimoda bugyō was technically the revival of an office abolished in 1720.

35. The policy is known in Japanese as the *agechirei*, or "land seizure order." The land claims for Edo and Osaka involved all lands within a 10 *ri* (24.4 mile) radius of the castle.

36. Mitani, *Escape from Impasse*, 50–52.

37. Ibid., 54–59.

38. Ravina, *Land and Lordship in Early Modern Japan*, 93–114.

39. Ibid., 128–153.

40. For peasant protests, see Stephen Vlastos, *Peasant Protests and Uprisings in Tokugawa Japan* (Berkeley: University of California Press, 1986); Anne Walthall, *Peasant Uprisings in Japan: A Critical Anthology of Peasant Histories* (Chicago: University of Chicago Press, 1991); Herbert Bix, *Peasant Protest in Japan: 1590–1884* (New Haven, CT: Yale University Press, 1986); James W. White, *Ikki: Social Conflict and Political Protest in Early Modern Japan* (Ithaca, NY: Cornell University Press, 1995).

41. Osamu Saitō, "The Labor Market in Tokugawa Japan: Wage Differentials and the Real Wage Level, 1727–1830," *Explorations in Economic History* 15 (1978).

42. Osamu Saitō, "Wages, Inequality, and Pre-Industrial Growth in Japan, 1727–1894," in *Living Standards in the Past: New Perspectives on Well-being in Asia and Europe*, ed. Robert C. Allen, Tommy Bengtsson, and Martin Dribe (Oxford: Oxford University, 2005). See also Howell, "Hard Times in the Kantō," esp. 357–364.

43. A famous period account of social decay is *Observations on Mundane Affairs* (Seji kenbunroku世事見聞録, 1816) reprinted in Buyō Inshi 武陽陰士, "Seji kenbunroku 世事見聞録," in *Nihon shomin seikatsu shiryō shūsei* 日本庶民生活史料集成, 8: 641–766, (Tokyo: San'ichi Shobō, 1969); or Buyō Inshi, *Lust, Commerce, and Corruption: An Account of What I Have Seen and Heard, by an Edo Samurai*, ed. Mark Teeuwen and Kate Wildman Nakai, trans. Mark Teeuwen et al. (New York: Columbia University Press, 2014). For a summary, see Susan L. Burns, *Before the Nation: Kokugaku and the Imagining of Community in Early Modern Japan* (Durham, NC: Duke University Press, 2003), 20–34.

44. Testuo Najita, "Ōshio Heihachirō (1793–1837)," in *Personality in Japanese History*, ed. Albert M. Craig and Donald H. Shively (Berkeley: University of California Press, 1970), 155–179.

45. J. R. R. Tolkien, *Beowulf: The Monsters and the Critics* (1936; reprint, London: Oxford University Press, 1963). See also Mary C. Wilson Tietjen, "God, Fate, and the Hero of 'Beowulf'," *Journal of English and Germanic Philology* 74, no. 2 (1975): esp. 159.

46. The historiography on Nativism is enormous. For an excellent overview, see Susan L. Burns, "The Politics of Philology in Japan: Ancient Texts, Language, and Japanese Identity," in *World Philology*, ed. Sheldon Pollock, Benjamin A. Elman, and Ku-ming Kevin Chang (Cambridge, MA: Harvard University Press, 2015). For greater detail, see Burns, *Before the Nation*; Peter Nosco, *Remembering Paradise: Nativism and Nostalgia in Eighteenth Century Japan* (Cambridge, MA: Council on East Asian Studies, Harvard University, 1990); Harry D. Harootunian, *Things Seen and Unseen: Discourse and Ideology in Tokugawa Nativism* (Chicago: University of Chicago Press, 1988); Harry D. Harootunian, *Toward Restoration: The Growth of Political Consciousness in Tokugawa Japan* (Berkeley: University of California, 1970); Peter Flueckiger, *Imagining Harmony: Poetry, Empathy, and Community in mid-Tokugawa Confucianism and Nativism* (Stanford, CA: Stanford University Press, 2011).

47. For a comparison of German and English mythologizing, see Maike Oergel, *The Return of King Arthur and the Nibelungen: National Myth in Nineteenth-Century English and German Literature* (Berlin: De Gruyter, 1997). For the Arthurian revival, see Rob Gossedge and Stephen Knight, "The Arthur of the Sixteenth to Nineteenth Centuries," in *The Cambridge Companion to the Arthurian Legend*, ed. Elizabeth Archibald and Ad Putter (Cambridge: Cambridge University Press, 2009), 103–119.

48. Harootunian, *Things Seen and Unseen*, esp. 27–28, 48, 151–154.

49. Donald Keene, "Hirata Atsutane and Western Learning," *T'oung Pao* 42, no. 5 (1954): 353–380; Richard Devine, "Hirata Atsutane and Christian Sources," *Monumenta Nipponica* 36, no. 1 (1981): 37–54.

50. Wilburn Hansen, "The Medium Is the Message: Hirata Atsutane's Ethnography of the World Beyond," *History of Religions* 45, no. 4 (2006), and Wilburn

Hansen, *When Tengu Talk: Hirata Atsutane's Ethnography of the Other World* (Honolulu: University of Hawaiʻi Press, 2008).

51. Harootunian, *Things Seen and Unseen*, esp. 27–28.

52. See Hirata's "Outline of the Ancient Way" (Kodo taii 古道大意), in Katō Totsudō 加藤咄堂, ed., *Kokumin shisō sōsho* 国民思想叢書, vol. 7 (Tokyo: Kokumin Shisō Sōsho Kankōkai, 1931), 286–287. For an English translation, see John Ordonic Walter, "Kodo taii, an Outline of the Ancient Way: An Annotated Translation with an Introduction to the Shinto Revival Movement and a Sketch of the Life of Hirata Atsutane" (Ph.D. diss., University of Pennsylvania, 1967), 65–66.

53. For an overview of Mito learning, see J. Victor Koschmann, *The Mito Ideology: Discourse Reform, and Insurrection in Late Tokugawa Japan, 1790–1864* (Berkeley: University of California Press, 1987).

54. Hayashi Shihei 林子平, *Kaikoku heidan* 海国兵談 (Tokyo: Tonansha, 1916), 175–178.

55. William Theodore De Bary, Carol Gluck, and Arthur Tiedemann, *Sources of Japanese Tradition*, Vol. 2: *1600 to 2000*, 2nd ed. (New York: Columbia University Press, 2005), 604–609. For Satō's overall economic thought, see Federico Marcon, "Satō Nobuhiro and the Political Economy of Natural History in Nineteenth-Century Japan," *Japanese Studies* 34, no. 3 (2014).

56. See *Kondō hisaku* 混同秘策, in Bitō and Shimazaki, eds., *Nihon shisō taikei 45: Andō Shōeki, Satō Nobuhiro*, 425–485. See also Satō's later work, *Legacy of a Secret Plan (Suitō hisaku* 垂統秘策) in ibid., 488–517. For Satō proposal to Mizuno, see Satō Nobuhiro 佐藤信淵, *Satō Nobuhiro kagaku zenshū* 佐藤信淵家学全集, ed. Takimoto Seiichi 滝本誠一, 3 vols. (Tokyo: Iwanami Shoten, 1925–26), 2:319–337.

57. Tōyama, "Chūkai injun roku," 115–117.

58. See "Ibuki oroshi 伊吹於呂志," in Hirata Atsutane 平田篤胤, *Hirata Atsutane zenshū* 平田篤胤全集, ed. Muromatsu Iwao 室松岩雄, 15 vols. (Tokyo: Itchidō shoten, 1911–18), 1:1–61, especially 1:24–29.

59. Leonard Blussé, "Bull in a China Shop: Pieter Nuyts in China and Japan (1627–1634)," in *Around and about Formosa: Essays in Honor of Professor Ts'ao Yung-ho*, ed. Yonghe Cao and Leonard Blussé (Taipei: Ts'ao Yung-ho Foundation for Culture and Education, 2003).

60. Koga Tōan 古賀侗庵, *Kaibō okusoku* 海防臆測, 2 vols. (Tokyo: Hidaka Nobuzane, 1880), 1:19.

61. Inoue Katsuo 井上勝生, *Bakumatsu ishin* 幕末・維新 (Tokyo: Iwanami Shoten, 2006), 121–122.

62. Bob Tadashi Wakabayashi, *Anti-foreignism and Western Learning in Early-modern Japan: The New Theses of 1825* (Cambridge, MA: Council on East Asian Studies, Harvard University, 1986), 184–185. I have also referred to the Japanese original in Imai Usaburō 今井宇三郎, Seya Yoshihiko 瀬谷義彦, and Bitō Masahide 尾藤正英, eds., *Nihon shisō taikei 53: Mitogaku* 日本思想体系 53: 水戸学日本思想体系 (Tokyo: Iwanami Shoten, 1973), 50–159.

63. Wakabayashi, *Anti-foreignism*, 158.

64. Adapted from ibid., 262 with reference to the original at Imai, Seya, and Bitō, eds., *Nihon shisō taikei 53: Mitogaku*, 145.

65. See *Tenchūki* 天柱記, in Bitō and Shimazaki, eds., *Nihon shisō taikei 45: Andō Shōeki, Satō Nobuhiro*, 361–423.

66. Ibid., 374–379. The Kojiki quote is "自其矛末垂落之鹽累積成嶋" from Book 1, Chapter 3. See Aoki Kazuo 青木和夫 et al., eds., *Nihon shisō taikei 1: Kojiki* 日本思想大系1:古事記 (Tokyo: Iwanami Shoten, 1982), 20–21. Translation from Donald L. Philippi, *Kojiki* (Princeton, NJ: Princeton University Press, 1968), 3.

67. The original phrase is "渾沌如鶏子" See Nihon shoki, Book 1, Part 1 in Sakamoto Tarō 坂本太郎 et al., eds., *Nihon shoki jō* 日本書紀・上, vol. 67 of *Nihon koten bungaku taikei* 日本古典文學大系 (Tokyo: Iwanami Shoten, 1967), 77. For a discussion of the *Nihon shoki* and the other five official "national histories," see Tarō Sakamoto, *The Six National Histories of Japan*, trans. John S. Brownlee (Vancouver: UBC Press, 1991).

68. Bitō and Shimazaki, eds., *Nihon shisō taikei 45: Andō Shōeki, Satō Nobuhiro*, 366–373. Satō's fragment of the Bible is the story of the creation of mankind from earth.

69. For this reading of Satō, I am indebted to Josephson, *The Invention of Religion in Japan*, 116–117.

70. Bettina Gramlich-Oka, "Tadano Makuzu and Her Hitori Kangae," *Monumenta Nipponica* 56, no. 1 (2001).

71. Ibid., quotes from 30.

72. Ibid., 32–33; Tadano Makuzu et al., "Solitary Thoughts: A Translation of Tadano Makuzu's Hitori Kangae (2)," *Monumenta Nipponica* 56, no. 2 (2001): 182–183.

CHAPTER 3

1. Conrad Totman, "Tokugawa Yoshinobu and Kobugattai: A Study of Political Inadequacy," *Monumenta Nipponica* 30, no. 4 (1975): 394.

2. After a formal reception in March 1868, Satow lamented that while "many of the guests were intelligent and well-behaved," the daimyo of Chōshū "drank more champagne than was good for him" and behaved like a "great baby." Ernest Mason Satow, *A Diplomat in Japan* (Philadelphia: J.B. Lippincott, 1921), 38, 371–372.

3. D. Colin Jaundrill, *Samurai to Soldier: Remaking Military Service in Nineteenth-century Japan* (Ithaca, NY: Cornell University Press, 2016), 49–66, 80–85; Thomas M. Huber, *The Revolutionary Origins of Modern Japan* (Stanford, CA: Stanford University Press, 1981), 122–124; Albert Craig, "The Restoration Movement in Choshu," *Journal of Asian Studies* 18, no. 2 (1959): 189–190.

4. Jaundrill, *Samurai to Soldier*, 66–72; Inoue, *Bakumatsu ishin*, 75–85. In Satsuma, the samurai estate included a type of rural vassal called *gōshi* (郷士).

5. For a general biography of Nariakira, see Kanbashi Norimasa 芳即正, *Shimazu Nariakira* 島津斉彬 (Tokyo: Yoshikawa Kōbunkan, 1993).

6. Mitani, *Escape from Impasse*, 74–76.

7. Hellyer, *Defining Engagement*, 161–162.

8. Kanbashi, *Shimazu Nariakira*, 117–122.

9. "Uraga bugyō jōshi sho 浦賀奉行上司書," 1849/6, in *Ishin shiryō kōhon* 維新史料稿本, 1巻 214頁, 嘉永2年6月是月(18490060660), manuscript 148/079, KA013-0667, quote from manuscript pp. 87–1. Permalink https://clioimg.hi.u-tokyo.ac.jp/viewer/image/idata/M00/M/20/KA013/0674.tif.

10. "Uraga bugyō ukagaisho 浦賀奉行伺書," 1849/12, in *Ishin shiryō kōhon* 維新史料稿本, 1巻 235頁, 嘉永2年12月是月(18490120660), manuscript 162/144, KA016-0390, quote from manuscript pp. 155–156. Permalink https://clio-img.hi.u-tokyo.ac.jp/viewer/image/idata/M00/M/20/KA016/0401.tif.

11. Mitani, *Escape from Impasse*, 104–105; Inoue, *Bakumatsu ishin*, 8–13.

12. Martha Chaiklin, "Monopolists to Middlemen: Dutch Liberalism and American Imperialism in the Opening of Japan," *Journal of World History* 21, no. 2 (2010): 262.

13. Mitani, *Escape from Impasse*, 104–115.

14. James Bradley, *Flyboys: A True Story of Courage* (Boston: Little, Brown, 2003), 36. There is a similar passage in Morison's biography of Perry, describing the US ships as "weird-looking aircraft from outer space." See Samuel Eliot Morison, *"Old Bruin": Commodore Matthew C. Perry, 1794–1858; The American Naval Officer Who Helped Found Liberia* (Boston: Little, Brown, 1967), 319.

15. S. Wells Williams, *A Journal of the Perry Expedition to Japan (1853–1854)*, ed. Frederick Wells Williams (Yokohama: Kelly & Walsh, 1910), 63–64, 102, 105.

16. Tessa Morris-Suzuki, *The Technological Transformation of Japan: From the Seventeenth to the Twenty-first Century* (Cambridge: Cambridge University Press, 1994), 61–63; Mitani, *Escape from Impasse*, 137; Adachi Hiroyuki 安達裕之, *Iyō no fune: yōshikisen dōnyū to sakoku taisei* 異様の船: 洋式船導入と鎖国体制 (Tokyo: Heibonsha, 1995), 173.

17. Mitani, *Escape from Impasse*, 136.

18. Ibid., 138–139

19. For an overview, see Inoue, *Bakumatsu ishin*, 23–38.

20. The official US account of Perry's action in Ryukyu is less belligerent than his personal diary. Note particularly the contrast between Hawks, ed., *Narrative of the Expedition*, 274–280, and Matthew Calbraith Perry, *The Japan Expedition, 1852–1854: The Personal Journal of Commodore Matthew C. Perry*, ed. Roger Pineau (1856; reprint, Washington, DC: Smithsonian Institution Press, 1968), 109–111. For instructions from Secretary of State Daniel Webster, see Millard Filmore, "Message from the President of the United States, communicating, in compliance with a resolution of the Senate, certain official documents relative to the Empire of Japan, and serving to illustrate the existing relations between

the United States and Japan," in *U. S. Senate Serial Set Vol. No. 620, Session Vol. No. 9. 32nd Congress, 1st Session. S.Exec.Doc. 59* (1852), 80–82. Webster was dead before Perry's departure, and Perry's own instructions for his mission are in Peter Booth Wiley and Korogi Ichiro, *Yankees in the Land of the Gods: Commodore Perry and the Opening of Japan* (New York: Penguin Books, 1991), 116–117. For Palmer's support and lobbying, see Aaron Haight Palmer, *Documents and facts illustrating the origin of the mission to Japan, authorized by government of the United States, May 10th, 1851* (Washington, DC: Henry Polkinhorn, 1857).

21. Perry, *The Japan Expedition*, 85–86.

22. Mitani, *Escape from Impasse*, 198–201.

23. This problem of treaty relations had been looming since at least 1844, when, in the wake of the Opium War, the shogunate quietly gave Satsuma permission for a treaty between France and Ryukyu if needed to avoid a war.

24. "Jin'in Rojin Karafuto ni kitari 壬寅魯人樺太に来り," 嘉永6年8月30日, in *Shiryō kōhon*史料稿本, 0201001 57782, 99編冊頁, 史料綱文, permalink https://clioimg.hi.u-tokyo.ac.jp/viewer/image/idata/T38/1853/34-3-1/5/0162.tif. See also Suzuki Hairin 鈴木楳林, *Suzuki daizasshū* 鈴木大雑集, ed. Hayakawa Junzaburō 早川純三郎, 5 vols., vol. 1 (Tokyo: Nihon Shiseki Kyōkai, 1919–1920), 212–218. For greater detail, see John J. Stephan, "The Crimean War in the Far East," *Modern Asian Studies* 3, no. 3 (1969), and Thierry Mormanne, "La prise de possession d'Urup par la flotte anglo-française en 1855," *CIPANGO Cahiers d'études japonaises* 11 (2004); Stephan, "The Crimean War in the Far East."

25. For an overview of the Ogasawara Islands, see David Chapman, "Different Faces, Different Spaces: Identifying the Islanders of Ogasawara," *Social Science Japan Journal* 14, no. 2 (2011); David Chapman, "Inventing Subjects: Early History of the 'Naturalized Foreigners' of the Bonin (Ogasawara) Islands 24," *Asia Pacific Journal* 24 (2009); and Russell Robertson, "The Bonin Islands," *Transactions of the Asiatic Society of Japan* 4 (1876)

26. Hawks, ed., *Narrative of the Expedition*, 211–214.

27. Matthew Calbraith Perry, *A Paper by Commodore M.C. Perry, U.S.N., read before the American Geographical and Statistical Society at a meeting held March 6th, 1856* (New York: D. Appleton, 1856), quote from 28–29.

28. Hakodate Shishi Hensanshitsu, ed., *Hakodate shishi: tsūsetsu hen*, 1:579–582.

29. Hellyer, *Defining Engagement*, 162–168, 177–206.

30. Conrad Totman, "Fudai Daimyo and the Collapse of the Tokugawa Bakufu," *Journal of Asian Studies* 34, no. 3 (1975): 583–584; Totman, *Collapse*, 11–21.

31. Townsend Harris, *The Complete Journal of Townsend Harris: First American Consul and Minister to Japan* (Rutland, VT: Charles E. Tuttle, 1959), 569–540. Notably, English observers such as Richard Cocks had referred to the Japanese emperor as the "pope of Japon" in the 1600s. See Michael Cooper, ed., *They Came to Japan: An Anthology of European Reports on Japan, 1543–1640* (Berkeley: University of California Press, 1965), 366, and Richard

Cocks, *Diary of Richard Cocks, Cape-merchant in the English Factory in Japan, 1615–1622*, ed. Edward Maunde Thompson, 2 vols. (London: Hakluyt Society, 1883), 1:311.

32. My reading here is informed by Burns, *Before the Nation*; Harootunian, *Things Seen and Unseen*; H. D. Harootunian, "Late Tokugawa Thought and Culture," in *The Cambridge History of Japan*, Vol. 5: *The Nineteenth Century*, ed. John Whitney Hall (Cambridge: Cambridge University Press, 1989).

33. Anne Walthall, "Off with Their Heads! The Hirata Disciples and the Ashikaga Shoguns," *Monumenta Nipponica* 50, no. 2 (1995); W. G. Beasley, *Select Documents on Japanese Foreign Policy, 1853–1868* (London: Oxford University Press, 1955), 35–43.

34. George M. Wilson, "The Bakumatsu Intellectual in Action: Hashimoto Sanai in the Political Crisis of 1858," in *Personality in Japanese History*, ed. Albert M. Craig and Donald H. Shively (Berkeley: University of California Press, 1970).

35. Tōkyō Daigaku Shiryō Hensanjo 東京大学史料編纂所, ed., *Bakumatsu gaikoku kankei monjo* 幕末外国関係文書 (Tokyo: Tōkyō Daigaku Shiryō Hensanjo, 1910–), 19:636–637. For an English translation see Beasley, *Select Documents*, 180–181.

36. For a thoughtful reevaluation of Ii, see Mori Yoshikazu 母利美和, *Ii Naosuke* 井伊直弼 (Tokyo: Yoshikawa Kōbunkan, 2006), esp. 149–183.

37. Hakodate Shishi Hensanshitsu, ed., *Hakodate shishi: tsūsetsu hen*, 3:583–585; *Ishin shiryō kōhon* 維新史料稿本, 1859/9/27, 3巻 221頁 安政6年9月27日, AN157-0448. Permalink https://clioimg.hi.u-tokyo.ac.jp/viewer/image/idata/M00/M/20/AN157/0448.tif. This arrangement was reversed after the Boshin War. See Kikuchi Isao 菊池勇夫, "Ezogashima to hoppō sekai 蝦夷島と北方世界," in *Ezogashima to hoppō sekai* 蝦夷島と北方世界, ed. Kikuchi Isao 菊池勇夫 (Tokyo: Yoshikawa kōbunkan, 2002), 82. For an overview of Ii's foreign policy, see Michael R. Auslin, *Negotiating with Imperialism: The Unequal Treaties and the Culture of Japanese Diplomacy* (Cambridge, MA: Harvard University Press, 2004), 45–50.

38. Rutherford Alcock, *The Capital of the Tycoon: A Narrative of a Three Years' Residence in Japan*, 2 vols. (New York: Longman, Green, Longman, Roberts, and Green, 1863), 1:347–359, quote from 1:348. The expatriate community seems to have learned of Ii's assassination in by late April. "The Rumored Assassination of the Tycoon of Japan," *New York Times*, June 13, 1860. See also *Ishin shiryō kōhon* 維新史料稿本, 1860/3/8, 3巻 282頁, 万延1年3月8日, MA005-0412, permalink https://clioimg.hi.u-tokyo.ac.jp/viewer/image/idata/M00/M/20/MA005/0412.tif, and 1860/i3/25, 3巻 303頁, 万延1年閏3月25日, MA007-1030, permalink https://clioimg.hi.u-tokyo.ac.jp/viewer/image/idata/M00/M/20/MA007/1030.tif.

39. Totman, *Collapse*, xx–xxii; Edwin B. Lee, "The Kazunomiya Marriage: Alliance between the Court and the Bakufu," *Monumenta Nipponica* 22, no. 3/4 (1967): 293–295; Tada Kōmon 多田好問, ed., *Iwakura-ko jikki* 岩倉公實記 (Tokyo: Iwakura-kō Kyūseki Hozonkai, 1927), 1:393–395.

40. "Bakufu Andō Nobumasa Kuze Hirochika nado o kenseki shi, taïin ses-himu　幕府、安藤信正・久世廣周等を譴責し、退隠せしむ,"　1862/8/16 文久2年8月16日, in *Shiryō kōhon*史料稿本, 020100160259, 99編冊頁,史料綱文, permalink https://clioimg.hi.u-tokyo.ac.jp/viewer/image/idata/T38/1862/34-7-2/5/0012.tif.

41. Matsudaira Yoshinaga Zenshū Hensan Iinkai 松平慶永全集編纂委員会, ed., *Matsudaira Shungaku zenshū* 松平春嶽全集 (Tokyo: Hara Shobō, 1973), 2:85–11. See also Kyu Hyun Kim, *The Age of Visions and Arguments: Parliamentarianism and the National Public Sphere in Early Meiji Japan* (Cambridge, MA: Harvard University Asia Center, 2007), 60.

42. Totman, "Tokugawa Yoshinobu and Kobugattai: A Study of Political Inadequacy," 393–403.

43. Mark Ravina, *The Last Samurai: The Life and Battles of Saigō Takamori* (Hoboken, NJ: John Wiley, 2004), 111–129.

44. Totman, *Collapse*, 208–214.

45. Ibid., 125–138, 168–172.

46. Conrad Totman, "From Reformism to Transformism: Bakufu Policy, 1853–1868," in *Conflict in Modern Japanese History: The Neglected Tradition*, ed. Tetsuo Najita and J. Victor Koschmann (Ithaca, NY: Cornell University Press, 1982), 77

47. Totman, *Collapse*, 332–339; Inaba Masakuni 稲葉正邦, ed., *Yodo Inaba-ke monjo* 淀稲葉家文書 (Tokyo: Nihon Shiseki Kyōkai, 1926), 467–478.

48. Totman, "From Reformism to Transformism," 71–74; Totman, *Collapse*, 342–354; Kumazawa Tōru 熊沢徹, "Bakumatsu ishinki no gunji to chōhei 幕末維新期の軍事と徴兵," *Rekishigaku kenkyū* 歴史学研究, no. 651 (1993).

49. Totman, *Collapse*, 355–357.

50. "Tokugawa kashu Tokugawa Yoshinobu, sho o Fukoku zenken kōshi Reon Rosshu ni okuri 徳川家主徳川慶喜、書を仏国全権公使レオン・ロッシュに贈り," 1866/8/27, in *Ishin shiryō kōhon* 維新史料稿本, 6巻　599頁, 慶応2年8月2 7日(18660080270), manuscript 2689/123, KE087-1156. Permalink https://clio-img.hi.u-tokyo.ac.jp/viewer/image/idata/M00/M/20/KE087/1156.tif.

51. Meron Medzini, *French Policy in Japan during the Closing Years of the Tokugawa Regime* (Cambridge, MA: East Asian Research Center, Harvard University, 1971), 125–134.

52. R. L. Sims, *French Policy towards the Bakufu and Meiji Japan, 1854–95* (Richmond, UK: Japan Library, 1998), 67; Totman, *Collapse*, 332–335.

53. Amy Aisen Kallander, *Women, Gender, and the Palace Households in Ottoman Tunisia* (Austin: University of Texas Press, 2013), esp. 125–149; Jean-Pierre Lehmann, "Léon Roches—Diplomat Extraordinary in the Bakumatsu Era: An Assessment of His Personality and Policy," *Modern Asian Studies* 14, no. 2 (1980). The English viewed Roches's colonial experiences differently. Mitford, for example, described him as "far more of a picturesque Spahi than a diplomatist." See Algernon Bertram Freeman-Mitford Redesdale, *Memories*, 2 vols.

(New York: E.P. Dutton, 1916), 1:377. For a thoughtful examination of Roches's orientalism, see Dana Irwin, "Sheikhs and Samurai: Léon Roches and the French Imperial Project," *Southeast Review of Asian Studies* 30 (2008).

54. Lehmann, "Léon Roches," 301–302.

55. Medzini, *French Policy*, 134–144.

56. Redesdale, *Memories*, 1:377–378.

57. Ravina, *The Last Samurai*, 131–135.

58. Grace Estelle Fox, *Britain and Japan, 1858–1883* (Oxford: Clarendon Press, 1969), 179–182; Satow, *A Diplomat in Japan*, 159–160.

59. Saigō Takamori detailed his meeting with Satow in an 1867/7/26 letter to Ōkubo Toshimichi. The letter is reproduced in Saigō Takamori Zenshū Henshū Iinkai 西郷隆盛全集編集委員会, ed., *Saigō Takamori zenshū* 西郷隆盛全集 (Tokyo: Yamato Shobō, 1976-80), 2:221–226.

60. "Marquis H. Ito: The Bismarck of Japan," *Phrenological Journal and Science of Health (1870–1911)* 104, no. 4 (1897); "Ito, the Pioneer of the New Nippon," *Current Literature (New York)* 39, no. 3 (1905); "Ito Hirobumi," *Outlook (1893–1924)*, May 4, 1901.

61. Katō's essay is especially interesting because of his later career and intellectual development. In the 1860s and 1870s, Katō emerged as a leading political philosopher and important advocate of natural rights theory. He was active in the Meirokusha, a prominent group of progressive intellectuals. In the late 1870s, he began a turn toward Social Darwinism and German political theory, and in 1881 he banned further publication of his earlier political writings. He was rewarded by the government with the presidency of Tokyo Imperial University. He later served in the House of Peers, the Privy Council, and the Genrōin. Thomas places Katō's intellectual transformation in the context his political opportunitism (Thomas, *Reconfiguring Modernity*, 84–110).

62. *Numayama taiwa* 沼山対話, in Satō Shōsuke 佐藤昌介, Uete Michiari 植手通有, and Yamaguchi Muneyuki 山口宗之, eds., *Nihon shisō taikei 55: Watanabe Kazan, Takano Chōei, Sakuma Shōzan, Yokoi Shōnan, Hashimoto Sanai* 日本思想体系 55:渡辺華山・高野長英・佐久間象山・横井小楠・橋本左内 (Tokyo: Iwanami Shoten, 1971), 496–511, esp. 505. "The nations of the world as one, a brotherhood of the four seas" is my translation of 万国一体四海兄弟, which resembles Analects 12:5 (Yan Yuan 顔淵). In Legge's translation, "Let the superior man never fail reverentially to order his own conduct, and let him be respectful to others and observant of propriety—then all within the four seas will be his brothers." James Legge, *Confucian Analects, the Great Learning, and the Doctrine of the Mean* (1893; reprint, New York: ACLS Humanities E-Book, 2012), 253.

63. *Kokuze sanron* 国是三論, in Satō, Uete, and Yamaguchi, eds., *Nihon shisō taikei 55: Watanabe Kazan, Takano Chōei, Sakuma Shōzan, Yokoi Shōnan, Hashimoto Sanai*, 438–465, esp. 448–449.

64. *Kokuze sanron*, esp. 448–450.

65. *Numayama kanwa* in Satō, Uete, and Yamaguchi, eds., *Nihon shisō taikei 55: Watanabe Kazan, Takano Chōei, Sakuma Shōzan, Yokoi Shōnan, Hashimoto Sanai*, 512–520, esp. 512–514.

66. "Ueda hanshi Akamatsu Kosaburō [Tomohiro] ikensho 上田藩士赤松小三郎「友裕」意見書" 1867/5/17, in *Ishin shiryō kōhon* 維新史料稿本, 7巻 127頁, 慶応3年5月17日 (18670050170), manuscript 2884/060. KE127-0827. Permalink https://clioimg.hi.u-tokyo.ac.jp/viewer/image/idata/M00/M/20/KE127/0827.tif.

67. Iwashita Tetsunori 岩下哲典, *Edo no Naporeon densetsu: Seiyō eiyū den wa dō yomareta ka* 江戸のナポレオン伝説: 西洋英雄伝はどう読まれたか (Tokyo: Chūō Kōron Shinsha, 1999), 69.

68. The Japanese National Diet Library has a useful brief summary of Koseki's work. See http://www.ndl.go.jp/nichiran/s2/s2_2.html. Accessed October 27, 2013. The smallpox text is Gyūtō shuho 牛痘種法.

69. Iwashita, *Edo no Naporeon densetsu*, 184–185.

70. There are several editions of Koseki's biography. I have here relied Koseki San'ei 小関三英, *Naporeon den* 那波列翁伝, 3 vols. (Seifūkan, 1857) in the Waseda University Rare Books Collection ヲ02 04764. The biography is also known as *Naporeon Bonaparute den* 那波列翁勃納把爾的伝. The quote is from volume 1, p. 2, of the main text.

71. Yoshida Shōin to Kitayama Yasuyo, in Yoshida Shōin 吉田松陰, *Yoshida Shōin zenshū* 吉田松陰全集, ed. Yamaguchi-ken Kyōikukai 山口県教育会, 10 vols. (Tokyo: Iwanami Shōin, 1934–36), 6:287–288.

72. See "Toward a Holy Alliance of the Peoples" (1849) in Giuseppe Mazzini, *A Cosmopolitanism of Nations: Giuseppe Mazzini's Writings on Democracy, Nation Building, and International Relations*, ed. Stefano Recchia and Nadia Urbinati, trans. Stefano Recchia (Princeton, NJ: Princeton University Press, 2009), 117–131, quote from 188. For Mazzini's broader influence, see C. A. Bayly and Eugenio F. Biagini, eds., *Giuseppe Mazzini and the Globalisation of Democratic Nationalism 1830–1920* (New York: Oxford University Press, 2008).

73. Stefano Recchia and Nadia Urbinati, "Giuseppe Mazzini's International Political Thought," in Mazzini, *A Cosmopolitanism of Nations*, 2; and "Concerning the Fall of the Roman Republic" (1849) in Mazzini, *A Cosmopolitanism of Nations*, 208–212.

74. Shibusawa Ei'ichi 渋沢栄一, *Tokugawa Yoshinobu-kō den* 徳川慶喜公伝, 8 vols. (Tokyo: Ryūmonsha, 1918), 4:71–74; Marius B. Jansen, *Sakamoto Ryōma and the Meiji Restoration* (Princeton, NJ: Princeton University Press, 1961), 312–335.

75. Sasaki Suguru 佐々木克, *Boshin sensō: haisha no Meiji ishin* 戊辰戦争: 敗者の明治維新 (Tokyo: Chūō Kōron Sha, 1977), 10–12; Dajōkan 太政官, ed., *Fukkoki* 復古記 (Tokyo: Naigai Shoseki, 1930), 1:10–11. See also Aoyama Tadamasa 青山忠正, *Bakumatsu ishin: honryū no jidai* 幕末維新:奔流の時代 (Tokyo: Bun'eidō, 1996), 184–189; Sasaki Suguru 佐々木克, "Taisei hōkan to tōbaku mitchoku 大政奉還と討幕密勅 " *Jinbun gakuhō (Kyōto Daigaku Jinbun*

Kagaku Kenkyūjo) 人文学報:京都大学人文科学研究所 80 (1997): 15; Totman, *Collapse*, 386–388.

76. In the early-modern era, the titles of Minister of the Right, Minister of the Left, and Inner Minister were often held simultaneously by several people.

77. For Kōmei's xenophobia, see Donald Keene, *Emperor of Japan: Meiji and His World, 1852–1912* (New York: Columbia University Press, 2002), 7–8, 16, 25, 34, 37, 38, 78–79.

78. Iwashita Tetsunori 岩下哲典 and Kobayashi Tetsuya 小林哲也, "Kōmei tennō wa tennentō de dokusatsu sareta 孝明天皇は天然痘で毒殺された," *Rekishitsū* 歴史通 20, no. 9 (2012): 202–203. For a thoughtful survey in English, see Keene, *Emperor of Japan: Meiji and His World, 1852–1912*, 94–97. For an overly credulous summary of the poisoning conspiracy theories, see Donald Calman, *The Nature and Origins of Japanese Imperialism* (London: Routledge, 1992), 90–92.

79. Totman, *Collapse*, 397.

80. The council meeting is known in Japanese as the *kogosho kaigi* 小御所会議. For summaries see Totman, *Collapse*, 398–400, and Sasaki, *Boshin sensō*, 12–15. For primary documents, see Dajōkan, ed., *Fukkoki*, 1:214–256, esp 214–222.

81. Sasaki, *Boshin sensō*, 17; US Department of State, *Executive documents printed by order of the House of Representatives during the third session of the fortieth Congress, 1868–69*, 14 vols., vol. 1 (US Government Printing Office, 1869), 607–609.

82. Dajōkan, ed., *Fukkoki*, 1:357.

83. Ravina, *The Last Samurai*, 148–149; Totman, *Collapse*, 408–415; M. William Steele, "Edo in 1868: The View from Below," *Monumenta Nipponica* 45, no. 2 (1990): 131–132; Ikai Takaaki 猪飼隆明, *Saigō Takamori: Seinan sensō e no michi* 西郷隆盛: 西南戦争への道 (Tokyo: Iwanami Shoten, 1992), 25–26; Sasaki, *Boshin sensō*, 21.

84. Totman, *Collapse*, 425–435; Sasaki, *Boshin sensō*, 20–31. The daimyo of Yodo, Inaba Masakuni, was a shogunal ally, but he was in Edo, serving as senior counselor. In his absence, Yodo's senior retainers betrayed shogunal forces.

85. US Department of State, *Executive documents 1868–69*, 619, 634.

CHAPTER 4

1. M. William Steele, "Against the Restoration: Katsu Kashū's Attempt to Reinstate the Tokugawa Family," *Monumenta Nipponica* 36, no. 3 (1981): 302–304; Totman, *Collapse*, 436–439; Sasaki, *Boshin sensō*, 51–55; Saigō Takamori Zenshū Henshū Iinkai, ed., *Saigō Takamori zenshū*, 2:431–440.

2. US Department of State, *Executive documents 1868–69*, 641–660.

3. "Brief History," *New York Times*, May 14, 1871.

4. Wealthier Japanese homes had rush mat flooring (tatami) and paper screen sliding doors (shōji), and decorum dictated removing one's shoes in a foyer. "Ee ja nai ka" dancers destroyed these homes by crashing about in wooden street clogs (geta).

5. The standard translation of yonaoshi is "world renewal" but it might also be translated as "world rectification" or "world repair." The common sense is a world out of order. See Stephen Vlastos, "Yonaoshi in Aizu," in *Conflict in Modern Japanese History*, ed. Tetsuo Najita and J. Victor Koschmann (Princeton, NJ: Princeton University Press, 1982); Vlastos, *Peasant Protests and Uprisings in Tokugawa Japan*. For an overview of 1860s protests, see Bix, *Peasant Protest in Japan: 1590–1884*, 161–214.

6. Sasaki, *Boshin sensō*, 54–56; Ravina, *The Last Samurai*, 155–157.

7. Sasaki, *Boshin sensō*, 111–133, esp. 132–133. Kitashirakawa's full title as prince was Kitashirakawa-no-miya Yoshihisa Shinnō (北白川宮能久親王). The adopted son of Emperor Ninkō (仁孝天皇, 1800–1846), he was also known as Rinnōji-no-miya (輪王寺宮).

8. Fujii Noriyuki 藤井徳行, "Meiji gannen iwayuru 'Tōhoku chōtei' sei-ritsu ni kansuru ichi kōsatsu: Rinnōjinomiya Kōgenhō Shinnō o megutte 明治元年・所謂「東北朝廷」成立に関する一考察・輪王寺宮公現法親王 をめぐって," in *Kindai Nihonshi no shinkenkyū*, Vol. 1 近代日本史の新研究 1, ed. Tezuka Yutaka 手塚豊 (Tokyo: Hokuju Shuppan, 1981), 228–314. For examples of the "Northern Mikado" in US diplomatic traffic, see Van Valkenburgh to Seward August 24 and September 17, 1868, in US Department of State, *Executive documents 1868–69*, 1:807–809, 1:819–20. I am thankful to Fabian Drixler for sharing his detailed understanding of the Northern Alliance.

9. Sasaki, *Boshin sensō*, 56–64; M. William Steele, "The Rise and Fall of the Shōgitai: A Social Drama," in *Conflict in Modern Japanese History*, ed. Tetsuo Najita and J. Victor Koschmann (Princeton, NJ: Princeton University Press, 1982).

10. Before leaving Edo, Enomoto wrote a diatribe dismissing the new government as a junta led by hoodlums and rogues (*shisei burai* 市井無頼) from Satsuma and Chōshū. Sasaki, *Boshin sensō*, 195–196; Dajōkan, ed., *Fukkoki*, 7:214–217.

11. See Van Valkenburgh for to Seward, July 3, 1868, in US Department of State, *Executive documents 1868–69*, 762–763.

12. Gaimushō 外務省, 1868/12, "Tokugawa dassō Eifu ryōgoku kōshi o keiyu shite tangansho teishutsu no ken 徳川脱徒英仏両国公使ヲ経由シテ嘆願書提出ノ件," B08090130200, 5-3-1-0-2(所蔵館:外務省外交史料館), Japan Center for Asian Historical Records JACAR(アジア歴史資料センター), frames 114–121. Enomoto's note is in Japanese, but with Dutch loan words such as "communicatie" for communication.

13. After the surrender of Edo, Brunet resigned his commission and joined the rebels. In a letter to Napoleon III, he insisted that he was serving France by repaying the trust of shogunal soldiers. Christian Polak

(Kurisuchan Porakku), "Buryune no hito to shōgai ブリユネの人と生涯," in *Hakodate no bakumatsu ishin: Furansu shikan Buryune no suketchi 100-mai* 函館の幕末・維新: フランス士官ブリユネのスケッチ 100枚, ed. Okada Shin'ichi 岡田新一 (Tokyo: Chūō Kōron Sha, 1988). For Enomoto's conversations in Dutch, see Richard Eusden to Harry Parkes, December 23, 1868, in MS British Foreign Office: Japan Correspondence, 1856-1905: Japan, Section II, F.O. 46/1-104, 1868–1890, Vol. 99:127, frames 204–208, The National Archives (Kew, United Kingdom), accessed through *Nineteenth Century Collections Online*, tinyurl.galegroup.com/tinyurl/4E3CQ7.

14. Tarō Matsudaira and Kamajirō Enomoto, "Kerais Exile's Tokonghava Aux Représentants Européens," in British Foreign Office: Japan Correspondence, 1856–1905: Japan, Section II, F.O. 46/1-104, 1868–1890, Vol. 99:1, frames 31–37, the National Archives (Kew, United Kingdom), accessed through *Nineteenth Century Collections Online*, tinyurl.galegroup.com/tinyurl/4E3EE1. For a Japanese discussion, see Hakodate Shishi Hensanshitsu, ed., *Hakodate shishi: tsūsetsu hen*, 2:238–241.

15. The letters of the various consuls to the Imperial government seem to have been closely coordinated. See Gaimushō 外務省, "Tokugawa dassō Eifu ryōgoku kōshi o keiyu shite tangansho teishutsu no ken 徳川脱徒英仏両国公使ヲ経由シテ嘆願書提出ノ件," frames 137–139, 142–144.

16. The phrase likely stems from an 1868/12/14 letter by Brunet to foreign consuls in which he promised that the Ezo government would chose its leaders in accordance with the principles of "universal suffrage." It seems Brunet made this promise without Enomoto's prior assent: there is no Japanese-language document anticipating Brunet's declaration. Nonetheless, the rebels promptly held an election the following day. The original French is "ces nomination faités a election on d'aprés le mode de suffrage universelle." An undated transcription of the French-language letter to the Hakodate consul is in Richard Eusden, "Eusden to Parkes, 1 February 1869 'Mr. Eusden reports latest intelligence respecting Tokugawa Kerais'" in British Foreign Office: Japan Correspondence, 1856–1905: Japan, Section II, F.O. 46/1-104, 1868–1890, Vol. 107:1, frames 65–70, the National Archives (Kew, United Kingdom), accessed through *Nineteenth Century Collections Online*, tinyurl.galegroup.com/tinyurl/4E3UU8. I have based the date of 1868/12/14 on Hakodate Shishi Hensanshitsu, ed., *Hakodate shishi: tsūsetsu hen*, 2:241–243. The phrase "Republic of Ezo" (*Ezo kyōwakoku*) seems to have originated in Francis Ottiwell Adams's adaptation of *Kinsé shiriaku*, Ernest Satow's translation of an early history of the Meiji Restoration by Yamaguchi Ken. In Yamaguchi's text, the 1868/12/15 election is described as *tōhyō kōsen* (投票公選) without any mention of foreign influence. Satow, however, added the gloss, "This was done in imitation of the practice observed in the United States of America, where these things are settled by the wish of the majority." Adams enhanced this

account one step further, inferring from the election that the Ezo government was a republic. See Yamaguchi Ken 山口謙 and Shozan Yashi 椒山野史, *Kinsei shiryaku* 近世史畧, 3 vols. (Tokyo: 1872), 3:39–40; Ken Yamaguchi, *Kinsé shiriaku: A history of Japan, from the first visit of Commodore Perry in 1853 to the capture of Hakodate by the Mikado's forces in 1869*, trans. Ernest Mason Satow (Yokohama: Japan Mail Office, 1873), 131–133; Francis Ottiwell Adams, *The History of Japan*, 2 vols. (London: Henry S. King, 1875), 2:173–175. This phrase "Republic of Ezo" thus appeared first in English in 1875 and was only later translated back into Japanese as "Ezo kyōwakoku" (蝦夷共和国).

17. For election results, see Hakodate Shishi Hensanshitsu, ed., *Hakodate shishi: tsūsetsu hen*, 2:238–241. For the banquet account, see *Kōsei nikki* 苟生日記, in Sudō Ryūsen 須藤隆仙, ed., *Hakodate sensō shiryōshū* 箱館戦争史料集 (Tokyo: Shin Jinbutsu Ōraisha, 1996), 173. Several refugees from the Northern Alliance had higher samurai rank than Enomoto, but they did not stand for office and played no role in the rebel government.

18. Dajōkan 太政官, June 1873, "Hakone funjō no saijosei Futsujin Buryūne nado menzai no gi ni tsuki ukagai 箱館紛擾ノ際助勢仏人ブリユーネ等免罪ノ儀ニ付伺," *Kōbunroku* 公文録, 本館-2A-009-00・公00826100, 件名番号 005, National Archives of Japan 国立公文書館; J. L. Brunet, *Les ordres de chevalerie et les distinctions honorifiques au Japon* (Paris: Actualités diplomatiques et coloniales, 1903). Japan's new imperial commendations were modeled on European practices such as the French Légion d'honneur, making the project especially appealing to Brunet.

19. A sole exception was Kitashirakawa Yoshihisa, the imperial prince, who was politically rehabilitated after several years in Europe.

20. Naikaku 内閣, 1870, "Shokuinroku, Meiji sannen, Hanmeiroku zen (Konshin ichi) 職員録・明治三年・藩銘録全 (坤震一)," A09054454500, 職B00023100, Japan Center for Asian Historical Records JACAR(アジア歴史資料センター).

21. Katsuta Masaharu 勝田政治, *Haihan chiken: "Meiji kokka" ga umareta hi* 廃藩置県:「明治国家」が生まれた日 (Tokyo: Kōdansha, 2000), 40.

22. John Breen, "The Imperial Oath of April 1868: Ritual, Politics, and Power in the Restoration," *Monumenta Nipponica* 51, no. 4 (1996): esp. 423–424; Suzuki Jun 鈴木淳, *Ishin no kōsō to tenkai* 維新の構想と展開 (Tokyo: Kōdansha, 2002), 12–14; Thomas, *Reconfiguring Modernity*, 60–62; Marius B. Jansen, *The Making of Modern Japan* (Cambridge, MA: Belknap Press of Harvard University Press, 2000), 336–341; Toby, *State and Diplomacy in Early Modern Japan*.

23. Matsuo Masahito 松尾正人, *Haihan chiken: kindai tōitsu kokka e no kumon* 廃藩置県―近代統一国家への苦悶 (Tokyo: Chūkō Shinsho, 1986), 34–38; Katsuta, *Haihan chiken*, 56–59; Dajōkan 太政官, *Dajōkan nisshi* 太政官日誌 (Tokyo: Dajōkan, 1876), for 1869/1/23 and 1/24.

24. Katsuta, *Haihan chiken*, 160–161.

25. Satow, *A Diplomat in Japan*, 264.

26. The incident is known in Japanese as the Kōgo Incident 庚午事変 for the zodiac signs of the year 1870. For a good overview, see Tokushima Kenritsu Monjokan 徳島県立文書館, ed., *Kōgo jihen no gunzō: tokubetsu kikakuten* 庚午事変の群像: 特別企画展 (Tokushima: Tokushima Kenritsu Monjokan, 2007). The incident is also summarized in Dajōkan 太政官, 1871, "Tokushima sōjō shimatsu 徳島騒擾始末," *Kōbunroku* 公文録, 公00434100, National Archives of Japan 国立公文書館.

27. For the memorial, see Kōshaku Hosokawa-ke Hensanjo 侯爵細川家編纂所, ed., *Higo-han kokuji shiryō* 肥後藩國事史料 (Kumamoto-shi: Kōshaku Hosokawa-ke Hensanjo, 1932), 10:775. For background, see Matsuo Masahito 松尾正人, "Haihan chiken no seijiteki chōryū 廃藩置県の政治的潮流," *Rekishigaku kenkyū* 歴史学研究 596, no. 8 (1989): 9–12; Inoue, *Bakumatsu ishin*, 186–187.

28. See, for example, "Tokushima hanpeitai tangansho 徳嶋藩兵隊歎願書," in Dajōkan 太政官, "Tokushima sōjō shimatsu 徳島騒擾始末."

29. Tokushima Kenritsu Monjokan, ed., *Kōgo jihen no gunzō: tokubetsu kikakuten*, 11.

30. Masahito, "Haihan chiken no seijiteki chōryū," 9–12; Andrew Fraser, "Hachisuka Mochiaki (1846–1918): A Meiji Domain Lord and Statesmen," *Papers on Far Eastern History (Canberra)* 2 (1970); Andrew Fraser, "Hachisuka Mochiaki (1846–1918): From Feudal Lord to Businessman," *Paper on Far Eastern History (Australian National University)* 37 (1988).

31. Katsuta, *Haihan chiken*, 120–123

32. My account of Hisamitsu's grievances draws on his detailed memorial of June 1873 in Nihon shiseki kyōkai 日本史籍協會, ed., *Shimazu Hisamitsu-kō jikki* 島津久光公實紀 (Tokyo: Tōkyō Daigaku Shuppankai, 1977), 3:211–225. For another account of these grievances, see Kunaichō rinji teishitsu henshūkyoku, ed., *Meiji tennō ki*, 3:89–90. For a summary of Hisamitsu's tirades against Saigō Takamori and Ōkubo Toshimichi, see Ravina, *The Last Samurai*, 170, 177–178.

33. Kasahara Hidehiko 笠原英彦, *Meiji rusu seifu* 明治留守政府 (Tōkyō: Keiō Gijuku Daigaku Shuppankai, 2010), 4–6.

34. Katsuta, *Haihan chiken*, 190–197.

35. Dajōkan 太政官, 1871/7/14, "Han o haishite ken o oku 藩ヲ廃シ県ヲ置ク," 太00062100 件名番号 122, National Archives of Japan 国立公文書館.

CHAPTER 5

1. The canonical origin of the phrase "parent of the people" is Mencius, King Hui of Liang Part 1:4 孟子・梁惠王上4. The Confucian paraphrase is from Analects 12:7.

2. George M. Beckmann, "Political Crises and the Crystallization of Japanese Constitutional Thought, 1871–1881," *Pacific Historical Review* 23, no. 3 (1954): 263.

3. *Japan Gazette*, November 1, 1873, 2.

4. Ian McArthur, *Henry Black: On Stage in Meiji Japan* (Clayton, Victoria, Australia: Monash University Publishing, 2013), esp. 30–37.

5. "First Fruits," *Japan Weekly Mail*, November 8, 1873. I am indebted to Scott Lightsey of Georgia State University for his help with these Bunyan references.

6. It is common in the standard historiography to neglect the Iwakura Mission's continuity with Tokugawa precedent. But the Tokugawa missions, despite considerably challenges, were well received in Europe and America. The US mission visited San Francisco; Washington, DC; Philadelphia; and New York, attracting large crowds at each destination. Press coverage was largely favorable. The *New York Times* reported that despite their exotic dress, the embassy leaders seemed to be "keen, sharp, intelligent men" (June 19, 1860).

7. I here follow the consensus that Verbeck's letter to Ōkuma Shigenobu was a major force behind the mission. See Ōkubo Toshiaki 大久保利謙, ed., *Iwakura shisetsu no kenkyū* 岩倉使節の研究 (Tokyo: Munetaka Shobō, 1976), 26–52, and Tanaka Akira 田中彰, *Iwakura Shisetsudan no rekishiteki kenkyū* 岩倉使節団の歴史的研究 (Tokyo: Iwanami Shoten, 2002), 69–73. A transcription of Verbeck's "Brief Sketch" can be found in Tanaka Akira 田中彰, ed., *Kaikoku* 開国, vol. 1 of *Nihon kindai shisō taikei* 日本近代思想体系 (Tokyo: Iwanami Shoten 1999), 364–371. I have also consulted the original letter in the Archives of the Reformed Church in America, Verbeck folder, "Brief Sketch," Japan Mission Box 737.3N. See also A. Hamish Ion, *American Missionaries, Christian Oyatoi, and Japan, 1859–73* (Vancouver: University of British Columbia Press, 2009), 143–144.

8. For an overview of Verbeck's life, see William Elliot Griffis, *Verbeck of Japan: A Citizen of No Country* (Edinburgh: Oliphant, Anderson & Ferrier, 1901).

9. Auslin, *Negotiating*, 170–172.

10. Ibid., 184. For Grant quote, see Grant to Fish, July 16, 1872, in Ulysses S. Grant, *The Papers of Ulysses S. Grant*, ed. John Y. Simon and John F. Marszalek, vol. 21, (Carbondale: Southern Illinois University Press, 1967), 202–204. For an overview of US diplomacy, see Robert L. Beisner, *From the Old Diplomacy to the New, 1865–1900*, 2nd. ed., (Arlington Heights, IL: Harlan Davidson, 1986), 72–95; Stephen McCullough, "Avoiding War: The Foreign Policy of Ulysses S. Grant and Hamilton Fish," in *A Companion to the Reconstruction Presidents 1865–1881*, ed. Edward O. Frantz (Chichester, West Sussex, UK: Wiley Blackwell, 2014), 311–317.

11. As Marlene Mayo notes, "Precisely what happened in Tokyo is difficult to disentangle." The caretaker government gave Ōkubo and Itō new credentials for Iwakura. But Mōri Toshihiko argues that the mission was still denied the authority to conclude treaties, and that this was just face-saving strategy for Ōkubo. See Marlene J. Mayo, "A Catechism of Western Diplomacy: The Japanese and Hamilton Fish, 1872," *Journal of Asian Studies* 26, no. 3 (1967): 406–408; Mōri Toshihiko 毛利敏彦, *Meiji roku-nen seihen* 明治六年政変 (Tokyo: Chūō Kōron Shinsha, 1979), 24–27. The mission's new credentials are in Gaimushō 外務省, *Dai Nihon gaikō bunsho* 大日本外交文書 (Tokyo: Nihon Kokusai Kyōkai, 1936–63), 5: 225–226.

12. Fish voiced strong opposition to a European conference when Mori Arinori first raised the subject on March 20, but Mori seems not to have fully appreciated Fish's position. When Iwakura raised the same issue in July, Fish responded in anger. The Fish quote is from Fish to Grant, July 11, 1872, in Grant, *The Papers of Ulysses S. Grant*, 21:202–204. See also Auslin, *Negotiating*, 187–191; Mayo, "Catechism," 404.

13. Kido's diary for 1872/6/17 (July 22, 1872) in Kido Takayoshi 木戸孝允, *Kido Takayoshi nikki* 木戸孝允日記, ed. Tsumaki Chūta 妻木忠太, 3 vols. (Tokyo: Hayakawa Ryōkichi, 1932–33), 2:201–202. See also Kido Takayoshi, *The Diary of Kido Takayoshi*, trans. Sidney DeVere Brown, 3 vols. (Tokyo: University of Tokyo Press, 1983), 2:186–187.

14. Ōkubo to Nishitoku Jirō, January 27, 1873, in Ōkubo Toshimichi 大久保利通, *Ōkubo Toshimichi bunsho* 大久保利通文書, 10 vols. (Tokyo: Nihon Shiseki Kyōkai, 1927–1929), 4:483–486.

15. Ōkubo to Saigō Takamori and Yoshii Tomozane, 1872/11/15 (November 15, 1872), in Ōkubo, *Ōkubo Toshimichi bunsho*, 4:447–451

16. Ōkubo to Saigō Takamori and Yoshii Tomozane, March 21, 1873 in Ōkubo, *Ōkubo Toshimichi bunsho*, 4:491–493.

17. Ōkubo to Ōyama Iwao, March 14, 1873 in Ōkubo, *Ōkubo Toshimichi bunsho*, 4:489–491 For the situation in France see Georges Valance, *Thiers: Bourgeois et Révolutionnaire* (Paris: Flammarion, 2007), 382–383.

18. Kim, *The Age of Visions and Arguments*, 62–63; and Ōkubo, *Ōkubo Toshimichi bunsho*, 1:442–443.

19. Ōkubo to Nishitoku Jirō, January 27, 1873 in Ōkubo, *Ōkubo Toshimichi bunsho*, 4:483–486.

20. "Discourse of Kido, Councillor of State, after his Return to Japan," *Japan Weekly Mail*, November 8, 1873. The article is reprinted in Walter Wallace McLaren, "Japanese Government Documents," *Transactions of the Asiatic Society of Japan* 42, Part I (1914): 567–577. There is no direct Japanese-language counterpart to this text, but in overall content it corresponds to a memorial submitted by Kido in July 1873. See "Kenpō seitei no kengensho 憲法制定の建言書," in Kido Takayoshi 木戸孝允, *Kido Takayoshi monjo* 木戸孝允文書, ed. Kido-kō Denki Hensanjo 木戸公伝記編纂所, 8 vols. (Tokyo: Nihon Shiseki Kankōkai, 1929–1931), 8:118–129.

21. Kido, *Kido Takayoshi monjo*, 8:126–127.

22. See Ōkubo, *Ōkubo Toshimichi bunsho*, 4:495–499.

23. Naikaku 内閣, 1872/11/28, "Chōhei kokuyu 徴兵告諭," *Chokugorui* 勅語類, 勅 00001100, 件名番号 032, National Archives of Japan 国立公文書館.

24. Mōri, *Meiji roku-nen miseihen*, 70–73; Fujimura Michio 藤村道生, "Chōheirei no seiritsu 徴兵令の成立," *Rekishigaku kenkyū* 歴史学研究, no. 428 (1976).

25. Etō was aware that Prussia had defeated France in 1871, but this did not diminish his faith in the Napoleonic Code. On the contrary, he defended French principles

in a classical Chinese poem. For a survey of Etō and the Meiji Justice Ministry (司法省), see Mōri Toshihiko 毛利敏彦, *Etō Shinpei: kyūshinteki kaikakusha no higeki* 江藤新平: 急進的改革者の悲劇, rev. and enlarged ed. (Tokyo: Chūō Kōron Shinsha, 1997), 138–185. Etō's most articulate defense of the Napoleonic Code is his 1873 letter threatening resignation. See Etō Shinpei 江藤新平, "Etō Shinpei jishoku gansho 江藤新平辞職願書," February 5, 1873, Request no. 4144-98, ID 00061115, Historiographical Institute, University of Tokyo (Tōkyō Daigaku Shiryō Hensanjo 東京大学史料編纂所).

26. The definitive study of the 1872–73 education reforms remains Kurasawa Takashi 倉沢剛, *Gakusei no kenkyū* 学制の研究 (Tokyo: Kōdansha, 1973). For background to the 1872 educational edict (学制 gakusei), see Brian Platt, *Burning and Building: Schooling and State Formation in Japan, 1750–1890* (Cambridge, MA: Harvard University Press, 2004), 131–134; and Benjamin C. Duke, *The History of Modern Japanese Education: Constructing the National School System, 1872–1890* (New Brunswick, NJ: Rutgers University Press, 2009), 67–74. For a translation of the edict, see Herbert Passin, *Society and Education in Japan* (New York: Studies of the East Asian Institute, Columbia University, 1965), 209–211. The original edict was published as Monbushō 文部省, *Gakusei* 学制 (Tokyo: Monbushō, 1872).

27. Kurasawa, *Gakusei no kenkyū*, 436–438.

28. Dajōkan 太政官, June 1872, "Gakusei hakkō no gi ukagai 学制発行ノ儀伺," *Kōbunroku* 公文録, 公00671100, 件名番号 011, Japan National Archvies 国立公文書館; Kurasawa, *Gakusei no kenkyū*, 420–424.

29. Etō, "Etō Shinpei jishoku gansho." For samurai self-actualization, see Eiko Ikegami, *The Taming of the Samurai* (Cambridge, MA: Harvard University Press, 1995).

30. Inoue co-authored his dissent with Shibusawa Eïchi, a finance ministry official better known for his later accomplishments as an entrepreneur. Remarkably, they published their dissent in a newspaper, the *Nisshin Shinjishi* 日新真事誌. See Inoue Kaoru 井上馨 and Shibusawa Eïchi 渋沢栄一, 1873, "Inoue Kaoru Shibusawa Eïchi no zaisei ni kansuru sōgi hyōron 井上馨・渋沢栄一ノ財政ニ関スル奏議評論," Waseda Daigaku Toshokan shozō Ōkuma Shigenobu kankei monjo 早稲田大学図書館所蔵大隈重信関係資料, i14_a1397 in Waseda University Rare Books Collection.

31. Terashima to Ōkubo, April 2, 1873, in Ōkubo, *Ōkubo Toshimichi bunsho*, 4:504–507.

32. For money supply, see Matsukata Masayoshi, *Report on the Adoption of the Gold Standard in Japan* (Tokyo: Government Press, 1899), 29, 97–98.

33. For an overview of the budget struggles, see Kasahara, *Meiji rusu seifu*, 88–109; Mōri, *Meiji roku-nen seihen*, 78–79.

34. Naikaku 内閣, "Chōhei kokuyu 徴兵告諭."

35. For hairstyles, see Suzanne G. O'Brien, "Splitting Hairs: History and the Politics of Daily Life in Nineteenth-Century Japan," *Journal of Asian Studies* 67, no. 4

(2008). For the emancipation of outcastes, see Daniel V. Botsman, "Freedom without Slavery? 'Coolies,' Prostitutes, and Outcastes in Meiji Japan's 'Emancipation Moment,'" *American Historical Review* 116, no. 5 (2011); Howell, *Geographies of Identity in Nineteenth-century Japan*, 79–109.

36. Hiroko Rokuhara, "Local Officials and the Meiji Conscription Campaign," *Monumenta Nipponica* 60, no. 1 (2005); cf. "Chōhei-rei hantai ikki 徴兵令反対一揆" in *Kokushi daijiten*.

37. For budget issues, see Kasahara, *Meiji rusu seifu*, 88–90, 103–109; Duke, *The History of Modern Japanese Education*, 134–140.

38. Duke, *The History of Modern Japanese Education*, 160–171; Platt, *Burning and Building*, 131–133.

39. Yukichi Fukuzawa, *An Encouragement of Learning*, trans. David A. Dilworth (New York: Columbia University Press, 2012), quote from 3; Duke, *The History of Modern Japanese Education*, 140–146; Earl H. Kinmonth, "Fukuzawa Reconsidered: Gakumon no Susume and Its Audience," *Journal of Asian Studies* 37, no. 4 (1978).

40. Paul Heng-Chao Ch'en, *The Formation of the Early Meiji Legal Order: The Japanese Code of 1871 and Its Chinese Foundation* (Oxford: New York, 1981), 3–11.

41. Ishii Ryōsuke 石井良助, "Minpō ketsugi' kaidai" 「民法決議」解題, in *Meiji bunka zenshū* 明治文化全集, ed. Meiji Bunka Zenshū Kenkyūkai 明治文化全集研究会 (Tokyo: Nihon Hyōron Shinsha, 1929), 13:39–41.

42. Georges Bousquet, *Le Japon de nos jours et les échelles de l'extrême Orient*, 2 vols. (Paris: Hachette, 1877), 2:56–58.

43. Kasahara Hidehiko 笠原英彦, "Etō Shinpei to Shihōshō: shihō seisaku no seijiteki haikei 江藤新平と司法省—司法政策の政治的背景," *Hōgaku kenkyū* 法学研究 64, no. 1 (1991); Suzuki Tsuruko 鈴木鶴子, *Etō Shinpei to Meiji Ishin* 江藤新平と明柏維新 (Tokyo: Asahi Shinbunsha, 1989). One of Etō's more comprehensive discussions of government is a manifesto threatening his resignation in February 1873. See Etō, "Etō Shinpei jishoku gansho."

44. For an overview of late-Tokugawa and Meiji-era attacks on Buddhism, see Yasumaru Yoshio 安丸良夫, *Kamigami no Meiji Ishin: shinbutsu bunri to haibutsu kishaku* 神々の明治維新: 神仏分離と廃仏毀釈 (Tokyo: Iwanami Shoten, 1979); and James Edward Ketelaar, *Of Heretics and Martyrs in Meiji Japan: Buddhism and Its Persecution* (Princeton, NJ: Princeton Univesity Press, 1990).

45. Helen Hardacre, "Creating State Shinto: The Great Promulgation Campaign and the New Religions," *Journal of Japanese Studies* 12, no. 1 (1986).

46. For the original edict, see Dajōkan 太政官, 1872/11/9, "Tai'inreki o haishi taiyōreki o okonau tsuki shōsho 太陰暦ヲ廃シ太陽暦ヲ行フ附詔書," 太00224100, 件名番号 041, National Archives of Japan 国立公文書館. For budgetary considerations, see Enjōji Kiyoshi 円城寺清, *Ōkuma-haku sekijitsutan* 大隈伯昔日譚 (Tokyo: Rikken Kaishintō Tōhōkyoku 1895), 604. The budget savings were arguably even larger. The traditional Japanese lunar-solar calendar, like the Chinese

and Jewish calendars, periodically added extra months. Those "leap months" kept lunar months in sync with the solar year. Since 1873 was scheduled to have thirteen months, the government eliminated one month of civil service salaries for both 1872 and 1873. See Okada Yoshirō 岡田芳朗, *Meiji kaireki: "toki" no bunmei kaika* 明治改暦:「時」の文明開化 (Tokyo: Taishūkan shoten, 1994); and Stefan Tanaka, *New Times in Modern Japan* (Princeton, NJ: Princeton University Press, 2004), 1–17.

47. Munakata Yasutomo 宗像靖共, Komorizawa Nagamasa 小森沢長政, and Furumi Nagayoshi 古海長義, 1868, "Heibushō shorui shōroku: maitsuki ichirokukyūjitsu sadame no kentachi 兵部省書類鈔録　毎月一六休日定の件達," Co9090002700, 海軍省·公文類纂-M1-2-2, Japan Center for Asian Historical Records JACAR (アジア歴史資料センター); and also Zōheishi 造兵司, June 1873, "Nichiyōbi kyūgyō ni kaisei ukagai 日曜日休業ニ改正伺," A03023212100, 公文別録·陸軍省衆規淵鑑抜粋·明治元年～明治八年·第十四巻、第十五巻·明治四年～明治八年, Japan Center for Asian Historical Records JACAR(アジア歴史資料センター). See also Ōkada, *Meiji kaireki: "toki" no bunmei kaika*, esp. 269–272.

48. Kaigunshō 海軍省, 1871, "Otsu 1 gō dai nikki, Ichirokukyū nichiyōbi ni kaitei no ken Ōkurashō kotae hoka 2 ken 乙1号大日記　一六休暇日曜日に改定の件大蔵省答他2件," Co9090195300, 公文類纂 M4-1-25, Japan Center for Asian Historical Records JACAR(アジア歴史資料センター).

49. The edict establishing Sundays is Shōgaku kyōsoku (shō) Meiji gonen kugatsu yōka Monbushō futatsu bangai 小学教則(抄)明治五年九月八日文部省布達番外 in Monbushō 文部省, *Gakusei hyakunen-shi* 学制百年史 (Tokyo: Teikoku Chihō Gyōseikai, 1972). See also http://www.mext.go.jp/b_menu/hakusho/html/others/detail/1318005.htm. The school regulations for 1873 show a curriculum based on weeks 週 but also feature the "one six holiday" schedule. Monbushō 文部省, *Shōgaku kyōsoku* 小学教則 (Tokyo: Izumoji Manjirō, 1873), 1.

50. Edict no. 21 for March 2, 1873, in Monbushō 文部省, *Monbushō futatsu zenshū* 文部省布達全書 (Tokyo: Monbushō, 1885), 2:29–30.

51. Ōki Takatō 大木喬任, April 1873, "Kyūkabi no gi ukagai 休暇日之義伺," A07060136300, 記00358100, Japan Center for Asian Historical Records JACAR(アジア歴史資料センター). Under the US Occupation, Empire Day was renamed National Foundation Day (*Kenkoku Kinen no Hi* 建国記念の日).

52. Well into the twentieth century, villagers and urban merchants continued to work on traditional holiday schedules. For the slow penetration of the official calendar, see Katsube Makoto 勝部眞人, "Meiji kaireki to shinreki no shintō katei 明治改暦と新暦の浸透過程," in *Kinsei kindai no chiiki shakai to bunka* 近世近代の地域社会と文化, ed. Rai Kīichi Sensei Taikan Kinen Ronshū Kankōkai 頼祺一先生退官記念論集刊行会 (Tokyo: Seibundō, 2004), 485–505.

53. Gyewon Kim, "Tracing the Emperor: Photography, Famous Places, and the Imperial Progresses in Prewar Japan," *Representations* 120, no. 1 (2012).

54. For a summary of the tour, see Keene, *Emperor of Japan: Meiji and His World, 1852–1912*, 210–216. Details of the tour, including discussions of flags and salutes, are in Dajōkan 太政官, 1872, "Jinshin Gojunkō zatsuroku 壬申・御巡幸雑録," *Kōbunroku* 公文録, 公00727100, National Archives of Japan 国立公文書館 国立公文書館. The instructions to Kyoto courtiers are in the subsection "Junkō nisshi 巡幸日誌." For changes in the public role of the emperor, see Takashi Fujitani, *Splendid Monarchy: Power and Pageantry in Modern Japan* (Berkeley: University of California Press, 1996), 42–55; and Carol Gluck, *Japan's Modern Myths* (Princeton, NJ: Princeton University Press, 1985), 77–80.

55. Robert Eskildsen, "Of Civilization and Savages: The Mimetic Imperialism of Japan's 1874 Expedition to Taiwan," *American Historical Review* 107, no. 2 (2002): 388–418. The term has antecedents in Peter Duus, *The Abacus and the Sword: The Japanese Penetration of Korea, 1895–1910* (Berkeley: University of California Press, 1995), 424–438.

56. The more standard English-language name for the agreement is Sino-Japanese Friendship and Trade Treaty. But the Qing drafters consciously choose the term 条規 rather than 条約 to distinguish the agreement from a Western-style treaty. Toshio Motegi, "A Prototype of Close Relations and Antagonism: From the First Sino-Japanese War to the Twenty-one Demands," in *Toward a History Beyond Borders: Contentious Issues in Sino-Japanese Relations*, ed. Daqing Yang and Andrew Gordon (Cambridge, MA: Harvard University Asia Center 2012), 27–28.

57. Lee Chi-Chang [Ri Keishō] 李啓彰, "Nisshin shūkō jōki seiritsu katei no saikentō: Meiji gonen Yanagihara Sakimitsu no Shinkoku haken mondai o chūshin ni 日清修好条規成立過程の再検討—明治5年柳原前光の清国派遣問題を中心に," *Shigaku zasshi* 史学雑誌 115, no. 7 (2006); Motegi, "A PROTotype of Close Relations and Antagonism," 20–52; Edwin Pak-Wah Leung, "The Quasi-War in East Asia: Japan's Expedition to Taiwan and the Ryūkyū Controversy," *Modern Asian Studies* 17, no. 2 (1983): 259–261.

58. Originally commissioned as the CSS *Stonewall* by the US Confederacy, the *Kōtestu* was deemed unbeatable by any wooden ship: in 1865, a Union naval force sent to stop the *Stonewall* from leaving Europe chose to retreat without firing a shot. J. Thomas Scharf, *History of the Confederate States Navy from its Organization to the Surrender of Its Last Vessel; Its Stupendous Struggle with the Great Navy of the United States; The Engagements Fought in the Rivers and Harbors of the South, and Upon the High Seas; Blockade-running, First Use of Iron-clads and Torpedoes, and Privateer History* (New York: Rogers & Sherwood, 1887), 804–806; Edwin Strong, Thomas Buckley, and Annetta St. Clair, "The Odyssey of the CSS *Stonewall*," *Civil War History* 30, no. 4 (1984): 318.

59. In the 1800s, ambassadors were commonly referred to as ministers, but I here use modern parlance.

60. For a bold revisionist account of Chinese diplomatic ritual, see James Louis Hevia, *Cherishing Men from Afar: Qing Guest Ritual and the Macartney Embassy of 1793* (Durham, NC: Duke University Press, 1995).

61. Wayne C. McWilliams, "East Meets East: The Soejima Mission to China, 1873," *Monumenta Nipponica* 30 (1975): 244–252; Tseng-Tsai Wang, "The Audience Question: Foreign Representatives and the Emperor of China, 1858–1873," *Historical Journal* 14, no. 3 (1971). McWilliams relies excessively on Soejima's own diary and should be used with caution.

62. "China. Court Formalities during the Imperial Reception of the Foreign Ambassadors," *New York Herald*, August 21, 1873.

63. For overviews of the incident, see Leung, "The Quasi-War in East Asia," 261–264; and Norihito Mizuno, "Early Meiji Policies Towards the Ryukyus and the Taiwanese Aboriginal Territories," *Modern Asian Studies* 43, no. 3 (2009): 688.

64. Leung, "The Quasi-War in East Asia," 264–271; and Mizuno, "Early Meiji Policies," esp. 711–712.

65. Le Gendre's involvement is discussed in John Shufelt's introduction to Charles William Le Gendre, *Notes of Travel in Formosa*, ed. Douglas L. Fix and John Shufelt (Tainan, Taiwan: National Museum of Taiwan History, 2012), xiii–xxxiv. See also Leung, "The Quasi-War in East Asia," 257–281; and Mizuno, "Early Meiji Policies," 705–708.

66. The text of the treaty can be found in Le Gendre, *Notes of Travel in Formosa*, 292. For Le Gendre's official account of the expedition and negotiations, see Le Gendre to Burlingame, November 7, 1867, in US Department of State, *Executive documents 1868–69*, 504–510. See also Thomas Francis Hughes, "Visit to Tok-e-Tok, Chief of the Eighteen Tribes, Southern Formosa," in George Taylor, *Aborigines of South Taiwan in the 1880s: Papers by the South Cape Lightkeeper George Taylor*, ed. Glen Dudbridge (Taipei: Shung Ye Museum of Formosan Aborigines, 1999), 22–32. Tokitok is also rendered as Tooke-toc, Tooke-tock, and Tauketok.

67. Eskildsen notes that the Paiwanese took all the Ryukyuans' belongings but offered them food and shelter. The villagers became enraged and killed the Ryukyuans only after they left the village without permission. The Paiwanese also assumed the Ryukyuans were Chinese and therefore not covered by the treaty with Le Gendre. Robert Esklidsen, *Recursive Imperialism* (forthcoming); Le Gendre, *Notes of Travel in Formosa*, 311, 314–315; Owen Rutter, *Through Formosa: An Account of Japan's Island Colony* (London: T. F. Unwin, 1923), 38–39. For a period ethnography, see George Taylor, "Formosa: Characteristic Traits of the Island and Its Aboriginal Inhabitants," *Proceedings of the Royal Geographical Society* 11, no. 4 (1889).

68. Le Gendre, *Notes of Travel in Formosa*, 309–333. For headhunting as a manhood rite, see "Notes of the Paiwan Tribe" in Taylor, *Aborigines of South Taiwan in the 1880s*, 65–69.

69. Charles William Le Gendre, *How to Deal with China: A Letter to De B. Rand. Keim, Esquire, Agent of the United States* (Amoy: Rozario, Marcal, 1871), 135–140. His later defense of Japan's claim to Taiwan is Charles Le Gendre, *Is Aboriginal Formosa a Part of the Chinese Empire?* (Shanghai: Lane, Crawford, 1874). See also Eskildsen, "Of Civilization and Savages."

70. Le Gendre had hoped to become US ambassador to Argentina, but the Senate would not ratify his appointment. Le Gendre, *Notes of Travel in Formosa*, xvii.

71. Gaimushō, *Dai Nihon gaikō bunsho*, 6:160–161, 178–179.

72. McWilliams, "East Meets East: The Soejima Mission to China, 1873," 274–275; Kasahara, *Meiji rusu seifu*, 115–121.

73. Enjōji, *Ōkuma-haku sekijitsutan*, 643–644.

74. Mizuno, "Early Meiji Policies," 702–703.

75. Shimazu Hisamichi 島津久道, "Toragari monogatari 虎狩物語," Kyōdo shiryō, K23/シ62 0130095557, Kagoshima kenritsu toshokan 鹿児島県立図書館. For its use in traditional education, see Kagoshima-ken kyōiku iinkai 鹿児島県教育委員会編, ed., *Kagoshima-ken kyōikushi* 鹿児島県教育史 (Kagoshima: Kagoshima Kenritsu Kenkyūjo, 1985), 98–99. ##

76. Hellyer, *Defining Engagement*, 200–204.

77. Totman, *Collapse*, 324–326.

78. For late Tokugawa arguments in favor of attacking Korea (*bakumatsu Seikanron* 幕末征韓論), see Takigawa Shūgo 瀧川修吾, "Tsushima-han no Seikanron ni kansuru hikaku kōsatsu: Bunkyū sannen, Genji gannen, Keiō yonnen no kenpakusho o chūshin ni 対馬藩の征韓論に関する比較考察--文久3年・元治元年・慶應4年の建白書を中心に," *Nihon Daigaku Daigakuin Hōgaku kenkyū nenpō* 日本大学大学院法学研究年報 35 (2005); Kimura Naoya 木村直也, "Bakumatsu no Nikkan kankei to Seikanron 幕末の日朝関係と征韓論," *Rekishi hyōron* 歴史評論, no. 516 (1993); Tsuchiya Wataru 土谷渉, "Bakumatsu Seikanron no genryū ni tsuite no ichi kōsatsu 幕末征韓論の源流についての一考察," *Kokushigaku kenkyū: Ryūkoku Daigaku Kokushigaku Kenkyūkai* 国史学研究・龍谷大学国史学研究会 29 (2006).

79. Mōri, *Meiji roku-nen seihen*, 108–111; Gaimushō, *Dai Nihon gaikō bunsho*, 6:276–283.

80. Morohoshi Hidetoshi 諸星秀俊, "Meiji roku-nen 'Seikanron' ni okeru gunji kōsō 明治六年「征韓論」における軍事構想," *Gunji Shigaku* 軍事史学 45, no. 1 (2009): 48–49; Kokuryūkai 黒竜会, ed., *Tōa senkaku shishi kiden* 東亜先覚志士記伝 (Tokyo: 1935), 1:27–34.

81. For an early reference to attacking Korea under international law, see Dajōkan 太政官, "Sada Hokubō hoka futari kichōgo mikomi kenpaku 佐田白茅外二人帰朝後見込建白," *Kōbunroku* 公文録, 本館-2A-009-00・公01697100, 件名番号 019, National Archives of Japan 国立公文書館.

82. Ōkubo, *Ōkubo Toshimichi bunsho*, 5: 53–64.

83. Mōri, *Meiji roku-nen seihen*, 82, 176–205; Ravina, *The Last Samurai*, 188–190; Ikai Takaaki, *Saigō Takamori*, 138–144.

84. Kokuryūkai 黒竜会, ed., *Seinan kiden* 西南記伝 (Tokyo: Kokuryūkai honbu, 1908-1911), vol. 1, appendix, 1–21.

CHAPTER 6

1. For an overview, see Mataji Miyamoto, Yōtarō Sakudō, and Yasukichi Yasuba, "Economic Development in Preindustrial Japan, 1859–1894," *Journal of Economic History* 25, no. 4 (1965).

2. Banno Junji 坂野潤治, *Mikan no Meiji Ishin* 未完の明治維新 (Tokyo: Chikuma Shōbō, 2007), 166–169, 197–208. Elsewhere Banno has observed "this way of thinking was remarkably similar to that of the 'development dictatorships' of many Asian countries after the Second World War." See Junji Banno, *Japan's Modern History, 1857–1937: A New Political Narrative*, trans. J. A. A. Stockwin (London: Routledge/Taylor & Francis Group, 2014), 75.

3. My figures for government revenue are from Sasaki Hiroshi 佐々木寛司, "Sozei kokka to chiso 租税国家と地租," in *Kindai Nihon no keisei to sozei* 近代日本の形成と租税 (Tokyo: Yūshisha, 2008), 12. Figures for the cost of the War of the Southwest are from Mōri Toshihiko 毛利敏彦, *Kokushi daijiten* 国史大事典, s.v. "Seinan sensō 西南戦争." Yoshikawa Kōbunkan, 1979–1997.

4. Dajōkan 太政官, April 14, 1875, "Genrōin daishin'in o oku mikotonori shigatsu jūyokka 元老院大審院ヲ置ク詔・四月十四日," Dajō ruiten 太政類典, 本館-2A-009-00・太0022310, 件名番号 031, National Archives of Japan 国立公文書館.

5. Fox, *Britain and Japan, 1858–1883*, 290–298.

6. Mizuno, "Early Meiji Policies," 724–730.

7. Japanese government memorandum, enclosure 3 in no. 76, Bingham to Fish, April 22, 1874, in US Department of State, *Executive documents printed by order of the House of Representatives, 1874–75*, 18 vols., vol. 1 (Washington, DC: US Government Printing Office, 1875), 679–680.

8. Mizuno, "Early Meiji Policies," 726; and Eskildsen, "Of Civilization and Savages," 396–397.

9. Robert Eskildsen, "An Army as Good and Efficient as Any in the World: James Wasson and Japan's 1874 Expedition to Taiwan," *Asian Cultural Studies* 36 (2010): esp. 53–55; Robert Eskildsen, "Suitable Ships and the Hard Work of Imperialism: Evaluating the Japanese Navy in the 1874 Invasion of Taiwan," *Asian Cultural Studies* 38 (2012): esp. 54.

10. F. Victor Dickins and Stanley Lane-Poole, *The life of Sir Harry Parkes: K.C.B., G.C.M.G., sometime Her Majesty's minister to China and Japan* (London: MacMillan, 1894), 194.

11. "New Oriental Diplomacy," *New York Times*, December 6, 1874, 6.

12. For the treaty text, see Gaimushō, *Dai Nihon gaikō bunsho*, 9:115–119.

13. Duus, *The Abacus and the Sword: The Japanese Penetration of Korea, 1895–1910*, 43–51; Takemichi Hara, "Korea, China, and Western Barbarians: Diplomacy in Early Nineteenth-Century Korea," *Modern Asian Studies* 32, no. 2 (1998); James

B. Palais, *Politics and Policy in Traditional Korea* (Cambridge, MA: Harvard University Press, 1975), 252–271.

14. "The Japanese Treaty with Corea," *Pall Mall Gazette*, March 20, 1876.

15. Gaimushō, *Dai Nihon gaikō bunsho*, 5: 373–384. My overall interpretation of the domestication of Ryūkyū is shaped by Araki Moriaki 安良城盛昭, "Ryūkyū shobun ron 琉球処分論," in *Ezochi to Ryūkyū: "Ikoku" no naikokuka to tōgō* 蝦夷地と琉球:「異国」の内国化と統合 (Tokyo: Yoshikawa Kōbunkan, 2001, originally published 1978), 184–186; and Yonaha Jun 與那覇潤, "Ryūkyū kara mita Ryūkyū shobun: 'kindai' no teigi o majime ni kangaeru 琉球からみた琉球処分ー「近代」の定義をまじめに考える," in *Ryūkyū kara mita sekaishi* 琉球からみた世界史, ed. Murai Shōsuke 村井章介 and Mitani Hiroshi 三谷博 (Tokyo: Yamakawa Shuppansha, 2011), 137–158.

16. Ōkubo Toshimichi 大久保利通, December 25, 1874, "Ryūkyū-han shobun kata no gi ni tsuki ukagai 琉球藩処分方ノ儀ニ付キ伺," *Kōbunroku* 公文録, A01100061700, Japan Center for Asian Historical Records JACAR(アジア歴史資料センター). A later version of Ōkubo's proposal in summarized in George H. Kerr, *Okinawa, the History of an Island People*, rev. ed. (Boston: Tuttle, 2000), 367–369.

17. Kerr, *Okinawa, the History of an Island People*, 370–376.

18. Sakurai Kigai 桜井基外, ed., *Ten no seisei* 天之聖声 (Wakkanai, Japan: Sakurai Kigai, 1910), 48–49.

19. Kerr, *Okinawa, the History of an Island People*, 376–377, 384–392; Richard T. Chang, "General Grant's 1879 Visit to Japan," *Monumenta Nipponica* 24, no. 4 (1969): 379–383.

20. "Riu Kiu: Memorandum upon the Diplomatic Question now pending between Japan and China, July 1879," part of "Official Correspondence between Japan and China relative to Loochoo," in MS British Foreign Office: Japan Correspondence, 1856–1905: Japan, Section II, F.O. 46/1-104, 1868–1890, Vol. 248:1, frames 147–151, National Archives (Kew, United Kingdom), accessed through *Nineteenth Century Collections Online*, tinyurl.galegroup.com/tinyurl/4E3bG1.

21. Kinjō Masaru 金城善, "Kindai Okinawa ni okeru koseki-hō no shikō 近代沖縄における戸籍法の施行," in *Okinawa kindaihō no keisei to tenkai* 沖縄近代法の形成と展開, ed. Tasato Osamu 田里修 and Mori Kenji 森謙二 (Okinawa-ken Ginowan-shi: Yōju Shorin, 2013); Kerr, *Okinawa, the History of an Island People*, 400–408

22. For late Tokugawa policies, see Howell, *Geographies of Identity in Nineteenth-century Japan*, 144–150. For Meiji policy, see Kaiho Yōko 海保洋子, " 'Ikoku' no naikokuka to tōgō 「異国」の内国化と統合," in *Ezochi to Ryūkyū* 蝦夷地と琉球, ed. Kuwabara Masato 桑原真人 and Gabe Masao 我部政男 (Tokyo: Yoshikawa Kōbunkan, 2001; originally published 1992), 132–136.

23. The ancient institution of the Azechi按察使was revived briefly in 1869–1870 by the Meiji government, but with the modern pronounciation

Ansatsu-shi. For similarities between the Ansatsu-shi and the Kaitakushi, see "Ansatsu-shi shokan no tōkyū wa Kaitakushi to dōitsu narashimu 按察使諸官ノ等級ハ開拓使ト同一ナラシム."

24. The tondenhei 屯田兵 are discussed in English in Harry D. Harootunian, "The Economic Rehabilitation of the Samurai in the Early Meiji Period," *Journal of Asian Studies* 19, no. 4 (1960): 435–439.

25. Kaiho, "'Ikoku' no naikokuka to tōgō," 126. For a period discussion of this problem, see Dajōkan 太政官, June 1873, "Goki hachidō no meishō kaitei no gi ukagai 五畿八道ノ名称改定ノ儀伺," *Kōbunroku* 公文録, 本館-2A-009-00・公00782100, 件名番号 007, National Archives of Japan 国立公文書館. The relocation of the capital, a subject of enormous complexity, is lucidly explored in Fujitani, *Splendid Monarchy*, 31–92.

26. Howell, *Geographies of Identity in Nineteenth-century Japan*, 149, 178–180. For an example of this shift, see the renaming of the position of Colonial Office Interpreter (開拓使通辞kaitakushi tsūji) to Manager of Aboriginal [Affairs] (土人取締 dojin torishimari). Dajōkan 太政官, 1872/7/8, "Tsūji no meishō wo haishi dojin torishimari to shōsu 通辞ノ名称ヲ廃シ土人取締ト称ス," Dajō ruiten 太政類典, 本館-2A-009-00・太00343100, 件名番号 027, National Archives of Japan 国立公文書館.

27. Brett L. Walker, "Meiji Modernization, Scientific Agriculture, and the Destruction of Japan's Hokkaido Wolf," *Environmental History* 9, no. 2 (2004).

28. I am indebted to Sidney Lu for bringing this image to my attention.

29. Alexis Dudden, "Japanese Colonial Control in International Terms," *Japanese Studies* 25, no. 1 (2005): 1–20; Sidney Xu Lu, "Colonizing Hokkaido and the Origin of Japanese Trans-Pacific Expansion, 1869–1894," *Japanese Studies* 36, no. 2 (2016).

30. John A. Harrison, "The Capron Mission and the Colonization of Hokkaido, 1868–1875," *Agricultural History* 25, no. 3 (1951): 137–138; Katsuya Hirano, "Thanatopolitics in the Making of Japan's Hokkaido: Settler Colonialism and Primitive Accumulation," *Critical Historical Studies* 2, no. 2 (2015): 198, 202–203.

31. For a highly critical evaluation of Capron, see Bogdan Mieczkowski and Seiko Mieczkowski, "Horace Capron and the Development of Hokkaido: A Reappraisal," *Journal of the Illinois State Historical Society (1908–1984)* 67, no. 5 (1974). See also Harrison, "The Capron Mission"; Donald Roden, "In Search of the Real Horace Capron: An Historiographical Perspective on Japanese-American Relations," *Pacific Historical Review* 55, no. 4 (1986).

32. Brett L. Walker, *A Concise History of Japan* (Cambridge: Cambridge University Press, 2015), 204–205.

33. Robertson, "The Bonin Islands," 138.

34. Chapman, "Inventing Subjects: Early History of the 'Naturalized Foreigners' of the Bonin (Ogasawara) Islands 24" http://apjjf.org/-David-Chapman/3169/article.html; Chapman, "Different Faces, Different Spaces: Identifying the Islanders

of Ogasawara." For Meiji deliberations on 1878 law, see Dajōkan 太政官, January 1882, "Ogawasawara-tō kikajin shobun no ken 小笠原島帰化人処分ノ件," *Kōbunroku* 公文録, 本館-2A-010-00・公03231100, 件名番号 022, National Archives of Japan 国立公文書館 and Naikaku 内閣, "Ogasawara-tō zaiseki kikajin ni taishi naichi ijū nado no kin wo toki ippan shinmin taru no kengi o yūseshimu 小笠原島在籍帰化人ニ対シ内地移住等ノ禁ヲ解キ一般臣民タルノ権義ヲ有セシム," 本館-2A-011-00・類00797100, 014, National Archives of Japan 国立公文書館.

35. A useful translation of Ōkubo's November 1873 opinion paper can be found in George M. Beckmann, *The Making of the Meiji Constitution: The Oligarchs and the Constitutional Development of Japan, 1868–1891* (Lawrence: University of Kansas Press, 1957), 111–119. For the original, see Ōkubo, *Ōkubo Toshimichi bunsho*, 5: 182–203.

36. See the Dajōkan (大史) edict of 1871/7/19 in Matsumoto Sannosuke 松本三之介 and Yamamuro Shin'ichi 山室信一, eds., *Genron to media* 言論とメディア, vol. 11 of *Nihon kindai shisō taikei* 日本近代思想体系 (Tokyo: Iwanami Shoten, 1990), 410–411. See also Kim, *The Age of Visions and Arguments*, 263–264.

37. See Dajōkan edict #352 of 1873 (新聞紙発行条目—日太政官布告第352号—1873/10/19) in Matsumoto and Yamamuro, eds., *Genron to media*, 411–412; and Kim, *The Age of Visions and Arguments*, 263–264.

38. See Dajōkan edict #12 of 1875 (新聞紙条例—日太政官布告第12号—1875/6/28) in Matsumoto and Yamamuro, eds., *Genron to media*, 412–415.

39. Dickins and Lane-Poole, *The Life of Sir Harry Parkes*, 244.

40. Kim, *The Age of Visions and Arguments*, 266–267.

41. See Kyōgaku seishi taishi (Meiji jūnin-nen) 教学聖旨大旨 (明治十二年), in Gakusei hyakunenshi: shiryōhen 学制百年史・資料編 at http://www.mext. go.jp/b_menu/hakusho/html/others/detail/1317935.htm.

42. Suzuki Jun 鈴木淳, "Kōbushō no jūgonen 工部省の十五年," in *Kōbushō to sono jidai* 工部省とその時代, ed. Suzuki Jun 鈴木淳 (Tokyo: Yamakawa Shuppansha, 2002), 3–22; Kashihara Hiroki 柏原宏紀, "Seikanron seihen-go no Kōbushō ni kansuru ichi kōsatsu 征韓論政変後の工部省に関する一考察," *Hōgaku kenkyū* 法学研究 82, no. 2 (2009): 487–510, esp. 502–503.

43. E. Sydney Crawcour, "Economic Change in the Nineteenth Century," in *Cambridge History of Japan*, Vol. 5: *The Nineteenth Century*, ed. Kozo Yamamura (Cambridge: Cambridge University Press, 1989), 610–614; E. Sydney Crawcour, "Industrialization and Technological Change, 1885–1920," in *Cambridge History of Japan*, Vol. 6: *The Twentieth Century*, ed. Peter Duus (Cambridge: Cambridge University Press, 1989), 423–424. For the Tomioka mill, see E. Patricia Tsurumi, *Factory Girls: Women in the Thread Mills of Meiji Japan* (Princeton, NJ: Princeton University Press, 1990), esp. 25–46.

44. Ōkurashō 大蔵省, *Kōbushō enkaku hōkoku* 工部省沿革報告 (Tokyo: Ōkurashō, 1889), 687–691.

45. Ōkubo, *Ōkubo Toshimichi bunsho*, 5: 561–566. Kamiyama describes this change in policy as a shift from direct to indirect support, which began in 1874 and accelerated in 1881 with Matsukata's policy of selling off government enterprises. Kamiyama Tsuneo 神山恒夫, "Shokusan kōgyō seisaku no tenkai 殖産興業政策の展開," in *Iwanami Kōza Nihon rekishi*, Vol. 15: *Kingendai 1* 岩波講座日本歴史. 第15巻(近現代1), ed. Ōtsu Tōru 大津透, Sakurai Eiji 桜井英治, and Fujii Jōji 藤井讓治 (Tokyo: Iwanami Shoten, 2014), 97–129.

46. Sasaki, "Sozei kokka to chiso," 2–15; Kozo Yamamura, "The Meiji Land Tax Reform," in *Japan in Transition: From Tokugawa to Meiji*, ed. Marius B. Jansen and Gilbert Rozman (Princeton, NJ: Princeton University Press, 1986). For the impact of Meiji reforms on common lands see Philip C. Brown, *Cultivating Commons: Joint Ownership of Arable Land in Early Modern Japan* (Honolulu: University of Hawai`i Press, 2011), esp. 177–187.

47. Sasaki Kanji 佐々木寛司 and Ochiai Hiroki 落合弘樹, "Zeisei kaikaku to rokusei haishi: chiso kaisei to chitsuroku shobun 税政改革と禄制廃止—地租改正と秩禄処分," in *Meiji ishin no keizai katei* 明治維新の経済過程, ed. Sasaki Kanji 佐々木寛司 and Katsube Makoto 勝部真人 (Tokyo: Yūshisha, 2013), 89–91.

48. D. Eleanor Westney, "The Military," in *Japan in Transition: From Tokugawa to Meiji*, ed. Marius B. Jansen and Gilbert Rozman (Princeton, NJ: Princeton University Press, 1988), 176–185; Rokuhara, "Local Officials and the Meiji Conscription Campaign," 81–88.

49. Ochiai Hiroki 落合弘樹, *Chitsuroku shobun* 秩禄処分 (Tokyo: Chūō Kōron Shinsha, 1999), 74–110.

50. Ibid., 112–134; Sasaki and Ochiai, "Zeisei kaikaku to rokusei haishi," 100–101.

51. Sasaki and Ochiai, "Zeisei kaikaku to rokusei haishi," 101.

52. Ibid., 101–103. For a detailed period guide, see Kondō Nobutaka 近藤信敬, ed., *Chitsuroku shobunhō* 秩禄処分法 (Nagoya: Kondō Nobutaka, 1897), esp. 17–24.

53. Sasaki and Ochiai, "Zesei kaikaku to rokusei haishi," 103–104.

54. Ravina, *Land and Lordship in Early Modern Japan*, 97–113.

55. For an overview of how samurai adapted, see Ochiai, *Chitsuroku shobun*, 194–203.

56. Ibid., 177–178. The Risshisha memorial is in Irokawa Daikichi 色川大吉 and Gabe Takao 我部政男, eds., *Meiji kenpakusho shūsei* 明治建白書集成 (Tokyo: Chikuma Shōbō, 1996), 5:334–343.

57. Akira Hayami and Satomi Kurosu, "Regional Diversity in Demographic and Family Patterns in Preindustrial Japan," *Journal of Japanese Studies* 27, no. 2 (2001): 295–321; Akira Hayami, "The Myth of Primogeniture and Impartible Inheritance in Tokugawa Japan," *Journal of Family History* 8, no. 1 (1983): 3–29.

58. Anne Walthall, "The Life Cycle of Farm Women in Tokugawa Japan," in *Recreating Japanese Women, 1600–1945*, ed. Gail Lee Bernstein (Berkeley: University of California Press, 1991).

59. Chizuko Ueno, "The Position of Japanese Women Reconsidered," *Current Anthropology* 28, no. 4 (1987): S75–S84.

60. Robert Epp, "The Challenge from Tradition: Attempts to Compile a Civil Code in Japan, 1866–78," *Monumenta Nipponica* 22, no. 1/2 (1967): 36–38. For a summary of Tokugawa law, see Carl Steenstrup, *A History of Law in Japan until 1868*, 2nd. ed. (New York: E. J. Brill, 1996), 124–159. For Ōkubo's own recognition that samurai inheritance practices were poorly suited to commoners, see Dajōkan 太政官, March 1876, "Heimin katoku sōzoku no gi ukagai 平民家督相続ノ儀伺," 請求番号 本館-2A-009-00・公01837100, 件名番号 059, National Archives of Japan 国立公文書館.

61. Mojuro Tonooka, "The Development of the Family Law in Modern Japan," *Comparative Law Review Hikaku hōgaku* 2, no. 2 (1966): 3–4; Wilhelm Röhl, *History of Law in Japan since 1868* (Leiden: Brill, 2005), 271–272.

62. Dajōkan 太政官, January 1873, "Mekake no meigi haishi ukagai 妾ノ名義廃止伺," *Kōbunroku* 公文録, 本館-2A-009-00・公00892100, 件名番号 008, National Archives of Japan 国立公文書館. I have translated 性法 (*seihō*) as "natural law," 天数 (*tensū*) as "heaven's law," and 犯姦 (*hankan*) as "adultery."

63. Dajōkan 太政官, June 1873, "Mekake o yatoïre to minasu no gi ukagai 妾ヲ雇入ト見做スノ儀伺," *Kōbunroku* 公文録, 本館-2A-009-00・公00902100, 件名番号 007, National Archives of Japan 国立公文書館.

64. Dajōkan 太政官, April 1884, "Mekake koseki no ken: keihō jitchi nochi ni tōki shitaru wa joseki seshimu 妾戸籍ノ件 (刑法実施後ニ登記シタルハ除籍セシム)," *Kōbunroku* 公文録, 本館-2A-010-00・公03694100, 件名番号 012, National Archives of Japan 国立公文書館.

65. Tonooka Mojūrō 外岡茂十郎, "Waga kuni ni okeru shiseishi-hō no tanjō to shiseishi no han'i 我國に於ける私生子法の誕生と私生子の範囲," *Waseda hōgaku (Waseda law review)* 早稲田法学 20 (1941): 1–58.

66. Keene, *Emperor of Japan: Meiji and His World, 1852–1912*, 350–351, 411–412.

67. Ibid., esp. 7, 52, 415; F. Cunliffe Owen, "The Mikado and the Reigning House of Japan," *Town and Country*, January 7, 1905. For the Meiji emperor and empress as an ideal couple, see Fujitani, *Splendid Monarchy*, 181–191.

68. Haru Matsukata Reischauer, *Samurai and Silk: A Japanese and American Heritage* (Cambridge, MA: Harvard University Press, 1986), 186–187; Clara A. Whitney, *Clara's Diary: An American Girl in Meiji Japan*, ed. M. William Steele and Tamiko Ichimata (Tokyo: Kodansha International, 1979), 9–23, 239–240.

69. The following draws on Ellen Nakamura, "Working the Siebold Network: Kusumoto Ine and Western Learning in Nineteenth-Century Japan," *Japanese Studies* 28, no. 2 (2008).

70. Ibid., 197–211. For Meiji-era medical and midwife regulations, see Yuki Terazawa, "The State, Midwives, and Reproductive Surveillance in Late Nineteenth- and Early Twentieth-Century Japan," *U.S.–Japan Women's Journal English Supplement*

24 (2003): 59–81; Aya Homei, "Birth Attendants in Meiji Japan: The Rise of a Medical Birth Model and the New Division of Labour," *Social History of Medicine* 19, no. 3 (2006): 407–424.

71. For the Seikantō manifesto, see "Declaration of War" (決戦之議 Kessen no gi) in Sugitani Akira 杉谷昭, Mōri Toshihiko 毛利敏彦, and Hirose Yoshihiro 広瀬順晧, eds., *Etō Shinpei kankei monjo* 江藤新平関係文書 (Tokyo: Hokusensha, 1989). Etō's English-language manifesto is in the same collection, but mislabeled as "Memorandum on International Law [English]" (国際法に関する覚書 (英文) Kokusaihō ni kansuru oboegaki [Eibun]) also in ibid., R 17–29.

72. Iwashita Tetsunori 岩下哲典, *Edo no kaigai jōhō nettowāku* 江戸の海外情報ネットワーク (Tokyo: Yoshikawa Kōbunkan, 2006), 108–134.

73. For the transformation of prints into quasi-newspapers, see Kinoshita Naoyuki 木下直之 and Yoshimi Shunya 吉見俊哉, *Nyūsu no tanjō: kawaraban to shinbun nishikie no jōhō sekai* ニュースの誕生: かわら版と新聞錦絵の情報世界 (Tokyo: Tōkyō Daigaku Shuppankai, 1999).

74. Matsumoto and Yamamuro, eds., *Genron to media*, 490; James L. Huffman, *Creating a Public: People and Press in Meiji Japan* (Honolulu: University of Hawaiʻi Press, 1997), 12–110.

75. Mark Ravina, "The Medieval in the Modern: Command and Consensus in Japanese Politics," *Medieval History Journal* 19, no. 2 (2016): 1–10; Yoshida Masahiko 吉田昌彦, "Gakushūin kengen seido no seiritsu to 'genro dōkaiʾ 学習院建言制度の成立と「言路洞開」," *Bulletin of the Graduate School of Social and Cultural Studies, Kyushu University* 比較社会文化 17 (2011); Rai Gyokusei [Lai Yujing] 頼鈺菁, "Bakumatsu-ki ni okeru 'kangen' to 'kengen'/'kenpaku': 'genro dōkaiʾ o megutte 幕末期における「諫言」と「建言」/「建白」:「言路洞開」をめぐって," *Kotoba to Bunka* 言葉と文化 14, no. 12 (2013).

76. For a discussion of the petition and reactions, see Kim, *The Age of Visions and Arguments*, 102–114. For Itagaki's links between democracy and organizational unity, see Thomas, *Reconfiguring Modernity*, 71–73. For the petition text, see Irokawa and Gabe, eds., *Meiji kenpakusho shūsei*, 3:22–25.

77. In the Song context, the phrase is often translated as "road of remonstrance." See Ari Daniel Levine, "Che-tsung's Reign (1085–1100) and the Age of Faction," in *The Cambridge History of China*, Vol. 5, Part 1: *The Sung Dynasty and Its Precursors, 907–1279*, ed. Denis Twichett and Paul Jakov Smith (Cambridge: Cambridge University Press, 2009).

78. Kim, *The Age of Visions and Arguments*, 101–254, esp. 125–134.

79. Prefectural assembly figures are from Naikaku tōkei kyoku 内閣統計局, *Dai-Nihon teikoku tōkei nenkan* 大日本帝國統計年鑑, vol. 2 (Tokyo: Naikaku Tōkei kyoku, 1883), 917–921. Police surveillance reports are from Dajōkan 太政官, "Seitō seisha torishirabesho narabi ni enzetsusha torishirabesho denran no ken 政党政社取調書並ビニ演説者取調書電覧ノ件," 本館-2A-037-00・雑00887100,

National Archives of Japan 国立公文書館. The report is described in Tersaki Osamu 寺崎修, "Seitō seisha torishirabesho: Meiji 15 nen 10 gatsu chōsa 政党政社取調書--明治15年10月調査," *Seijigaku ronshū* 政治学論集, no. 43 (1996). Regional differences in leadership are discussed in Kim, *The Age of Visions and Arguments*, 193–215. The impact of demography on domain-level politics is explored in Ravina, *Land and Lordship in Early Modern Japan*, esp. 46–70.

80. Huffman, *Creating a Public*, 81–82.

81. Kim, *The Age of Visions and Arguments*, 154–156. The title *Meiroku Zasshi* means "1873 Journal," reflecting the year of its inception.

82. Dajōkan 太政官, April 1875, "Rikken seitai no shōsho gofukoku an 立憲政体 ノ詔書御布告案," *Kōbunroku* 公文録, 本館-2A-009-00・公01372100, 件名番号 001, National Archives of Japan 国立公文書館. Genrō might more directly be translated as Council of Elders, although the word Senate is etymologically related to terms for "elder" such as senior. The 1875 Genrōin is unrelated to a later, informal institution known as the Genrō.

83. Andrew Fraser, "The Osaka Conference of 1875," *Journal of Asian Studies* 26, no. 4 (1967); Kim, *The Age of Visions and Arguments*, 119–125.

84. Osterhammel, *The Transformation of the World*, 59–62, 585–605.

85. Ibid.; Ikai Takaaki 猪飼隆明, *Seinan sensō: sensō no taigi to dōinsareru minshū* 西南戦争—戦争の大義と動員される民衆 (Tokyo: Yoshikawa Kōbunkan, 2008), 6–18.

86. Edward S. Morse, *Japan Day by Day*, 2 vols. (Boston: Houghton Mifflin, 1917), 1:269. For Saigō in popular lore, see Mark Ravina, "The Apocryphal Suicide of Saigō Takamori: Samurai, Seppuku and the Politics of Legend," *Journal of Asian Studies* 69, no. 3 (2010).

87. Ravina, *The Last Samurai*, 197–198.

88. Ikai, *Seinan sensō*, 23–28; Ochiai, *Chitsuroku shobun*, 147–175

89. "Some Hopeful Signs of the Times," *Tokio Times*, September 1, 1877.

90. Ikai, *Seinan sensō*, 72–77.

91. Mutsu's translation of Bentham was published in 1883–84 under the title *Rigaku seisō* 利学正宗.

92. Tsunoda Kurō 角田九郎, *Ōe Taku kun no ryakuden* 大江卓君之略伝 (Ichinoseki, Iwate, Japan: Tsunoda Kurō, 1890), 41–42. Research on the 1877 Tosa conspiracy remains astonishingly thin. For an overview, see Fukuchi Atsushi 福地惇, "Risshisha no kyohei keikaku ni tsuite 立志社の挙兵計画について," *Nihon rekishi* 日本歴史 531 (1992): 91–97.

93. *Japan Daily Herald*, September 25, 1877.

94. Ravina, *The Last Samurai*, 177, 193–196; Ravina, "The Apocryphal Suicide of Saigō Takamori," 711–712.

95. See, for example, Marius B. Jansen, *The Japanese and Sun Yat-sen* (Cambridge, MA: Harvard University Press, 1954), 39; Sidney DeVere Brown, "Crisis of

1873," in *Modern Japan: An Encyclopedia of History, Culture, and Nationalism*, ed. James L. Huffman (New York: Garland, 1998), 40.

96. Kojima Tokuya 小島徳弥, *Meiji ikō daijiken no shinsō to hanrei* 明治以降大事件の真相と判例 (Tokyo: Kyōbunsha, 1934), 83–90. See also Katsuta Masaharu 勝田正治, *"Seijika" Ōkubo Toshimichi: kindai Nihon no sekkei-sha* 「政治家」大久保利通:近代日本の設計者 (Tokyo: Kōdansha, 2003), 212–213.

97. Kim, *The Age of Visions and Arguments*, 296–298, 307. For the details of financial policy see Steven J. Ericson, "The 'Matsukata Deflation' Reconsidered: Financial Stabilization and Japanese Exports in a Global Depression, 1881–85, " *Journal of Japanese Studies* 40, no. 1 (2014), 1–28.

98. For an overview of the 1881 Political Crisis, see Kazuhiro Takii, *The Meiji Constitution: The Japanese Experience of the West and the Shaping of the Modern State*, trans. David Noble (Tokyo: International House of Japan, 2007), 51–52. For details, see Kim, *The Age of Visions and Arguments*, 207–223. The popular movement is detailed in Daikichi Irokawa, *The Culture of the Meiji Period*, translation edited by Marius B. Jansen (1969; reprint, Princeton, NJ: Princeton University Press, 1985), esp. 76–122, 151–218.

99. Joyce Chapman Lebra, "Okuma Shigenobu and the 1881 Political Crisis," *Journal of Asian Studies* 18, no. 4 (1959): 477–478; Andrew Fraser, "The Expulsion of Ōkuma from the Government in 1881," *Journal of Asian Studies* 26, no. 2 (1967): 218–219.

100. Hirobumi Itō 伊藤博文, 1881, "Sōgi (an) 奏議(案)," 本館-2A-037-00・雑00630100 行政文書—内閣・総理府—太政官・内閣関係—諸雑公文書—(諸雑公文書[狭義]), National Archives of Japan 国立公文書館; Kim, *The Age of Visions and Arguments*, 276–278.

101. Kim, *The Age of Visions and Arguments*, 278–285; George Akita, *Foundations of Constitutional Government in Modern Japan, 1868–1900* (Cambridge, MA: Harvard University Press, 1967), 31–57; Lebra, "Okuma Shigenobu," 478.

102. Kim, *The Age of Visions and Arguments*, 288–328; Huffman, *Creating a Public*, 115–120; Lebra, "Okuma Shigenobu," 482–483.

103. Kim, *The Age of Visions and Arguments*, 318–325; Lebra, "Okuma Shigenobu," 484–485. The exact details of the crisis remain obscure because contemporaneous records are fragmentary and the later recollections of the participants are contradictory.

104. Kim, *The Age of Visions and Arguments*, 324.

105. G. R. Searle, *The Quest for National Efficiency: A Study in British Politics and Political Thought, 1899–1914* (Berkeley: University of California Press, 1971), 57–59.

106. H. G. Wells, *A Modern Utopia* (1905; reprint, Lincoln: University of Nebraska Press, 1967).

107. Robert Stephenson Smyth Baden-Powell, *Boy Scouts beyond the Seas; "My World Tour"* (London: C. Arthur Pearson, 1913), 86–100; Michael Rosenthal, *The*

Character Factory: Baden-Powell and the Origins of the Boy Scout Movement (New York: Pantheon Books, 1986), 125–130. For a valuable overview of British views of Japan see Sheldon Garon, *Beyond Our Means: Why America Spends While the World Saves* (Princeton, NJ: Princeton University Press, 2011), 119–121.

108. Itō 伊藤博文, "Sōgi (an) 奏議(案)," 本館-2A-037-00, National Archives of Japan 国立公文書館.

109. Dajōkan 太政官, October 12, 1881, "Kokkai kaisetsu no chokuyu 国会開設之勅諭," *Chokugorui* 勅語類, 本館-2A-030-09・附A00304115, National Archives of Japan 国立公文書館.

CONCLUSION

1. Kevin J. Cooney and Alex Scarbrough, "Japan and South Korea: Can These Two Nations Work Together?" *Asian Affairs* 35, no. 3 (2008): 173–192; "Uneasy Partners Japan, S Korea Join US Air Drills," *New Zealand Herald*, August 22, 2013.

2. See, for example, June 5, 2010 press release by the Japanese Ministry of Defense of a meeting between Kitazawa Toshimi 北澤俊美 (Japan's defense minister) and Gim Tae-yeong 金泰榮 (Chairman of the Joint Chiefs of State, ROKA) http://www.mod.go.jp/j/press/youjin/2010/06/05d.pdf.

3. See, for example, Jonathan W. Best, *A History of the Early Korean Kingdom of Paekche: Together with an Annotated Translation of the Paekche Annals of the Samguk Sagi* (Cambridge, MA: Harvard University Asia Center, 2006). Hyung Il Pai, *Constructing "Korean" Origins: A Critical Review of Archaeology, Historiography, and Racial Myth in Korean State-formation Theories* (Cambridge, MA: Harvard University Asia Center, 2000).

4. For a theoretical consideration of national anthems and national flags, see Karen A. Cerulo, "Symbols and the World System: National Anthems and Flags," *Sociological Forum* 8, no. 2 (1993).

5. A literal translation of Nihon would be "origin of the sun."

6. "The United Nations Flag Code and Regulations, ST/SGB/132," (1967). The flag of Nepal, with its dual pennant shape, represents the sole exception to this rule.

7. Gerry J. Simpson, *Great Powers and Outlaw States: Unequal Sovereigns in the International Legal Order* (Cambridge: Cambridge University Press, 2004), 1–131, 165–193. Kang notes the how membership in the OECD reflects status hierarchies. Kang, *East Asia before the West*, 21–22. Howland explores how Meiji leaders appealed to the more egalitarian face of the modern international order through membership in administrative unions such as the International Telegraph Union and the Universal Postal Union. Douglas Howland, "Japan and the Universal Postal Union: An Alternative Internationalism in the 19th Century," *Social Science Japan Journal* 17, no. 1 (2014), 23-39; Douglas Howland, "An Alternative Mode of International Order: The International Administrative Union in the Nineteenth Century," *Review of International Studies* 41, no. 1 (2015), 161–83.

8. For a survey of the dispute, see Seokwoo Lee, *Territorial Disputes among Japan, China and Taiwan Concerning the Senkaku Islands* (Durham, UK: International Boundaries Research Unit, Department of Geography, University of Durham, 2002); Unryu Suganuma, *Sovereign Rights and Territorial Space in Sino-Japanese Relations: Irredentism and the Diaoyu/Senkaku Islands* (Honolulu: University of Hawai'i Press, 2000). For a political science perspective on such non-borders, see Kang, *East Asia before the West*, 140–141.

9. Peter Bol, "Creating a GIS for the History of China," in *Placing History: How Maps, Spatial Data, and GIS are Changing Historical Scholarship*, ed. Anne Kelly Knowles and Amy Hillier (Redlands, CA: ESRI Press, 2008), 42.

10. For a discussion of the relationship between cartography, empire, and national consciousness, see Brett L. Walker, "Mamiya Rinzō and the Japanese exploration of Sakhalin Island: Cartography and Empire," *Journal of Historical Geography* 33 (2007). For the Chinese case see Laura Hostetler, *Qing Colonial Enterprise: Ethnography and Cartography in Early Modern China* (Chicago: University of Chicago Press, 2001).

11. For an overview of the dispute, see Min Gyo Koo, "Economic Dependence and the Dokdo/Takeshima Dispute between South Korean and Japan," *Harvard Asia Quarterly* 9, no. 4 (2005); and Alexis Dudden, *Troubled Apologies among Japan, Korea, and the United States* (New York: Columbia University Press, 2008), 1–30.

12. Samuel P. Huntington, "The Clash of Civilizations?" *Foreign Affairs* 72, no. 3 (1993).

13. Fogel has suggested the term "Sinosphere" to capture Chinese culture as an "organizing model or ideology" rather than a direct exercise of imperial power. Fogel, *Articulating the Sinosphere*, 1–6.

14. For an English translation of the Mongol epistle, see Susumu Ishii, "The Decline of the Kamakura Bakufu," in *The Cambridge History of Japan*, Vol. 3: *Medieval Japan*, ed. Kozo Yamamura (Cambridge: Cambridge University Press, 1990), 132. The Japanese text is reproduced in Kamakura ibun 鎌倉遺文, document #9564.

15. Hanawa Hokinoichi 塙保己一, ed., *Zoku gunsho ruijū* 続群書類従, Vol. 30, Part 1 (Tokyo: Zoku Gunsho Ruijū Kanseikai, 1925), 404.

16. My observation here is historical, but informed by Anthony Giddens's theory of structuration and social reproduction. As Giddens observes, "Structure is not to be equated with constraints but is always both constraining and enabling." See Anthony Giddens, *The Constitution of Society* (Berkeley: University of California Press, 1984), 25. For a brief, but lively summary, see Anthony Giddens and Christopher Pierson, *Conversations with Anthony Giddens: Making Sense of Modernity* (Stanford, CA: Stanford University Press, 1998), 75–93.

Glossary

Abe Masahiro 阿部正弘 (1819–1857): Chair of the shogunal council of elders (*rōjū shuza* 老中首座) from 1845 to 1855. Abe attempted to create a national unity government by seeking the counsel and support of daimyo such as Tokugawa Nariaki and Shimazu Nariakira. Resigned in favor of Hotta Masayoshi.

Brunet, Jules ジュール・ブリュネ (1838–1911): French army officer and advisor to the shogunate; fled with Enomoto Takeaki to Hokkaido and served with "Republic of Ezo."

Chamber of the Left (*sa'in* 左院): A council under the dajōkan system.

Chamber of the Right (*u'in* 右院): A council under the dajōkan system.

Chōshū 長州: A tozama daimyo domain in southwestern Honshu, also known as Hagi and Yamaguchi. Ruling house was the Mōri 毛利. The shogunate and allied domains invaded and defeated Chōshū in 1864, but the domain pushed back a second attack in 1866, publicly revealing shogunal weakness. In alliance with Satsuma, Chōshū led the coalition that overthrew Tokugawa Yoshinobu in 1868. Many key Meiji leaders were from Chōshū, including Kidō Takayoshi, Inoue Kaoru, Yamagata Aritomo, and Itō Hirobumi.

Council of State (*dajōkan* 太政官): An early Meiji government structure based on Nara-Heian-era Japanese and Tang-era Chinese models. Revived in 1868, it was replaced in 1885 by a modern cabinet system. The main organ of the Council of State was the Grand Chamber (*sei'in*) comprising a Grand Minister (*dajō daijin*), Minister of the Left (*sadaijin*), Minister of the Right (*udaijin*), and four grand councilors (*sangi*), who commonly served concurrently as heads of ministries. Beneath the Grand Chamber were two deliberative bodies, the Chamber of the Left and Chamber of the Right, which had little effective power.

Dajōkan: see Council of State.

Enomoto Takeaki 榎本武揚 (1836–1908): Shogunal naval commander (*kaigun fukusōsai* 海軍副総裁) and advocate of military reform and modernization. In 1868, Enomoto rejected the shogunate's surrender and fled with eight of the government's best ships to Hokkaido. Defeated and then imprisoned from 1869 to 1872, he was pardoned and rehabilitated, later serving as ambassador to Russia, ambassador to China, minister of post and communications, and foreign minister.

eta 穢多: One of the major outcaste groups in Tokugawa society. The eta were associated with animal slaughter, leather work, and the execution of criminals, activities considered ritually unclean. Legal restrictions on the eta, such as limits on place of residence, were formally lifted in 1871.

Etō Shinpei 江藤新平 (1834–1874): Politician active in early Meiji legal and education reform. Born in Saga domain, he led troops in the Boshin War. In the Meiji government, he rose to the rank of grand councilor, served as vice-minister of education (*monbu taifu*文部大輔) and minister of justice (*shihōkyō* 司法卿), and advocated the swift adoption of a new civil code based on the Napoleonic Code. Etō quit the government as part of the 1873 Political Crisis and signed the 1874 petition for an elected national assembly (*minsen giin kenpakusho* 民選議院建白書). After returning to Saga he led an anti-government rebellion and was captured and executed in April 1874.

Grand Chamber (*sei'in* 正院): The main chamber of the Council of State (*dajōkan*).

Grand councilor (*sangi* 参議): A high-ranking position in the Grand Chamber.

hinin 非人: Literally "non-person," one of the major outcaste groups in Tokugawa society. Hinin were largely street entertainers and beggars. Legal restrictions on hinin were formally lifted in 1871.

Hirata Atsutane 平田篤胤 (1776–1843): Influential nativist (*kokugaku*) scholar, known for his public lectures advocating the revival of Japan's "ancient way." Although Hirata styled himself as Motoori Norinaga's disciple, he never studied with Norinaga and revised key aspects of his scholarship.

Hotta Masayoshi 堀田正睦 (1810–1864): Chair of the shogunal council of elders (*rōjū shuza* 老中首座) from 1855 to 1860. Struggled to win imperial support for unpopular foreign treaties.

Inoue Kaoru 井上馨 (1836–1915): Chōshū samurai and Meiji-era politician, early advocate of replacing samurai stipends with government bonds. As vice-minister of finance (*ōkura taifu* 大蔵大輔) in the caretaker government, Inoue rejected budget demands for a new national school system and court system.

Itagaki Taisuke 板垣退助 (1837–1919): Tosa samurai, government official, and political activist. Itagaki fought in the Boshin War and later served in the caretaker government. After resigning during the 1873 Political Crisis, he founded the Public Patriot Party (*Aikoku Kōtō* 愛国公党) and signed the famous 1874 petition for an elected national assembly (*minsen giin setsuritsu kenpakusho* 民撰議院設立建白書). He briefly rejoined the government in 1875 as a grand councilor.

Itō Hirobumi 伊藤博文 (1841–1909): Chōshū samurai and Meiji government official. Studied in Britain in 1863–64 and traveled to the United States in 1870 to examine financial systems. Promoted to grand councilor in 1873, he emerged as a dominant figure in civil administration after the death of Ōkubo in 1878.

Iwakura Mission: An eighteen-month embassy to the United States and Europe (1871–73) that included leading members of the early Meiji government.

Iwakura Tomomi 岩倉具視 **(1825–1883):** Imperial court noble, important in late Tokugawa and early Meiji politics. Instrumental in the 1867/12/9 (January 3, 1868) palace coup that abolished the Tokugawa shogunate. Highest ranking member of the Iwakura Mission (1871–1873) and a key figure in forcing the resignations of caretaker government leaders in the 1873 Political Crisis.

Matsudaira Yoshinaga 松平慶永 **(1828–1890):** Daimyo of Fukui. Also known as Matsudaira Keiei and Matsudaira Shungaku 松平春岳. Important for his attempts to gather daimyo in a national unity government.

Mito 水戸: A collateral domain of the Tokugawa house, Mito daimyo were descendants of the first shogun Tokugawa Ieyasu's eleventh son Yorifusa. Because Mito lords were distant cousins of the shogun, they could provide heirs for the Tokugawa main line when a shogun had no suitable successor. The last shogun, Tokugawa Yoshinobu, was the son of Tokugawa Nariaki, daimyo of Mito.

Mizuno Tadakuni 水野忠邦 **(1794–1851):** Daimyo and shogunal reformer. As chair of the shogun's council of elders (*rōjū shuza* 老中首座), Mizuno sought to strengthen the shogunate by seizing and consolidating daimyo lands around Edo. Stiff opposition forced him from office.

Motoori Norinaga 本居宣長 **(1730–1801):** Influential Tokugawa-era philosopher, known for his commentaries on ancient Japanese texts and his rejection of Chinese learning.

Nariaki: see Tokugawa Nariaki.

Nariakira: see Shimazu Nariakira.

Nativism (kokugaku 国学**):** A Tokugawa-era intellectual and political movement focusing on ancient Japanese texts, the recovery of ancient "ways," and the rejection of Chinese learning.

Ogyū Sorai 荻生徂徠 **(1666–1728):** Influential Tokugawa-era philosopher. Sorai advocated radical reforms but based his proposals on exacting readings of ancient Chinese texts.

Ōkubo Toshimichi 大久保利通 **(1830–1878):** Satsuma samurai and Meiji government official. After helping to establish key structures of the early Meiji state, he left Japan on the Iwakura Mission. Between the 1873 Political Crisis and his assassination in 1878, Ōkubo was Japan's single most powerful political figure.

Ōkuma Shigenobu 大隈重信 **(1838–1922):** Hizen samurai, served as grand councilor and minister of finance in the Meiji government. During the 1881 Political Crisis, Ōkuma advocated the swift promulgation of a constitution with a parliamentary cabinet system and was forced from office.

Roches, Léon (1809–1901): French diplomat and minister plenipotentiary to the Tokugawa shogunate, ally of Tokugawa Yoshinobu.

Saigō Takamori 西郷隆盛 **(1827–1877):** Satsuma samurai, leader of Satsuma's efforts to topple the shogunate. After leaving Meiji government in the 1873 Political Crisis, Saigō retired to Satsuma. In 1877 led Satsuma forces against the central government in the War of the Southwest. Died in battle in September 1877.

Sanjō Sanetomi 三条実美 **(1837–1891):** Imperial court noble, important in late Tokugawa and early Meiji politics. Official titles include minister of the right (udai-jin 右大臣) and grand minister (dajō daijin 太政大臣). Sanjō was nominally the leader of the caretaker government, but he struggled to contain factional rivalries.

Satō Nobuhiro 佐藤信淵 **(1769–1850):** Agronomist and philosopher who advised shogunal senior councilor Mizuno Tadakuni. Satō advocated a strong central government, the conscription of commoners, and an overseas Japanese empire.

Satsuma 薩摩: A tozama daimyo domain in southwestern Kyushu. Ruling house was the Shimazu 島津. Because of its conquest of Ryukyu in 1609, the domain received embassies from Ryukyuan kings and the Shimazu held distinct status within the Tokugawa order. In alliance with Chōshū, Satsuma overthrew the last shogun, Tokugawa Yoshinobu, in 1868. Many key Meiji leaders were from Satsuma, including Ōkubo Toshimichi, Saigō Takamori, and Saigō Tsugumichi.

Shimazu Hisamitsu 島津久光 **(1817–1887):** De facto daimyo of Satsuma, although technically only regent to his son, the daimyo Shimazu Tadayoshi (1840–97). In contrast to his predecessor and half-brother, Nariakira, Hisamitsu rejected many Western-oriented reforms. Although Satsuma troops helped establish the Meiji state, Hisamitsu was a strident critic of the new government.

Shimazu Nariakira 島津斉彬 **(1809–1858):** Daimyo of Satsuma, known for his modernizing reforms including Western-style factories and ships. Half-brother and rival to his successor, Shimazu Hisamitsu.

Sorai: see Ogyū Sorai.

Terashima Munenori 寺島宗則 **(1832–1893):** Satsuma samurai, served as vice-minister of foreign affairs (*gaimu daibu* 外務大輔) in the caretaker government, and foreign minister in the Ōkubo administration.

Tokugawa Kamenosuke 徳川亀之助 **(1863–1940):** Also known as Tayasu Kamenosuke 田安亀之助 and Tokugawa Iesato 徳川家達. Heir to the last Tokugawa shogun, Tokugawa Yoshinobu.

Tokugawa Nariaki 徳川斉昭 **(1800–1860):** Daimyo of Mito domain, known for his embrace and patronage of Mito-learning (Mitogaku), a distinct fusion of Western learning and nativist thought. Abe Masahiro recruited Nariaki as an advisor, but he was purged in 1858 under Ii Naosuke and confined to his residence in Mito. Father of Tokugawa Yoshinobu.

Tokugawa Yoshimune 徳川吉宗 **(1684–1751):** Eighth Tokugawa shogun, known for his reformist policies.

Tokugawa Yoshinobu 徳川慶喜 **(1837–1913):** The last Tokugawa shogun. Also known by the family name Hitotsubashi 一橋 and the given name Keiki. Son of Tokugawa Nariaki. Rejected in the 1858 shogunal succession dispute, Yoshinobu gained power during the mid-1860s and formally succeeded as shogun in 1867. He undertook aggressive centralizing and Westernizing reforms but was outmaneuvered by the Satsuma-Chōshū imperial loyalist alliance.

Yoshimune: see Tokugawa Yoshimune.

Yoshinobu: see Tokugawa Yoshinobu.

Works Consulted

ARCHIVES AND MAJOR ARCHIVAL SOURCES

Archives of the Reformed Church in America, Gardner A. Sage Library of New Brunswick Theological Seminary, New Brunswick, NJ

British Foreign Office, *Japan Correspondence, 1856–1905*, National Archives, Kew, United Kingdom. Accessed through *Nineteenth Century Collections Online*

Historiographical Institute, University of Tokyo (Tōkyō Daigaku Shiryō Hensanjo 東京大学史料編纂所). Electronic access via http://www.hi.u-tokyo.ac.jp/

    *Ishin shiryō kōhon*維新史料稿本, manuscript of the unpublished document collection *Dai Nihon Ishin shiryō*大日本維新史料

    *Shiryō kōhon*史料稿本, manuscript of the partially published document collection *Dai Nihon shiryō*大日本史料

JACAR (Japan Center for Asian Historical Records, Ajia Rekishi Shiryō Sentā アジア歴史資料センター), a division of the National Archives of Japan 国立公文書館. Electronic access via http://www.jacar.go.jp/

Kagoshima Prefectural Library (Kagoshima Kenritsu Toshokan 鹿児島県立図書館)

National Archives of Japan (Kokuritsu kōmonjokan 国立公文書館). Electronic access via http://www.digital.archives.go.jp/

Sapporo Municipal Central Library (Sappro-shi Chūō Toshokan札幌市中央図書館). Electronic access via http://gazo.library.city.sapporo.jp/index.php

Waseda University Rare Books Collection (Waseda Daigaku Toshokan Tokubetsu Shiryōshitsu早稲田大学図書館特別資料室). Electronic access via http://www.wul.waseda.ac.jp/kotenseki/about.html

PUBLISHED SOURCES

Adachi Hiroyuki 安達裕之. *Iyō no fune: yōshikisen dōnyū to sakoku taisei* 異様の船: 洋式船導入と鎖国体制. Tokyo: Heibonsha, 1995.

Adams, Francis Ottiwell. *The History of Japan*. 2 vols. London: Henry S. King, 1875.

Akita, George. *Foundations of Constitutional Government in Modern Japan, 1868–1900*. Cambridge, MA: Harvard University Press, 1967.

Alcock, Rutherford. *The Capital of the Tycoon: A Narrative of a Three Years' Residence in Japan.* 2 vols. New York: Longman, Green, Longman, Roberts, and Green, 1863.

Amino Yoshihiko 網野善彦. *"Nihon" to wa nani ka* 「日本」とは何か. Tokyo: Kōdansha, 2008.

Anderson, Benedict. *Imagined Communities: Reflection on the Origins and Spread of Nationalism.* 2nd ed. London: Verso, 1991.

Anderson, Benedict. *The Spectre of Comparisons: Nationalism, Southeast Asia, and the World.* London: Verso, 1998.

Anghie, Antony. *Imperialism, Sovereignty, and the Making of International Law.* Cambridge: Cambridge University Press, 2004.

Aoki Kazuo 青木和夫, Ishimoda Shō 石母田正, Kobayashi Yoshinori 小林芳規, and Saeki Arikiyo 佐伯有清, eds. *Nihon shisō taikei 1: Kojiki* 日本思想大系1:古事記. Tokyo: Iwanami Shoten, 1982.

Aoyama Tadamasa 青山忠正. *Bakumatsu ishin: honryū no jidai* 幕末維新:奔流の時代. Tokyo: Bun'eidō, 1998.

Arai Hakuseki 新井白石. *Gojiryaku* 五事略. Edited by Takenaka Kunika 竹中邦香. 2 vols. Tokyo: Hakusekisha, 1883.

Araki Moriaki 安良城盛昭. "Ryūkyū shobun ron 琉球処分論." In *Ezochi to Ryūkyū: "Ikoku" no naikokuka to tōgō* 蝦夷地と琉球:「異国」の内国化と統合, edited by Kuwabara Masato 桑原真人 and Gabe Masao 我部政男, 184–214. Tokyo: Yoshikawa Kōbunkan, 2001. Originally published 1978.

Arano, Yasunori. "The Formation of a Japanocentric World Order." *International Journal of Asian Studies* 2, no. 2 (2005): 185–216.

Arano Yasunori 荒野泰典. *Kinsei Nihon to Higashi Ajia* 近世日本と東アジア. Tokyo: Tōkyō Daigaku Shuppankai, 1988.

Arano Yasunori 荒野泰典. *"Sakoku" o minaosu* 「鎖国」を見直す. Kawasaki: Kawasaki Shimin Akademī Shuppanbu, 2003.

Asao Naohiro 朝尾直弘. *Nihon kinseishi no jiritsu* 日本近世史の自立. Tokyo: Azekura Shobō, 1988.

Atwell, William S. "Another Look at Silver Imports into China, ca. 1635–1644." *Journal of World History* 16, no. 4 (2005): 467–489.

Auslin, Michael R. *Negotiating with Imperialism: The Unequal Treaties and the Culture of Japanese Diplomacy.* Cambridge, MA: Harvard University Press, 2004.

Baden-Powell, Robert Stephenson Smyth. *Boy Scouts beyond the Seas: "My World Tour."* London: C. Arthur Pearson, 1913.

Banno, Junji. *Japan's Modern History, 1857–1937: A New Political Narrative.* Translated by J. A. A. Stockwin. London: Routledge/Taylor & Francis Group, 2014.

Banno Junji 坂野潤治. *Mikan no Meiji Ishin* 未完の明治維新. Tokyo: Chikuma Shobō, 2007.

Batten, Bruce L. "Foreign Threat and Domestic Reform: The Emergence of the Ritsuryō State." *Monumenta Nipponica* 41, no. 2 (1986): 199–219.

Bayly, C. A. *The Birth of the Modern World, 1780–1914: Global Connections and Comparisons.* Malden, MA: Blackwell, 2004.

Bayly, C. A. and Eugenio F. Biagini, eds. *Giuseppe Mazzini and the Globalisation of Democratic Nationalism 1830–1920.* New York: Oxford University Press, 2008.

Beasley, W. G. *Select Documents on Japanese Foreign Policy, 1853–1868.* London: Oxford University Press, 1955.

Beasley, W. G. *The Meiji Restoration.* Stanford, CA: Stanford University Press, 1972.

Beckmann, George M. *The Making of the Meiji Constitution: The Oligarchs and the Constitutional Development of Japan, 1868–1891.* Lawrence: University of Kansas Press, 1957.

Beckmann, George M. "Political Crises and the Crystallization of Japanese Constitutional Thought, 1871–1881." *Pacific Historical Review* 23, no. 3 (1954): 259–270.

Beisner, Robert L. *From the Old Diplomacy to the New, 1865–1900.* 2nd. ed. Arlington Heights, IL: Harlan Davidson, 1986.

Benton, Lauren A. *A Search for Sovereignty: Law and Geography in European Empires, 1400–1900.* Cambridge: Cambridge University Press, 2010.

Benyowsky, Maurice Auguste, comte de. *Memoirs and travels of Mauritius Augustus Count de Benyowsky; magnate of the kingdoms of Hungary and Poland, one of the chiefs of the confederation of Poland, &c. &c. Consisting of his military operations in Poland, his exile into Kamchatka, his escape and voyage . . . through the northern Pacific Ocean, . . . Written by himself. Translated from the original manuscript. In two volumes.* 2 vols. London: G. G. J. and J. Robinson, 1790.

Berry, Mary Elizabeth. *Hideyoshi.* Cambridge, MA: Harvard University Press, 1982.

Best, Jonathan W. *A History of the Early Korean Kingdom of Paekche: Together with an Annotated Translation of the Paekche Annals of the Samguk Sagi.* Cambridge, MA: Harvard University Asia Center, 2006.

Birt, Michael P. "Samurai in Passage: The Transformation of the Sixteenth-Century Kanto." *Journal of Japanese Studies* 11, no. 2 (1985): 369–399.

Bitō Masahide 尾藤正英 and Shimazaki Takao 島崎隆夫, eds. *Nihon shisō taikei 45: Andō Shōeki, Satō Nobuhiro* 日本思想体系45:安藤昌益, 佐藤信淵. Tokyo: Iwanami Shoten, 1977.

Bix, Herbert. *Peasant Protest in Japan: 1590–1884.* New Haven, CT: Yale University Press, 1986.

Blussé, Leonard. "Bull in a China Shop: Pieter Nuyts in China and Japan (1627–1634)." In *Around and about Formosa: Essays in Honor of Professor Ts'ao Yung-ho,* edited by Yonghe Cao and Leonard Blussé, 95–110. Taipei: Ts'ao Yung-ho Foundation for Culture and Education, 2003.

Bol, Peter. "Creating a GIS for the History of China." In *Placing History: How Maps, Spatial Data, and GIS Are Changing Historical Scholarship,* edited by Anne Kelly Knowles and Amy Hillier, 27–59. Redlands, CA: ESRI Press, 2008.

Bolitho, Harold. *Treasures among Men: The Fudai Daimyo in Tokugawa Japan.* New Haven, CT: Yale University Press, 1974.

Botsman, Daniel V. "Freedom without Slavery? 'Coolies,' Prostitutes, and Outcastes in Meiji Japan's 'Emancipation Moment.'" *American Historical Review* 116, no. 5 (2011): 1323–1347.

Bousquet, Georges. *Le Japon de nos jours et les échelles de l'extrême Orient.* 2 vols. Paris: Hachette, 1877.

Bradley, James. *Flyboys: A True Story of Courage.* Boston: Little, Brown, 2003.

Breen, John. "The Imperial Oath of April 1868: Ritual, Politics, and Power in the Restoration." *Monumenta Nipponica* 51, no. 4 (1996): 407–429.

"Brief History of the Government Troubles and Their Result—Our Intercourse with the Country—Remarks of Gov. Ito of Jeddo." *New York Times*, May 14, 1871, 1.

Brown, Philip C. "The Mismeasure of Land. Land Surveying in the Tokugawa Period." *Monumenta Nipponica* 42, no. 2 (1987): 115–155.

Brown, Philip C. "Practical Constraints on Early Tokugawa Land Taxation: Annual versus Fixed Assessments in Kaga Domain." *Journal of Japanese Studies* 14 no. 2 (1988): 369–401.

Brown, Philip C. *Central Authority and Local Autonomy in the Formation of Early Modern Japan: The Case of Kaga Domain.* Stanford, CA: Stanford University Press, 1993.

Brown, Philip C. *Cultivating Commons: Joint Ownership of Arable Land in Early Modern Japan.* Honolulu: University of Hawai`i Press, 2011.

Brown, Sidney DeVere. "Crisis of 1873." In *Modern Japan: An Encyclopedia of History, Culture, and Nationalism,* edited by James L. Huffman, xxxiii. New York: Garland, 1998.

Brunet, J. L. *Les ordres de chevalerie et les distinctions honorifiques au Japon.* Paris: Actualités diplomatiques et coloniales, 1903.

Burns, Susan L. *Before the Nation: Kokugaku and the Imagining of Community in Early Modern Japan.* Durham, NC: Duke University Press, 2003.

Burns, Susan L. "The Politics of Philology in Japan: Ancient Texts, Language, and Japanese Identity." In *World Philology,* edited by Sheldon Pollock, Benjamin A. Elman, and Ku-ming Kevin Chang, 245–263. Cambridge, MA: Harvard University Press, 2015.

Butler, Lee A. "Tokugawa Ieyasu's Regulations for the Court: A Reappraisal." *Harvard Journal of Asiatic Studies* 54, no. 2 (1994): 509–551.

Buyō Inshi 武陽陰士. "Seji kenbunroku 世事見聞録." In *Nihon shomin seikatsu shiryō shūsei* 日本庶民生活史料集成, edited by Miyamoto Tsuneichi 宮本常一, Haraguchi Torao 原口虎雄, and Higa Shunchō 比嘉春潮, 8: 641–766. Tokyo: San'ichi Shobō, 1969. Originally published 1816.

Buyō Inshi 武陽陰士. *Lust, Commerce, and Corruption: An Account of What I Have Seen and Heard, by an Edo Samurai.* Translated by Mark Teeuwen, Kate Wildman Nakai, Miyazaki Fumiko, Anne Walthall, and John Breen. Edited by Mark Teeuwen and Kate Wildman Nakai. New York: Columbia University Press, 2014.

Calman, Donald. *The Nature and Origins of Japanese Imperialism.* London: Routledge, 1992.

Cerulo, Karen A. "Symbols and the World System: National Anthems and Flags." *Sociological Forum* 8, no. 2 (1993): 243–271.

Ch'en, Paul Heng-Chao. *The Formation of the Early Meiji Legal Order: The Japanese Code of 1871 and Its Chinese Foundation.* New York: Oxford University Press, 1981.

Chaiklin, Martha. "Monopolists to Middlemen: Dutch Liberalism and American Imperialism in the Opening of Japan." *Journal of World History* 21, no. 2 (2010): 249–269.

Chakrabarty, Dipesh. "Towards a Discourse on Nationalism." Review of *Nationalist Thought and the Colonial World: A Derivative Discourse* by Partha Chatterjee. *Economic and Political Weekly* 22 (1987): 1137–1138.

Chang, Richard T. "General Grant's 1879 Visit to Japan." *Monumenta Nipponica* 24, no. 4 (1969): 373–392.

Chapman, David. "Different Faces, Different Spaces: Identifying the Islanders of Ogasawara." *Social Science Japan Journal* 14, no. 2 (2011): 189–212.

Chapman, David. "Inventing Subjects: Early History of the 'Naturalized Foreigners' of the Bonin (Ogasawara) Islands." *Asia Pacific Journal* 7: 24 (2009). http://apjjf. org/-David-Chapman/3169/article.html.

Chatterjee, Partha. *Nationalist Thought and the Colonial World: A Derivative Discourse.* London: Zed Books, 1986.

Clark, Donald N. "Sino-Korean Tributary Relations under the Ming." In *The Cambridge History of China 8 part I.* edited by Denis C. Twitchett and Frederick W. Mote, 272-300. Cambridge: Cambridge University Press, 1998

Clulow, Adam. *The Company and the Shogun: The Dutch Encounter with Tokugawa Japan.* New York: Columbia University Press, 2014.

Clulow, Adam. "From Global Entrepôt to Early Modern Domain: Hirado, 1609–1641." *Monumenta Nipponica* 65, no. 1 (2010): 1–35.

Cocks, Richard. *Diary of Richard Cocks, Cape-merchant in the English Factory in Japan, 1615–1622.* Edited by Edward Maunde Thompson. 2 vols. London: Hakluyt Society, 1883.

Conlan, Thomas. *Weapons & Fighting Techniques of the Samurai Warrior, 1200–1877 AD.* London: Amber Books, 2008.

Cooney, Kevin J. and Alex Scarbrough. "Japan and South Korea: Can These Two Nations Work Together?" *Asian Affairs* 35, no. 3 (2008): 173–192.

Cooper, Frederick. *Colonialism in Question: Theory, Knowledge, History.* Berkeley: University of California Press, 2005.

Cooper, Michael, ed. *They Came to Japan: An Anthology of European Reports on Japan, 1543–1640.* Berkeley: University of California Press, 1965.

Craig, Albert. "The Restoration Movement in Choshu." *Journal of Asian Studies* 18, no. 2 (1959): 187–197.

Craig, Albert. *Chōshū in the Meiji Restoration.* Cambridge, MA: Harvard University Press, 1961.

Cranmer-Byng, J. L. "Russian and British Interests in the Far East 1791–1793." *Canadian Slavonic Papers/Revue Canadienne des Slavistes* 10, no. 3 (1968): 357–375.

Crawcour, E. Sydney. "Economic Change in the Nineteenth Century." In *Cambridge History of Japan*, Vol. 5: *The Nineteenth Century*, edited by Kozo Yamamura, 569–617. Cambridge: Cambridge University Press, 1989.

Crawcour, E. Sydney. "Industrialization and Technological Change, 1885–1920." In *Cambridge History of Japan*, Vol. 6: *The Twentieth Century*, edited by Peter Duus, 385–450. Cambridge: Cambridge University Press, 1989.

Cumings, Bruce. *Korea's Place in the Sun: A Modern History*. New York: Norton, 1997.

Dajōkan 太政官. *Dajōkan nisshi* 太政官日誌. Tokyo: Dajōkan, 1876.

Dajōkan 太政官, ed. *Fukkoki* 復古記. 15 vols. Tokyo: Naigai Shoseki, 1930–1931.

Davis, Winston. *The Moral and Political Naturalism of Baron Katō Hiroyuki*. Berkeley: Institute of East Asian Studies, University of California, 1996.

De Bary, William Theodore, Carol Gluck, and Arthur Tiedemann. *Sources of Japanese Tradition*, Vol. 2: *1600 to 2000*. 2nd ed. New York: Columbia University Press, 2005.

de Heer, Philip. "Three Embassies to Seoul: Sino-Korean Relations in the 15th Century." In *Conflict and Accommodation in Early Modern East Asia: Essays in Honour of Erik Zurcher*, edited by Leonard Blussé and Harriet T. Zurndorfer, 240–257. Leiden: E. J. Brill, 1993

Devine, Richard. "Hirata Atsutane and Christian Sources." *Monumenta Nipponica* 36, no. 1 (1981): 37–54.

Dickins, F. Victor and Stanley Lane-Poole. *The Life of Sir Harry Parkes: K.C.B., G.C.M.G., sometime Her Majesty's Minister to China and Japan*. London: Macmillan, 1894.

Duara, Prasenjit. "Civilizations and Nations in a Globalizing World." In *Reflections on Multiple Modernities: European, Chinese, and Other Interpretations*, edited by Dominic Sachsenmaier and S. N. Eisenstadt, 79–99. Leiden: Brill, 2002.

Duara, Prasenjit. *Rescuing History from the Nation: Questioning Narratives of Modern China*. Chicago: University of Chicago Press, 1995.

Duara, Prasenjit. *Sovereignty and Authenticity: Manchukuo and the East Asian Modern*. Lanham: Rowman & Littlefield, 2003.

Dudden, Alexis. "Japanese Colonial Control in International Terms." *Japanese Studies* 25, no. 1 (2005): 1–20.

Dudden, Alexis. *Troubled Apologies among Japan, Korea, and the United States*. New York: Columbia University Press, 2008.

Duke, Benjamin C. *The History of Modern Japanese Education: Constructing the National School System, 1872–1890*. New Brunswick, NJ: Rutgers University Press, 2009.

Duus, Peter. *The Abacus and the Sword: The Japanese Penetration of Korea, 1895–1910*. Berkeley: University of California Press, 1995.

Elisonias, Jurgis. "Christianity and the Daimyo." In *The Cambridge History of Japan*, Vol. 4: *Early Modern Japan*, edited by John Whitney Hall, 301–372. Cambridge: Cambridge University Press, 1991.

Emura Eiichi 江村栄一, ed. *Nihon kindai shisō taikei 9: Kenpō kōsō* 日本近代思想体系9:憲法構想. Tokyo: Iwanami Shoten, 1989.

Enjōji Kiyoshi 円城寺清. *Ōkuma-haku sekijitsutan* 大隈伯昔日譚. Tokyo: Rikken Kaishintō Tōhōkyoku 1895.

Epp, Robert. "The Challenge from Tradition: Attempts to Compile a Civil Code in Japan, 1866–78." *Monumenta Nipponica* 22, no. 1/2 (1967): 15–48.

Ericson, Steven J. "Orthodox Finance and 'The Dictates of Practical Expediency': Influences on Matsukata Masayoshi and the Financial Reform of 1881–1885." *Monumenta Nipponica* 71, no. 1 (2016): 83–117.

Ericson, Steven J. "The 'Matsukata Deflation' Reconsidered: Financial Stabilization and Japanese Exports in a Global Depression, 1881–85." *The Journal of Japanese Studies* 40, no. 1 (2014): 1–28.

Eskildsen, Robert. "An Army as Good and Efficient as Any in the World: James Wasson and Japan's 1874 Expedition to Taiwan." *Asian Cultural Studies* 36 (2010): 45–62.

Eskildsen, Robert. "Of Civilization and Savages: The Mimetic Imperialism of Japan's 1874 Expedition to Taiwan." *American Historical Review* 107, no. 2 (2002): 388–418.

Eskildsen, Robert. "Suitable Ships and the Hard Work of Imperialism: Evaluating the Japanese Navy in the 1874 Invasion of Taiwan." *Asian Cultural Studies* 38 (2012): 47–60.

Eskildsen, Robert. *Recursive Imperialism.* forthcoming.

Ferguson, Niall. *Civilization: The West and the Rest.* London: Allen Lane, 2011.

Fiala, Karel. "First Contacts of Czechs and Slovaks with Japanese Culture (Up to World War I): The Major Publications and Personalities." *Japan Review: Journal of the International Research Center for Japan Studies* 3 (1992): 45–71.

Filmore, Millard. "Message from the President of the United States, communicating, in compliance with a resolution of the Senate, certain official documents relative to the Empire of Japan, and serving to illustrate the existing relations between the United States and Japan." In *U.S. Senate Serial Set Vol. No. 620, Session Vol. No.9. 32nd Congress, 1st Session. S.Exec.Doc. 59,* 1852, 80–82.

Flueckiger, Peter. *Imagining Harmony: Poetry, Empathy, and Community in Mid-Tokugawa Confucianism and Nativism.* Stanford, CA: Stanford University Press, 2011.

Flynn, Dennis O. and Arturo Giráldez. "Arbitrage, China, and World Trade in the Early Modern Period." *Journal of the Economic and Social History of the Orient* 38, no. 4 (1995): 429–448.

Flynn, Dennis O. and Arturo Giráldez. "Born with a 'Silver Spoon': The Origin of World Trade in 1571." *Journal of World History* 6, no. 2 (1995): 201–221.

Flynn, Dennis O. and Arturo Giráldez. "Cycles of Silver: Global Economic Unity through the Mid-Eighteenth Century." *Journal of World History* 13, no. 2 (2002): 391–427.

Fogel, Joshua A. "2011 Arthur O. Lovejoy Lecture The Gold Seal of 57 CE and the Afterlife of an Inanimate Object." *Journal of the History of Ideas* 73, no. 3 (2012): 351–369.

Fogel, Joshua A. *Articulating the Sinosphere: Sino-Japanese Relations in Space and Time*. Cambridge, MA: Harvard University Press, 2009.

Fox, Grace Estelle. *Britain and Japan, 1858–1883*. Oxford, UK: Clarendon Press, 1969.

Frantz, Edward O., ed. *A Companion to the Reconstruction Presidents 1865–1881*. Chichester, West Sussex, UK: Wiley Blackwell, 2014.

Fraser, Andrew. "The Expulsion of Ōkuma from the Government in 1881." *Journal of Asian Studies* 26, no. 2 (1967): 213–236.

Fraser, Andrew. "Hachisuka Mochiaki (1846–1918): A Meiji Domain Lord and Statesmen." *Papers on Far Eastern History (Canberra)* 2 (1970): 43–61.

Fraser, Andrew. "Hachisuka Mochiaki (1846–1918): From Feudal Lord to Businessman." *Paper on Far Eastern History (Australian National University)* 37 (1988): 93–104.

Fraser, Andrew. "The Osaka Conference of 1875." *Journal of Asian Studies* 26, no. 4 (1967): 589–610.

Fróis, Luís. *Historia de Japam*. Edited by Josef Wicki. 5 vols. 1583–1587. Reprint, Lisbon: Biblioteca Nacional de Lisboa, 1976.

Fromkin, David. "The Great Game in Asia." *Foreign Affairs* 58, no. 4 (1980): 936–951.

Fujii Noriyuki 藤井徳行. "Meiji gannen iwayuru 'Tōhoku chōtei' seiritsu ni kansuru ichi kōsatsu: Rinnōjinomiya Kōgenhō Shinnō o megutte 明治元年・所謂「東北朝廷」成立に関する一考察・輪王寺宮公現法親王をめぐって." In *Kindai Nihonshi no shinkenkyū*, Vol. 1 近代日本史の新研究 1, edited by Tezuka Yutaka 手塚豊, 219–316. Tokyo: Hokuju Shuppan, 1981.

Fujimura Michio 藤村道生. "Chōheirei no seiritsu 徴兵令の成立." *Rekishigaku kenkyū* 歴史学研究, no. 428 (1976): 1–18.

Fujino Tamotsu 藤野保. *Shintei bakuhan taiseishi no kenkyū* 新訂幕藩体制史の研究. Tokyo: Yoshikawa Kōbunkan, 1975.

Fujita Satoru 藤田覚. "Bakufu Ezo-chi seisaku no tenkan to Kunashiri-Menashi jiken 幕府蝦夷地政策の転換とクナシリ・メナシ事件." In *Jūhasseiki Nihon no seiji to gaikō* 十八世紀日本の政治と外交,, edited by Fujita Satoru 藤田覚, 215–234. Tokyo: Yamakawa Shuppansha, 2010.

Fujita Satoru 藤田覚. *Kinsei kōki seijishi to taigai kankei* 近世後期政治史と対外関係. Tokyo: Tōkyō Daigaku Shuppankai, 2005.

Fujita Satoru 藤田覚. *Kinsei no san dai-kaikaku* 近世の三大改革. Tokyo: Yamakawa Shuppansha, 2002.

Fujitani, Takashi. *Splendid Monarchy: Power and Pageantry in Modern Japan*. Berkeley: University of California Press, 1996.

Fukuchi Atsushi 福地惇. "Risshisha no kyohei keikaku ni tsuite 立志社の挙兵計画について." *Nihon rekishi* 日本歴史 531 (1992): 91–97.

Fukuzawa, Yukichi. *An Encouragement of Learning*. Translated by David A. Dilworth. New York: Columbia University Press, 2012.

Gaimushō 外務省. *Dai Nihon gaikō bunsho* 大日本外交文書. Tokyo: Nihon Kokusai Kyōkai, 1936–63.

Garon, Sheldon. *Beyond Our Means: Why America Spends While the World Saves.* Princeton, NJ: Princeton University Press, 2011.

Gellner, Ernst. *Nations and Nationalism.* Ithaca, NY: Cornell University Press, 1983.

Giddens, Anthony. *The Constitution of Society.* Berkeley: University of California Press, 1984.

Giddens, Anthony. *The Nation-State and Violence,* Vol. 2 of *A Contemporary Critique of Historical Materialism.* Berkeley: University of California Press, 1985.

Giddens, Anthony and Christopher Pierson. *Conversations with Anthony Giddens: Making Sense of Modernity.* Stanford, CA: Stanford University Press, 1998.

Ginsburg, Tom. "Eastphalia and East Asian Regionalism." *University of California Davis Law Review* 44, no. 3 (2010): 859–877.

Gluck, Carol. "The End of Elsewhere: Writing Modernity Now." *American Historical Review* 116, no. 3 (2011): 676–687.

Gluck, Carol. *Japan's Modern Myths.* Princeton, NJ: Princeton University Press, 1985.

Golovnin, Vasilii Mikhailovich and Petr Ivanovich Rikord. *Narrative of My Captivity in Japan, during the Years 1811, 1812 & 1813.* 2 vols. London: Henry Colburn, 1818.

Gossedge, Rob and Stephen Knight. "The Arthur of the Sixteenth to Nineteenth Centuries." In *The Cambridge Companion to the Arthurian Legend,* edited by Elizabeth Archibald and Ad Putter, 103–119. Cambridge: Cambridge University Press, 2009.

Goswami, Manu. "Rethinking the Modular Nation Form: Toward a Sociohistorical Conception of Nationalism." *Comparative Studies in Society and History* 44, no. 4 (2002): 770–799.

Gotō Yasushi 後藤靖. *Kokushi daijiten* 国史大事典, s.v. "Shinpūren no ran 神風連の乱." Tokyo: Yoshikawa kōbunkan, 1979–1997.

Gramlich-Oka, Bettina. "Tadano Makuzu and Her Hitori Kangae." *Monumenta Nipponica* 56, no. 1 (2001): 1–20.

Grant, Ulysses S. *The Papers of Ulysses S. Grant.* Edited by John Y. Simon and John F. Marszalek. 31 vols. Carbondale: Southern Illinois University Press, 1967–2009.

Griffis, William Elliot. *Verbeck of Japan: A Citizen of No Country.* Edinburgh: Oliphant, Anderson & Ferrier, 1901.

Gulik, R. H. van. "Kakkaron 隔鞾論: A Japanese Echo of the Opium War." *Monumenta Serica* 4, no. 2 (1940): 478–545.

Haboush, JaHyun Kim. *A Heritage of Kings: One Man's Monarchy in the Confucian World.* New York: Columbia University Press, 1988.

Hakodate Shishi Hensanshitsu 函館市史編さん室, ed. *Hakodate shishi: tsūsetsu hen* 函館市史 通説編. 3 vols. Hakodate: Hakodate-shi, 1980.

Hall, John Whitney. *Tanuma Okitsugu, 1719–1788: Forerunner of Modern Japan.* Cambridge, MA: Harvard University Press, 1955.

Hanawa Hokinoichi 塙保己一, ed. *Zoku gunsho ruijū* 続群書類従. Vol. 30, part 1. Tokyo: Zoku Gunsho Ruijū Kanseikai, 1925.

Hanley, Susan B. "A High Standard of Living in Nineteenth-Century Japan: Fact or Fantasy?" *Journal of Economic History* 43, no. 1 (1983): 183–192.

Hansen, Wilburn. "The Medium Is the Message: Hirata Atsutane's Ethnography of the World Beyond." *History of Religions* 45, no. 4 (2006): 337–372.

Hansen, Wilburn. *When Tengu Talk: Hirata Atsutane's Ethnography of the Other World.* Honolulu: University of Hawai'i Press, 2008.

Hara Nensai 原念斎, Minamoto Ryōen 源了圓, and Maeda Tsutomu 前田勉, eds. *Sentetsu sōdan* 先哲叢談. Tokyo: Heibonsha, 1994.

Hara, Takemichi. "Korea, China, and Western Barbarians: Diplomacy in Early Nineteenth-Century Korea." *Modern Asian Studies* 32, no. 2 (1998): 389–430.

Harada Nobuo 原田信男. *Edo no ryōrishi: ryōribon to ryōri bunka* 江戸の料理史: 料理本と料理文化. Tokyo: Chūō Kōron Sha, 1989.

Hardacre, Helen. "Creating State Shinto: The Great Promulgation Campaign and the New Religions." *Journal of Japanese Studies* 12, no. 1 (1986): 29–63.

Harootunian, Harry D. "Late Tokugawa Thought and Culture." In *The Cambridge History of Japan*, Vol. 5: *The Nineteenth Century*, edited by John Whitney Hall, 168–258. Cambridge: Cambridge University Press, 1989.

Harootunian, Harry D. "Remembering the Historical Present." *Critical Inquiry* 33, no. 3 (2007): 471–494.

Harootunian, Harry D. "The Economic Rehabilitation of the Samurai in the Early Meiji Period." *Journal of Asian Studies* 19, no. 4 (1960): 433–444.

Harootunian, Harry D. *Things Seen and Unseen: Discourse and Ideology in Tokugawa Nativism.* Chicago: University of Chicago Press, 1988.

Harootunian, Harry D. *Toward Restoration: The Growth of Political Consciousness in Tokugawa Japan.* Berkeley: University of California Press, 1970.

Harris, Townsend. *The Complete Journal of Townsend Harris: First American Consul and Minister to Japan.* Rutland, VT: Charles E. Tuttle, 1959.

Harrison, John A. "The Capron Mission and the Colonization of Hokkaido, 1868–1875." *Agricultural History* 25, no. 3 (1951): 135–142.

Hawks, Francis L., ed. *Narrative of the Expedition of an American Squadron to the China Seas and Japan, performed in the years 1852, 1853, and 1854, under the command of Commodore M.C. Perry, United States Navy, by order of the government of the United States. Compiled from the original notes and journals of Commodore Perry and his officers at his request, and under his supervision.* Washington, DC: A.O.P. Nicholson, 1856.

Hayami, Akira. "The Myth of Primogeniture and Impartible Inheritance in Tokugawa Japan." *Journal of Family History* 8, no. 1 (1983): 3–29.

Hayami, Akira and Satomi Kurosu. "Regional Diversity in Demographic and Family Patterns in Preindustrial Japan." *Journal of Japanese Studies* 27, no. 2 (2001): 295–321.

Hayashi Shihei 林子平. *Kaikoku heidan* 海国兵談. Tokyo: Tonansha, 1916.

Hellyer, Robert I. *Defining Engagement: Japan and Global Contexts, 1640–1868.* Cambridge, MA: Harvard University Asia Center, 2009.

Hellyer, Robert I. "The Missing Pirate and the Pervasive Smuggler: Regional Agency in Coastal Defence, Trade, and Foreign Relations in Nineteenth-Century Japan." *International History Review* 27, no. 1 (2005): 1–24.

Hevia, James Louis. *Cherishing Men from Afar: Qing Guest Ritual and the Macartney Embassy of 1793*. Durham, NC: Duke University Press, 1995.

Hevia, James Louis. *English Lessons: The Pedagogy of Imperialism in Nineteenth-Century China*. Durham, NC: Duke University Press, 2003.

Higashionna Kanjun 東恩納寬惇. *Higashionna Kanjun zenshū* 東恩納寬惇全集. Vol. 1. Edited by Ryūkyū Shinpōsha 琉球新報社. Tokyo: Daiichi Shobō, 1978.

Hirakawa Arata 平川新. *Kaikoku e no michi* 開国への道: Shōgakkan, 2008.

Hirano, Katsuya. "Thanatopolitics in the Making of Japan's Hokkaido: Settler Colonialism and Primitive Accumulation." *Critical Historical Studies* 2, no. 2 (2015): 191–218.

Hirata Atsutane 平田篤胤. *Hirata Atsutane zenshū* 平田篤胤全集. Edited by Muromatsu Iwao 室松岩雄. 15 vols. Tokyo: Itchidō shoten, 1911–18.

Hobsbawm, E. J. "Introduction: Inventing Traditions." In *The Invention of Tradition*, edited by E. J. Hobsbawm and T. O. Ranger, 1–14. Cambridge: Cambridge University Press, 1983.

Hokkaidō chō 北海道庁, ed. *Shinsen Hokkaidō shi* 新撰北海道史. 7 vols. Sapporo: Hokkaidō chō, 1936–37.

Homei, Aya. "Birth Attendants in Meiji Japan: The Rise of a Medical Birth Model and the New Division of Labour." *Social History of Medicine* 19, no. 3 (2006): 407–424.

Hostetler, Laura. *Qing Colonial Enterprise: Ethnography and Cartography in Early Modern China*. Chicago: University of Chicago Press, 2001.

Howe, Stephen. *Empire: A Very Short Introduction*. Oxford: Oxford University Press, 2002.

Howell, David L. *Geographies of Identity in Nineteenth-century Japan*. Berkeley: University of California Press, 2005.

Howell, David L. "Hard Times in the Kantō: Economic Change and Village Life in Late Tokugawa Japan." *Modern Asian Studies* 23, no. 2 (1989): 349–371.

Howland, Douglas. "Japan and the Universal Postal Union: An Alternative Internationalism in the 19th Century." *Social Science Japan Journal* 17, no. 1 (2014): 23-39.

Howland, Douglas. "An Alternative Mode of International Order: The International Administrative Union in the Nineteenth Century." *Review of International Studies* 41, no. 1 (2015): 161–183.

Huber, Thomas M. *The Revolutionary Origins of Modern Japan*. Stanford, CA: Stanford University Press, 1981.

Huffman, James L. *Creating a Public: People and Press in Meiji Japan*. Honolulu: University of Hawai'i Press, 1997.

Hui, Victoria Tin-bor. *War and State Formation in Ancient China and Early Modern Europe*. Cambridge: Cambridge University Press, 2005.

Huntington, Samuel P. "The Clash of Civilizations?" *Foreign Affairs* 72, no. 3 (1993): 22–49.

Ikai Takaaki 猪飼隆明. *Seinan sensō: sensō no taigi to dōinsareru minshū* 西南戦争―戦争の大義と動員される民衆. Tokyo: Yoshikawa Kōbunkan, 2008.

Ikai Takaaki 猪飼隆明. *Saigō Takamori: Seinan sensō e no michi* 西郷隆盛:西南戦争への道. Tokyo: Iwanami Shoten, 1992.

Ikegami, Eiko. *The Taming of the Samurai*. Cambridge, MA: Harvard University Press, 1995.

Ikeuchi Satoshi 池内敏. *Taikun gaikō to "bui": kinsei Nihon no kokusai chitsujo to Chōsen-kan* 大君外交と「武威」―近世日本の国際秩序と朝鮮観. Nagoya: Nagoya Daigaku Shuppankai, 2006.

Imai Usaburō 今井宇三郎, Seya Yoshihiko 瀬谷義彦, and Bitō Masahide 尾藤正英, eds. *Nihon shisō taikei 53: Mitogaku* 日本思想体系 53: 水戸学. 日本思想体系. Tokyo: Iwanami Shoten, 1973.

Imaizumi Teisuke 今泉定介 and Ichishima Kenkichi 市島謙吉, eds. *Arai Hakuseki zenshū* 新井白石全集. 6 vols. Tokyo: Yoshikawa Hanshichi, 1905–1907.

Inaba Masakuni 稲葉正邦, ed. *Yodo Inaba-ke monjo* 淀稲葉家文書. Tokyo: Nihon Shiseki Kyōkai, 1926.

Inagaki Reiko 稲垣令子. "Kinsei Ezochi ni okeru girei shihai no tokushitsu: uimamu, omusha no hensen o tōshite 近世蝦夷地における儀礼支配の特質・ウイマム・オムシャの変遷を通して." In *Minshū seikatsu to shinkō shisō* 民衆生活と信仰・思想, edited by Minshūshi Kenkyūkai 民衆史研究会. Tokyo: Yūzankaku, 1985.

Innes, Robert LeRoy. "The Door Ajar: Japan's Foreign Trade in the Seventeenth Century." Ph.D. diss., University of Michigan, 1980.

Inobe Shigeo 井野邊茂雄. *Ishin zenshi no kenkyū* 維新前史の研究. Rev. ed. Tokyo: Chūbunkan, 1942.

Inoue Katsuo 井上勝生. *Bakumatsu ishin* 幕末・維新. Tokyo: Iwanami Shoten, 2006.

Ion, A. Hamish. *American Missionaries, Christian Oyatoi, and Japan, 1859–73*. Vancouver: University of British Columbia Press, 2009.

Irokawa, Daikichi. *The Culture of the Meiji Period*. Translation edited by Marius B. Jansen. 1969. Reprint, Princeton, NJ: Princeton University Press, 1985.

Irokawa Daikichi 色川大吉 and Gabe Takao 我部政男, eds. *Meiji kenpakusho shūsei* 明治建白書集成. 9 vols. Tokyo: Chikuma Shobō, 1987–2000.

Irwin, Dana. "Sheikhs and Samurai: Léon Roches and the French Imperial Project." *Southeast Review of Asian Studies* 30 (2008): 23–40.

Ishii Ryōsuke 石井良助. "'Minpō ketsugi' kaidai 「民法決議」解題." In *Meiji bunka zenshū* 明治文化全集, edited by Meiji Bunka Zenshū Kenkyūkai 明治文化全集研究会, 13:39–41. Tokyo: Nihon Hyōron Shinsha, 1929.

Ishii Ryōsuke 石井良助, ed. *Tokugawa kinreikō* 德川禁令考. Enlarged ed. 11 vols. Tokyo: Sōbunsha, 1959–1961.

Ishii, Susumu. "The Decline of the Kamakura Bakufu." In *The Cambridge History of Japan*, Vol. 3: *Medieval Japan*, edited by Kozo Yamamura. Translated by Jeffrey

P. Mass and Hitomi Tonomura, 128–174. Cambridge: Cambridge University Press, 1990.

Ishii, Yoneo. *The Junk Trade from Southeast Asia: Translations from the Tōsen fusetsu-gaki, 1674–1723*. Singapore: Institute of Southeast Asian Studies, 1998.

"Ito Hirobumi." *Outlook (1893–1924)*, May 4, 1901, 77.

Itō, Tasaburō. "The Book Banning Policy of the Tokugawa Shogunate." *Acta Asiatica* 22 (1972): 36–61.

"Ito, the Pioneer of the New Nippon." *Current Literature (New York)* 39, no. 3 (1905): 325–327.

Iwai Shigeki 岩井茂樹. "Shindai no goshi to 'chinmoku gaikō' 清代の互市と「沈黙外交」." In *Chūgoku Higashi Ajia gaikō kōryū-shi no kenkyū* 中国東アジア外交交流史の研究, edited by Fuma Susumu 夫馬進, 354–390. Kyoto: Kyōto Daigaku Gakujutsu Shuppankai, 2007.

Iwao Seiichi 岩生成一. "Nanyō Nihonmachi no kenkyū 南洋日本町の研究." In *Yamada Nagamasa shiryō shūsei* 山田長政資料集成, edited by Yamada Nagamasa Kenshōkai 山田長政顕彰会, 259–302. Shizuoka: Yamada Nagamasa Kenshōkai, 1974.

Iwashita Tetsunori 岩下哲典. *Edo no kaigai jōhō nettowāku* 江戸の海外情報ネットワーク. Tokyo: Yoshikawa Kōbunkan, 2006.

Iwashita Tetsunori 岩下哲典. *Edo no Naporeon densetsu: Seiyō eiyū den wa dō yomareta ka* 江戸のナポレオン伝説: 西洋英雄伝はどう読まれたか. Tokyo: Chūō Kōron Shinsha, 1999.

Iwashita Tetsunori 岩下哲典 and Kobayashi Tetsuya 小林哲也. "Kōmei tennō wa tennentō de dokusatsu sareta 孝明天皇は天然痘で毒殺された." *Rekishitsū* 歴史通 20, no. 9 (2012): 194–205.

Izui Asako 泉井朝子. "Tashidaka-sei ni kansuru ichi kōsatsu 足高制に関する一考察." *Gakushūin shigaku* 学習院史学, no. 2 (1965): 70–88.

Jansen, Marius B. *The Japanese and Sun Yat-sen*. Cambridge, MA: Harvard University Press, 1954.

Jansen, Marius B. *The Making of Modern Japan*. Cambridge, MA: Belknap Press of Harvard University Press, 2000.

Jansen, Marius B. *Sakamoto Ryōma and the Meiji Restoration*. Princeton, NJ: Princeton University Press, 1961.

Jaundrill, D. Colin. *Samurai to Soldier: Remaking Military Service in Nineteenth-century Japan*. Ithaca, NY: Cornell University Press, 2016.

Jennings, Justin. *Globalizations and the Ancient World*. Cambridge: Cambridge University Press, 2011.

Josephson, Jason Ānanda. *The Invention of Religion in Japan*. Chicago: University of Chicago Press, 2012.

Kagoshima-ken kyōiku iinkai 鹿児島県教育委員会編, ed. *Kagoshima-ken kyōikushi* 鹿児島県教育史. Reprint ed. Kagoshima: Kagoshima Kenritsu Kenkyūjo, 1985

Kaiho Yōko 海保洋子. "'Ikoku' no naikokuka to tōgō 「異国」の内国化と統合." In *Ezochi to Ryūkyū* 蝦夷地と琉球, edited by Kuwabara Masato 桑原真人 and Gabe Masao 我部政男, 120–151. Tokyo: Yoshikawa Kōbunkan, 2001. Originally published 1992.

Kallander, Amy Aisen. *Women, Gender, and the Palace Households in Ottoman Tunisia.* Austin: University of Texas Press, 2013.

Kamiya Nobuyuki 紙屋敦之. *Ryūkyū to Nihon, Chūgoku* 琉球と日本・中国. Tokyo: Yamakawa Shuppansha, 2003.

Kamiyama Tsuneo 神山恒夫. "Shokusan kōgyō seisaku no tenkai 殖産興業政策の展開." In *Iwanami Kōza Nihon rekishi*, Vol. 15: *Kingendai 1* 岩波講座日本歴史. 第15巻(近現代1), edited by Ōtsu Tōru 大津透, Sakurai Eiji 桜井英治, and Fujii Jōji 藤井讓治, 97–129. Tokyo: Iwanami Shoten, 2014.

Kanbashi Norimasa 芳即正. *Shimazu Nariakira* 島津斉彬. Tokyo: Yoshikawa Kōbunkan, 1993.

Kanbashi Norimasa 芳即正. *Shimazu Shigehide* 島津重豪. Tokyo: Yoshikawa Kōbunkan, 1980.

Kang, David C. *East Asia before the West: Five Centuries of Trade and Tribute.* New York: Columbia University Press, 2010.

Kang, Etsuko Hae-jin. *Diplomacy and Ideology in Japanese-Korean Relations: From the Fifteenth to the Eighteenth Century.* London: Macmillan Press, 1997.

Kasahara Hidehiko 笠原英彦. "Etō Shinpei to Shihōshō: shihō seisaku no seijiteki haikei 江藤新平と司法省—司法政策の政治的背景." *Hōgaku kenkyū* 法学研究 64, no. 1 (1991): 33–55.

Kasahara Hidehiko 笠原英彦. *Meiji rusu seifu* 明治留守政府. Tōkyō: Keiō Gijuku Daigaku Shuppankai, 2010.

Kasaya Kazuhiko 笠谷和比古. *Tokugawa Yoshimune* 徳川吉宗. Tokyo: Chikuma Shobō, 1995.

Kashihara Hiroki 柏原宏紀. "Seikanron seihen-go no Kōbushō ni kansuru ichi kōsatsu 征韓論政変後の工部省に関する一考察." *Hōgaku kenkyū* 法学研究 82, no. 2 (2009): 487–510.

Katō Totsudō 加藤咄堂, ed. *Kokumin shisō sōsho* 国民思想叢書. 12 vols., vol. 7. Tokyo: Kokumin Shisō Sōsho Kankōkai, 1931.

Katō Yūzō 加藤祐三. "Kurobune zengo no seikai 7: 'keiken to fūsetsu' Morison-gō jiken to Ahen sensō jōhō 黒船前後の世界 (7) <経験と風説>モリソン号事件とアヘン戦争情報." *Shisō* 思想, no. 719 (1984): 44–67.

Katsube Makoto 勝部眞人. "Meiji kaireki to shinreki no shintō katei 明治改暦と新暦の浸透過程." In *Kinsei kindai no chiiki shakai to bunka* 近世近代の地域社会と文化, edited by Rai Kïichi Sensei Taikan Kinen Ronshū Kankōkai 頼祺一先生退官記念論集刊行会, 485–505. Tokyo: Seibundō, 2004.

Katsuta Masaharu 勝田政治. *Haihan chiken: "Meiji kokka" ga umareta hi* 廃藩置県：「明治国家」が生まれた日. Tokyo: Kōdansha, 2000.

Katsuta Masaharu 勝田政治. *"Seijika" Ōkubo Toshimichi: kindai Nihon no sekkeisha* 「政治家」大久保利通:近代日本の設計者. Tokyo: Kōdansha, 2003.

Keene, Donald. *Emperor of Japan: Meiji and His World, 1852–1912.* New York: Columbia University Press, 2002.

Keene, Donald. *Frog in the Well: Portraits of Japan by Watanabe Kazan, 1793–1841.* New York: Columbia University Press, 2006.

Keene, Donald. "Hirata Atsutane and Western Learning." *T'oung Pao* 42, no. 5 (1954): 353–380.

Keene, Donald. *The Japanese Discovery of Europe, 1720–1830.* Rev. ed. Stanford, CA: Stanford University Press, 1969.

Kerr, George H. *Okinawa, the History of an Island People.* Rev. ed. Boston: Tuttle, 2000.

Ketelaar, James Edward. *Of Heretics and Martyrs in Meiji Japan: Buddhism and its Persecution.* Princeton, NJ: Princeton University Press, 1990.

Kido Takayoshi 木戸孝允. *Kido Takayoshi monjo* 木戸孝允文書. Edited by Kido-kō Denki Hensanjo 木戸公伝記編纂所. 8 vols. Tokyo: Nihon Shiseki Kankōkai, 1929–1931.

Kido Takayoshi 木戸孝允. *Kido Takayoshi nikki* 木戸孝允日記. Edited by Tsumaki Chūta 妻木忠太. 3 vols. Tokyo: Hayakawa Ryōkichi, 1932–33.

Kido Takayoshi 木戸孝允. *The Diary of Kido Takayoshi.* Translated by Sidney DeVere Brown. 3 vols. Tokyo: University of Tokyo Press, 1983.

Kikuchi Isao 菊地勇夫. *Bakuhan taisei to Ezochi* 幕藩体制と蝦夷地. Tokyo: Yūzankaku, 1984.

Kikuchi Isao 菊地勇夫. "Ezogashima to hoppō sekai 蝦夷島と北方世界." In *Ezogashima to hoppō sekai* 蝦夷島と北方世界, edited by Kikuchi Isao 菊池勇夫, 7–89. Tokyo: Yoshikawa kōbunkan, 2002.

Kim, Gyewon. "Tracing the Emperor: Photography, Famous Places, and the Imperial Progresses in Prewar Japan." *Representations* 120, no. 1 (2012): 115–150.

Kim, Kyu Hyun. *The Age of Visions and Arguments: Parliamentarianism and the National Public Sphere in Early Meiji Japan.* Cambridge, MA: Harvard University Asia Center, 2007.

Kimura Naoya 木村直也. "Bakumatsu no Nikkan kankei to Seikanron 幕末の日朝関係と征韓論." *Rekishi hyōron* 歴史評論, no. 516 (1993): 26–37.

Kinjō Masaru 金城善. "Kindai Okinawa ni okeru koseki-hō no shikō 近代沖縄における戸籍法の施行." In *Okinawa kindaihō no keisei to tenkai* 沖縄近代法の形成と展開, edited by Tasato Osamu 田里修 and Mori Kenji 森謙二, 327–382. Okinawa-ken Ginowan-shi: Yōju Shorin, 2013.

Kinmonth, Earl H. "Fukuzawa Reconsidered: Gakumon no Susume and Its Audience." *Journal of Asian Studies* 37, no. 4 (1978): 677–696.

Kinoshita Naoyuki 木下直之 and Yoshimi Shunya 吉見俊哉. *Nyūsu no tanjō: kawaraban to shinbun nishiki no jōhō sekai* ニュースの誕生: かわら版と新聞錦絵の情報世界. Tokyo: Tōkyō Daigaku Shuppankai, 1999.

Kinsei meishi shashin hanpukai 近世名士写真頒布会, ed. *Kinsei meishi shashin* 近世名士写真. 2 vols. Osaka: Kinsei meishi shashin hanpukai, 1935.

Kodama Kōta 児島幸多 and Kitajima Masamoto 北島正元, eds. *Hanshi sōran* 藩史総覧. Tokyo: Shinjinbutsu Ōraisha, 1977.

Koga Tōan 古賀侗庵. *Kaibō okusoku* 海防臆測. 2 vols. Tokyo: Hidaka Nobuzane, 1880.

Kojima Tokuya 小島徳弥. *Meiji ikō daijiken no shinsō to hanrei* 明治以降大事件の真相と判例. Tokyo: Kyōbunsha, 1934.

Kokuryūkai 黒竜会, ed. *Seinan kiden* 西南記伝. 3 vols. Tokyo: Kokuryūkai honbu, 1908–1911.

Kokuryūkai 黒竜会, ed. *Tōa senkaku shishi kiden* 東亜先覚志士記伝. 2 vols. Tokyo, 1935.

Kondō Nobutaka 近藤信敬, ed. *Chitsuroku shobunhō* 秩禄処分法. Nagoya: Kondō Nobutaka, 1897.

Kōno Tsunekichi 河野常吉. "Kunashiri Etorofu no kenpyō ni kansuru dan'an 国後択捉の建標に関する断案." *Sapporo Hakubutsu Gakkai Kaihō* 札幌博物学会会報 4, no. 1 (1912): 43–50.

Koo, Min Gyo. "Economic Dependence and the Dokdo/Takeshima Dispute between South Korean and Japan." *Harvard Asia Quarterly* 9, no. 4 (2005): 24–35.

Koschmann, J. Victor. *The Mito Ideology: Discourse Reform, and Insurrection in Late Tokugawa Japan, 1790–1864.* Berkeley: University of California Press, 1987.

Koseki San'ei 小関三英. *Naporeon den* 那波列翁伝. 3 vols: Seifūkan, 1857.

Kōshaku Hosokawa-ke Hensanjo 侯爵細川家編纂所, ed. *Higo-han kokuji shiryō* 肥後藩國事史料. Rev. ed. 10 vols. Kumamoto-shi: Kōshaku Hosokawa-ke Hensanjo, 1932.

Kraehe, Enno E. "A Bipolar Balance of Power." *American Historical Review* 97, no. 3 (1992): 707–715.

Kristiansen, Roald. "Western Science and Japanese Neo-Confucianism: A History of Their Interaction and Transformation." *Japanese Religions* 21, no. 2 (1996): 253–282.

Kumazawa Tōru 熊沢徹. "Bakumatsu ishinki no gunji to chōhei 幕末維新期の軍事と徴兵." *Rekishigaku kenkyū* 歴史学研究, no. 651 (1993): 118–129.

Kunaichō rinji teishitsu henshūkyoku 宮内省臨時帝室編修局, ed. *Meiji tennō ki* 明治天皇記. 13 vols. Tokyo: Yoshikawa Kōbunkan, 1968–1977.

Kurasawa Takashi 倉沢剛. *Gakusei no kenkyū* 学制の研究. Tokyo: Kōdansha, 1973.

Kurimoto Joun (Hōan) 栗本鋤雲 (匏庵). *Hōan jisshu* 匏菴十種. 2 vols. Tokyo: Kyūsenkan, 1869.

Kuwahata Hajime 桑波田興. *Kokushi daijiten* 国史大事典, s.v. "Shimazu Yoshihiro 島津義弘." Tokyo: Yoshikawa Kōbunkan, 1979–1997.

Le Gendre, Charles William. *Is Aboriginal Formosa a Part of the Chinese Empire?* Shanghai: Lane, Crawford, 1874.

Le Gendre, Charles William. *How to Deal with China: A Letter to De B. Rand. Keim, Esquire, Agent of the United States.* Amoy: Rozario, Marcal, 1871.

Le Gendre, Charles William. *Notes of Travel in Formosa.* Edited by Douglas L. Fix and John Shufelt. Tainan, Taiwan: National Museum of Taiwan History, 2012.

Lebra, Joyce Chapman. "Okuma Shigenobu and the 1881 Political Crisis." *Journal of Asian Studies* 18, no. 4 (1959): 475–487.

Lee Chi-Chang [Ri Keishō] 李啓彰. "Nisshin shūkō jōki seiritsu katei no saikentō: Meiji gonen Yanagihara Sakimitsu no Shinkoku haken mondai o chūshin ni 日清修好条規成立過程の再検討—明治5年柳原前光の清国派遣問題を中心に." *Shigaku zasshi* 史学雑誌 115, no. 7 (2006): 1281–1292.

Lee, Edwin B. "The Kazunomiya Marriage: Alliance between the Court and the Bakufu." *Monumenta Nipponica* 22, no. 3/4 (1967): 290–304.

Lee, Hoon. "The Repatriation of Castaways in Chosŏn Korea-Japan Relations, 1599–1888." *Korean Studies* 30, no. 1 (2006): 65–88.

Lee, John. "Trade and Economy in Preindustrial East Asia, c. 1500–c. 1800: East Asia in the Age of Global Integration." *Journal of Asian Studies* 58, no. 1 (1999): 2–26.

Lee, Seokwoo [Yi Sŏg-u]. *Territorial Disputes among Japan, China and Taiwan concerning the Senkaku Islands.* Durham, UK: International Boundaries Research Unit, Department of Geography, University of Durham, 2002.

Legge, James. *Confucian Analects, the Great Learning, and the Doctrine of the Mean.* 1893. Reprint, New York: ACLS Humanities E-Book, 2012.

Lehmann, Jean-Pierre. "Léon Roches—Diplomat Extraordinary in the Bakumatsu Era: An Assessment of His Personality and Policy." *Modern Asian Studies* 14, no. 2 (1980): 273–307.

Lensen, George Alexander. *The Russian Push toward Japan: Russo-Japanese Relations, 1697–1875.* Princeton, NJ: Princeton University Press, 1959.

Leung, Edwin Pak-Wah. "The Quasi-War in East Asia: Japan's Expedition to Taiwan and the Ryūkyū Controversy." *Modern Asian Studies* 17, no. 2 (1983): 257–281.

Levine, Ari Daniel. "Che-tsung's Reign (1085–1100) and the Age of Faction." In *The Cambridge History of China,* Vol. 5, Part 1: *The Sung Dynasty and Its Precursors, 907–1279,* edited by Denis Twichett and Paul Jakov Smith, 484–555. Cambridge: Cambridge University Press, 2009.

Lewis, James Bryant. *Frontier Contact between Chosŏn Korea and Tokugawa Japan.* London: Routledge Curzon, 2003.

Lewis, James Bryant. "The Pusan Japan House (Waegwan) and Chosôn Korea: Early Modern Korean Views of Japan through Economic, Political, and Social Connections." Ph.D. diss., University of Hawai'i at Manoa, 1994.

Lidin, Olaf G., ed. *Ogyū Sorai's Discourse on Government (Seidan): An Annotated Translation.* Wiesbaden: Harrassowitz Verlag, 1999.

Lieberman, Victor. *Strange Parallels: Southeast Asia in Global Context, c. 800–1830,* Vol. 2: *Mainland Mirrors: Europe, Japan, China, South Asia, and the Islands.* Cambridge: Cambridge University Press, 2009.

Lieberman, Victor. "Transcending East-West Dichotomies: State and Culture Formation in Six Ostensibly Disparate Areas." In *Beyond Binary*

Histories: Re-imagining Eurasia to c.1830, edited by Victor Lieberman, 19–102. Ann Arbor: University of Michigan Press, 1999.

Lu, Sidney Xu. "Colonizing Hokkaido and the Origin of Japanese Trans-Pacific Expansion, 1869–1894." *Japanese Studies* 36, no. 2 (2016): 251–274.

Maddison, Angus. *Contours of the World Economy, 1–2030 AD: Essays in Macroeconomic History.* New York: Oxford University Press, 2007.

Maier, Charles S. "Consigning the Twentieth Century to History: Alternative Narratives for the Modern Era." *American Historical Review* 105, no. 3 (2000): 807–831.

Makuzu, Tadano, Janet R. Goodwin, Bettina Gramlich-Oka, Elizabeth A. Leicester, Yuki Terazawa, and Anne Walthall. "Solitary Thoughts: A Translation of Tadano Makuzu's Hitori Kangae (2)." *Monumenta Nipponica* 56, no. 2 (2001): 173–195.

Mamdani, Mahmood. *Citizen and Subject: Contemporary Africa and the Legacy of Late Colonialism.* Princeton, NJ: Princeton University Press, 1996.

Marcon, Federico. "Inventorying Nature: Tokugawa Yoshimune and the Sponsorship of Honzōgaku in Eighteenth-Century Japan." In *Japan at Nature's Edge: The Environmental Context of a Global Power,* edited by Brett L. Walker, Julia Adeney Thomas, and Ian Jared Miller, 189–206. Honolulu: University of Hawaiʻi Press, 2013.

Marcon, Federico. *The Knowledge of Nature and the Nature of Knowledge in Early Modern Japan.* Chicago: University of Chicago Press, 2015.

Marcon, Federico. "Satō Nobuhiro and the Political Economy of Natural History in Nineteenth-Century Japan." *Japanese Studies* 34, no. 3 (2014): 265–287.

"Marquis H. Ito: The Bismarck of Japan." *Phrenological Journal and Science of Health (1870–1911)* 104, no. 4 (1897): 190.

Maruyama, Masao. *Studies in the Intellectual History of Tokugawa Japan.* Translated by Mikiso Hane. Princeton, NJ: Princeton University Press, 1974.

Maruyama Yasunari 丸山雍成. *Sankin kōtai* 参勤交代. Tokyo: Yoshikawa Kōbunkan, 2007.

Matsuo Masahito 松尾正人. "Haihan chiken no seijiteki chōryū 廃藩置県の政治的潮流." *Rekishigaku kenkyū* 歴史学研究 596, no. 8 (1989): 1–17, 27.

Matsudaira Yoshinaga Zenshū Hensan Iinkai 松平慶永全集編纂委員会, ed. *Matsudaira Shungaku zenshū* 松平春嶽全集. 4 vols. 1939. Reprint, Tokyo: Hara Shobō, 1973.

Matsukata Masayoshi. *Report on the Adoption of the Gold Standard in Japan.* Tokyo: Government Press, 1899.

Matsumoto Sannosuke 松本三之介 and Yamamuro Shin'ichi 山室信一, eds. *Genron to media* 言論とメディア. Vol. 11 of *Nihon kindai shisō taikei* 日本近代思想体系. Tokyo: Iwanami Shoten, 1990.

Matsuo Masahito 松尾正人. *Haihan chiken: kindai tōitsu kokka e no kumon* 廃藩置県―近代統一国家への苦悶. Tokyo: Chūkō Shinsho, 1986.

Mayo, Marlene J. "A Catechism of Western Diplomacy: The Japanese and Hamilton Fish, 1872." *Journal of Asian Studies* 26, no. 3 (1967): 389–410.

Mayo, Marlene J. "Nationalist Revolution in Japan." Review of *The Meiji Restoration* by W. G. Beasley. *Monumenta Nipponica* 29 (1974): 83–91.

Mazzini, Giuseppe. *A Cosmopolitanism of Nations: Giuseppe Mazzini's Writings on Democracy, Nation Building, and International Relations.* Translated by Stefano Recchia. Edited by Stefano Recchia and Nadia Urbinati. Princeton, NJ: Princeton University Press, 2009.

McArthur, Ian. *Henry Black: On Stage in Meiji Japan.* Clayton, Victoria, Australia: Monash University Publishing, 2013.

McClain, James L., John M. Merriman, and Kaoru Ugawa, eds. *Edo and Paris: Urban Life and the State in the Early Modern Era.* Ithaca, NY: Cornell University Press, 1994.

McCullough, Stephen. "Avoiding War: The Foreign Policy of Ulysses S. Grant and Hamilton Fish." In *A Companion to the Reconstruction Presidents 1865–1881,* edited by Edward O. Frantz, 311–327. Chichester, West Sussex, UK: Wiley Blackwell, 2014.

McEwan, J. R. *The Political Writings of Ogyū Sorai.* Cambridge: Cambridge University Press, 1962.

McLaren, Walter Wallace. "Japanese Government Documents." *Transactions of the Asiatic Society of Japan* 42, Part I (1914): xiv–681.

McWilliams, Wayne C. "East Meets East: The Soejima Mission to China, 1873." *Monumenta Nipponica* 30 (1975): 237–281.

Medzini, Meron. *French Policy in Japan during the Closing Years of the Tokugawa Regime.* Cambridge, MA: East Asian Research Center, Harvard University, 1971.

Meyer, John W. "World Society, Institutional Theories, and the Actor." *Annual Review of Sociology* 36 (2010): 1–20.

Meyer, John W., John Boli, and George M. Thomas. "Ontology and Rationalization in the Western Cultural Account." In *Institutional Structure: Constituting State, Society, and the Individual,* edited by George M. Thomas, 11–37. Newbury Park, CA: Sage, 1987.

Meyer, John W., John Boli, George M. Thomas, and Francisco O. Ramirez. "World Society and the Nation-State." *American Journal of Sociology* 103, no. 1 (1997): 144–181.

Mieczkowski, Bogdan and Seiko Mieczkowski. "Horace Capron and the Development of Hokkaido a Reappraisal." *Journal of the Illinois State Historical Society (1908–1984)* 67, no. 5 (1974): 487–504.

Mitani, Hiroshi. *Escape from Impasse: The Decision to Open Japan.* Translated by David Noble. Tokyo: International House of Japan, 2006.

Mitani Hiroshi 三谷博. *Meiji ishin o kangaeru* 明治維新を考える. Tokyo: Yūshiya, 2006.

Mitani Hiroshi 三谷博. *Meiji ishin to nashonarizumu: bakumatsu no gaikō to seiji hendō* 明治維新とナショナリズム: 幕末の外交と政治変動. Tokyo: Yamakawa Shuppansha, 1997.

Miyamoto Mataji 宮本又次. *Kōnoike Zen'emon* 鴻池善右衛門. Tokyo: Yoshikawa Kōbunkan, 1958.

Miyamoto Mataji 宮本又次. Ōsaka no kenkyū 大阪の研究. 5 vols. Osaka: Seibundō Shuppan, 1967.

Miyamoto, Mataji, Yōtarō Sakudō, and Yasukichi Yasuba. "Economic Development in Preindustrial Japan, 1859–1894." *Journal of Economic History* 25, no. 4 (1965): 541–564.

Mizruchi, Mark S. and Lisa C. Fein. "The Social Construction of Organizational Knowledge: A Study of the Uses of Coercive, Mimetic, and Normative Isomorphism." *Administrative Science Quarterly* 44, no. 4 (1999): 653–683.

Mizuno, Norihito. "China in Tokugawa Foreign Relations: The Tokugawa Bakufu's Perception of and Attitudes toward Ming-Qing China." *Sino-Japanese Studies* 15 (2003): 103–144.

Mizuno, Norihito. "Early Meiji Policies Towards the Ryukyus and the Taiwanese Aboriginal Territories." *Modern Asian Studies* 43, no. 03 (2009): 683–739.

Monbushō 文部省. *Gakusei* 学制. Tokyo: Monbushō, 1872.

Monbushō 文部省. *Gakusei hyakunen-shi* 学制百年史 Tokyo: Teikoku Chihō Gyōseikai, 1972.

Monbushō 文部省. *Monbushō futatsu zenshū* 文部省布達全書. Tokyo: Monbushō, 1885.

Monbushō 文部省. *Shōgaku kyōsoku* 小学教則. Tokyo: Izumoji Manjirō, 1873.

Mōri Toshihiko 毛利敏彦. *Etō Shinpei: kyūshinteki kaikakusha no higeki* 江藤新平: 急進的改革者の悲劇. Rev. and enlarged ed. Tokyo: Chūō Kōron Shinsha, 1997.

Mōri Toshihiko 毛利敏彦. *Meiji roku-nen seihen* 明治六年政変. Tokyo: Chūō Kōron Shinsha, 1979.

Mōri Toshihiko 毛利敏彦. *Kokushi daijiten* 国史大事典, s.v. "Seinan sensō 西南戦争." Tokyo: Yoshikawa Kōbunkan, 1979–1997.

Mori Yoshikazu 母利美和. *Ii Naosuke* 井伊直弼. Tokyo: Yoshikawa Kōbunkan, 2006.

Morison, Samuel Eliot. *"Old Bruin": Commodore Matthew C. Perry, 1794–1858; the American Naval Officer who Helped Found Liberia.* Boston: Little, Brown, 1967.

Mormanne, Thierry. "La prise de possession d'Urup par la flotte anglo-française en 1855." *CIPANGO Cahiers d'études japonaises* 11 (2004): 209–239.

Morohoshi Hidetoshi 諸星秀俊. "Meiji roku-nen 'Seikanron' ni okeru gunji kōsō 明治六年「征韓論」における軍事構想." *Gunji Shigaku* 軍事史学 45, no. 1 (2009): 43–62.

Morris-Suzuki, Tessa. *The Technological Transformation of Japan: From the Seventeenth to the Twenty-first Century.* Cambridge: Cambridge University Press, 1994.

Morse, Edward S. *Japan Day by Day.* 2 vols. Boston: Houghton Mifflin, 1917.

Motegi, Toshio. "A Prototype of Close Relations and Antagonism: From the First Sino-Japanese War to the Twenty-one Demands." In *Toward a History beyond Borders: Contentious Issues in Sino-Japanese Relations*, edited by Daqing Yang and Andrew Gordon. Translated by Matthew Fraleigh, 20–52. Cambridge, MA: Harvard University Asia Center 2012.

Naikakutōkeikyoku 内閣統計局. *Dai-Nihon teikoku tōkei nenkan* 大日本帝國統計年鑑. Vol. 2. Tokyo: Naikaku Tōkei kyoku, 1883.

Najita, Tetsuo. "Ōshio Heihachirō (1793–1837)." In *Personality in Japanese History*, edited by Albert M. Craig and Donald H. Shively, 155–179. Berkeley: University of California Press, 1970.

Najita, Tetsuo, ed. *Tokugawa Political Writings*. Cambridge: Cambridge University Press, 1998.

Nakai, Kate Wildman. *Shogunal Politics: Arai Hakuseki and the Premises of Tokugawa Rule*. Cambridge, MA: Council on East Asian Studies, Harvard University, 1988.

Nakajima, Gakushō. "The Invasion of Korea and Trade with Luzon: Katō Kiyomasa's Scheme of the Luzon Trade in the Late Sixteenth Century." In *The East Asian Mediterranean: Maritime Crossroads of Culture, Commerce and Human Migration*, edited by Angela Schottenhammer, 145–168. Wiesbaden: Harrassowitz, 2008.

Nakamura, Ellen. "Working the Siebold Network: Kusumoto Ine and Western Learning in Nineteenth-Century Japan." *Japanese Studies* 28, no. 2 (2008): 197–211.

Nakamura Kunimitsu 中村邦光. "Kyōho kaikaku no okeru 'kinsho kanwa': Nihon kagaku-shi jō no gokai 享保改革における<禁書緩和>—日本科学史上の誤解." *Butsurigaku-shi nōto* 物理学史ノート 9 (2005): 53–67.

Nakamura Yasuhiro 中村安宏. "Muro Kyūsō to Shushigaku: Kyōho kaikaku, kagaku dōnyū hantairon o chūshin ni 室鳩巣と朱子学・享保改革—科学導入反対論を中心に." *Nihon shisōshi kenkyū* 日本思想史研究 31 (1999): 31–44.

Nakane, Chie and Shinzaburō Ōishi, eds. *Tokugawa Japan: The Social and Economic Antecedents of Modern Japan*. Translation edited by Conrad D. Totman. Tokyo: University of Tokyo Press, 1990.

Namikawa Kenji 浪川健治. *Ainu minzoku no kiseki* アイヌ民族の軌跡. Tokyo: Yamakawa Shuppansha, 2004.

"New Oriental Diplomacy." *New York Times*. December 6, 1874, 6.

Nihon shiseki kyōkai 日本史籍協會, ed. *Shimazu Hisamitsu-kō jikki* 島津久光公實紀. 3 vols. Tokyo: Tōkyō Daigaku Shuppankai, 1977.

Nishijima Sadao 西嶋定生 and Yi Sŏng-si [Ri Sonshi] 李成市, eds. *Kodai higashi Ajia sekai to Nihon* 古代東アジア世界と日本. Tokyo: Iwanami Shoten, 2000.

Nishikawa Joken 西川如見. *Nishikawa Joken isho* 西川如見遺書. Edited by Nishikawa Tadasuke 西川忠亮. 18 vols. Tokyo: Nishikawa Tadasuke, 1898–1907.

Nishikawa Nagao 西川長夫. *Kokkyō no koekata: kokumin kokka ron josetsu* 国境の越え方: 国民国家論序説. 2nd ed. Tokyo: Heibonsha, 2001.

Nishikawa Nagao 西川長夫. "Nihongata kokumin kokka no keisei: hikakushiteki kanten kara 日本型国民国家の形勢—比較史的観点から." In *Bakumatsu Meiji-ki no kokumin kokka keisei no bunka hen'yō* 幕末・明治期の国家形成と文化変容, edited by Nishikawa Nagao 西川長夫 and Matsumiya Hideharu 松宮秀治, 3–42. Tokyo: Shin'yōsha, 1995.

Nishikawa Nagao 西川長夫 and Matsumiya Hideharu 松宮秀治, eds. *Bakumatsu Meiji-ki no kokumin kokka keisei to bunka hen'yō* 幕末・明治期の国民国家の形成と文化変容. Tokyo: Shin'yōsha, 1995.

Nosco, Peter. *Remembering Paradise: Nativism and Nostalgia in Eighteenth Century Japan.* Cambridge, MA: Council on East Asian Studies, Harvard University, 1990.

O'Brien, Suzanne G. "Splitting Hairs: History and the Politics of Daily Life in Nineteenth-Century Japan." *Journal of Asian Studies* 67, no. 4 (2008): 1309–1339.

Ochiai Hiroki 落合弘樹. *Chitsuroku shobun* 秩禄処分. Tokyo: Chūō Kōron Shinsha, 1999.

Oergel, Maike. *The Return of King Arthur and the Nibelungen: National Myth in Nineteenth-Century English and German Literature.* Berlin: De Gruyter, 1997.

Ōishi Manabu 大石学. "Nihon kinsei kokka no yakusō seisaku: Kyōho kaikaku o chūshin ni 日本近世国家の薬草政策—享保改革期を中心に." *Reikishigaku kenkyū* 歴史学研究 639 (1992): 11–23.

Ōishi Manabu 大石学. *Edo no gaikō senryaku* 江戸の外交戦略. Tokyo: Kadokawa Gakugei Shuppan, 2009.

Ōishi Shinzaburō 大石慎三郎. *Tanuma Okitsugu no jidai* 田沼意次の時代. Tokyo: Iwanami Shoten, 1991.

Okada Yoshirō 岡田芳朗. *Meiji kaireki: "toki" no bunmei kaika* 明治改暦:「時」の文明開化. Tokyo: Taishūkan shoten, 1994.

Ōkubo Toshiaki 大久保利謙, ed. *Iwakura shisetsu no kenkyū* 岩倉使節の研究. Tokyo: Munetaka Shobō, 1976.

Ōkubo Toshimichi 大久保利通. *Ōkubo Toshimichi bunsho* 大久保利通文書. 10 vols. Tokyo: Nihon Shiseki Kyōkai, 1927–1929.

Ōkurashō 大蔵省. *Kōbushō enkaku hōkoku* 工部省沿革報告. Tokyo: Ōkurashō, 1889.

Ooms, Herman. *Imperial Politics and Symbolics in Ancient Japan: The Tenmu Dynasty, 650–800.* Honolulu: University of Hawaiʻi Press, 2009.

Osiander, Andreas. "Sovereignty, International Relations, and the Westphalian Myth." *International Organization* 55, no. 2 (2001): 251–287.

Osterhammel, Jürgen. "Globalizations." In *The Oxford Handbook of World History*, edited by Jerry H. Bentley, 89–104. Oxford: Oxford University Press, 2011.

Osterhammel, Jürgen. *The Transformation of the World: A Global History of the Nineteenth Century.* Princeton, NJ: Princeton University Press, 2014.

Owen, F. Cunliffe. "The Mikado and the Reigning House of Japan." *Town and Country*, January 7, 1905, 17.

Ōyama Genshi Den Hensan Iin 大山元帥伝編纂委員, ed. *Genshi kōshaku Ōyama Iwao* 元帥公爵大山巌. Tokyo: Ōyama Genshi Den Kankōkai, 1935.

Pai, Hyung Il. *Constructing "Korean" Origins: A Critical Review of Archaeology, Historiography, and Racial Myth in Korean State-formation Theories.* Cambridge, MA: Harvard University Asia Center, 2000.

Palais, James B. *Politics and Policy in Traditional Korea.* Cambridge, MA: Harvard University Press, 1975.

Palmer, Aaron Haight. *Documents and facts illustrating the origin of the mission to Japan, authorized by government of the United States, May 10th, 1851*. Washington, DC: Henry Polkinhorn, 1857.

Park, Saeyoung. "Reordering the Universe: The Unyō Crisis of 1875 and the Death of Eastphalia." Unpublished manuscript, 2015.

Passin, Herbert. *Society and Education in Japan*. New York: Studies of the East Asian Institute, Columbia University, 1965.

Peng Hao [Hō Kō] 彭浩. "Nagasaki bōeki ni okeru shinpai seido to Shinchō no taiō 長崎貿易における信牌制度と清朝の對應." *Tōhōgaku* 東方学 119 (2010): 73–90.

Perry, Matthew Calbraith. *The Japan Expedition, 1852–1854: The Personal Journal of Commodore Matthew C. Perry*. Edited by Roger Pineau. 1856. Reprint, Washington, DC: Smithsonian Institution Press, 1968.

Perry, Matthew Calbraith. *A Paper by Commodore M.C. Perry, U.S.N., read before the American Geographical and Statistical Society at a meeting held March 6th, 1856*. New York: D. Appleton, 1856.

Philippi, Donald L. *Kojiki*. Princeton, NJ: Princeton University Press, 1968.

Platt, Brian. *Burning and Building: Schooling and State Formation in Japan, 1750–1890*. Cambridge, MA: Harvard University Press, 2004.

Polak, Christian (Kurisuchan Porakku). "Buryune no hito to shōgai ブリュネの人と生涯." In *Hakodate no bakumatsu ishin: Furansu shikan Buryune no suketchi 100-mai* 函館の幕末・維新: フランス士官ブリュネのスケッチ 100枚, edited by Okada Shin'ichi 岡田新一, 81–88. Tokyo: Chūō Kōron Sha, 1988.

Pratt, Edward E. *Japan's Protoindustrial Elite: The Economic Foundations of the Gōnō*. Cambridge, MA: Harvard University Asia Center, 1999.

Rai Gyokusei [Lai Yujing] 賴鈺菁. "Bakumatsu-ki ni okeru 'kangen' to 'kengen'/'kenpaku': 'genro dōkai' o megutte 幕末期における「諫言」と「建言」/「建白」:「言路洞開」をめぐって." *Kotoba to Bunka* 言葉と文化 14, no. 12 (2013): 145–163.

Ravina, Mark. "The Apocryphal Suicide of Saigō Takamori: Samurai, Seppuku and the Politics of Legend." *Journal of Asian Studies* 69, no. 3 (2010): 691–721.

Ravina, Mark. "Japanese State Making in Global Context." In *State Making in Asia*, edited by Richard Boyd and Tak-Wing Ngo, 31–46. London: Routledge, 2006.

Ravina, Mark. *Land and Lordship in Early Modern Japan*. Stanford, CA: Stanford University Press, 1999.

Ravina, Mark. *The Last Samurai: The Life and Battles of Saigō Takamori*. Hoboken, NJ: John Wiley, 2004.

Ravina, Mark. "The Medieval in the Modern: Command and Consensus in Japanese Politics." *Medieval History Journal* 19, no. 2 (2016): 1–21.

Ravina, Mark. "State-Making in Global Context: Japan in a World of Nation-States." In *The Teleology of the Modern Nation-State*, edited by Joshua Fogel, 87–104. Philadelphia: University of Pennsylvania Press, 2005.

Ravina, Mark. "Tokugawa, Romanov, and Khmer: The Politics of Trade and Diplomacy in Eighteenth-Century East Asia." *Journal of World History* 26, no. 2 (2016): 267–292.

Recchia, Stefano and Nadia Urbinati. "Giuseppe Mazzini's International Political Thought." In *A Cosmopolitanism of Nations: Giuseppe Mazzini's Writings on Democracy, Nation Building, and International Relations*, edited by Stefano Recchia and Nadia Urbinati, 1–30. Princeton, NJ: Princeton University Press, 2009.

Redesdale, Algernon Bertram Freeman-Mitford. *Memories*. 2 vols. New York: E.P. Dutton, 1916.

Reed, Edward J. *Japan: Its History, Traditions, and Religions, with the Narrative of a Visit in 1879*. London: J. Murray, 1880.

Reid, Anthony. "The Unthreatening Alternative: Chinese Shipping to Southeast Asia, 1567–1842." *Review of Indonesian and Malaysian Affairs* 27 (1993): 13–32.

Reischauer, Haru Matsukata. *Samurai and Silk: A Japanese and American Heritage*. Cambridge, MA: Harvard University Press, 1986.

Robertson, Russell. "The Bonin Islands." *Transactions of the Asiatic Society of Japan* 4 (1876): 111–143.

Roden, Donald. "In Search of the Real Horace Capron: An Historiographical Perspective on Japanese-American Relations." *Pacific Historical Review* 55, no. 4 (1986): 549–575.

Röhl, Wilhelm. *History of Law in Japan since 1868*. Leiden: Brill, 2005.

Rokuhara, Hiroko. "Local Officials and the Meiji Conscription Campaign." *Monumenta Nipponica* 60, no. 1 (2005): 81–110.

Rosenthal, Michael. *The Character Factory: Baden-Powell and the Origins of the Boy Scout Movement*. New York: Pantheon Books, 1986.

Rowe, William T. *China's Last Empire: The Great Qing*. Cambridge, MA: Harvard University Press, 2009.

Rubinger, Richard. *Popular Literacy in Early Modern Japan*. Honolulu: University of Hawai'i Press, 2007.

Rutter, Owen. *Through Formosa: An Account of Japan's Island Colony*. London: T. F. Unwin, 1923.

Saigō Takamori Zenshū Henshū Iinkai 西郷隆盛全集編集委員会, ed. *Saigō Takamori zenshū* 西郷隆盛全集. 6 vols. Tokyo: Yamato Shobō, 1976–80.

Saitō, Osamu. "The Labor Market in Tokugawa Japan: Wage Differentials and the Real Wage Level, 1727–1830." *Explorations in Economic History* 15 (1978): 84–100.

Saitō, Osamu. "Wages, Inequality, and Pre-Industrial Growth in Japan, 1727–1894." In *Living Standards in the Past: New Perspectives on Well-being in Asia and Europe*, edited by Robert C. Allen, Tommy Bengtsson, and Martin Dribe, 77–97. Oxford: Oxford University Press, 2005.

Sakai Kenkichi 坂井健吉. *Satsumaimo* さつまいも. Tokyo: Hōsei Daigaku Shuppankyoku, 1999.

Sakamoto, Tarō. *The Six National Histories of Japan*. Translated by John S. Brownlee. Vancouver: University of British Columbia Press, 1991.

Sakamoto Tarō 坂本太郎, Inoue Mitsusada 井上光貞, Ienaga Saburō 家永三郎, and Ōno Susumu 大野晋, eds. *Nihon shoki jō* 日本書紀・上. Vol. 67 of *Nihon koten bungaku taikei* 日本古典文學大系. 102 vols. Tokyo: Iwanami Shoten, 1967.

Sakurai Kigai 桜井基外, ed. *Ten no seisei* 天之聖声. Wakkanai, Japan: Sakurai Kigai, 1910.

Sasaki Hiroshi 佐々木寛司. "Sozei kokka to chiso 租税国家と地租." In *Kindai Nihon no keisei to sozei* 近代日本の形成と租税, 2–15. Tokyo: Yūshisha, 2008.

Sasaki Kanji 佐々木寛司 and Ochiai Hiroki 落合弘樹. "Zeisei kaikaku to rokusei haishi: chiso kaisei to chitsuroku shobun 税政改革と禄制廃止―地租改正と秩禄処分." In *Meiji ishin no keizai katei* 明治維新の経済過程, edited by Sasaki Kanji 佐々木寛司 and Katsube Makoto 勝部真人, 81–108: Tokyo: Yūshisha, 2013.

Sasaki Shirō 佐々木史郎. *Hoppō kara kita kōekimin: kinu to kegawa to Santanjin* 北方から来た交易民: 絹と毛皮とサンタン人. Tokyo: Nihon Hōsō Shuppan Kyōkai, 1996.

Sasaki Suguru 佐々木克. *Boshin sensō: haisha no Meiji ishin* 戊辰戦争:敗者の明治維新. Tokyo: Chūō Kōron Sha, 1977.

Sasaki Suguru 佐々木克. "Taisei hōkan to tōbaku mitchoku 大政奉還と討幕密勅." *Jinbun gakuhō (Kyōto Daigaku Jinbun Kagaku Kenkyūjo)* 人文学報:京都大学人文科学研究所 80 (1997): 1–32.

Satō Nobuhiro 佐藤信淵. *Satō Nobuhiro kagaku zenshū* 佐藤信淵家学全集. Edited by Takimoto Seiichi 滝本誠一. 3 vols. Tokyo: Iwanami Shoten, 1925–26.

Satō Shōsuke 佐藤昌介, Uete Michiari 植手通有, and Yamaguchi Muneyuki 山口宗之, eds. *Nihon shisō taikei 55: Watanabe Kazan, Takano Chōei, Sakuma Shōzan, Yokoi Shōnan, Hashimoto Sanai* 日本思想体系55:渡辺華山・高野長英・佐久間象山・横井小楠・橋本左内. Tokyo: Iwanami Shoten, 1971.

Satō, Tsuneo. "Tokugawa Villages and Agriculture." In *Tokugawa Japan: The Social and Economic Antecedents of Modern Japan*, edited by Chie Nakane and Shinzaburō Ōishi. Translated by Conrad D. Totman, 37–80. Tokyo: University of Tokyo Press, 1990.

Satow, Ernest Mason. *A Diplomat in Japan*. Philadelphia: J. B. Lippincott, 1921.

Scharf, J. Thomas. *History of the Confederate States Navy from its Organization to the Surrender of its Last Vessel; Its Stupendous Struggle with the Great Navy of the United States; The Engagements Fought in the Rivers and Harbors of the South, and Upon the High Seas; Blockade-running, First Use of Iron-clads and Torpedoes, and Privateer History*. New York: Rogers & Sherwood, 1887.

Schottenhammer, Angela. "Japan—The Tiny Dwarf? Sino-Japanese Relations from the *Kangxi* to the *Qianlong* Reigns." In *East Asian Mediterranean: Maritime Crossroads of Culture, Commerce and Human Migration*, edited by Angela Schottenhammer, 331–388. Wiesbaden: Harrassowitz, 2008.

Schroeder, Paul W. "Did the Vienna Settlement Rest on a Balance of Power?" *American Historical Review* 97, no. 3 (1992): 683–706.

Searle, G. R. *The Quest for National Efficiency: A Study in British Politics and Political Thought, 1899–1914*. Berkeley: University of California Press, 1971.

Secretary-General of the United Nations. "The United Nations Flag Code and Regulations, ST/SGB/132." 1967. http://www.un.org/ga/search/view_doc.asp?symbol=st/sgb/132.

Shalev, Eran. *Rome Reborn on Western Shores: Historical Imagination and the Creation of the American Republic.* Charlottesville: University of Virginia Press, 2009.

Shibusawa Eïichi 渋沢栄一. *Tokugawa Yoshinobu-kō den* 徳川慶喜公伝. 8 vols. Tokyo: Ryūmonsha, 1918.

Shigeshita Kazuo 繁下和雄, Satō Tetsuo 佐藤徹夫, and Oyama Sakunosuke 小山作之助, eds. *Kimigayo shiryō shūsei* 君が代史料集成. 5 vols. Tokyo: Ōzorasha, 1991.

Shisō mondai kenkyūjo 思想問題研究所. *Kokugō kokki kokka no yurai to seishin* 国号国旗国歌の由来と精神. Tokyo: Higashiyama Shobō, 1937.

Simpson, Gerry Jason. *Great Powers and Outlaw States: Unequal Sovereigns in the International Legal Order.* Cambridge: Cambridge University Press, 2004.

Sims, R. L. *French Policy towards the Bakufu and Meiji Japan, 1854–95.* Richmond, UK: Japan Library, 1998.

Sippel, Patricia. "Abandoned Fields. Negotiating Taxes in the Bakufu Domain." *Monumenta Nipponica* 53, no. 2 (1998): 197–223.

Smith, George. *Lewchew and the Lewchewans; being a Narrative of a Visit to Lewchew, or Loo Choo, in October, 1850.* London: T. Hatchard, 1853.

Smith, George. *Ten Weeks in Japan.* London: Longman, Green, Longman and Roberts, 1861.

Smith, Thomas C. *The Agrarian Origins of Modern Japan.* Stanford, CA: Stanford University Press, 1959.

Smits, Gregory. *Visions of Ryukyu: Identity and Ideology in Early-modern Thought and Politics.* Honolulu: University of Hawaiʻi Press, 1999.

"Some Hopeful Signs of the Times," *Tokio Times*, September 1, 1877, 116.

Steele, M. William. "Against the Restoration: Katsu Kashū's Attempt to Reinstate the Tokugawa Family." *Monumenta Nipponica* 36, no. 3 (1981): 299–316.

Steele, M. William. "Edo in 1868: The View from Below." *Monumenta Nipponica* 45, no. 2 (1990): 127–155.

Steele, M. William. "The Rise and Fall of the Shōgitai: A Social Drama." In *Conflict in Modern Japanese History*, edited by Tetsuo Najita and J. Victor Koschmann, 128–144. Princeton, NJ: Princeton University Press, 1982.

Steenstrup, Carl. *A History of Law in Japan until 1868.* 2nd. ed. New York: E. J. Brill, 1996.

Stephan, John Jason. "The Crimean War in the Far East." *Modern Asian Studies* 3, no. 3 (1969): 257–277.

Stephan, John Jason. "Ezo under the Tokugawa Bakufu 1799–1821: An Aspect of Japan's Frontier History." Ph.D. diss., University of London, 1969.

Strong, Edwin, Thomas Buckley, and Annetta St. Clair. "The Odyssey of the CSS *Stonewall*." *Civil War History* 30, no. 4 (1984): 306–323.

Sudō Ryūsen 須藤隆仙, ed. *Hakodate sensō shiryōshū* 箱館戦争史料集. Tokyo: Shin Jinbutsu Ōraisha, 1996.

Suematsu [Suyematsu], Kenchō. *A Fantasy of Far Japan or Summer Dream Dialogues.* London: Archibald Constable, 1905.

Suganuma, Unryu. *Sovereign Rights and Territorial Space in Sino-Japanese Relations: Irredentism and the Diaoyu/Senkaku Islands.* Honolulu: University of Hawaiʻi Press, 2000.

Sugitani Akira 杉谷昭, Mōri Toshihiko 毛利敏彦, and Hirose Yoshihiro 広瀬順晧, eds. *Etō Shinpei kankei monjo* 江藤新平関係文書.Tokyo: Hokusensha, 1989.

Suzuki Hairin 鈴木楳林. *Suzuki daizasshū* 鈴木大雑集. Edited by Hayakawa Junzaburō 早川純三郎. 5 vols. Vol. 1. Tokyo: Nihon Shiseki Kyōkai, 1918.

Suzuki Jun 鈴木淳. *Ishin no kōsō to tenkai* 維新の構想と展開. Tokyo: Kōdansha, 2002.

Suzuki Jun 鈴木淳. "Kōbushō no jūgonen 工部省の十五年." In *Kōbushō to sono jidai* 工部省とその時代, edited by Suzuki Jun 鈴木淳, 3–22. Tokyo: Yamakawa Shuppansha, 2002.

Suzuki Tsuruko 鈴木鶴子. *Etō Shinpei to Meiji Ishin* 江藤新平と明治維新. Tokyo: Asahi Shinbunsha, 1989.

Swope, Kenneth M. "Crouching Tigers, Secret Weapons: Military Technology Employed during the Sino-Japanese-Korean War, 1592–1598." *Journal of Military History* 69, no. 1 (2005): 11–41.

Swope, Kenneth M. "Deceit, Disguise, and Dependence: China, Japan, and the Future of the Tributary System, 1592–1596." *International History Review* 24, no. 4 (2002): 757–782.

Tabohashi Kiyoshi 田保橋潔. *Kindai Nissen kankei no kenkyū* 近代日鮮関係の研究. 2 vols. Seoul: Chōsen Sōtokufu Chūsūin, 1940.

Tada Kōmon 多田好問, ed. *Iwakura-ko jikki* 岩倉公實記. 3 vols. Tokyo: Iwakura-kō Kyūseki Hozonkai, 1927.

Takagi Hiroshi 高木博志. "Nihon no kindaika to 'dentō' no sōshutsu 日本の近代化と「伝統」の創出." In *"Dentō" no sōzō to bunka hen'yō* 「伝統」の創造と文化変容, edited by Parutenon Tama パルテノン多摩, 81–122. Tama: Parutenon Tama, 2001.

Takigawa Shūgo 瀧川修吾. "Tsushima-han no Seikanron ni kansuru hikaku kōsatsu: Bunkyū sannen, Genji gannen, Keiō yonnen no kenpakusho o chūshin ni 対馬藩の征韓論に関する比較考察—文久3年・元治元年・慶應4年の建白書を中心に." *Nihon Daigaku Daigakuin Hōgaku kenkyū nenpō* 日本大学大学院法学研究年報 35 (2005): 389–420.

Takii, Kazuhiro. *The Meiji Constitution: The Japanese Experience of the West and the Shaping of the Modern State.* Translated by David Noble. Tokyo: International House of Japan, 2007.

Tanaka Akira 田中彰. *Iwakura Shisetsudan no rekishiteki kenkyū* 岩倉使節団の歴史的研究. Tokyo: Iwanami Shoten, 2002.

Tanaka Akira 田中彰, ed. *Kaikoku* 開国, Vol. 1 of *Nihon kindai shisō taikei* 日本近代思想体系. Tokyo: Iwanami Shoten, 1999.

Tanaka, Stefan. *New Times in Modern Japan*. Princeton, NJ: Princeton University Press, 2004.

Taylor, Brian D. and Roxana Botea. "Tilly Tally: War-Making and State-Making in the Contemporary Third World." *International Studies Review* 10, no. 1 (2008): 27–56.

Taylor, George. *Aborigines of South Taiwan in the 1880s: Papers by the South Cape Lightkeeper George Taylor*. Edited by Glen Dudbridge. Taipei: Shung Ye Museum of Formosan Aborigines, 1999.

Taylor, George. "Formosa: Characteristic Traits of the Island and its Aboriginal Inhabitants." *Proceedings of the Royal Geographical Society* 11, no. 4 (1889): 224–239.

Teeuwen, Mark and Fabio Rambelli. *Buddhas and Kami in Japan: Honji suijaku as a Combinatory Paradigm*. London: RoutledgeCurzon, 2003.

Tersaki Osamu 寺崎修. "Seitō seisha torishirabesho: Meiji 15 nen 10 gatsu chōsa 政党政社取調書—明治15年10月調査." *Seijigaku ronshū* 政治学論集, no. 43 (1996): 107–178.

Terazawa, Yuki. "The State, Midwives, and Reproductive Surveillance in Late Nineteenth- and Early Twentieth-Century Japan." *U.S.–Japan Women's Journal English Supplement* 24 (2003): 59–81.

Thomas, Julia Adeney. "Reclaiming Ground: Japan's Great Convergence." *Japanese Studies* 34, no. 3 (2014): 253–263.

Thomas, Julia Adeney. *Reconfiguring Modernity: Concepts of Nature in Japanese Political Ideology*. Berkeley: University of California Press, 2001.

Tietjen, Mary C. Wilson. "God, Fate, and the Hero of 'Beowulf'." *Journal of English and Germanic Philology* 74, no. 2 (1975): 159–171.

Tilly, Charles. *Coercion, Capital, and European States, AD 990–1992*. Rev. paperback ed. Cambridge, MA: Blackwell, 1992.

Tilly, Charles. "Reflection on the History of European State-making." In *The Formation of National States in Western Europe*, edited by Charles Tilly and Gabriel Ardant, 3–83. Princeton, NJ: Princeton University Press, 1975.

Toby, Ronald P. "Contesting the Centre: International Sources of Japanese National Identity." *International History Review* 7, no. 3 (1985): 347–363.

Toby, Ronald P. "Mapping the Margins of Japan." In *Cartographic Japan*, edited by Kären Wigen, Fumiko Sugimoto, and Cary Karacas, 24–27. Chicago: University of Chicago Press, 2016.

Toby, Ronald P. *State and Diplomacy in Early Modern Japan*. Princeton, NJ: Princeton University Press, 1984.

Tokushima Kenritsu Monjokan 徳島県立文書館, ed. *Kōgo jihen no gunzō: tokubetsu kikakuten* 庚午事変の群像: 特別企画展. Tokushima: Tokushima Kenritsu Monjokan, 2007.

Tōkyō Daigaku Shiryō Hensanjo 東京大学史料編纂所, ed. *Bakumatsu gaikoku kankei monjo* 幕末外国関係文書. 51 vols. Tokyo: Tōkyō Daigaku Shiryō Hensanjo, 1910–.

Tolkien, J. R. R. *Beowulf: The Monsters and the Critics*. 1936. Reprint, London: Oxford University Press, 1963.

Tonooka, Mojuro. "The Development of the Family Law in Modern Japan." *Comparative Law Review Hikaku hōgaku* 2, no. 2 (1966): 198–224.

Tonooka Mojūrō 外岡茂十郎. "Waga kuni ni okeru shiseishi-hō no tanjō to shiseishi no han'i 我國に於ける私生子法の誕生と私生子の範圍." *Waseda hōgaku (Waseda law review)* 早稲田法学 20 (1941): 1–58.

Totman, Conrad. *The Collapse of the Tokugawa Bakufu, 1862–1868.* Honolulu: University of Hawaiʻi Press, 1980.

Totman, Conrad. *Early Modern Japan.* Berkeley: University of California Press, 1993.

Totman, Conrad. "From Reformism to Transformism: Bakufu Policy, 1853–1868." In *Conflict in Modern Japanese History: The Neglected Tradition,* edited by Tetsuo Najita and J. Victor Koschmann, 62–80. Ithaca, NY: Cornell University Press, 1982.

Totman, Conrad. "Fudai Daimyo and the Collapse of the Tokugawa Bakufu." *Journal of Asian Studies* 34, no. 3 (1975): 581–591.

Totman, Conrad. "Tokugawa Yoshinobu and Kobugattai: A Study of Political Inadequacy." *Monumenta Nipponica* 30, no. 4 (1975): 393–403.

Tōyama Kagemichi 遠山景晋. "Chūkai injun roku 籌海因循録." In *Nihon kaibō shiryō sōsho* 日本海防史料叢書, edited by Sumita Shōichi 住田正一, 10 vols., 4: 113–122. Tokyo: Kaibō Shiryō Kankōkai, 1932–1933. Originally published 1824.

Tsuchiya Wataru 土谷渉. "Bakumatsu Seikanron no genryū ni tsuite no ichi kōsatsu 幕末征韓論の源流についての一考察." *Kokushigaku kenkyū: Ryūkoku Daigaku Kokushigaku Kenkyūkai* 国史学研究・龍谷大学国史学研究会 29 (2006): 1–33.

Tsunoda Kurō 角田九郎. *Ōe Taku kun no ryakuden* 大江卓君之略伝. Ichinoseki, Iwate, Japan: Tsunoda Kurō, 1890.

Tsunoda, Ryusaku, William Theodore De Bary, and Donald Keene, eds. *Sources of Japanese Tradition.* 2 vols. New York: Columbia University Press, 1958.

Tsurumi, E. Patricia. *Factory Girls: Women in the Thread Mills of Meiji Japan.* Princeton, NJ: Princeton University Press, 1990.

Tucker, John Allen. *Ogyū Sorai's Philosophical Masterworks: The Bendō and Benmei.* Honolulu: University of Hawaiʻi Press, 2006.

US Department of State. *Executive documents printed by order of the House of Representatives during the third session of the fortieth Congress, 1868–69.* 14 vols., Vol. 1. Washingon, DC: US Government Printing Office, 1869.

US Department of State. *Executive documents printed by order of the House of Representatives, 1874–75.* 18 vols., Vol. 1. Washington, DC: US Government Printing Office, 1875.

Uehara Kenzen 上原兼善. "Chūgoku ni taisuru Ryūnichi kankei no inpei seisaku to 'michi no shima' 中国に対する琉日関係の隠蔽政策と「道之島」." In *Rettōshi no minami to kita* 列島史の南と北, edited by Isao Kikuchi 菊池勇夫 and Maehira Fusaaki 真栄平房昭, 35–56. Tokyo: Yoshikawa Kōbunkan, 2006.

Ueno, Chizuko. "The Position of Japanese Women Reconsidered." *Current Anthropology* 28, no. 4 (1987): S75–S84.

Valance, Georges. *Thiers: Bourgeois et Révolutionnaire.* Paris: Flammarion, 2007.

Vaporis, Constantine N. "Samurai and Merchant in Mid-Tokugawa Japan: Tani Tannai's Record of Daily Necessities (1748–54)." *Harvard Journal of Asiatic Studies* 60, no. 1 (2000): 205–227.

Vaporis, Constantine N. *Tour of Duty: Samurai, Military Service in Edo, and the Culture of Early Modern Japan.* Honolulu: University of Hawai'i Press, 2008.

Verwayen, F. B. "Tokugawa Translations of Dutch Legal Texts." *Monumenta Nipponica* 53, no. 3 (1998): 335–358.

Vlastos, Stephen. *Peasant Protests and Uprisings in Tokugawa Japan.* Berkeley: University of California Press, 1986.

Vlastos, Stephen. "Yonaoshi in Aizu." In *Conflict in Modern Japanese History,* edited by Tetsuo Najita and J. Victor Koschmann, 164–175. Princeton, NJ: Princeton University Press, 1982.

Vlastos, Stephen, ed. *Mirror of Modernity: Invented Traditions of Modern Japan.* Berkeley: University of California Press, 1998.

von Glahn, Richard. "Myth and Reality of China's Seventeenth-Century Monetary Crisis." *Journal of Economic History* 56, no. 2 (1996): 429–454.

Wakabayashi, Bob Tadashi. *Anti-foreignism and Western Learning in Early-modern Japan: The New Theses of 1825.* Cambridge, MA: Council on East Asian Studies, Harvard University, 1986.

Wakabayashi, Bob Tadashi. "Katō Hiroyuki and Confucian Natural Rights, 1861–1870." *Harvard Journal of Asiatic Studies* 44, no. 2 (1984): 469–492.

Wakabayashi, Bob Tadashi. "Opium, Expulsion, Sovereignty: China's Lessons for Bakumatsu Japan." *Monumenta Nipponica* 47, no. 1 (1992): 1–25.

Walker, Brett L. *A Concise History of Japan.* Cambridge: Cambridge University Press, 2015.

Walker, Brett L. *The Conquest of Ainu Lands: Ecology and Culture in Japanese Expansion, 1590–1800.* Berkeley: University of California Press, 2001.

Walker, Brett L. "The Early Modern Japanese State and Ainu Vaccinations: Redefining the Body Politic 1799–1868." *Past & Present,* no. 163 (1999): 121–160.

Walker, Brett L. "Mamiya Rinzō and the Japanese exploration of Sakhalin Island: Cartography and Empire." *Journal of Historical Geography* 33 (2007): 283–313.

Walker, Brett L. "Meiji Modernization, Scientific Agriculture, and the Destruction of Japan's Hokkaido Wolf." *Environmental History* 9, no. 2 (2004): 248–274.

Walter, John Ordonic. "Kodo taii, an Outline of the Ancient Way: An Annotated Translation with an Introduction to the Shinto Revival Movement and a Sketch of the Life of Hirata Atsutane." Ph.D. diss., University of Pennsylvania, 1967.

Walthall, Anne. "The Life Cycle of Farm Women in Tokugawa Japan." In *Recreating Japanese Women, 1600–1945,* edited by Gail Lee Bernstein, 42–70. Berkeley: University of California Press, 1991.

Walthall, Anne. "Off with Their Heads! The Hirata Disciples and the Ashikaga Shoguns." *Monumenta Nipponica* 50, no. 2 (1995): 137–170.

Walthall, Anne. *Peasant Uprisings in Japan: A Critical Anthology of Peasant Histories.* Chicago: University of Chicago Press, 1991.

Walthall, Anne. "Village Networks. Sodai and the Sale of Edo Nightsoil." *Monumenta Nipponica* 43, no. 3 (1988): 279–303.

Wang, Tseng-Tsai. "The Audience Question: Foreign Representatives and the Emperor of China, 1858–1873." *Historical Journal* 14, no. 3 (1971): 617–626.

Watanabe, Miki. "An International Maritime Trader—Torihara Sōan: The Agent for Tokugawa Ieyasu's First Negotiations with Ming China, 1600." In *The East Asian Mediterranean: Maritime Crossroads of Culture, Commerce and Human Migration,* edited by Angela Schottenhammer, 169–176. Wiesbaden: Harrassowitz, 2008.

Wells, David N. *Russian Views of Japan, 1792–1913: An Anthology of Travel Writing.* New York: RoutledgeCurzon, 2004.

Wells, H. G. *A Modern Utopia.* 1905. Reprint, Lincoln: University of Nebraska Press, 1967.

Westney, D. Eleanor. "The Military." In *Japan in Transition: From Tokugawa to Meiji,* edited by Marius B. Jansen and Gilbert Rozman, 168–194. Princeton, NJ: Princeton University Press, 1988.

White, James W. *Ikki: Social Conflict and Political Protest in Early Modern Japan.* Ithaca, NY: Cornell University Press, 1995.

Whitney, Clara A. *Clara's Diary: An American Girl in Meiji Japan.* Edited by M. William Steele and Tamiko Ichimata. Tokyo: Kodansha International, 1979.

Wiley, Peter Booth and Korogi Ichiro. *Yankees in the Land of the Gods: Commodore Perry and the Opening of Japan.* New York: Penguin Books, 1991.

Williams, S. Wells. *A Journal of the Perry Expedition to Japan (1853–1854).* Edited by Frederick Wells Williams. Yokohama: Kelly & Walsh, 1910.

Wills, John E. "Relations with Maritime Europeans, 1514–1662." In *The Cambridge History of China,* Part 2, Vol. 8: *The Ming Dynasty, 1368–1644,* edited by Denis Twitchett and Frederick W. Mote, 333–375. Cambridge: Cambridge University Press, 1998.

Wilson, George M. "The Bakumatsu Intellectual in Action: Hashimoto Sanai in the Political Crisis of 1858." In *Personality in Japanese History,* edited by Albert M. Craig and Donald H. Shively, 234–263. Berkeley: University of California Press, 1970.

Wilson, Noell. *Defensive Positions: The Politics of Maritime Security in Tokugawa Japan.* Cambridge, MA: Harvard University Asia Center, 2015.

Wilson, Noell. "Tokugawa Defense Redux: Organizational Failure in the *Phaeton* Incident of 1808." *Journal of Japanese Studies* 36, no. 1 (2010): 1–32.

Wong, Roy Bin. *China Transformed: Historical Change and the Limits of European Experience.* Ithaca, NY: Cornell University Press, 1997.

Yamaguchi Keiji山口啓二and Sasaki Junnosuke 佐々木潤之介. *Taikei Nihon rekishi 4: Bakuhan taisei* 体系・日本歴史4:幕藩体制. Tokyo: Nihon hyōronsha, 1971.

Yamaguchi, Ken. *Kinsé shiriaku: A history of Japan, from the first visit of Commodore Perry in 1853 to the capture of Hakodate by the Mikado's forces in 1869.* Translated by Ernest Mason Satow. Yokohama: Japan Mail Office, 1873.

Yamaguchi Ken 山口謙 and Shozan Yashi 椒山野史. *Kinsei shiryaku* 近世史畧. 3 vols. Tokyo, 1872.

Yamamoto Hirofumi 山本博文. *Sankin kōtai* 参勤交代. Tokyo: Kodansha, 1998.

Yamamura, Kozo. "The Increasing Poverty of the Samurai in Tokugawa Japan, 1600–1868." *Journal of Economic History* 31, no. 2 (1971): 378–406.

Yamamura, Kozo. "The Meiji Land Tax Reform." In *Japan in Transition: from Tokugawa to Meiji*, edited by Marius B. Jansen and Gilbert Rozman, 382–399. Princeton, NJ: Princeton University Press, 1986.

Yamamura, Kozo. "Toward a Reexamination of the Economic History of Tokugawa Japan, 1600–1867." *Journal of Economic History* 33, no. 3 (1973): 509–546.

Yamashita Tsuneo 山下恒夫, ed. *Daikokuya Kōdayū shiryōshū* 大黒屋光太夫史料集. 4 vols. Tokyo: Nihon hyōronsha, 2003.

Yasumaru Yoshio 安丸良夫. *Kamigami no Meiji Ishin: shinbutsu bunri to haibutsu kishaku* 神々の明治維新: 神仏分離と廃仏毀釈. Tokyo: Iwanami Shoten, 1979.

Yonaha Jun 與那覇潤. "Ryūkyū kara mita Ryūkyū shobun: 'kindai' no teigi o majime ni kangaeru 琉球からみた琉球処分—「近代」の定義をまじめに考える." In *Ryūkyū kara mita sekaishi* 琉球からみた世界史, edited by Murai Shōsuke 村井章介 and Mitani Hiroshi 三谷博, 137–158. Tokyo: Yamakawa Shuppansha, 2011.

Yoshida Masahiko 吉田昌彦. "Gakushūin kengen seido no seiritsu to 'genro dōkai' 学習院建言制度の成立と「言路洞開」." *Bulletin of the Graduate School of Social and Cultural Studies, Kyushu University* 比較社会文化 17 (2011): 37–50.

Yoshida Shōin 吉田松陰. *Yoshida Shōin zenshū* 吉田松陰全集. Edited by Yamaguchi-ken Kyōikukai 山口県教育会. 10 vols., Vol. 6. Tokyo: Iwanami Shōin, 1934–36.

Yoshikawa Kōjirō 吉川幸次郎, Maruyama Masao 丸山‖真男, Nishida Taichirō 西田太一郎, and Tsuji Tatsuya 辻達也, eds. *Nihon shisō taikei 36: Ogyū Sorai* 日本思想体系 36: 荻生徂徠. Tokyo: Iwanami Shoten, 1973.

Index

Lightning Source UK Ltd.
Milton Keynes UK
UKHW041504070622
403979UK00009B/261